The Police State of Louis Napoleon Bonaparte, 1851–1860

Louis

The
Police
State of

Napoleon Bonaparte
1851-1860

BY HOWARD C. PAYNE

UNIVERSITY OF WASHINGTON PRESS · *Seattle*

To Adelheid

Preface

THIS STUDY attempts no major revision of the French Second Empire's history; nor is it immediately concerned with whether Louis Napoleon Bonaparte was a "good" or "bad" ruler. It seeks to call attention to a neglected aspect of the authoritarian regime of the 1850's and, by extension, of the French state since the early nineteenth century.

Many writers have referred to the continuity of centralized public administration in France. They have generalized about its effects upon political stability and aspirations toward democratic government. But few have lingered to inquire closely into the historical roles of the administrators who have tended that part of the institutional leviathan which lies below the surface of political events in the modern French state. This book may possibly be a suggestive beginning of such an inquiry into the most authoritarian years of the Second Empire.

The historical evaluation of Louis Napoleon's dictatorship, and in particular his use of political police methods, are matters of controversy. I have therefore investigated the activities and attitudes of the administrative officials who were most involved in political police service. I have also tried to clarify concepts and mechanisms of political police functions within the French system of public administration which may not be altogether familiar to the reader. To my knowledge no other systematic archival research has been undertaken for this specific purpose. Administrators and their acts in the 1850's have largely remained people and practices without a history.

This effort is necessarily incomplete. Source problems confront the researcher because of the large-scale destruction of political police documents at the end of the Second Empire and during the Paris Commune. The considerable materials remaining in Parisian archives are disconnected by tantalizing gaps. Not the least problem is the lack of available direct evidence of Louis Napoleon's personal attitude and influence with regard to political police. Adrien Dansette's current use of the Bonaparte family papers may cast some welcome light upon such questions.*

Meanwhile, further use of provincial archives, which I was able to consult only in the Midi and at Grenoble, should uncover many new details. For the investigator of provincial archives, French administrative centralization has a distinct advantage. Copies of directives and policy statements from the ministries in Paris, whose originals may now be missing, went out uniformly to officials throughout the country. Regional archives also show the details of compliance with central instructions. Especially in the case of the prefects, whose correspondence is imperfectly preserved in Paris, the outlying archives contain copies or minutes of reports to the ministries.

I have not attempted here to examine all the facets of political police operations in the fifties. Much more information could be assembled on the topics touched by this study and also on the policing of the theater, printing, bookselling, colportage (the peddling of literary and artistic materials), the foreign press in France and abroad, workers' activities, and organizations of various kinds. This investigation deals primarily with the work of officials responsible to the Ministry of the Interior and, to a lesser extent, with those under the Ministry of Justice. Further study of these and other ministerial bureaucracies would undoubtedly yield many new insights into the general history of the period.

Above all I express my gratitude to Professor Emeritus Franklin C. Palm of the University of California at Berkeley for long ago suggesting the topic of this inquiry, and to Professor David L. Dowd of the University of Florida for his encouragement to pursue it. Without the aid of a Fulbright Research Award in

---

* Adrien Dansette, *Louis-Napoléon à la conquête du pouvoir* (Paris, 1961), brings a projected multivolume history of the Second Empire to December, 1851.

1953–54 the work could not have begun. During that year Edouard Morot-Sir, director of the Fulbright program in Paris, was exceedingly helpful. My thanks go also to Marcel Le Clère, Commissaire Divisionnaire aux Délégations Judiciaires in Paris, for graciously introducing me to the archives of the Préfecture de Police. Washington State University has generously assisted the completion of my study through grants-in-aid. Professors Raymond Muse, Edward Bennett, Stephen Mitchell, and Mr. Gary Ross of Washington State University very kindly read and criticized portions of the manuscript. I am greatly indebted to the staffs of the Bibliothèque Nationale, the Service Historique de l'Armée at Vincennes, the archives of the Préfecture de Police, and the Archives de France in Paris, Marseille, Aix-en-Provence, and Grenoble. The Institut de France kindly made available the Baroche papers in the Bibliothèque Thiers. The archivists of the British Public Record Office were equally helpful in my use of Foreign Office documents. All imperfections in the work are, of course, my sole responsibility.

I acknowledge with thanks the publishers' permission to use portions of my previously published material on the gendarmerie and the *commissaires* in Frederick J. Cox (ed.), *Studies in modern European history in honor of Franklin Charles Palm* (New York: Bookman Associates, now Twayne Publishers, Inc., 1956) and in my article, "The French commissaire of police in the mid-nineteenth century," *Police* (Springfield, Illinois: Charles C. Thomas, Publisher), issues of September–October and November–December, 1960.

HOWARD C. PAYNE

Pullman, Washington
September 5, 1964

Contents

Maps

The Police State of Louis Napoleon Bonaparte, 1851–1860

Introduction: The Administrative Legacy, Instrument of Dictatorship

LOUIS NAPOLEON had neither to innovate nor to "return" to the First Empire to acquire political police controls over France. An instrument of dictatorship lay ready at hand—only temporarily dislocated by the revolution of 1848—long before he became president of the Second Republic at the end of that same year, seized dictatorial power in his coup d'état three years later, and, in 1852, launched the Second Empire.

This instrument was the already flourishing theory and practice of political police—the centralized public administration of the French state and the traditions, routine procedures, and developing jurisprudence underlying it, of the nineteenth century.

Rooted in the Old Regime, French administrative centralization was remolded into its modern form by the Revolution and the first Napoleon, and retouched in detail by various later regimes. Under Louis Napoleon, no fundamental innovation was required. The instrument was already operational, and only minor adjustments could amplify its potential, once it was surrounded by a more congenial constitutional and legislative milieu after the coup d'état of 1851.

FROM ADMINISTRATIVE THEORY TO POLITICAL POLICE

During much of the Old Regime, the term police had meant "administration" and "administrative law" before the latter expressions came into use.[1] The accepted reasoning ran as follows: To ensure society's freedom to pursue its rightful interests in

3

security, a sovereign government, "a single power requiring obedience by the entire country," and a supporting army and judiciary, were natural necessities. But further to satisfy the "collec-
tive needs of society for which neither individual nor group
initiative could well provide," a unified public administration
should uniformly provide "measures of police, surveillance, and
forethought." Sovereign authority spoke through "administrative
regulations, a kind of secondary legislation." Administrative officials acted as "a series of direct agents" of the government, responsible for "all the exigencies of the general interest" on
society's behalf.[2]

All nineteenth-century French constitutions placed the executive
power—in whatever form it might be conceived—unequivocally
in charge of the administrative services. Chief of government, the
executive was also the "supreme administrator of the state," who
normally delegated his sovereign administrative authority,
through the ministers, "to the lower degrees of the hierarchy."[3]
By the same token, the executive might also have been dubbed
"first policeman of the state," police functions being part of the
comprehensive administrative mission.

Louis Napoleon, as President of the Republic after December,
1848, or Emperor after December, 1852, was therefore bound
by administrative theory and law to assume control of the public
administration and its built-in centralized police system. Constitutionally, the ministers depended upon him. They had "no
jurisdiction other than that which he is pleased to delegate to
them." With or without the sort of constitution introduced in
1852, it could be legitimately said that "in the administrative
sphere, all authority emanates from the Emperor . . . and his
prerogatives extend through the entire administration," being expressed "by a transmission from superior to inferior, down to the
most remote points of the empire. . . ."[4]

Police powers being inseparable from general administration,
French theorists found a doctrine of police in the very assump-
tions underlying administrative centralization itself. Police authority sprang from society's right to existence and hence its
"right of legitimate defense" against potential or actual threats

to individual and group interests. The term police referred primarily to an administrative *function*, as well as to certain *personnel* specializing in the function. "Police" signified broadly "the whole of the means employed by a government to protect everyone," ranging from the guarding of individuals and their property to the "legitimate defense" of the state against subversion. The police function was "tutelary and protective, watching providentionally over society." Officials of the Second Empire could quote the historian, Augustin Thierry, with the approval due a familiar doctrine : " 'The police is the most solid foundation of civilization, watching over the morality, safety, and peace of the people.' "[5]

Within this broad definition, administrative theory more precisely delineated the basic types of police function. The Law of 3 Brumaire Year IV (October 24, 1796) distinguished between *administrative,* or "preventive," and *judiciary,* or "repressive," police.[6] The former belonged primarily, though not entirely, to the Minister of the Interior and his subordinate bureaucracy; the latter primarily, though not entirely, to the Minister of Justice and his subordinates. Administrative police embraced the general surveillance of society and the maintenance of public order and security. The judiciary police function dealt with the full investigation of offenses and the prosecution of their authors before the proper courts, in the name of the executive power. Inevitably, the two functions overlapped. But the theoretical distinction, important in police theory and practice from the Revolution to the present day, was rigorously maintained during the Second Empire. An imperial prosecutor in 1869 stood upon very correct doctrine when arguing that the government's obligation to guarantee the security of persons and property,

without which guarantee society would not exist, is obtained in two . . . different ways: by suppressing the causes of troubles in advance, and by punishing those responsible for disorder. Hence the natural and logical distinction of two polices, administrative and judiciary.[7]

Administrative police included the subdivisions of *municipal* and *general* police functions. Municipal police, directed by the mayors of communes under the *tutelle* of the Ministry of the In-

terior, included what an American or Englishman would probably
consider "ordinary" police duties, ranging from traffic control to
the routine lookout for crime and disorder. General police was a
different though related matter, with sweeping political implica-
tions. Directed by the Ministry of the Interior's hierarchy—the
prefects of the *départements* and the Paris Prefect of Police—
general police upheld the *sûreté générale,* or the security of the
state itself and public order throughout the country.[8] It was the
special responsibility of the executive, bound by the principle of
"legitimate defense" to uphold the *sûreté générale,* to decide in a
given instance what "measures of *sûreté générale*" were required
by the circumstances. Long after the Second Empire, twentieth-
century writers continued to hold that

> General police has no limited objective. It is charged with decreeing,
> according to day-to-day needs, all the measures required for the maintenance
> of order in general. Nor are the rights permitted to it defined by statutes.
> . . . Those general police powers which are . . . so excessive with respect to
> the common law are warranted solely by the aim for which the governing
> power may use them.[9]

Certain practical restraints usually limited the exercise of such
undefined executive power: constitutional and legislative law as
interpreted by the judiciary, public opinion, the executive's own
sense of political expediency and, not least, administrators' attitudes toward their own proper functions. A constitutionally
strong and politically ambitious executive could easily drive the
powers of general police to an excessive point unless restrained by
its own scruples. This possibility, often noted by writers on administrative law, was not overlooked by police authorities of the
Second Empire. A memorandum prepared in the Ministry of the
Interior in 1853 pointedly concluded that the concept of general
police had in the past led to "the most complete arbitrariness"
because it allowed police authorities "to enter into a share of the
prerogatives of sovereignty itself, which protects the police with
its own inviolability."[10]

Not all general police activities habitually undertaken in the
name of the *sûreté générale* were politically significant. However,

many were, and consequently the practice of *political police* was recognized as an aspect of the general police function and continued by all French regimes after the Revolution. The term "political police" has often been superficially equated only with "secret police," or applied narrowly to a special segment of police personnel, or linked only to certain periods or institutions in French history.[11] Such interpretations ignore some of the most fundamental qualities of French administrative theory and practice.

A pattern of security activities included in the general police function comprised the political police in nineteenth-century France, especially though not exclusively entrusted to the Ministry of the Interior and its agents. Security activities were carried out routinely by various administrative officials along with their other nonpolitical duties. These functions involved periodic and special reports at all levels of the administrative hierarchy on anything the executive power deemed politically interesting or significant.

In particular, political police engaged in constant surveillance of and opportune action upon public opinion, the press in all its forms, and associations of all kinds. Its business included police operations ranging from the suppression of rebellions to arrests for political conspiracy or other activities legally defined as subversive or considered to be so by the authorities entrusted with the protection of the *sûreté générale*. Political police maintained surveillance of the national frontiers, and of persons or groups abroad, for reasons considered politically relevant to the state's security. Sometimes the political police operated secretly through specialists in undercover work or part-time informers. But its essence was inseparable from the routine performance of certain functionaries whose general police powers formed only part of their broader administrative assignments.

ADMINISTRATIVE CENTRALIZATION

Nineteenth-century French police theory and practice can be understood only in the context of general administration and

administrative law. Public administration rested upon the Law of
28 Pluviôse Year VIII (February 17, 1800), a veritable charter
of centralized administrative powers. Various ministerial bureaucracies, directed from Paris under delegated executive authority,
thereafter extended their jurisdictions uniformly into all the regional divisions, or *départements,* which the Revolution had substituted for the ancient provinces. Within each of the eighty-six
départements of the 1850's—and in their administrative subdivisions, *arrondissements, cantons,* and *communes*—agents of the
centralized bureaucracies policed, taxed, superintended, regulated,
and reported aspects of provincial life, activities that in a less
unitary state would have belonged to regional and local governments.

Regional and local representative assemblies already existed:
the "general council" of the *département,* the *"arrondissement*
council," and the communal "municipal council." All obeyed central supervision and control. After 1833, for instance, the general
councils were forbidden to discuss political matters by a legal interdiction that remained until after the Second Empire.[12] Police,
public works, finances, economic development, education, the
function of public prosecutor, and other public services were
ultimately subject to central administrative control, or *tutelle.*
"The *départements* are considered minors," a nineteenth-century
administrative treatise emphasized, "placed under the *tutelle* of
the government and unable to act except with its approval."[13]

Despite some reforms of detail after 1815, the centralized
system of 1800 remained essentially intact. A mid-nineteenth-century observation that the system "entirely sacrificed . . . local life
to the omnipotence of the central government," echoed into the
twentieth century: "Local life is effaced as under the Revolution,
its resources are monopolized by the state as during the Empire,
and local government finds itself reduced to a fictitious situation."[14]

At one time or another during the nineteenth century, nearly
every political group attacked administrative centralization, yet
none did much to change it. Paul Deschanel, quoting Alexis de
Tocqueville, concluded in 1895:

"Most of those in France who talk against centralization do not really wish to destroy it—some because they hold power, others because they count upon obtaining it." . . . It is such a convenient instrument of domination! [15]

The revolution of 1848 only briefly disturbed the "normality" of administrative centralization, which remained the bedrock beneath succeeding governments. Historians, while recognizing its existence, have perhaps neglected this tenacious influence within the French body politic, leaving the subject mainly to specialists in administrative organization and law.[16]

ADMINISTRATIVE LAW

The *tutelle* found its justification in the evolving concepts of nineteenth-century administrative law as distinguished from constitutional and legislative law. Administrative law grew apart from the common laws, ordinary courts, and the legislative process. It was most simply defined as "the *ensemble* of rules regulating the relations between . . . the administrative authority and the citizenry."[17] Those "rules" arose as administrators, responsible solely to the executive power, developed a body of detailed regulations, procedures, and interpretations during their daily task of enforcing the general prescriptions of constitutional and legislative law. Such "rules," issued under the aegis of the executive authority, acquired an autonomous force of law by an inductive and gradual process of systematization and acceptance.[18]

Remaining uncodified in the land of the Napoleonic Codes, administrative law evolved through the course of routine administrative practice, the "doctrine" promulgated by ministers and their agents, the writings of influential jurists,[19] decisions of the Council of State (the highest administrative court), and those of the Court of Cassation (the highest civil court of appeal), which consistently recognized its validity. Although subordinate in theory to constitutional and legislative authority, administrative law in reality was equally important to French citizens in daily confrontation with the *tutelle*.

Administrative law thus took its place beside the Napoleonic Codes, the growth of its autonomous domain uninterrupted by political upheavals and changes of regime. It legitimized the

paternalistic administrative *tutelle*. And it was also the matrix of
a theory of police—and particularly of political police—that in
the hands of Louis Napoleon represented not innovation but historical continuity. In administrative law, police powers were an
integral part of administrative *tutelle,* distributed by delegation
from the executive through the ministers—especially those of the
Interior and Justice—down the bureaucratic hierarchy to local
functionaries.

Two other features of French administrative law and practice
ensured the continuing effectiveness of the political police function.
The related concepts of "administrative jurisdiction" and "separation of powers" provided the bedrock of an imposing autonomy
which the executive and its administrative agents enjoyed while
performing their political duties.

Administrative Jurisdiction

Until after the Second Empire, the administration itself enjoyed exclusive control over citizens' attempts to obtain relief
against competent "administrative acts" and their consequences.
The administration was the ultimate judge in its own case. Citizens seeking judicial remedy could apply only to separate administrative courts—the "prefectorial council" in each *département*
and the national Council of State—answerable only to the executive power and entirely apart from ordinary courts. Nonpolitical
cases were accepted routinely and decided under administrative
law, the question being whether the administrative acts in question
had been "in excess of power."

But against an "act of government," that is, a politically mo-
tivated administrative action on behalf of the *sûreté générale,* no
recourse whatever was possible. The Council of State upheld this
principle until 1875, even though its chief legal foundation—
Article 75 of the Constitution of the Year VIII, or 1800—was
finally repealed soon after the fall of the Second Empire in 1870.
Article 75 had decreed: "Agents of the government, other than
the ministers, cannot be prosecuted for matters relating to their
functions, except by virtue of a decision of the Council of
State. . . ."[20]

Political police measures were "acts of government" by qualified executive agents sharing in the immunity of sovereignty
itself. That immunity survived the revolution of 1848. In 1849
Alexandre Vivien, noted authority on administration and spokes-
man for a parliamentary commission studying new administrative legislation, told the National Assembly:

In a representative government . . . there are circumstances wherein,
because of high public necessity, the ministers resort to measures harmful to
private rights. . . . To make them justiciable . . . would be to paralyze actions undertaken on behalf of the common interest and would create within
the state a new power that would threaten all the others. Measures of
sûreté générale . . . do not come within [even] administrative court jurisdiction, even though private rights might thereby be affected.[21]

When Napoleon III's Council of State refused to admit judicial
review of "acts of government" in the administrative or ordinary
courts, it acted in full harmony with earlier laws and administrative doctrine.[22]

While engaged in "acts of government" ordered by competent
authority, administrators became "agents of the government" by
executive delegation and hence immune from prosecution. A law
of August 16, 1790, placed all functionaries in this category.
Later, the quality of "agent" was narrowed to prefects, subprefects, mayors and their adjoints, *commissaires* of police, and
certain officials of the ministries of Finance and Public Works.
Lesser police officers, such as gendarmes and the ordinary urban
and rural policemen, were excluded.

However, the Court of Cassation on May 3, 1838, held that
the immunity of an "agent of the government" derived not from
his status of administrator as such, but only from the nature of
the function being performed. He must be "the depository of a
part of governmental authority," acting under the government's
immediate or mediate direction. Another decision of March 31,
1864, further clarified what might be termed the "function-not-
person" doctrine by stressing that immunity from prosecution for
"acts of government" was intended to safeguard administrative
independence in the performance of certain vital public functions,
and not to protect functionaries as individuals. To receive im-

munity, the agent must limit himself to those actions essential to his proper function as "agent of the government." Otherwise he was personally liable. The administration might also extend immunity to lesser functionaries when they were immediately engaged in an "act of government" delegated to them by a recognized "agent of the government." [23]

This point was successfully argued, for example, in defense of six Paris policemen who were sued for rough handling of private citizens during an arrest under the Second Empire. The judiciary police insisted that "it is the . . . nature of the act which creates the quality of agent. The same functionary can be, alternately, an agent of the government or not. It is the fact which characterizes the agent." In other cases the Council of State consistently denied recourse against "acts of government," such as that resulting from the seizure of the Orléans family properties in 1852, an attempted action by the Duc d'Aumale against the Prefect of Police, in 1867, and another by the newspaper, *Gazette de France,* in 1865. In the latter case, as in others, the administration defended "a political act with respect to which the law has meant to arm the government with a discretionary power, and which by its very nature excludes in the most absolute manner any possibility of recourse. . . ."[24]

The Separation-of-Powers Doctrine

Administrative jurisdiction gained further independence in administrative law by the principle of "separation" of executive and judiciary in administrative affairs. Explicitly stated in revolutionary legislation of 1790, the doctrine of separation imposed an "interdiction to the courts against taking cognizance of administrative acts." This meant in practice that the ordinary courts were forbidden "ever to acquire administrative functions or to summon before themselves the administrators by reason of their functions." The judiciary, when called upon to assist the enforcement of administrative acts, must do so "without the power to decide upon their justice, timeliness, or substance."[25]

But the doctrine had another side. The executive could not intervene in nonadministrative matters within the proper jurisdiction of the courts, where justice was rendered in the executive's *name* by delegation, but not by the executive as such. Here was a guarantee of judicial independence and due process of law, once the administration turned over a case to the judiciary police for prosecution before the regular courts. The Second Empire held to both aspects of the "separation-of-powers" doctrine, which was explicitly contained in Article 7 of the Constitution of 1852.[26]

"Separation of powers" not only prevented judicial interference in administrative matters; it also left the executive, and hence the administration, free to decide whether certain cases involving administrative functionaries belonged to administrative or ordinary court jurisdiction. Aside from "acts of government," which could always be withheld from even the administrative courts, officials were constantly involved in disputes with citizens who claimed grounds for trial before the regular courts. In such ambiguous cases the balance of power was always with the administration. Moreover, even though a disgruntled citizen was allowed to seek remedy in an administrative court, the "due process" he would find there was still conditional upon a final decision by the executive power. Administrative courts lacked judicial independence, giving only advisory decisions.

Prefectorial Councils and the Council of State

Private legal actions against administrative acts and the functionaries performing them were made at two levels. The prefectorial councils were appointive boards of review presided over by the prefect of each *département*. They were administrative courts of first instance in the realm of *contentieux administratif,* or recourse against nonpolitical administrative acts. The supreme administrative court was the Council of State, created in 1800 on the older model of the King's Council and retained by all governments after 1814.[27]

Except between 1849 and 1852, the Council of State was appointed by the executive. It settled disputes within the administration, judged prosecutions launched by citizens against administrative acts and functionaries, and decided whether such actions belonged to administrative or ordinary court jurisdiction. Reflecting the separation-of-powers doctrine, the Council's function rested upon a legal distinction which described its administrative jurisdiction as "retained justice" (*justice retenue*) exercised by the chief of state, in contrast to "delegated justice" (*justice déléguée*) dispensed in the regular courts. In other words, the Council of State lacked the status of court in its own right, rendering only advisory decisions to the executive, whose verdict was final. But in fact governments after 1800 consistently followed the Council's recommendations.[28]

From 1849 to 1852 the Council of State's status changed temporarily. By the Constitution of 1848 members were named by the National Assembly. A newly created Tribunal of Conflicts, composed equally of members of the Council of State and the Court of Cassation, decided conflicts between administrative and ordinary court jurisdiction. A law of March, 1849, gave the Council the power of "delegated justice" in administrative cases, increasing its autonomy. These changes weakened the executive's arbitrary authority in administrative jurisdiction. Indeed, the Council of State under the Second Republic favored the Assembly in its conflict with President Louis Napoleon. The latter, after the coup d'état of December, 1851, abolished the Tribunal of Conflicts and reorganized the Council of State on its old bases, returning deliberately to the model of the First Empire, Restoration, and July Monarchy.[29] Only in this one instance did Louis Napoleon inherit a serious impairment of the executive's supremacy in administration.

THE POLICE HIERARCHY

Throughout the nineteenth century, the general police function was administered by variously organized central agencies. From its creation in 1790 until 1818, the Ministry of the Interior and its provincial hierarchy shared general police powers either with ministries of general police or special supervisory police agencies under various names. With the abolition of the police ministry in 1818, the Ministry of the Interior took full control of general police. Through eleven intramural reorganizations between December, 1818, and August, 1851, general police was vested in either a special "directorship" or a simple "division" of the Ministry. In Paris and the Seine after 1800, all police powers belonged to the Prefect of Police, nominally subordinate to the Ministry of the Interior but virtually independent in reality. Continuing the pattern of 1818–51, the Second Empire also introduced organizational changes within the system in quest of greater efficiency. Except for a seventeen-month interim in 1852–53, general police in the *départements* was the Minister of the Interior's responsibility through the prefects, who were the most important "agents of the government" in the administrative system.

The Prefects and General Police

Heir of the Old Regime *intendant*—"the king present in the provinces"—the nineteenth-century prefect was "the depository" and the "direct representative of the executive power in the *département.*" The prefect, "armed with the entire administrative power," wielded an authority that in varying degrees penetrated all the ministerial bureaucracies. He was the subministerial agent most responsible for initiating and supervising measures of *sûreté générale*. His *tutelle* indirectly controlled municipal police. Responsibility for the general security made him chief of general police, into whatever administrative domain this duty might lead him. As a result, the prefect directed political police activities, open and secret, everywhere in the *département*. For the safety of the state, administrative doctrine prescribed that "all must converge into the one center, the prefecture. The prefect must know everything."[30]

Knowing meant receiving and making reports on anything relevant to the *sûreté générale*. The prefecture received, synthesized, and relayed to Paris the most varied information submitted by police officers and administrators of all sorts. The prefect must also act. He issued detailed *règlements* or more general *arrêtés* (to assure execution of the laws and his own *règlements*) that were legally binding upon communes throughout the *département*. His "circulars" instructed lesser agents, usually in order to implement more general ministerial circulars which he himself received from Paris. As the superior among administrators, he might annul or modify others' actions if they conflicted with his own interpretations, instructions, or administrative edicts. Such prefectorial powers were entrenched long before the post-1848 reaction and the Second Empire, which continued, with some detailed embellishments, the prefects' traditional rights. Thus, when the prefect of the Haute-Marne, by an *arrêté* of October, 1851, invoked his general police power to impose a *règlement général de police* upon the municipalities of his *département,* he could cite earlier precedents "and the general right belonging to me as delegate of the executive power" to override municipal police autonomy if in his view the *sûreté générale* required it.[31]

After inauguration of the prefectorial system in 1800, the prefects assumed a place among the country's elite. Under Napoleon I and the Restoration, the prefectures were filled by men recruited from the country's "notables," though the Bourbons replaced many servants of the Empire. The revolution of 1830 led to a wholesale renewal of prefects and other functionaries. These changes re-emphasized the Napoleonic administrative tradition, drawing heavily on ex-servants of the First Empire, and entrenched upper-bourgeois elements in all levels of public administration. Career administrators thereafter moved up the lower rungs of the hierarchy into the prefectures. Ex-prefects, in turn, increasingly staffed the commanding positions of the state in a trend uninterrupted by either the Second Empire or the Third Republic. In an ever more complex society, the prefects' powers steadily multiplied in detail. The revolution of 1848 brought a brief "prefectorial crisis" by the abolition of the system on February 25. It was immediately restored, however, in a new form under so-called *commissaires* of the Republic. On May 20, 1848, the prefectorial system formally resumed its sway in its older form. Within six months the prefectorial corps was reconstituted about evenly with old men and new. And a stable, conservative group emerged to serve the Second Republic in 1849–51 and the Second Empire as well, in the traditional spirit.[32]

Immediately subordinate to the prefect in every *arrondissement* of the *département* (except that of the prefect's residence) was a subprefect. The subprefects were delegates of the prefectorial authority in general administrative and police matters. As the chief "intermediaries" between the prefect and mayors of communes, the subprefects were "agents of the government" though not themselves autonomous administrators, the prefect alone retaining full responsibility. They could on occasion act independently, as when the prefect expressly delegated certain powers, or in those rare emergencies when time prevented communication with the prefect.[33]

The Mayors

In the more than thirty-seven thousand communes of France, the mayors and their assistants, or *adjoints,* played very complex administrative and police roles, depending upon the matter at hand. The mayor, "a municipal magistrate and chief of the communal association," presided over the elected municipal council in local administration. Or, as an administrative police officer, he commanded both the municipal and rural police—the former composed of agents of police, *sergents de ville,* and *commissaires* of police; the latter including the *gardes champêtres* and *gardes forestiers.* The mayor was also "the representative and agent of the government," with general police powers under the direction of the prefect or subprefect. In nonpolitical operations of strictly municipal and rural police, the mayor was in theory supreme within his commune. But always, whether appointed or elected, he submitted to prefectorial *tutelle* in police and other administrative functions. The mayor and his local police personnel were always at the prefects' disposal for the needs of the *sûreté générale,* as defined by the prefect himself. A prefect of the Second Empire spoke characteristically and traditionally when he declared:

It is through surveillance of the municipal police that the most effective implementation of political and administrative police can be made. Everything converges and is linked together in this service.[34]

In practice the municipal and general police functions so overlapped that no one could define precisely their reciprocal spheres of action. In political police activities no effective gap prevailed in the hierarchy between prefect and mayor.

Finally, the mayor was also an officer of judiciary police under the supervision of the Ministry of Justice and its provincial agents. As such he acted as magistrate in the communal police court. A sympathetic nineteenth-century observer very aptly noted:

> The mayor is . . . a corporal without an army. He supports all the weight of the administrative hierarchy. Upon his back falls the execution of all the orders that descend, level by level, from the central sanctuary of laws and decrees.[35]

The Commissaires of Police

The *commissaire de police*, for whom the English term "commissioner" would be misleading, was wedged into a unique position in the administrative hierarchy. Endowed with a venerable ancestry arising in Roman Gaul, one-time owner of hereditary office during the Old Regime, abolished by the Revolution only to be reincarnated in 1790–91, the *commissaire* occupied the most crucial workaday position in the French police system.[36]

Serving the Paris Prefecture of Police and the larger provincial cities, the *commissaires* wore various official hats according to the police function being performed at a given moment. They were "the auxiliaries and subordinates of the mayors for municipal police, and of the prefects for general police." They could call out the gendarmerie, a military police force administered by the Ministry of War. As officers of judiciary police, the *commissaires* were linked to the bureaucratic chain of command under the Ministry of Justice. But most fundamentally, they were agents of the executive power within the prefectorial hierarchy, "one of the most important branches of that tutelary tree under whose branches all society confidently takes shelter."[37]

Less metaphorically, the *commissaires* of police performed municipal or rural police functions under the mayors' orders. But in the general police they were agents of the government under the prefects' command and could themselves issue orders to the mayors. In 1838 the Court of Cassation upheld the doctrine that the *commissaires* "exercise by direct delegation . . . a part of the sovereign public authority." During the Second Empire these officers continued their traditional roles, being repeatedly reminded by their superiors that they were "above all, political functionaries placed under the direct and immediate authority of the prefect." Writers on police doctrine exhorted them to be "the ever-open eyes of the government" in political police, with competence in "all things relevant to justice and society. . . ."[38] In the manner of its predecessors, the Second Empire relied heavily upon the *commissaires* and increased their numbers. The overworked officers continued to provide a crucial administrative link between the prefects and all branches of police activity in the *départements*.

The Second Empire inherited three types of "special *commissaires* of police," assigned not to communes but to certain specialized police duties important in political police, for which they were responsible directly to the Ministry of the Interior. In 1851, twelve special *commissaires* were stationed in Paris and other large cities for surveillance of printers, the book trade, and the peddling, especially in rural areas, of books, brochures, almanacs, emblems, and the like. Another group, posted at frontier points, examined all incoming printed materials from the viewpoint of public order, morality, and literary rights.[39] A third kind of special police agent arrived with the railways, and a royal ordinance of November 25, 1846, established several "special *commissaires* of railway police." These officers were responsible for the safety and good order of trains. Beyond that, in their railway jurisdictions they shared the typical attributes of *commissaires* generally, including powers of judiciary, general, and political police. Their status as officers of general police was left ambiguous by the reforms of 1848, but the Ministry of the Interior never lost interest in the railway *commissaires* as useful political police agents. The Second Empire considerably developed their service as a natural outgrowth of the expansion of rail mileage and the consequent new dimension for political police surveillance.[40]

The Paris Prefecture of Police

In the *département* of the Seine, the Prefect of Police ruled a centralized domain that in many respects was a microcosm of the national administrative system—a "government within a government," according to one Prefect of Police. Created in its modern form in 1800, the Prefecture of Police was the lineal descendant of the Lieutenancy-General of Police established by Louis XIV in 1674.[41]

The nineteenth-century Prefect of Police was a direct agent of the government, responsible to the executive through the ministers, and after March, 1848, specifically through the Ministry of the Interior. But in fact the Prefecture's affairs were more complex than those of many ministries. The Prefect's prestige enabled him to act in a virtually autonomous way, conferring directly with the chief of state. In the capital the extent of his powers prompted the conclusion, "the history of the Paris police . . . would be the history of the city itself." [42]

The legislation of 1800 partitioned the Seine between the Prefect of Police and the departmental prefect. Alone among his colleagues the prefect of the Seine lacked general police powers. They were concentrated in the hands of the Prefect of Police for the entire *département,* along with most general administrative powers for the city of Paris. The Prefect of Police was also an officer of judiciary police; in fact if not in name he was mayor of the capital. His work ranged from the most complex political police operations in France to supervision of markets, river navigation, parks, prisons, and the price of bread. Little in Parisian life failed to come somehow within the official cognizance of the Prefecture of Police. With reason the Prefecture has been judged an institution "unique in France, the only part of the French administrative organization to sanction such an absolute state system" within the state.[43]

Lyon

An analogous, though not identical, police jurisdiction was established in Lyon on the eve of Louis Napoleon's coup d'état.

Legislation of June and September, 1851, created a "strong and unique police" under the prefect of the Rhône. This prefect henceforth acted as "prefect of police" in a jurisdiction known as the *agglomération lyonnaise,* including the city and a dozen suburban communes. Here the prefect of the Rhône wielded the same powers given the Paris Prefect of Police in 1800, delegating police affairs to a special Secretary-General Charged with Police, who managed a staff of about nine hundred and fifty office workers and policemen in the prefect's name. In this industrial area, long agitated by political radicalism and secret societies, political police was of special concern.[44]

The Gendarmerie

Administrators before and during the Second Empire almost unanimously attested the indispensability of the national gendarmerie in policing France. With an ancestry, under other names, reaching back to the tenth century, the modern gendarmerie dated from a law of 1791 and a royal ordinance of September, 1815. Gendarmes were uniformed troops, members of a special army branch administered by one of the seven directorships in the Ministry of War. They permanently assisted the civil police authorities. In December, 1848, about eighteen thousand gendarmes patrolled the *départements*—one "legion" to each *département* commanded by a colonel or lieutenant-colonel. For routine police duty, the gendarmes were deployed in companies and small brigades under their own officers. They reported through their military hierarchy to the Minister of War, keeping other police authorities generally informed. Their officers enjoyed the powers of judiciary police. By formal requisition, the gendarmerie could be summoned for special duties by agents of the government among the administrative and judiciary police. Because of the scarcity and frequent incompetence of municipal and rural police in small communes, the villages and countryside of France depended upon the gendarmerie as their only truly effective policemen.

Although in theory the gendarmerie was a nonpolitical police corps, it was in fact deeply involved in political police, before and

during the Second Empire. Gendarmerie officers reported regularly on political conditions and public opinion to the Minister of
War, who often relayed important information for action to
other ministers. They reported diverse matters to the prefects.
Moreover, the right of civil authorities to requisition the gendarmerie for special services necessarily involved the corps in
political police activities. Baron Haussmann, as prefect of the
Var in 1849, had nothing but praise for the salutary prestige of
"the gendarme's cap," which cowed the radical secret societies
more than any other symbol of authority.[45]

The Paris Republican Guard, a special branch of the gendarmerie, was kept at the exclusive disposal of the Prefect of
Police and the Minister of the Interior. Maintained by various
post-Napoleonic governments under different names and in several
forms, the Guard was full integrated into the national gendarmerie in 1849 after loyally serving against the insurgents in the
"June Days" of 1848. Its strength was set officially at 2,130 men,
organized in eighteen infantry companies and three mounted
squadrons, but the force remained somewhat below complement
in 1851.[46]

The national budget of 1852, prepared in 1851, projected an
expansion of the gendarmerie to 788 officers, 13,798 cavalry, and
10,073 foot soldiers. Especially favored by Louis Napoleon, the
gendarmerie was to play an important role in the political police
of the Second Empire.

The Judiciary Police and the Procureurs-Généraux

The term *police judiciaire* in administrative parlance denoted
a function as well as the hierarchy of civil servants primarily
associated with the function. The judiciary police function, performed mainly by the bureaucracy of the Ministry of Justice—
assisted by gendarmerie officers, prefects, *commissaires* of police,
and mayors—included legal paperwork such as the issuance or
certification of arrest and search warrants and *procès-verbaux,*
or official reports of the circumstances and evidence leading to
arrest. It included, after arrest, the further investigation of the
offenses and the questioning of defendants and their prosecution

before the proper courts in the name of the executive power. Officials of three ministries shared various aspects of the judiciary
police function. But the personnel principally involved in the
function belonged to a nonpermanent magistracy responsible to
the executive power through the Minister of Justice.

At the top of the judiciary police hierarchy in the *départements*
were twenty-seven (after 1860, twenty-eight) *procureurs-généraux*, the highest-ranking public prosecutors, who directed judiciary police activities through an orderly chain of command
extending down to the communes. The *procureurs-généraux* and
their subordinate agents belonged to the *magistrature debout*, as
distinguished from the *magistrature assise*. The latter, descrip-
tively named, were irremovable judges whose positions on the
bench were nonpolitical and beyond the arbitrary control of the
executive. But the *magistrature debout*, from the *procureurs* on
down, were state functionaries without tenure. As judiciary police,
they represented the *ministère public* in the courts, which is to say
they were appointive investigators and public prosecutors representing the state's interests. Collectively, they were regarded in
administrative law as "the organ of the executive power attached
to [*auprès de*] the courts." Judiciary police functionaries thus
belonged to the national scheme of administrative centralization.

Their organization was geared to certain levels in the national
judicial structure. French court jurisdictions reflected a three-level
legal definition of criminal offenses in order of their gravity.
Contraventions, the least serious, were tried in two kinds of lower
courts: "simple police tribunals," where the mayor or a *commissaire* of police represented the *ministère public;* and the cantonal
"police tribunals," where the justices of the peace, judiciary police
functionaries, played the same role. *Délits* (the second category
of offenses) and appeals from the police courts were tried before
"correctional tribunals" in every *arrondissement*. To each of the
correctional courts were assigned a *procureur de la république*
(under the Second Empire, *procureur impérial*) and a staff of
assistants. *Crimes* went to the "assize courts," one to each *département*, the only French criminal courts using the jury. Finally,
twenty-seven (after 1860, twenty-eight) appellate courts, known

during the Second Empire as *cours impériales,* sat in as many
regional districts, or *ressorts,* each of which (except that of
Paris) included from two to four *départements.* The Paris court
of appeal covered seven *départements.*

At each court of appeal was a *procureur-général* and his staff,
constituting the *parquet,* or establishment of judiciary police. As
head of the *parquet* and administrative chief of all the other
judiciary police personnel in his *ressort,* the *procureur-général,*
answering to the Minister of Justice, presided over a considerable bureaucracy.[47] Their duties brought the *procureurs* into frequent contact with those members of the prefectorial hierarchy
who performed both general and judiciary police functions. Within their own domains they played a role somewhat analogous
to that of the prefects, though they were not officers of general
police. Their attitudes toward law, public order and morality,
and political orthodoxy during the Second Republic and Empire
closely paralleled those of the prefects, with whom differences
often arose from the *procureurs'* more meticulous concern for the
correctness of legal and judicial procedures. The *procureurs* necessarily cooperated with the prefects in political, as well as other
aspects of police. They received regular reports from their own
subordinates and were often able to provide information to
assist the prefects' "preventive" police actions. Their activity in
the investigation of alleged political offenses and their systematic
reports to the Minister of Justice on the social, moral, economic,
and political situation of their *ressorts,* provided a wealth of detail and perceptive generalization to further political police operations during the Second Republic and Empire.[48]

"Interpenetration" of Police Functions

On the surface, the nineteenth-century French police system
seems complex and unwieldy. Police officials belonged to three
separate ministerial bureaucracies. The police function itself was
partitioned by legal and doctrinal definition into several sub-
categories. However, these divisions were sharper in theory than
in practice. The system operated with an effective degree of cen-

tralized unity because of a so-called interpenetration among the
various police branches.

Within the prefectorial hierarchy, the *commissaires* of police
had one foot in municipal police, another in general police; they
could also call upon the gendarmerie and perform the functions
of judiciary police. The judiciary police function, though concentrated in the *procureurs'* bureaucracy, extended in certain respects to officers of gendarmerie, mayors and their adjoints,
commissaires, prefects, and the Paris Prefect of Police. Prefects
could request officers of judiciary police "to take all necessary
actions for verifying criminal offenses and turning over the offenders to the courts." They could use the gendarmerie in general
police measures. In Paris the gendarmerie, judiciary, and administrative police functions were all controlled by the Prefect of
Police. The first was administratively part of the Ministry of
War; the other two were combined in the Prefecture. This mixed
police system, full of overlapping jurisdictions and procedures
which blurred many neat theoretical distinctions, nurtured countless occasions for administrative conflict. Built into the system,
such conflict often smoldered and occasionally flared openly.

The system's capstone lay in the special prerogatives of the
executive power, its decisive motive force, and the integrative role
of the executive's chief administrative agents, the prefects. The
executive was the ultimate commander-in-chief of the gendarmerie, officers of judiciary police, and the prefectorial hierarchy.
Direct executive intervention in general administration was in
many ways circumscribed by law, custom, and expediency. The
nonadministrative courts and the judicial process were autonomous. But administrative law and the separation-of-powers doctrine allowed the executive's agents great latitude in interpreting
and applying the law, giving them a significant practical influence
in the making, as well as the carrying out, of governmental policy
in the day-to-day sense. Administrative *tutelle* over local or regional initiative made the executive's interpretation of legislative
intent (after filtering through the prefects' views and instructions) uniformly applicable throughout the country.

Of all the executive's prerogatives, the most important politically were those deriving from his responsibility for initiating all measures necessary for upholding the *sûreté générale*. This undefined right, translated into the powers of general police and enforced by prefects and other agents of the government immune from prosecution for their acts, cut through the boundaries of the various bureaucracies and the fine delineations among municipal, judiciary, and other types of police jurisdiction. The limits of political police therefore fluctuated with the executive's strength and sense of expediency. In this fact the elements of a police state existed in nineteenth-century France.

THE REACTION OF 1849–51

Louis Napoleon was elected President of the Second Republic on December 10, 1848. Thereafter, three fateful forces—the President's resolution to hold and consolidate power, the "red specter" of messianic republican radicalism, and a public reaction against the specter—began a consequential three-year interaction. From it arose an "administrative renaissance" and a dictatorship which, more frankly than any government since 1814, drew upon the potential of traditional police theory.

The "Red Specter" of 1848–51

The temporary relaxation of legal and administrative restraints in the revolutionary honeymoon of early 1848 coincided with an eruption of varied messianic revolutionary aspirations passionately expressed in radical newspapers, political clubs, and popular slogans. Of the latter, the cry for "the democratic and social republic!" became the tocsin of disparate radical groups joined together less by precision of doctrine or program than by the generalized intent to drive the revolution beyond political reform into the realization of eschatological social visions. Their inexperienced utopianism, promising imminent dissolution of the old social order, mingled with threats of vengeance for past social injustices.

Not too surprisingly, the external, comprehensive simplicity of the goals of "democratic and social" republicanism was soon reflected in the fears of those Frenchmen who saw (as did their counterparts elsewhere in the Europe of 1848) a nihilistic "red specter" gnawing at the economic, social, and religious bonds of civilized life. The revolutionary Messiahs were "socialists," unprincipled "anarchists" and "demagogues"; distinctions between moderate and utopian republicanism were increasingly blurred for those under the spell of the "red specter." In the bloody "June Days" of 1848, the forces of "order" simultaneously crushed a proletarian insurrection and confirmed their own fears. Wholesale proscriptions, the reconstitution of the prefectorial system, and a return to repressive legislation against the press and political association spearheaded a post-June reaction against the republican Left.

Louis Napoleon, swept into the presidency by the conservative groundswell and, in part, by the magic of his patronymic among segments of the Left, found in the "red specter" both opportunity and challenge. Not until the summer of 1849 did he abandon earlier hopes of building national support among both Left and Right. The elections of May, 1849, a victory for the "party of order," likewise saw unexpected gains for the radical Left, followed in June by another abortive insurrection touched off by Ledru-Rollin. As De Tocqueville recalled, "the terror was universal." The "red specter" flared anew during a second phase of reactionary legislation. At this point, Louis Napoleon systematically aligned against "socialist" republicanism and based an increasingly personal policy on a rejuvenated administration headed by prefects and *procureurs,* prepared energetically to strike subversives with their political police powers and to further presidential prestige and policies.

By the end of 1850, the "red" menace seemed physically curbed, at least on the surface. But the "specter" itself arose again to hover over the growing political tension of 1851—a tension whose elements focused upon the presidential and parliamentary elections slated for the spring of 1852. Louis Napoleon's relationship with the Legislative Assembly grew increasingly ambivalent. The "red specter" pulled conservatives toward him while his determination to revise the constitution and become eligible for re-election in 1852 repelled them. Meanwhile, during 1851 the "red specter" itself rose to its third peak since 1848 in a setting of surface calm. By 1851, moderate republicanism, ground between years of reaction on the one hand and messianic radicalism on the other was obscured by the fear of "democratic and social" republicans at home and abroad. French political refugees from nearby foreign havens incited their counterparts in France, who went underground into secret societies to prepare for the "échéance de 1852," the reckoning which their propaganda promised would coincide with the selecting of a new president and legislature.

This "great test of 1852," as the *procureur* at Grenoble phrased it, envisaged an electoral victory by radical minorities secretly organized and tactically united against the divided factions of "order." Rumors of the impending crisis of 1852 sped through France. As a detached observer, Walter Bagehot noted late in 1851 that "the tradespeople talked of May, '52, as if it were the end of the world." Identical alarms were typical of administrative reports through 1851. Officials warned their ministers and one another of the perilous unpredictability projected into 1852 by the "party of disorder, with which no truce is possible."[49]

Louis Napoleon decided in August, 1851, that no alternative but a coup d'état remained to end his grappling with the Assembly. In the concurrent and newest phase of the "red specter," he found a suitable pretext for justifying an audacious act of "legitimate defense" of society before the expected dénouement of 1852 arrived. In planning a coup, he could count upon the support of a police system armed by the Assembly's repressive legislation, seasoned by more than two years' intensive practice of its political police arts, and itself convinced that the "red specter" was real.

The Administration's "Invitation" of 1851

Long before ex-prefect August Romieu deliberately exacerbated public fears in 1851 with his influential pamphlet, *Le spectre rouge de 1852,* police functionaries from prefects and *procureurs* on down almost universally recorded their convictions that the "specter" was genuine. In the France of 1849–51, they typically saw only the two alternatives of severe police repression or catastrophic upheaval. Using the new restrictive legislation and their prerogatives under administrative law, they struck effectively at the outward signs of the menace, encouraged and directed by such men as Jules Baroche, Eugène Rouher, and Pierre Carlier—Louis Napoleon's hand-picked chiefs of the Ministries of the Interior and Justice and the Prefecture of Police. The result was "a vast inquisition," a systematic political police operation against the "communist" threat.[50]

Despite their considerable successes, provincial police authorities looked to the immediate future with foreboding, referring repeatedly to the "crisis of 1852," before which the prevailing calm of 1851 masked only a tactical interlude of the reds. The *procureur* at Nancy spoke for many: "one feels that order exists only on the surface."[51] By no means overwhelmingly "Bonapartist" in any doctrinaire sense, police officials showed a characteristic tendency to see in Louis Napoleon the way to a more lasting administrative alternative to chaos. Under an authoritarian executive, the rational processes of administrative control would stamp out the smoldering remains of the "red specter" and restore the nation's social continuity. A distinction was drawn between the great majority and active "demagogic" leaders. Purge the revolutionary firebrands, ran the prevailing administrative view, and the people at large would "without constraint or mental reservations yield to their instincts for order and their profound need of authority."[52] Administrative reports during 1851 elaborated heavily upon this theme, amounting to an invitation for Louis Napoleon to lead administrators and public alike into a more secure polity.

"In the current state of opinion," wrote the *procureur* at Limoges, "the mission of authority seems greater. . . . People are growing accustomed to see it as a continual and necessary protection." His colleagues at Nancy and Douai agreed, observing that universal suffrage had produced no stable democracy. Rather, by dividing "men of order" through the conflict between executive and legislature, the republic left unsatisfied the majority's longing for security from "evil passions."⁵³ These and other officials, either subtly or bluntly, urged the dramatic consolidation of central power to satisfy mass desires and ensure public security under the aegis of an administration free to pursue its paternalistic mission. The repression begun in 1849 must go to its logical conclusion! It was time "to apply a great remedy" to the national illness, the *procureur* at Montpellier advised, and the people knew the only available doctor: "They are saying it only half-aloud still, but they are saying it. Louis Napoleon alone is . . . the keystone of the social order." The crisis of 1852 could be averted through resolute, direct action, "despite all difficulties and moral inhibitions, if you please!"⁵⁴

As such "invitations" were almost rhythmically reiterated by many administrators during 1851, Louis Napoleon prepared his coup d'état, secure in the assumption that his political police bureaucracy would serve loyally and with conviction.

The Army, Gendarmerie, and Administration Aligned for the Coup

For a coup d'état, Louis Napoleon needed reliable men to head the army and gendarmerie, the Ministry of the Interior, and the Prefecture of Police. Foreseeing little opposition after nearly three years of political repression by these agencies, the President could realistically expect automatic responses once the command to act was flashed from Paris. Thus in the autumn of 1851 he was able to plan a nationwide seizure of power with hardly more than a half-dozen other men sharing the secret.

Louis Napoleon's constant advisers during the planning stage were Colonel Emile Fleury, an aide-de-camp; Fialin de Persigny, old comrade and counselor; Comte Charles de Morny, the President's half-brother; Eugène Rouher, an able strategist; and perhaps his private secretary Mocquard. Through Fleury's mediation the young Algerian veteran, General Leroy de Saint-Arnaud, after some wavering, agreed to command the army and gendarmerie as Minister of War for the coup. As for the gendarmerie itself, since 1849 Louis Napoleon had won the open and enthusiastic support of its leaders—made evident in the official

Journal de la gendarmerie de France—through various benevolent gestures including promises of increased personnel and improved service conditions. Gendarmerie officers had also become an important source of political police intelligence for the Elysée, supplementing that provided by normal administrative channels. The Comte de Morny agreed to take the Ministry of the Interior at the moment of the coup d'état. And at the Prefecture of Police, Pierre Carlier, the energetic Prefect since 1849, joined the plot initially as its chief tactician. But Carlier, convinced foe of the "red specter" and a leader in the post-1848 reaction, withdrew from the conspiracy in mid-September because of differences, principally with Morny, over the timing and other details of the coup.

Carlier's successor was Charlemagne-Emile de Maupas, named Prefect of Police on October 26, his appointment coinciding with Saint-Arnaud's entry into the Ministry of War. Maupas, an experienced administrator, began his career in 1840 as a minor official in the Ministry of the Interior. He was a subprefect by 1844 and thereafter earned a reputation for efficiency and authoritarian zeal. Avowing strong allegiance to the Orléans regime and to the revolution of 1848 in its turn, he was nonetheless turned out by the Provisional Government. Undaunted, Maupas won reinstatement as subprefect at Boulogne in January, 1849, aided by political influence and his marriage into a solid administrative family. He joined the reaction with unflagging enthusiasm and identified himself with the Bonapartist cause. In late 1849 he was prefect of the Allier; in March, 1851, he moved into the more important Haute-Garonne. In both posts he successfully sought Louis Napoleon's attention and favor. By mid-1850 his confidential political reports to the ministry were being relayed to the desk of the President himself. During the summer of 1851, Maupas was daring to urge Louis Napoleon to seize power by a coup d'état, because "all parliamentary and strictly lawful methods were powerless."[55] When Carlier withdrew, Louis Napoleon, after further appraisal, chose Maupas to command the Paris police. New plans were rapidly completed and the coup d'état, after several postponements, was set for December 2, anniversary of Austerlitz.

Convinced that resistance to the coup would be concentrated in Paris, Maupas insisted upon the preliminary arrests of certain deputies, anti-Bonapartist generals, and political leaders who might organize the opposition. Prompted by an active jealousy of Morny and the legal subordination of the Prefecture to the Ministry of the Interior, Maupas further demanded and received a written agreement assuring him of autonomous control over the Paris police during the coup d'état. At the end of November, with Carlier's well-oiled police mechanism under his control, Maupas was ready to follow a precise timetable for the early-morning capture of Paris on December 2. The control of France was assumed already to be an administrative *fait accompli*.[56]

CONCLUSION

No French government in the nineteenth century, except possibly that of Louis Napoleon during an interim following the coup d'état of December, 1851, attempted to rule by a literal application of the theoretically boundless executive powers embodied in the doctrines of "legitimate defense," *sûreté générale*, and general police. Political police methods were subject to many variable legal and practical limitations. Still, nineteenth-century France retained both the instrument and the doctrinal sanction of "police state" activity as a normal aspect of public life. If a "police state" be defined as a national polity in which the executive possesses both the formal right to decree and the institutionalized means of enforcing arbitrary coercive measures without the approval or review of a legislature or judiciary, then France before the Second Empire displayed the elements of a "police state." The upheaval of 1848 brought only partial and momentary interruption of this "normality." Indeed, the apparent inability of the new republican order to conduct national affairs peacefully without centralized administrative and police action led almost immediately to the re-establishment and intensification of the traditional system.

Invoking the imperative of the *sûreté générale* in December,

1851, Louis Napoleon briefly and arbitrarily removed the existing constitutional restraints upon unfettered police action. Then he surrounded the traditional system with the new constitutional and partly new legal framework of the dictatorial Republic and the Second Empire. The system operated with fewer practical restraints but still in accord with past theory and practice, without essential changes in established administrative attitudes and organization. In fact, the continuity of French administration, including the attitudes of career administrators toward their own functions, determined in great part the conduct of political police under the Second Empire, becoming on occasion a barrier to certain innovations desired by the regime's leaders.

2

The Coup d'État and an Interim of Extraordinary Police Powers, December 2, 1851–March 29, 1852

BEFORE DAWN on December 2, Morny took over the Ministry of the Interior. Coolly confident and decisive, he invoked fully the theoretically enormous and undefined general police powers open to the executive in a national emergency. In the most audacious political police action in nineteenth-century French history, he manipulated the authorities of eighty-six *départements* with instructions, inquiries, and admonitions that hummed over the telegraph lines during most of December. Flanked in Paris by Maupas at the Prefecture of Police and aided where needed by Saint-Arnaud's troops, Morny (until his resignation on January 22) was the executive officer of a coup d'état launched as Louis Napoleon's last resort in defense of the *sûreté générale*. Thus justified, nearly four months of "extraordinary" political police powers followed Morny's first telegram to the prefects before Louis Napoleon proclaimed the return to formal legality in late March, 1852.

During this turbulent interim, two major activities proceeded concurrently. In an arbitrary, *ad hoc* fashion, police authorities dramatically completed the more restrained reaction of 1849–51 in a vast purge of real and fancied enemies of public order. They arrested suspects on the grand scale, disposed of the prisoners by unusual procedures, purged administrative ranks, and struck severely at political societies and newspapers. Meanwhile, the legal and institutional cornerstones of a constitutional dictatorship were established to define a wider area wherein traditional political police activities could normally proceed solely by administrative fiat. The plebiscite of December 20–21 legitimized

34

all extraordinary measures through the retroactive mystique of delegated popular sovereignty. A new constitution magnified the executive's role and, as a consequence, the administration's. A series of presidential decree-laws—particularly those of December 8 on secret societies and of February 17 on the press—armed the political police with more permissive legality. And on January 22, for the fourth time since the birth of its prototype in 1796, a special Ministry of General Police appeared beside that of the Interior. The administration was not only the chief mechanism of the coup. When the interim ceased on March 29, 1852, it emerged as a major beneficiary of the new order as well, its traditional structure and outlook essentially intact, its freedom to act less impeded by the courts or legislature.

REIGN OF THE *SÛRETÉ GÉNÉRALE*

Morny's first dispatches to the prefects on December 2 invoked the executive's "higher right" of "legitimate defense" against anyone suspected of "fomenting plots" against public security. He delegated full, extraordinary powers until further notice. Arbitrary "measures of *sûreté générale*" superseded normal administrative and judicial procedures, and transcended all legal and customary restraints. Morny ordered the prefects to post and enforce the proclamations of the coup, to purge dubious functionaries forthwith, and to silence all forms of criticism expediently. Many prefects hesitated, perhaps incredulously, to accept such limitless delegation at face value. Morny had to reassure them repeatedly: "Your unswerving aim must be to disorganize the forces of anarchy. Apply your fullest zeal and activity. . . ." In the present emergency, he insisted, one must "eliminate the formalities which delay execution of public security measures."

By authorizing the prefects to announce that anyone found armed or building a barricade would be immediately shot, Morny for the moment plumbed general police theory to its ultimate definition. He modified the prefects' extraordinary mission in but one detail. Probably because of a jurisdictional dispute with the Minister of Justice, he told the prefects publicly to leave the

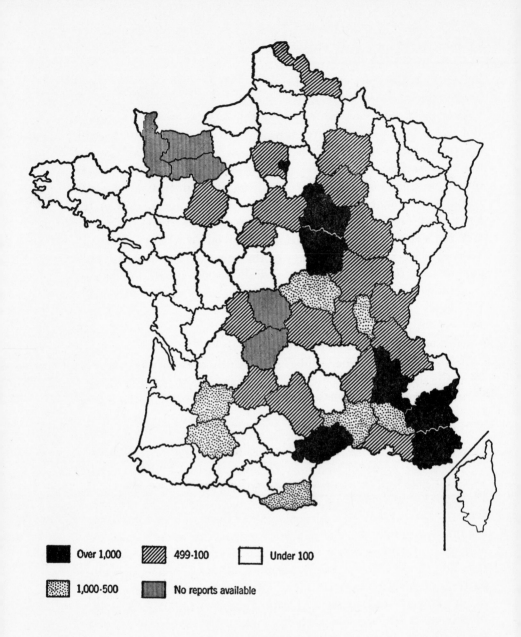

Over 1,000 499-100 Under 100

1,000-500 No reports available

MAP 1

Regional distribution of arrests in connection with the coup d'état of December, 1851

purging of judiciary police personnel to the *procureurs,* who would listen to prefectorial advice before acting.[1]

It is unnecessary here to retell the full story of the coup d'état.[2] Police officials were undoubtedly surprised by the extent of popular resistance which, by no means general throughout the country, was formidable enough to require more than anticipated use of extraordinary powers. The events in Paris are familiar— Maupas' preparations and the arrests of parliamentarians while Louis Napoleon's proclamations were posted; an ominous calm and the waiting for expected popular resistance, which erupted after three days; support of the police against insurgents on the part of General Magnan's troops; and Morny's caustic messages to Maupas, who lacked the composure of his nominal chief. Provincial resistance burgeoned after December 5, just as Morny was authorizing the prefects to announce that "the combat has ceased . . . and France is saved from anarchy."[3]

Many *départements* saw little resistance. Corsica reported no incident. But outside Paris, opposition serious enough to merit the administration's "insurrection" category flared in a dozen rural *départements*. These formed a triangle from the Center (Loiret, Yonne, Nièvre, Saône-et-Loire), southeast to the Drôme, Basses-Alpes, Var, and Vaucluse; then west through the Gard and Hérault, with an island of violence in the Lot-et-Garonne and Gers still farther west. In some of these areas, as Philippe Vigier has recently shown, insurrection was less in defense of the Second Republic or against Louis Napoleon than a regionally organized social protest movement of disaffected peasants and artisans. Unable to make such distinctions, administrators, and conservatives generally, found in the unexpectedly heavy pattern of insurgency an apparent confirmation of their fears of an ambient "red specter." Despite some intramural tensions, the various police and military authorities collaborated to disperse the resistance. National Guards participated in some areas; elsewhere Morny, doubting their loyalty, dissolved them.[4]

In over thirty *départements* put under siege, jurisdictional conflicts between military and civil police authorities were more frequent. A law of 1849 allowed the executive to decree a state

of siege to protect the *sûreté générale*. All police power passed
to the military. Commanders could personally direct police operations or leave them in usual channels. In the latter case, the
administration kept all the political police initiative which the
military did not pre-empt. However, the state of siege categorically obliged civil agents to cooperate with all military orders.[5]

The generals in December used their authority variously. In
the Var, the judiciary police and the courts proceeded normally,
except in Toulon where a military tribunal ruled. In the Basses-
Alpes, the judiciary police fully submitted to military jurisdiction.
The military's repressive measures varied regionally in severity,
ranging up to that in the Haute-Saône and other *départements*
where, prompted by Saint-Arnaud, officers placarded the warning: "All who resist [will] be shot in the name of society in
legitimate defense."[6]

Civil-military tensions often emerged from jurisdictional sensi-
tivities like that displayed at Lyon by General de Castellane,
siege commander, who angrily protested the prefect's use of the
words, "armed with the full powers confided in me. . . ." When
the prefect of the Lot presumed to order extra wine rations for
the Cahors garrison, he ultimately provoked a stern remonstrance
by Saint-Arnaud to Morny deploring this "new and strange
abuse" of extraordinary powers.[7] As for the gendarmerie, their
exemplary role brought only praise from military and civil superiors alike, epitomized by a divisional general: "The gendarmerie acted with its customary élan and vigor." The present writer
found only one complaint against the gendarmerie, and that appeared to be rooted in a prefect's personal grudge.

In the Bouches-du-Rhône and a few other southern *départements,* the prefects and the military combined their extraordinary
powers in the use of "mobile columns" of infantry, cavalry, and
police agents. In the Vaucluse, the column was sent "to scour the
département, reassuring the public and punishing the insurgents
severely." In the Bouches-du-Rhône, each column included a
commissaire of police for making arrests, five gendarmes, and
thirty infantrymen. They captured secret society suspects, hunted
fugitives, closed cafés and other public houses, effaced "seditious"

inscriptions and emblems, and uprooted "so-called trees of liberty."[8]

To supplement other police forces, Morny named four *commissaires extraordinaires* for brief tours as trouble shooters in about fifteen *départements* between December 6 and 13. Empowered to initiate and coordinate all forms of police work, they intervened locally at will and according to Morny's telegraphed advice. They acted against newspapers, public employees, and individual citizens by peremptory orders to officials in all the provincial services or through delegation of their blanket authority to other functionaries. Maurice Duval, one of these extraordinary *missi dominici,* persuaded a bishop to support the coup within the limits of "sacerdotal prudence." He cashiered the prefect of Ille-et-Vilaine, temporarily placing the mayor of Nantes in charge; he gave a subprefect command of the Finistère when its former chief defected. In the Yonne, Pierre Carlier (Maupas' predecessor as Prefect of Police) freely ordered arrests and required all police officers to collaborate with an *ad hoc commission d'instruction* which he created to speed the handling of political prisoners. Carlier told this body to punish the leaders and free the others, "especially those who will reveal who has indoctrinated them." In the Nièvre, he joined the prefect in rewarding those functionaries and notables who most ably abetted the "triumph of order over insurrection."[9]

Mobile columns and special *commissaires* were ephemeral extensions of ordinary political police techniques, in use for only a few days. Otherwise, the December collaboration among military, administrative, and judiciary police forces was the abruptly intensified climax of a repression underway since the June Days of 1848. The state of siege was repeatedly used after 1848, notably in the Rhône. For three years, the prefects and *procureurs* had strained at legal restrictions in their severity toward all expressions of opinion they regarded as subversive. They entered the coup prepared with lists of suspects against whom incriminating evidence, by judicial standards, was either lacking altogether or too circumstantial normally to justify arrest and trial. These lists probably accounted for most of the December arrests, excluding culprits taken in acts of resistance. General de Castellane ascribed the relative ease of the coup at Lyon to the systematic repression and administrative preparation undertaken before December. In Marseille, the archives attest the prefect's diligent surveillance of the suspects who could be gathered in when and if the needs of the *sûreté générale,* rigorously construed, would permit.[10] The authorities particularly yearned to complete their three-year crusade against those who, if not technically guilty of a specific offense under the pre-December republic, were identified with that nebulous cluster of messianic republican aspirations making up the "red specter" of 1848. The residue of that "specter," so recurrently cited in official correspondence before the coup d'état, was thought to live underground by secret organization, eluding normal police methods and the niceties of judicial procedure.

The War on Secret Societies

The December police actions aimed primarily at real or imagined secret political societies. No aspect of the popular political ferment released in 1848 had so disturbed both the conservative public and officialdom alike. By 1851, it was not an overt, spontaneous demonstration toward the "red specter" on the part of people as individuals that the latter feared. Police officials attributed the real social danger to secret societies, heirs of the radical clubs, wherein a hard-core minority organized their disciples and proselytized the gullible in preparation for resumption of a social war begun in June, 1848.

By no means all imaginary,[11] secret societies were sufficiently extravagant in their symbolism, threats, and prophecies to nourish an inflated image of a continuing "red specter." Those who were perplexed, awed, or terrified by visions of a once-inchoate mass learning purposefully to deploy its energies against the existing political and social order envisioned secret societies harboring the general staff and the shock troops of revolutionary nihilism. The threat was as vibrant in the unpublished, confidential reports of administrators as it was in the public jeremiads of frightened conservatives or opportunistic press agents of Bonapartism.

Officials were overinclined to attribute individual radicalism and isolated instances of public discontent to the machinations of occult organization. An outspoken critic here, a radical newspaper there, or groups of men conversing in low voices in a café—all might be the visible clues to a united underground. Men involved in such activities, and their associates, became suspect. In the trite synonyms of administrative jargon, they became members of the "demagogic party," the "demagoguery," "socialists," "anarchists," or "reds." They were assumed to be affiliates of a secret society and duly noted as such in police dossiers, though the evidence against them might be insufficient to justify an arrest. Thousands of these persons were swept up in the coup d'état and its aftermath, especially when open resistance erupted to reconfirm the authorities' preconceived image of an organized conspiracy against society.

The Decree of December 8, 1851

Against endemic secret conspiracy, the extraordinary powers of December were useful but temporary. Louis Napoleon, inspired by Morny, provided the decree-law of December 8 as a special double-edged sword for permanent use. No law of the Second Empire more expressly perpetuated the coup's arbitrary powers.

The decree revised the criminal code to permit the prefects to transport to an overseas penal colony, for periods of between five and ten years, anyone "recognized guilty" of membership in a secret society. In other words, merely by their own decision, the administration might rearrest (after an earlier punishment had been endured) and transport a former offender without new evidence or judicial procedure. The same penalty applied to persons placed under formal police surveillance who were guilty of *rupture de ban* (violating fixed residence conditions imposed by the police). Furthermore, those who had duly completed sentences of formal police surveillance would thereafter have their residence fixed by the administration. In all three cases, the punitive action was by simple measure of *sûreté générale*, without judicial review. The law thus allowed multiple punishment for thousands who were thrust into its relevant categories by the extraordinary events of December, 1851, and for those in future whom it might strike by more regular procedures.[12]

Morny publicly declared that the draconian law of December 8 "must not become a dead letter" until France was permanently rid of the secret scourge. Privately, he enjoined the prefects to use full powers against those not touched by the new decree but who were suspected of secret society membership. Legal criteria of evidence, he reiterated, were quite irrelevant.[13] Long convinced of the danger, provincial authorities needed little prodding. One victim of the December rigors later recalled:

Denounced, we were tracked into our homes, into the fields and woods. Treason crept into our secret society. . . . The red cravat . . . produced in the gendarmes and *mouchards* [police spies] the same sensations as the *muleta* in a Spanish bull.[14]

Meanwhile, Morny and Eugène Rouher, Minister of Justice, disputed the meaning of the ambiguous phrasing, "recognized guilty," upon which much of the decree's import hinged. Morny insisted upon using the law against all who fell into the specified categories, regardless of whether the original penalty was imposed by the courts or by extraordinary administrative measure. Rouher held that the original offense must have been established by competent tribunals *after* December 8. Morny argued from the premise of "legitimate defense" and the executive's right to use "salutary terror" against "those who mislead public-minded persons and prepare revolutions." He added the argument of expediency, warning that the "ordinary delays of a judicial investigation" would dilute the potential impact of a measure intended as "a salutary example" to the country. In rebuttal, Rouher was led to observe that "perhaps the administration misunderstands what we might call the imprescriptible rules of justice." His position won out by early 1852, being enforced by his successor, Abbatucci, and by Maupas as Minister of Police, whose responsibility it was to authorize the prefects' use of the new law.[15] Even so, the prefects' authority under the decree of December 8 remained imposing.

Morny defined secret societies as "all political associations" not authorized by a law of July 28, 1848. It was left to the prefects to define the meaning of "political associations"—an important question because many nonpolitical groups not registered under the 1848 law were in fact suspected of clandestine political agitation. The Ministry of Justice agreed with the prefects that "disguised political societies" could be legally dissolved. The Ministry successfully insisted that in such cases the decree of December 8 could not be invoked, by the fact of dissolution, against all members of such groups. Not guilt by association but individual incrimination, judicially established, must be shown before the law of December 8 applied.[16]

Despite this new reservation, the prefects retained unequivocal jurisdiction over legally condemned secret society offenders and culprits under formal police surveillance. Lists of such persons were maintained. In consultation with the *procureurs,* the prefects might invoke the decree of December 8 for those considered "dangerous" at the termination of their sentences. Or they could hold such unfortunates "by administrative measure" pending final decision. *Surveillés* could be moved about at will if the prefects regarded them as "sources of uneasiness in their communes."[17]

Although Morny urged that the decree of December 8 be applied without hesitation, its use declined after 1852. This moderation, of course, did not alleviate the hardships of those against whom the administration chose to invoke it. The law stood among the most-hated symbols of tyranny in the eyes of Louis Napoleon's enemies and as a reflection of officialdom's fear of the "red specter" in 1851–52.

The December Arrests and Aftermath

Under the decree of December 8 and by extraordinary measures, 26,884 persons were arrested in the coup d'état, over two thousand of whom were in Paris. This total, impressive enough, fell short of contemporary estimates broadcast by such French republican refugees as Victor Schoelcher and Hippolyte Magen, who wrote of over one hundred thousand arrests in the provinces and another twenty-six thousand in the capital.[18] Stories of insurgents wantonly massacred and of babes, sleeping women, and old men cut down by soldiers appear to have been equally unfounded. More credible was Magen's charge that arrests occurred "at random . . . without pretext or warrant," though the statement cannot be accepted whole. Extraordinary powers made arrest warrants (issued only by judiciary police authority) unnecessary. Sometimes they were used, sometimes not. No doubt warrants were already prepared for many persons marked for arrest before December 2. Others encountered the police unexpectedly, perhaps in some cases even "at random." It is difficult to establish the exact count of arrests by region. Many prisoners taken without evidence were let go before any formal recording or investigation. And the statistics of various regional officials disagreed, though discrepancies were usually slight.[19]

Arrest orders numbered more than twenty-seven thousand, including those issued for more than twenty-five hundred persons in flight, some of whom were never caught (the figures later incompletely reported for eighty-one *départements* by the *procureurs*). Of this number, seventeen thousand five hundred were by warrants of judiciary police and nearly seven thousand by "administrative measure" alone.[20]

The judiciary police released over three thousand six hundred, and the prefects released over three thousand—not a substantial reduction despite the number of people. Over twenty-five hundred of those arrested by administrative order were freed by the same means. In all, over nine thousand, or one third, of those arrested were eventually released.

The extent of political arrests during late December and January is indicated in the numbers of prisoners brought in—nineteen thousand four hundred persons. A breakdown of these arrests reveals the major trouble areas.

Arrests were most numerous where open resistance flared. The Var was the major trouble spot, with eighty-seven insurrectionary communes. Total arrests in the Var added up to more than twenty-five hundred. The Hérault provided only a little over a hundred less arrests. The Seine was next with more than two thousand, the Basses-Alpes reported fifteen hundred, and the Nièvre, less than fifteen hundred.

Of the eighty-one *départements* reported by the *procureurs,* fourteen recorded over five hundred arrests, forty-seven counted one hundred or less, and thirty-one, less than fifty. Lozère and Finistère each reported one arrest; Corsica, none.

On a smaller scale, the coup's momentum carried its aftermath into the early spring of 1852. On January 7, Morny asked the prefects to submit new lists of "leaders and principal members of the socialist party" who might later be capable of "insurrection and revolt." Typifying the general spirit of compliance, the prefect of the Moselle sent lists of suspects for each subprefecture, declaring that although no known secret society remained in his area, the new suspects were "just as dangerous as members of such societies and could very well organize if not subjected to an active surveillance." In the Gers, the gendarmerie, administrative, and judiciary police joined in compiling a roster of men "capable of prejudicing the government's interests" and another of outstandingly loyal citizens. Earlier governments, the prefect observed, had made "the unfortunate mistake of not becoming precisely informed upon both their friends and enemies."[21]

Paradoxically, even while reporting the enormous success of December's purge, many *procureurs* and prefects could not shake off their dread of secret societies, which they predicted would revive with Hydra-headed tenacity. The *procureur-général* at Paris blamed the recent "insurrection" exclusively on a secret "army of the apostles of socialism" which, in 1851, was poised for the conquest of society. For the moment dispersed, the army would surely reorganize. Far away in Lyon, General de Castellane agreed. Secret societies, he declared, "have always been, are now, and will always be our country's plague, the haunt of all disorderly men, the laboratory of revolutionaries." In January, 1852, a majority of the *procureurs,* especially those of the Midi, reached similar conclusions. From Lyon came massive documentation including revolutionary manifestos of the *Jeune Montagne* and other groups, embellished with violent slogans and hand-drawn insignia like those of "The Revolutionary Committee of the South," complete with carpenter's level and a Phyrgian bonnet.[22] The secret society specter outlived December to harry police officials throughout the 1850's.

Lest the motto "Liberty, Equality, Fraternity" abet the aspirations of secret organizers, it too fell victim to the coup. The *Moniteur* on January 7 printed Morny's order to efface it from public view. The motto was "a touching device," the Minister conceded, but it was too dangerous in unsettled times. Public buildings, monuments, official flags, and churches were shorn of the incriminating words, though the tricolor, wordless, survived. In the Isère, the prefect explained that removal of the inscription from communal flags was ordained because "the tricolor must remain a national emblem in whose shadow *everyone* can and must unite." He promised to deliver "eagles" as more fitting symbols. With an irony probably unknown to those arrested for "seditious cries," including "Liberty, Equality, Fraternity," the police frugally continued to report such offenses under old letterheads bearing the same expression neatly ruled through once or twice with a fine-pointed pen.[23]

The Threat of Political Refugees

Fear of the activities of French and other political refugees abroad was a corollary of the officials' preoccupation with secret societies at home. Since 1848, international colonies of refugees had appeared in Switzerland, Belgium, and above all, in England. Persistent in their divergent visions of the "democratic and social republic," the leaders of these expatriates dreamed of a new revolution in France to provide the catalyst for an international upheaval. Mazzini, Kossuth, Ledru-Rollin, and other refugee heroes never resolved their own differences; much less were they able to achieve unified control of the French secret societies. Yet the frustrated veterans of 1848 sent enough propaganda and secret agents into France to convince police that the domestic underground was at least partly inspired, directed—and when broken up, renewed—from abroad. In the 1850's, several refugee organizations, especially Mazzini's "European Democratic Central Committee" in London, did have connections inside France. Louis Blanc, Caussidière, Considérant, Delescluze, Pyat, Martin-

Bernard, and Ledru-Rollin were only a few of the French exiles who before December, 1851, expected the French elections of 1852 to signal their return and the "beginning of the democratic republic."[24]

In retrospect, the refugees' optimism now may seem overdrawn. But it was matched by the exaggerated credence which the French government and administration gave to the threat. In 1851, the Prefect of Police and the ministers of Justice and the Interior worried at length about the dangers of newspaper articles and brochures written by the refugees. Scattered but frequent alarms—like that sounded by the *procureur* at Nancy, warning that "socialists" were financing an emissary to seek the refugees' *mot d'ordre* in London—received immediate attention at the highest administrative levels.[25] Before the coup d'état, the French government compiled a documented portrait of "the European conspiracy," drawn from years of political police reports from throughout the country. This and ministerial pressures led Jules Baroche as Minister of Foreign Affairs to importune London for more stringent controls over refugees and for prosecution of the Democratic Central Committee's leaders. Louis Napoleon's propagandic use of the same documentation in a published apologia for the coup should not obscure the seriousness with which such evidence was evaluated in 1851. Even the British Foreign Office in December confided to the Paris embassy its belief that the Parisian secret societies alone could muster nearly twenty thousand "organized and armed" men who were expecting the return, already beginning, "of the greater part of the French refugees in London."[26]

While the police in France were harassing known and suspected members of real and imaginary secret societies, the threat of the refugees' return harassed French authorities. Many dispatches relayed news and rumors of "invasion" by "demagogues" from England and Belgium. From Paris, Morny directed an intensive surveillance of land frontiers and the Channel coast. The Ministry of Marine lent its facilities to prevent "illicit disembarkations." Morny waged an international police offensive against hundreds of London refugees reportedly converging on France through Belgium, using the prefects, the mediation of Fialin de

Persigny on special mission to Lille, and direct correspondence
with the Belgian government. Simultaneously, he tried to check
fugitives from the coup who were in flight to Belgium. Belgian
authorities cooperated in blocking this two-way traffic by dis-
persing some of the "demagogues" and delivering those without
papers to French police at border points.[27]

Much energy was wasted against the "invaders" in December.
The urgent circulation of misinformation and wild rumors bor-
dered often on the ludicrous—which itself attested the gravity of
the problem in French eyes.[28]

Only a negligible few refugees could have "invaded" France
in December, 1851; certainly they had no discernible effect upon
the coup d'état. Indeed, the latter exacerbated the refugee problem by driving new fugitives abroad. Successful repression of the
"red specter" in France intensified French authorities' worry over
its continued propagation beyond their reach. The British ambassador was shocked to overhear a French general mutter, during
an Elysée reception, "We must go and crush them in Switzerland."

French diplomatic protests and demands went to London and
other capitals in December and thereafter. Clearly France chose
to regard its neighbors' harboring of political refugees as a major
problem of both diplomacy and political police. On December 5,
Lord Normanby accurately predicted that the new *emigrés,* determined "to avail themselves of the neighboring shores to make
their voices heard," would create tensions demanding "more than
the usual caution" in British foreign policy.[29]

Morny could act more directly against foreign political refugees on French soil. Beginning a policy that lasted through the
fifties, he allowed the prefects to expel (after ministerial approval) all foreigners "whose presence appears to be politically
dangerous."[30]

Newspapers in the Coup d'État

Along with secret societies, the "demagogic" press was another
prime target of extraordinary police operations. Since 1848, open
criticism of the social order and secret subversion had become

intimately linked in the administrative mind. Moreover, freedom or control of the newspaper press had been central issues since the Great Revolution. Restrictive press laws of varying severity —opening newspapers to outright censorship, prosecution, and a host of lesser administrative controls—had vied successfully with the tenacious if abstract principle of press freedom. For both administrators and conservative citizens, the brief flowering of an unrestricted and ebullient press in 1848 was a disturbing rupture of "normal" press surveillance and regulation. New press laws during the repression of 1849–51 allowed the administration to prosecute, fine, and otherwise harass into oblivion many radical papers whose usually precarious finances made them easy prey to such additional pressures. Early in 1851, the *procureur* at Aix-en-Provence reported the demise of the last outlet for "demagogic opinion" in his district, six months after his colleague at Lyon declared that "neither a socialistic nor Montagnard paper, nor even any kind of opposition journal" survived in his three *départements*.[31]

Yet the *procureurs* and prefects still deplored the remaining legal barriers to arbitrary suppression of troublesome newspapers. Prosecution for the most serious offenses, such as incitement to armed rebellion, required evidence that could meet judicial standards. Furthermore, a law of 1849 assigned press cases to the assize courts, where unpredictable juries often thwarted the intentions of the judiciary police. As the *procureur* at Aix complained, police were "powerless" in courts which rejected "moral proofs alone." Authorities brushed aside the distinctions between a revolutionary and a merely critical editor. Like popular political organization itself, they distrusted a varied and autonomous press. Both were dangerous "abuses" of freedom. Shortly before the coup d'état, the veteran *procureur* at Lyon nostalgically longed for the return of more severity against "the popular habit of feverishly reading newspapers." If one could again "accustom the nation to aspire only to public order and security," then "the destiny of the country would be less uncertain."[32]

In December, the administration translated such hopes into action—and not only against the "socialist" press. Morny pub-

licly empowered the prefects to suspend or suppress any overly
argumentative paper regardless of its political bias. Suspected
editors were to be summarily arrested. Prefects were to authorize
or forbid publication solely upon their decision as to whether the
results "would tend to diminish or to weaken governmental authority." Authorized papers must submit proofs for preliminary
approval. In confidential instructions, Morny was more explicit.
Above all, the prefects must "permit no discussion regarding the
legality of the events just completed." At greater length he outlined what was to become a basic press policy of the authoritarian
Empire:

> You should tolerate only those newspapers which conform to the prescrip-
> tions I have already outlined. . . . If some of them seem disposed to assist
> the liberating action of the government, . . . treat them with just favor. As
> for those journals that solicit permission to reappear, approval must not be
> readily given. Although a formerly hostile and dangerous paper might be
> restrained through fear and become more circumspect, it would still cater
> to its old confederates . . . whom it would regroup into a kind of alliance
> and over whom it would retain an influence that we would be wiser to elim-
> inate.[33]

A decree of December 31, ostensibly to assure speedier justice,
shifted press cases from the courts of assizes (and their juries)
to the correctional courts.[34] In the latter, the judiciary police need
contend only with a tribunal presumably more disposed, if legal
technicalities permitted, to decide for the prosecution. This
change reappeared later in the definitive press law of February
17, 1852.

In December, the police reports told of newspapers suspended,
editors in custody or in flight, presses seized, premises closed,
and the more pliant editors submitting to the prefectorial will.
The new administrative freedom was reflected in the commonest
reasons given for punitive action, such as the belief that a paper
or its editor was "dangerous," that a journal was known as "an
organ of the demagogy," or that a prefect "heard" that a paper
planned to protest against the coup. A few prefects' zeal seemed
tepid to the vigilant Morny, who prodded them by peremptory
telegrams like that to the Côtes-du-Nord: "Suppress . . . *La Foi*

bretonne. It is incredible that you let its number of the 4th pass. It is more than ever imperative that you act with extreme energy and rigor." Other prefects, though zealous enough, seemed misguided to the Minister, who countermanded their local decisions. When the Isère's prefect (who buoyantly asked that his new powers "be extended for a long time") demanded suppression of the legitimist *L'Ami de l'ordre,* Morny refused, explaining: "It is run by men of the moderate party. If it consents to reappear under your control, give it authorization."

Many prefects authorized papers whose editors were willing to abandon earlier political views in support of the new regime. The prefect of the Côte d'Or permanently suppressed two of nine political papers, both "anarchical." Two others, the legitimist *Ordre* and the Catholic *Spectateur,* were also suppressed and then reinstated in return for written promises of cooperation. Of the other five, only one was solidly Bonapartist; four Orleanist and legitimist papers "rallied" to Louis Napoleon. Two of these —the *Union Bourguignone* and *La Côte d'Or*—as well as the formerly suppressed *Spectateur,* were temporarily exempted from the stamp tax and allowed to print special daily editions in anticipation of the December plebiscite. The prefect grumblingly tolerated a degree of Orleanist criticism from the *Côte d'Or.* On behalf of the *Union Bourguignone,* he promoted a subscription drive "to pay the costs of this useful publication."[35]

In Paris, the leading newspapers were suspended for a few days, then allowed to reappear under close police scrutiny. The oppositionist *Siècle,* for example, received permission to print the full texts of governmental proclamations without preliminary authorization. But the editor was sternly reminded that he might do so only "under your personal responsibility, the administration reserving its full right to act against your paper in case this sort of publication should appear to be made with an intent hostile to the government." An entire issue of *L'Opinion Publique* was seized on January 7 because one article was unsigned. Such rigors imposed a humbling experience upon spirited Parisian journalists. The large *Assemblée Nationale* became so cautious by February that its editor asked permission to reprint a letter of Daniel

Webster from *Le Constitutionnel,* an officially favored journal.[36]

The ranks of opposition newspapers and the political press generally were thinned, though not to the extent suggested by an historian's assertion that in 1853 only fourteen daily political papers remained in France.[37] Reports from eighty-three *départements* (excluding Paris, the Bouches-du-Rhône, and the Var) indicated that 258 political newspapers were continuing to publish in late 1852. Twenty-three more survived in Paris following the disappearance of fourteen others in December and January.

Of only 210 provincial papers whose periodicity the present writer was able to verify, twenty-one were dailies and twenty-three published six times weekly; another six in both categories were in Paris. Moreover, in the early 1850's, few French papers aspired to publish daily; far more typical were schedules of three times weekly or less. Of the incomplete total of 258 provincial papers checked, the authorities regarded 136 as safely progovernment, though not necessarily Bonapartist, 102 as opposition (including only six listed as republican), and twenty as neutral. Eighty-seven papers in seventy-nine *départements* reporting were permanently suppressed by extraordinary power; seventy-one of these were labeled "republican," "socialistic," "demagogic," or "anarchical." In thirty-four *départements* (five of which had no political journals even before December) there were neither suspensions nor suppressions. Up to July, 1852, thirty-seven papers, nine being progovernment, voluntarily quit publication for various reasons, principally financial, and because of discouragement in the face of intensified press controls.[38]

Officials were more severe in some *départements* than in others. In the Haute-Garonne, eight out of nine papers were suppressed. One of these had been Bonapartist, and the reason for its suppression was not made clear. The lone survivor, *Le Journal de Toulouse,* was Orleanist and by no means uncritical, though circumspect. To "balance" it, the administration founded *L'Aigle* in 1852. This situation continued until 1868. In the thinly populated Basses-Alpes, *L'Ami de l'Ordre* survived the coup not because it showed Napoleonic sympathies but simply because it was the sole political paper in the *département.* In the nearby Hautes-Alpes, no political paper had existed since 1850. The prefect used two nonpolitical papers to broadcast thirty thousand "Yes" bulletins for the plebiscite and to inspire a front-page editorial headed, "Why Not Say YES?" The prefect of the Ardennes believed complete suspension of the political press "less inconvenient" than preliminary censorship. He almost was able to realize his belief without the use of extraordinary powers. Two of the Ardennes' three political journals collapsed a full year before the coup d'état, leaving only the *Courrier de la Semaine* in Charleville, established in 1850 by a local "association for anti-socialist propaganda." This paper renamed itself *Courrier des Ardennes* in December and was solidly governmental.[39] In the Moselle, two opposition papers survived, along with an Orleanist journal devoted to "order," because in the prefect's opinion the editors feared the "red specter" more than Louis Napoleon.[40]

In the Nord, whose twenty-seven political newspapers on the eve of December 2 outnumbered the press of any other *département* outside the Seine, a varied press survived a relatively mild attrition. The prefect suspended seven papers—six republican and one legitimist—and sealed their presses. Three of these were soon reinstated. The other four, all "ardently democratic," disappeared. Of the remaining twenty-three, *L'Abeille Lilloise* changed to nonpolitical status in April, 1852. Hence the Nord entered the new era with twenty-two political journals, three of them dailies, representing the spectrum of opinion from non-socialist republicanism to Bonapartism. Only five were classified as "very devoted" to the new regime. In terms of their June, 1852, circulation figures, the unequivocally progovernment papers in the Nord counted only 69,384 out of the total circulation of 478,168 for the entire departmental political press.

However, the prefect was in a better position than these figures indicated. Besides the "very devoted" category, he could reasonably depend upon the non-Bonapartist but "rallied" group with a circulation of just under three hundred thousand. In his other categories, the "accept but won't serve" class sold over fifty thousand and the outright opposition somewhat less. No frankly Bonapartist papers appeared among the top five in circulation,

which were: the Orleanist *Liberté* (daily, "rallied," 290,535);
the republican *Echo du Nord* (daily, "neutral," 56,158); the
republican *Courrier du Nord* (three times weekly, "rallied," 32,-
174); the legitimist *Gazette de Flandre et d'Artois* (daily, "hostile," 25,550); and the Orleanist *Dunkerquoise* (three times
weekly, "unreliable," 22,137). Among the "very devoted," the
Echo de la Frontière at Valenciennes and the *Observateur d'Avesnes,* neither dailies, could claim the highest circulations of 15,520
and 14,603, respectively.[41]

Generally speaking, the December police action was intended
to destroy newspapers considered irreconcilable, not to eliminate
the opposition press altogether. Rather, lacking a widespread
Bonapartist press, the prefects sought to gain control over newspapers of diverse opinions, thus at once creating a tolerable
medium for official propaganda while preserving the appearance
of a press "balanced" by moderately critical opposition. Most
papers were authorized if their editors agreed to follow administrative tutelage or at least to refrain from systematic hostility.
A few formerly radical republican journals collaborated, but
legitimist, Orleanist, and moderate liberal editors were far more
compliant.

In the Gers, for example, the prefect regarded the three political papers as "unanimous in attacking the President's policy. . . ."
Two of these were "Montagnard"; they were suppressed on
December 4. The Orleanist survivor, *L'Opinion* at Auch, "immediately offered to abstain from any hostility or even from all
political discussion." Its stockholders installed new journalists
"devoted to the government," which allowed the prefect to pre-
dict that he could rely upon it absolutely.[42] Some editors implored
the prefects to authorize their papers in such terms as, "Mindful
that it is being a good republican to sacrifice one's personal prefer-
ences . . . to the general welfare, I shall in no way attack the
government's actions." This request was refused. Others resisted
all prefectorial blandishments yet were allowed to publish if their
critical tone remained moderate. Thus the *procureur* at Marseille
noted confidently that most of the city's diversified press now was
led by the sense of common danger to support the new order

"without reservations." If the *Gazette du Midi* continued to mix its denunciation of the "red specter" with "indirect and mitigated" opposition, the authorities could easily afford to tolerate it.[43]

In December, the government was anxious to rally the press into a posture of unanimity for the plebiscite and the later elections to the Corps Législatif, and yet preserve a semblance of press "freedom" and diversity. After Morny, Fialin de Persigny left the prefects largely to their own ingenuity in this difficult assignment: "the law is obscure and equity alone can guide the hand of justice."[44]

The prefect of the Calvados used his latitude to suppress one "socialist" paper and to allow two republican and two "moderate" journals to stand by while two other "conservative" (though not frankly Bonapartist) papers took the initiative in stimulating the public for the plebiscite. On December 12, the legitimist *Intérêt Public* at Caen portrayed the coup as the triumph of public morality and logic in accord with an "innate sentiment of popular reason" invoked by Louis Napoleon as he averted "the most frightful civil war." In the Ille-et-Vilaine, the prefect entered the coup with only one reliable paper (*L'Auxiliaire Breton* at Rennes).

He suspended, then reinstated, three other unfriendly journals: the legitimist *Journal de Rennes,* the more moderate legitimist *Petit Courrier de la Bretagne,* and the "advanced republican" and "democratic" *Progrès.* Postponing the *Journal's* revival until after the plebiscite, he allowed the *Progrès* and *Courrier* meanwhile to publish under preliminary censorship and to discuss the plebiscite "so as not to appear to be compromising liberty of expression." But, he informed Morny, only "a simple declaration without provocative analyses" was allowed. Although the prefect intended to tolerate both papers after the plebiscite, he assured the Minister that all political discussion other than "a simple statement of official . . . facts will be strictly forbidden and at the least infraction, repression will be immediate and complete." When the *Journal de Rennes* was subsequently reinstated, it agreed to use no material "tending to discuss the legality of the events just accomplished or to diminish governmental authority."[45]

When extraordinary powers ended in March, 1852, the hostile press was severely pared away though not fully eliminated. A severe new press law of February 17 was already making its weight felt. Under it, the more pliable opposition papers lived on as the prefects disciplined and groomed them for a moderate opposition, neutral, or progovernment role under the Second Empire.

The Administration and the Plebiscite of December, 1851

The administration's intensified political police activities were indispensable in making the coup d'état; they were also useful in securing popular endorsement of Louis Napoleon's decision and, incidentally, of the administration's own extraordinary operations. To make the plebiscite of December 20–21 into "a veritable national festival," as Maupas described it, functionaries from the prefects on down worked to bring out the most favorable vote. Their intervention was thorough and systematic, short of direct coercion at the polls or falsification of the results. Morny and the prefects stressed the guarantee of a "free vote" and rigid adherence to meticulously prescribed voting procedures. On December 4, a decree introduced the secret ballot. Perhaps this decision owed something to reports like that of the prefect of the Doubs, who noted that even "the most devoted citizens" showed a "fear of inquisition" and thus "unanimously" desired a secret vote. However, Morny made it clear that the prefects must advertise the "President's thinking" to the electorate.[46]

On this cue, the Interior and Justice functionaries mobilized their varied means of ensuring a resounding "yes" vote, not least of which was the prefects' control of the press. Officials' zeal doubtless sometimes exceeded the letter and even the spirit of ministerial instructions. Generally, the administration concentrated on reducing abstentions and exhorting voters with patriotic appeals and visions of the "red specter" in a situation wherein the opposition lacked the means and temerity to speak out. No special "terror," other than that already felt by the coup's enemies, was generated for the occasion. But informal psychological pressures could be and were applied, particularly in smaller communes where neighbors had few major secrets from one another. Suspects just freed from arrest sometimes voted openly, though not required to do so, fearing police reprisals otherwise.[47]

Obeying ministerial orders, the judiciary police helped bring out the vote. Justices of the peace verified and updated electoral lists. One justice, crusading against "the fatal system of abstention," told of house-to-house visits in six communes, where he checked voter's cards and warned the citizenry not to ignore such an important election because this was not to be "a political vote, but a vote related to a truly social question." In the Sarthe, the prefect branded abstainers, and even criminals, as sluggards, because their inaction possibly furthered "the suicide of the fatherland." Louis-Hippolyte Dieu, one of the era's most aggressive prefects, instructed all functionaries in the Haute-Saône to enforce electoral regularity and a free vote. But he also publicized Louis Napoleon's proclamations and others written by local electoral committees, business groups, and himself—all urging a "yes" vote as the only sane choice between "peace or the most frightful civil war . . . the prosperity of labor or the overthrow of the entire social order." Scrupulously reminding citizens that theirs was a free choice, he expressed his confidence in their "good sense, love of the good, . . . and patriotism." And he predicted that "you will vote for order because all of you know that the country's safety lies in supporting Louis Napoleon."[48]

That support was indeed forthcoming, by a majority of over six million eight hundred thousand.

THE FOURTH MINISTRY OF GENERAL POLICE

By February, 1852, though extraordinary police powers continued in force, most of the legal and institutional pillars that would stabilize the new dictatorship were settled in position. The December plebiscite conferred the national blessing on the coup d'état, the decrees accompanying it, and a new constitution whose strong executive power ensured more arbitrary administrative centralization. Specific aids to the political police function—in addition to the decree of December 8 and the press law of February 17—appeared in the statute books, usually based upon traditional precedents.

Most specific of all in Louis Napoleon's re-emphasis on the executive's responsibility for political police was his creation of a Ministry of General Police on January 22. Charlemagne-Emile de Maupas, Prefect of the Police during the coup, headed the new ministry. Ironically, the Interior's hierarchy, in its apparent moment of aggrandizement, saw the supreme control of its political police functions lodged in a new administrative superstructure with general police jurisdiction over all France. This was the fourth experiment with an institution which, after its prototype of 1796, had reached its apogee, despite a brief interruption, under Napoleon I, and had lived a third and briefer life under the Bourbons until 1818.

Louis Napoleon's private motives for reviving the ministry remain a matter of conjecture. Maupas attributed the move solely to his chief's "very understandable veneration" of the First Empire.[49] An editor of *La Patrie* praised it as a necessary counterattack against the "red specter"—that is, the "new dangers and passions still threatening civilization with total destruction." Some considered the new ministry purely temporary; others thought it was meant to be an integral part of the new order. The Prince-President himself stated his public motives in an open letter to Maupas printed in the *Moniteur* on January 23.

Taken at face value, with a little reading between lines, Louis Napoleon's own statement seems plausible enough. He admitted that the new regime's dependence upon widened administrative powers—particularly those of general police in the Ministry of the Interior—might threaten his own personal control as a benevolent dictator. Effective centralization required some check upon "the sole political ministry" lest the latter become too autonomous and self-centered. Without such a check, the executive would have no reliable source of complete and objective information on the activities of the various ministries. Only a specialized agency devoted to constant surveillance of the whole administration and in unique contact with himself could "provide the government with the means of doing good" for the nation. The chief of state must have *direct* control; only thus could he give symmetry to an otherwise imperfect edifice of centralization. It seems reasonable to speculate that Louis Napoleon intended the ministry to become a permanent feature of the authoritarian Empire.

The ministry as constituted could succeed only at the expense of the Interior's time-hardened leadership in general police functions. Success would depend upon the prefects' cooperation with the new minister and his skeleton staff of supervisory personnel who numbered only a small fraction of the functionaries commanded by the prefects. As predicted three years earlier by Léon Faucher, an ex-minister of the interior, conflict between the prefectorial corps and a specialized police ministry was inevitable, and tension between the minister himself and other ministers very likely. Faucher had observed that the French police function was so integrated with general administration that control of the two activities was inseparable. Two ministries attempting to share such authority would contend for supremacy in both police and administration. He predicted further that a minister of police would seek arbitrary power within the state: "the *lettre de cachet* is the cornerstone of the institution, or the institution is nothing."[50]

Maupas' appointment was the product of dissension among the captains of the coup d'état. By January a behind-scenes rift had opened between Morny and Louis Napoleon over seizure of the Orléans properties and the policy of reviving a police ministry. Another conflict emerged between Morny on the one hand, Maupas and Persigny on the other. Personality clashes among these men of firm convictions and considerable egos were perhaps as consequential as divergence over policies. On January 22, when he announced Maupas' elevation to a ministry, Louis Napoleon accepted Morny's resignation and moved Persigny into the Ministry of the Interior. Persigny, who had sought the portfolio of Foreign Affairs (this was retained by the Marquis de Turgot, the original choice for the police ministry), undertook his new duties with little respect for Maupas. The two men's relationship could hardly improve so long as Persigny's hierarchy held the very

powers Maupas must absorb if his own apparatus were to achieve
its mission.

Even before Maupas had completed his agency's organization
in early February, rumors of internecine conflict filtered through
governmental and business circles in Paris. In mid-February a
police officer stationed at the Bourse reported that no one expected the new ministry to be more than a passing "ministry of
circumstance." And prophetically, old Chancelier Pasquier
quipped, "There is a child who can't live but who can give his
parents a lot of trouble before dying."[51]

DISPOSAL OF THE DECEMBER PRISONERS

Maupas took office just in time to become involved in the final
disposition of the prisoners taken in the coup d'état. By the end
of December it had become clear that what had begun by extraordinary measures required unusual means of liquidation. Unexpected resistance during the coup more than filled the jails in
some *départements*. No plans were made in advance for emptying
them. Normal judicial procedures, if used, were sure to be overwhelmed by more than twenty-six thousand cases awaiting solution. In January, the government faced the disposal problem only
tentatively, amid confusion and conflicts among authorities. In
the *départements* under siege, the military went their way; the
prefects were in charge elsewhere. The judiciary police attempted,
often disgruntledly, to assist both generals and prefects. Not until
February were tentative procedures scrapped and the three kinds
of authorities brought into a concerted solution of the problem.

The Decrees of January 9, 1852

Eighty-nine arrested ex-representatives of the defunct National
Assembly received separate and unequal punishment by three
presidential decrees on January 9. Promoted by Morny with
Maupas' support, the decrees were intended as temporary meas-
ures (according to Granier de Cassagnac) to be rescinded when
regularized government returned. Five men were transported.
Sixty-six, including such luminaries as Victor Hugo, Victor
Schoelcher, Raspail, and Esquiros—all branded as known leaders

of "socialism"—were expelled from French soil under pain of transportation for illegal return. Another eighteen, capable of endangering the country by "agitation," suffered temporary exile. This group included such varied personalities as Duvergier de Hauranne, Adolphe Thiers, Émile de Girardin, Edgar Quinet, Pascal Duprat, and Generals Changarnier, Lamoricière, and Le Flô.

The *Moniteur* announced on January 19 that the expellees and exiles were given time to settle their affairs before being taken to the frontier or abroad by policemen in "bourgeois" dress. This escort service had its ironies. Unlike hundreds of refugees who fled from the police into Belgium, General Changarnier, using the name "Leblanc," was taken to Mons by two officers and told to remain there. Ex-representative Baze passed through Belgian customs as "Lasalle," the servant of his police escort, bound for Aix-la-Chapelle.[52]

Indecision during January

Regarding other prisoners, consultation among the ministers of War, Justice, and Interior in late December produced no consistent policy. Rouher confided to the *procureurs* that the government was still undecided on appropriate measures. During most of January each minister steered his own course.

Morny, apparently using the decrees of January 9 as his model, asked the prefects for lists of prisoners arranged in the same three categories, plus a fourth rubric for persons to be temporarily banished from their home *départements*. This last group was reserved for the suspects who the prefects *believed* had favored "known leaders of socialism"! Such a vague criterion of culpability, Morny reminded the prefects, remained legitimate and morally justifiable as long as extraordinary powers continued to uphold the *sûreté générale*. Ordinary judicial procedures were inadequate for the mass of cases; anyway, open trials "would constitute a new public danger."[53]

Rouher requested the *procureurs* to send posthaste all relevant information on the prisoners and to recommend action in each case. The response showed that most of the December arrests were made for incitement to civil war, affiliation with a secret society, seditious words, detention in the interest of "tranquility," and mere suspicion without specific charge.[54] The *procureurs'* recommendations for disposal of the cases varied greatly in kind and severity including: unconditional release, release under "caution" or after preventive detention, expulsion from the *département* or region, internment in a fixed residence, detention to await trial, application of "severest measures," and transportation under the decree of December 8 or simply by measure of *sûreté générale*. Reduced to fewer specific categories, these suggestions apparently became the guide for the kinds of punishment later meted out (by the Mixed Commissions) in February and March. The *procureurs'* information also enabled the Ministry of Justice to decide upon thirty-six legal charges which, if extraordinary powers were not finally used, could be invoked against the prisoners in court. These ranged from political to criminal offenses such as looting, spreading false news, murder, theft, arson, moral charges, destruction of harvests and trees, and "attempted crimes or misdemeanors uncompleted because of circumstances beyond the control of their authors."[55]

In areas under siege, Saint-Arnaud, between December 19 and January 17, gradually generalized the use of three-officer "military commissions." Prisoners were classified according to recommendations for release, transportation, and trial by courts martial. Each divisional general autonomously fixed the policies and procedures governing the commissions in his district. From Lyon, General de Castellane ordered his commissioners to make new arrests; he also added a fourth punitive category for unwanted foreigners who would be expelled by the gendarmerie. He directed that only those whose conviction was certain be sent to military courts. Others, denounced either by the police or the public, were to be punished arbitrarily in the name of the *sûreté générale*, especially if they were suspected secret society members. The General emphatically declared that in their exceptional role the military commissions need not bother with "material proofs." Routine justice found it "nearly always impossible in a regular court to confront [such culprits] with *material proofs* of their *affiliation* with these infamous societies."[56]

Castellane's appointees were actually less severe than their instructions permitted. In the Isère, where many persons had in December been denounced on the merest hearsay along with real secret society militants, the commission sent those considered "very dangerous" on shaky evidence back to the judiciary police in hopes that investigation would yield sounder bases for punishment. Pressed by the distractions of haste, the three officers at Grenoble apparently strove conscientiously, within their own sphere of reference, to be discriminatingly just. Those not seriously incriminated could go free by an expression of repentance combined with the appearance of a person "without influence" or of "little intelligence."

Where the military were in charge, they often clashed with civilian officials. Prefect Guérin in the Eure-et-Loire fulminated against the leniency of the general commanding his *département* because he released most of the prisoners after investigation by the judiciary police. Thus, according to the prefect, those actually given to the military commissions "were nearly all obscure agitators pushed by their leaders into culpable activities." Had the prefect been left in control, he would have swiftly rooted out "the most incriminated agents of the socialist party"!

In the Aveyron and Hérault, the *procureur* at Montpellier worked harmoniously with General Rostolan. There the military commissions took only cases arising from insurrection. Others were left to the prefects and judiciary police. But the *procureur* at Nîmes complained bitterly that the military commissions, during their "usurpation" of his own functions, treated the judiciary police as mere underlings. The *procureur* retaliated by refusing to deliver certain dossiers, and he defied the army's insistence that he issue arrest warrants against men who "were not compromised by even the slightest trace of evidence."

On January 19, the Minister of War told the military commissions to be more moderate. They must not confuse the "imitative and flighty followers" with the truly "inveterate conspirators." All the accused must undergo a second interrogation and review of their cases.[57] Within two weeks thereafter, the military commissions disappeared in favor of a more coordinated solution of the disposal problem.

Louis Napoleon on January 29 opened a brief "liberation" period announced by Persigny in the *Moniteur* of January 30. Now the prefects, *procureurs,* and generals were to join in freeing all prisoners who were "merely misled and whose liberation cannot cause society any danger." The Prince-President's generosity was now offered to all "misguided men who were led into revolt only by weakness or ignorance." Saint-Arnaud's similar instructions were more laconic. Because the jails were too full, the generals must release all prisoners named by the prefects, whether systematic investigations of their cases had begun or not. In the ensuing exodus, the Vaucluse, an extreme example, saw half of its prisoners go free. The liberation policy displeased General de Castellane, who feared that the civil functionaries' use of such clemency unjustly thrust the odium of recent severities upon the army.[58] Persigny's published circular of January 29 had an unpublicized sequel. Confidentially, he later chided the prefects for following his counsel of moderation so literally as to release potentially dangerous men. But, he pointed out, extraordinary powers still permitted the prefects to rearrest suspects if the *sûreté générale* required it.[59]

The Mixed Commissions

The new "liberation" policy soon gave way to another. On February 3, more than a month of indecision in Paris ended with a coordinated solution. In each *département,* the ministers of War, Justice, and Interior jointly convened "a sort of mixed tribunal" including the prefect, the general of the military subdivision, and a *procureur.* These "departmental commissions"—the official designation, which never caught on—would finally judge those "pernicious elements" still in custody. The mixed tribunals were enjoined to combine the needs of justice, the *sûreté générale,* and humanitarianism in "careful deliberation." They could render verdicts for dismissal, formal surveillance or internment in France under the Ministry of Police, temporary or indefinite expulsion from French territory, transportation to penal colonies in Algeria or Cayenne, and transfer for trial before either a court martial or tribunal of correctional police. They could not impose sentences of imprisonment, hard labor, or death.[60]

Created solely by ministerial directive, the Mixed Commissions, according to one's perspective, were either illegal kangaroo courts or responsible guardians of the *sûreté générale* invested with the imperium of the "legitimate defense" doctrine. Leaders and advocates of the new regime of course took the latter view. In a decree of March 5, Louis Napoleon buttressed the commissions' legality by authorizing the execution of their decisions. This act by a chief of state empowered by plebiscite to enact decree-laws later induced the Court of Cassation to uphold the Mixed Commissions' legality even after the fall of the Second Empire.[61]

In hardly more than a month, the Mixed Commissions penalized almost twenty thousand persons. Slightly more than half were transported to Algeria (9,581) or Cayenne (239); over eight thousand were interned or placed under formal police surveillance in France; the rest were expelled from French soil or temporarily exiled.[62] The Commissions followed diverse procedures and sometimes differed on the concepts that should govern their mission of political expediency. In the Morbihan, the commission rejected its wide discretionary powers even after Maupas ordered it to proceed; that of the Loir-et-Cher sat only under protest. Many *procureurs* were "visibly embarrassed" by what they regarded as irregular procedure and excessive powers. The chief of the *parquet* at Aix-en-Provence declared it unjust that the Commissions judge cases arising from arrests which the prefects had allegedly ordered "without proofs and mostly on the basis of slanderous denunciations."

The diversity of operating principles probably explains the frequent discrepancy between the severity of the Mixed Commissions' sentences and the degree of resistance or radical ferment in a given *département* during December. Generally the decisions seem to have aimed primarily at the "leaders of socialism" (whatever this might have meant from one region to another) instead of men "without influence." The majority of cases were peasants, artisans, innkeepers, doctors, lawyers, journalists, and teachers. Members of esteemed families in some instances enjoyed special indulgence.[63]

The Mixed Commissions' edicts were executed immediately. *Proscrits* sailed from Toulon to Cayenne under the auspices of the naval authorities. The prefects handled transportees to Algeria under the Ministry of War. Maupas had to intervene on behalf of foreigners swept into the exodus. He reminded the prefects that the Mixed Commissions lacked the authority to transport foreigners without due judicial process. Hence they must be shifted into the categories of expellees or interned in France.

Expellees, internees, and *surveillés* fell within the jurisdiction of the Ministry of Police. Maupas decided that expellees to England or Belgium must leave within eight days after notification by the prefects, who supplied "free" passports for an obligatory itinerary out of France. Those preferring another country might go there if their motives had no "political character" and if they could obtain a visa within ten days after receipt of their "free" French passports. Maupas immediately met difficulties. Except for England and Belgium, neighboring states refused to accept expellees other than their own nationals.[64]

In March, Maupas directed that France's rejected persons cease to be sent to Sardinia, Switzerland, or Spain. Spain later relented by accepting a few expellees if they were financially solvent and settled away from the border. The Kingdom of Sardinia accepted its own subjects but allowed other Italians to cross its territory only if they had money for the trip. Others were turned back at the frontier. They congregated in the Var, much to the wrath of the prefect, whose protests forced Maupas to forbid the prefect of the Bouches-du-Rhône to expel Italians who could not meet the Sardinian conditions. Ruefully, Maupas admitted to one prefect that "England is the only country . . . that consents to receive the expellees." By mid-April this admission became policy when he instructed that the remaining expellees go to England only, even Belgium having become inhospitable.[65]

Maupas thus became party to a paradox in being since June,

1848. To join the thousands of refugees who voluntarily found haven abroad before and after December, 1851, the government now officially sent some sixteen hundred more. Yet nothing caused French police, who were confident they could repress subversion at home, more frustrated concern than the concentration of still-obdurate, messianic, political revolutionaries abroad.

Maupas also had to deal with the thousands of persons whom the Mixed Commissions sentenced to internment or formal police surveillance. Neither punishment was new in 1852 for political and criminal offenders. In administrative law, such persons were subject to the *haute police* function. But the sudden expansion of these categories forced Maupas to issue new regulations and to plead for effective enforcement. In the *Moniteur* on April 16, he explained that internees lived in residences fixed by the police. *Surveillés* continued in their chosen residence but were restricted in their movements. Both groups regularly reported to police authorities and carried passports indicating their status. By regulations accumulated since 1849, Paris and other large cities were off-limits to them. To these forbidden areas, Maupas added the environs of presidential residences, twenty-three communes served by the Orléans-Bourges railway, and nine *départements*.[66]

The prefects could change the residence of internees under certain conditions. *Surveillés* must be "continually observed and followed," Maupas ordered. Persons under internment or surveillance endured the double jeopardy permitted by the decree of December 8. Once their sentences had expired, they could again be placed under surveillance and their residence assigned. Maupas advised the prefects to use this additional weapon freely. Such stringent regulations were enforced when the prefects were zealous enough or had the time and means to carry them out. When the *procureurs* occasionally criticized such severity, the protest was against the method, not the prefects' political intent or their power to act.

Administrative law and doctrine clearly sided with the prefects. The *procureur* at Rouen, for example, declared the minute regulations imposed in the Eure upon internees and *surveillés* to be both unjust and illegal. He predicted that some of the victims would

seek legal remedy. But he reminded his staff that the Mixed Commissions' decisions were "acts of a quite exceptional nature"
undertaken in the name of the *sûreté générale*. Therefore "separation of powers" prevailed; no court could accept an action
for recourse unless the police themselves submitted the case. The
Minister of Justice agreed that such political police measures
were "entirely foreign to the judicial authority."[67]

The problem was soon alleviated. Hardly had the Mixed Commissions handed in their decisions when Louis Napoleon began
their wholesale revision, using the same executive powers earlier
invoked to justify the punishments.

Revision of the Mixed Commissions' Decisions

Louis Napoleon began his presidential career in December,
1848, by pardoning the 483 *proscrits* who were the residue of
thousands condemned earlier in the year for political reasons.
Now in March, 1852, he launched a larger-scale clemency which
began with administrative confusion and dissension recalling that
preceding the Mixed Commissions.

On March 9, the Minister of Justice informed his colleagues
of Police, Interior, and War that he was appointing a Committee
on Political Pardons, a six-man board representing the four ministries, to advise the chief of state. The Committee met on March
15; its first proposals went to Louis Napoleon within four days.

Two weeks later the President appointed three Extraordinary
Commissaires of the Government to a six-weeks mission of revision in areas where the Mixed Commissions had been most active.
They had *carte blanche* in the revision of sentences and they could
release persons awaiting trial on political charges "whose liberty
would not seem dangerous for public security."[68] The three executive agents worked concurrently with the Committee on Political Pardons but without any liaison. Extraordinary *Commissaires*
General Canrobert and Colonel Espinasse were aides-de-camp of
the Prince-President. Alexandre Quentin-Bauchart, the third
commissaire, was an ex-liberal of the 1847–1848 period who supported Louis Napoleon after the June Days, until the arrests of
representatives in the coup. Forgiven for his protests on that

occasion, in March, 1852, he was a newly appointed Councilor of State.

Assigned to twelve of the most disturbed *départements* of December, Quentin-Bauchart was the most liberal and active of the three men in revising sentences. He freed 1,377 out of 3,020 transportees and commuted the sentences of 1,047 others to lesser penalties. Others were later amnestied on his recommendations. General Canrobert liberated 727 out of 4,076. Colonel Espinasse was content with two hundred pardons and one hundred commutations out of slightly more than four thousand cases.[69] Dissension ensued within the administration as to the wisdom of such a clemency policy in general and the liberality of Quentin-Bauchart in particular. Colonel Espinasse himself viewed the entire procedure gloomily. In his report he portrayed the revisions as producing "the worst effect" upon the public. The Mixed Commissions, he believed, had punished only the guiltiest men. If they erred, it was on the side of excessive indulgence, for the Colonel estimated that more than one hundred twenty thousand secret society members still roamed in three designated *départements* alone. He urged his chief to grant no further pardons that were not based upon specific petitions by regional administrative authorities.[70]

Liberally given or not, the Extraordinary *Commissaires'* revisions had strings attached. To accept clemency was technically to admit original guilt. Recipients signed oaths to Louis Napoleon formally promising to abjure secret societies and to obey the law. Even those with full pardons could become the objects of police surveillance.

Dissension over the revisions also arose in the Committee on Political Pardons and in the Ministry of Justice. One of the latter's very annoyed delegates on the Committee deplored the "very regrettable misunderstandings" mischievously generated by two uncoordinated and overlapping clemency jurisdictions. The Minister of Justice prevailed. After April 26, all subsequent revisions of the Mixed Commissions' decisions depended on his recommendation, with the advice of the Minister of Police and, after June, 1853, that of the Minister of the Interior.[71] Thereafter,

individual pardons and commutations were granted in this fashion, supplemented intermittently by more comprehensive group
amnesties. During the fifties, individuals not recommended by
the administration or included in amnesties could petition the
Minister of Justice for reconsideration of their plight. However
obtained, executive clemency merely made the recipient *eligible*
for pardon. First he must make an "act of submission" accepting
the Napoleonic regime and submitting to whatever conditions of
surveillance the police deemed necessary.[72] Most of the eligibles
accepted the required conditions.

THE END OF EXTRAORDINARY POWERS

A decree of March 27 ended the interim of extraordinary
powers. It raised the state of siege, abolished extraordinary police
measures, dissolved the Mixed Commissions, and declared that
in future no arrests or prosecutions would be undertaken outside
ordinary laws and procedures. Abbatucci, Minister of Justice,
announced that the time had come "to give the common laws all
their rightful scope" now that public order and civilization itself
were safe. Two days later, Maupas directed the prefects to ex-
ecute the decree. Anyone under arrest by administrative measure
would immediately be released or sent to the proper court.[73] As
Maupas' circular went out to the prefects, Louis Napoleon
opened the Senate and Legislative Body with the message that
France now reposed upon "institutions appropriate to its needs";
hence "the dictatorship which the people confided to me ceases
today. Things will resume their normal course."

Normality for the administrative and judiciary police implied
a freer use of their traditional political police powers in the
institutional setting constructed during the interim since December 2. Expressions of satisfaction converged upon Paris from the
provincial administration, possibly contributing to the euphoria
detected by Count Hübner, the Austrian ambassador, at a meeting
attended by Maupas and other leaders: "around an enormous
table one saw nothing but satisfaction, or rather, men who count
upon all sorts of satisfactions. . . . It is their honeymoon. Everyone hopes."

It was generally agreed that the coup had effectively consoli-
dated power for an era of constructive authoritarianism. So reported Piétri, the new Prefect of Police, throughout 1852. Piétri
considered the administrative "consolidation of power" increasingly secure because of a new "respect for authority" sweeping
through the population. Even the "demagogic" leaders knew now
they would need years to rebuild a mass following. The legitimists
and Orléanists were resigned to present realities.

Similar views reached Paris from the departmental administrative heads. In certain regions the legitimists were regarded, next
to the "red specter," as the most formidable though not truly
dangerous opposition group of the future. The prefect of the Ille-
et-Vilaine, a heavily legitimist area, predicted that all but a few
of the most stubborn legitimists would find in the fact that "some
chateaux were burned . . . a sufficient motive for at least temporary fusion" with other partisans of order, as in 1848—because
"the social question dominates over the political." This prefect
hoped that moderate liberals and republicans would "instinctively
feel that the flag of '89 is now borne by the chief of state" and
would move neither to the Left nor toward the ultra-royalists.
The clergy would surely follow the bishops, added the prefect,
and if prodded could be eased into "a more active role" on behalf
of the new order.[74]

The "red specter," *procureurs* and prefects almost unanimously
agreed, would require authoritarian administration for years to
come. An official at Marseille very typically saw no outward sign
of political disorder in May, 1852. "But we must have no illusions
about this apparent calm," he warned. The hard-core leaders of
subversion—"not resigned to their defeat in any final way"—
would surely reorganize "in the shadows," hoping in more favorable times "to resume their work of destruction."[75] This theme
appeared endlessly in administrative reports during the 1850's.

Meanwhile, in 1852 the administration anticipated some specific satisfactions along with its general satisfaction, as Count
Hübner had noted. It expected rewards—an attitude not lost on
Louis Napoleon whose address of March 29 mentioned that improvements in the material welfare of "the greater part of the

principal functionaries" were already in progress. The administration expected further to administer freely on behalf of its chosen "mission" of preserving public order. But problems lay ahead.

In the spring of 1852 the most immediate obstacle to the realization of greater administrative autonomy was not the "red specter." It was the newest administrative creation of the interim just ending—the Ministry of General Police.

3

Administrative Conflict and the Demise of the Ministry of General Police, January, 1851–June, 1853

HAVING COME victoriously through the coup d'état, administrators entered the year 1852 in anticipation of a more nearly ideal administrative state. "The administration, assisted by the army," wrote one advocate of such a new era, "has just saved France!" Its "sacred mission" would now be recognized and rewarded, he told his colleagues: "Today your task is accomplished and that of the government is about to begin. Its first duty will be to strengthen your power and improve your position."[1]

HERALDS OF A NEW ADMINISTRATIVE ERA

The administration's case in anticipation of a "new era" was presented at greater length by Pierre Conquet, editor of the newly founded *Moniteur Administratif* in early 1852. In a series of editorials he reviewed the "neglect" and alleged injustices experienced by the administration during "the long period of parliamentary government." For eighteen years, public functionaries had suffered the indignities of the "partisan spirit" in public life. Its national mission unrespected and its needs ignored, the administration had been "a center of exploitation beset by all the ambitions and incapacities" of party politics. No wonder that "profound and legitimate discouragement" had gradually set in over the years. Nonetheless, the public servants clung to "duty before all else . . . because in our administrative services the principle of authority plays a traditional role."

The functionaries had lived on their "faith in the future of the

73

administration." In times of crisis, the editor declared, "the functionary alone is riveted by duty to a fixed place; his assigned
official residence is his battle station." And there indeed the
country found him, to its salvation, during the troubles endured
since 1848. Conquet predicted that such fidelity would be rewarded and its claim to "distributive justice" acknowledged in
compensation for past wrongs. Perhaps soon, he dared to hope,
"our admirable administrative structure, formerly . . . one of the
Empire's glories, will be rejuvenated." Already one could see
signs of the "government's solicitude" and a responsive new
"vigor and regularity in the functioning of the administrative
machine."[2]

Many prefects and *procureurs* recorded similar hopes. "Authority is now the sole aristocracy," concluded the prefect of the
Rhône. But with authority went grave responsibilities. From the
Dordogne came the observation that the forthcoming transition
from republic to empire would impose "new duties and rigorous
obligations upon those functionaries especially responsible for
directing and sheltering the national will." The new obligations
in great part rested upon the police function. Thus one writer
hailed the coup d'état as a *"chef-oeuvre* of political science" bringing to a climax the renaissance of political police that began in
1849 and would now free the police function to achieve its highest
traditional goals. In future the police would construct as well
as repress and deserve to be "powerful and honored" in French
life. In similar vein, the *procureur* at Douai praised the coup
for having at last renewed "the means and will to assure order
and security founded upon solid bases." Welcoming the return
to "principles of authority so profoundly dislocated by the shock
of 1848," he noted that "ideas of order, social hierarchy, and
submission to authority are beginning to prevail in the masses . . . ,
who seem little disposed to let themselves be taken in again by
mad utopias. . . ."[3]

Clearly the directors of the administrative and judiciary police
expected to become the preferred political guardians of society
under the presidential (and after December, 1852, the imperial)
dictatorship. This they regarded as their natural and traditional

function. In principle they might have been expected to welcome any new emphasis on the political police function. But after January 22 they greeted with chagrin and mounting irritation the new Ministry of General Police which Louis Napoleon unexpectedly placed over *themselves* as the supreme custodian of the *sûreté générale*. Undoubtedly for that reason, among others, Maupas' ministry was the most ephemeral of the Napoleonic revivals introduced by the Second of December. It survived only seventeen months before its death by decree on June 21, 1853.

THE DECLINE AND FALL OF THE MINISTRY OF POLICE

When Charlemagne-Emile de Maupas left the Ile de la Cité and the Prefecture of Police for new quarters in the Rue de Varennes as the fifteenth Minister of General Police, his assigned mission was to give the general police function "a simple and uniform organization obeying only one direction." His ministry embodied the familiar concept of political police powers woven into a centralized administration. But in this case, Maupas' hierarchy was grafted into an older and far more massive organism which must support and tolerate the intruder. The Minister had nationwide responsibility for political police. But, as in the past, that activity would actually continue to be performed in detail by the functionaries responsible to the ministries of the Interior, Justice, and War, and to the Paris Prefect of Police. In his own Paris headquarters, Maupas could muster only thirty-nine officials above the rank of office employee. His only field agents in the *départements* were twenty-one supervisory inspectors. All his staff, including the lowliest office boy, did not exceed one hundred and fifty. His budget was more impressive, amounting to plans for nearly four million francs for 1853, much of which came at the expense of the Ministry of the Interior.[4]

Portents of Conflict

Obviously, Maupas had to win the cooperation of the Ministry of the Interior, eighty-six prefects and their subordinates, and the Paris Prefecture. The latter alone had personnel and facilities that dwarfed those of Maupas in the nation at large. Not only must he induce these officials to take his Ministry's orders and to submit reliable reports, but they must also accept his ministry's surveillance and evaluation of their own political reliability and administrative competence. Being obliged to report directly to Louis Napoleon on these matters, Maupas would presumably use confidential means of assessing and reporting the activities of the entire administration, including the prefectorial system and the Paris Prefecture. Both were systems long accustomed to an autonomous monopoly of political police and personnel evalua-tion within their respective domains. There remained the question of the Ministry's relationships with the gendarmerie and pro-cureurs-généraux. As a departmental prefect and, during the coup, Prefect of Police, Maupas had already displayed both zeal and boldness. But the role he assumed on January 22 required in addition considerable tact and diplomacy, qualities for which he was less noted.

In a conflict with other authorities, Maupas would face worthy antagonists. Fialin de Persigny, already at odds with Maupas, replaced Morny at the Interior on the same day that the Ministry of Police appeared. Persigny was close to Louis Napoleon. But he was not the sort to be complacent about seeing "the sole polit-ical ministry," as the Prince-President described it, placed under the surveillance of another. The addition of jurisdiction over agriculture and commerce to the Interior's functions (which ac-companied the reshuffling of January 22) hardly compensated for the loss of supreme control over general police activities and funds. The special police ministry must have come as a surprise in the Interior. Only a month before Persigny's appointment, Morny had begun a reorganization of his ministry's central ad-ministration designed to emphasize the function of general police.[5]

Pierre-Marie Piétri, Corsican lawyer, ex-prefect, and a Bona-partist since 1847, became Prefect of Police on January 27. As energetically opportunistic as Maupas, Piétri had more experi-ence, flexibility, and subtlety. Like Persigny he was unlikely to suffer placidly any major encroachment upon his own terrain. At the Ministry of War, General Saint-Arnaud commanded the gendarmerie, an indispensable police force known for its efficiency and its officers' sensitive pride. Since December, Saint-Arnaud had been an unfriendly critic of Maupas. Within the Ministry of War, a newly established Committee of the Gendarmerie directly administered the elite corps. Its officer-members were vigilant custodians of the gendarmes' autonomy in their relations with civilian authorities. Especially so was General of Division La Ruë, Inspector-General of the Gendarmerie, and future president of the Committee. Achille Fould, who in December, 1852, became Minister of State, joined Persigny and Saint-Arnaud in the cabinet to form a triumvirate of opposition against Maupas, though Fould's position was not such as to create jurisdictional disputes with the Ministry of Police.

Perhaps most decisive among the interested critics of the police ministry were the prefects, with whom Maupas must work constantly and directly. Certainly unopposed either to centralized, vigorous political police, or as a group to Maupas personally, it was they who expected to inherit the administrative state after December, 1851. Aware of their own indispensability, the prefects immediately looked with skepticism upon the new agency now looming as a tutelary superstructure over themselves. Their attitudes were apparently widely shared by the *procureurs-généraux,* but the judiciary police were in less frequent direct conflict with the police ministry.

Even before his ministry was fully operational, Maupas asked the prefects to correspond directly with him all in general police affairs. But one day earlier, in a mood soon shared by many colleagues, Prefect du Suleau of the Bouches-du-Rhône queried Persigny on a "grave question" raised by the advent of the new ministry. Since 1800, he wrote, the "unity of administrative powers" in the *départements* had depended upon the prefects' control. Was this unity now to be disrupted? Predicting trouble if Maupas' agents aspired to become "prefects of police" in the provinces, Suleau criticized the ambiguity of the Ministry's founding decree. He urged forcefully that the ambiguity be clarified in favor of the prefects before Maupas launched his activities.[6]

A look at the organization of the Ministry of Police reveals
the sources of Suleau's concern. It is further apparent from
Maupas' first instructions why the prefects suspected intentions
on his part that were all too explicit for their liking.

Organization of the Ministry

Maupas' new central administration, headed by experienced
and competent men, consisted of the *Cabinet de Ministre,* a Secretary-General, three Divisions, and three Directors-General. To
the Minister's office was attached a special Bureau of Political
Police under Eugène Blanchet, a former Parisian *commissaire*
(who arrested General Lamorcière the night of December 2)
and writer on police doctrine. The original Secretary-General,
Cambacérès, an ex-prefect, also headed the First Division. He
was replaced in May, 1852, by another ex-prefect, Bourgeois
d'Orvannes, who in turn yielded to Pierre-Marie Collet-Meygret,
subprefect at St. Etienne in December, 1851, and destined to play
an important role in political police after the Ministry's downfall.

In addition to Blanchet's specifically political bureau, the Second and Third Divisions (for the *sûreté-générale* and the press,
respectively) had essentially political police assignments. Heading
the Third Division was the young publicist Pierre-Celestin Latour-Dumoulin, who alone among the Ministry's officials lacked
an administrative background. The three Directors-General, all
ex-prefects, rounded out the central administration. From Paris
each Director-General supervised a territorial *arrondissement.*
Balland (replaced May 22, 1852, by General Inspector of Police
Delesvaux) had forty-seven *départements* and Tonnet, former
head of the division of *sûreté générale* in the Ministry of the Interior, thirty-eight *départements.* Prefect of Police Piétri was the
third Director-General of the Ministry of Police, charged with
surveillance over his own police administration of Paris and certain communes of the Seine-et-Oise. Piétri's appointment was
realistic because of the practical importance of the Paris police.
It was also a prudent tactic, in view of Maupas' ambiguous jurisdictional situation, to associate the Prefect of Police with the new

ministry. However, one General Inspector of Police directly responsible to Maupas was posted in Paris.

Maupas' provincial agents consisted of nine General Inspectors of Police and twelve Special Inspectors stationed throughout the country. Each General Inspector presided over a group of *départements*. All were experienced administrators and outstanding ex-prefects or ex-representatives. They established headquarters in Paris, Lille, Metz, Lyon, Marseille, Toulouse, Bordeaux, Nantes, and Bourges.[7] The Special Inspectors, immediately responsible to the General Inspectors, were assigned to principal cities other than those of their chiefs: Rouen, Chalons-sur-Marne, Strasbourg, Besançon, Montpellier, Perpignan, Bayonne, Rennes, Bastia, Tours, Clermont-Ferrand, and Limoges.[8]

The new ministry's structure bore a certain resemblance to Napoleon I's Ministry of Police at its height in 1811, when there had been five Directors-General, all for areas outside France proper; thirteen *Commissaires-Généraux* in France and others outside; and eight *Commissaires-Spéciaux* in France plus others outside. In 1852, both grades of police inspectors received ceremonial rank like that accorded to the *commissaires* of 1811. General Inspectors ranked two degrees below prefects and "immediately after the bishops"; Special Inspectors followed the presidents of courts of the first instance. The inspectors' cities of residence paid the costs of their lodging and office space.[9]

On February 26, the General Inspectors left for their posts and the Special Inspectors shortly thereafter. Known for their loyalty to Louis Napoleon, they were for the most part relatively moderate men who apparently tried diligently to carry out their difficult assignments. The majority found successful administrative and political careers following their brief tenure under Maupas.[10] Their problems arose principally from the competition with departmental authorities into which they were forced by their Minister's interpretations of his very generalized mandate under the organizational decree of January 30.

The decree made Maupas the supreme chief of general police without defining what that was to mean in detailed administrative relationships. The General Inspectors were to "correspond" with prefects, mayors, the judiciary police, and gendarmerie officers. The decree produced a crucial source of dissension by placing the *commissaires* of police directly under the inspectors' orders for general police while continuing their responsibility to the prefects as well.

These agents had been formerly subject only to the prefects in general police work. Now the prefects resisted what they regarded as a demoralizing penetration of the Ministry of Police into the prefectorial hierarchy. Moreover, the decree left few other aspects of general administration beyond the police inspectors' reach. The General Inspectors were told to "extend their surveillance . . . especially to everything affecting public opinion, morality, and security." They must "correct false news and rumors and attend to the general efficiency of public administration in order to assure execution of the Minister's orders." They must scrutinize "publications of all kinds, booksellers, theaters, prisons, public instruction, political and economic organizations." The Special Inspectors received a similar assignment under the supervision of their immediate superiors. They also could give orders to *commissaires* of police and correspond directly with other public functionaries. General Inspectors could order arrests only after advising the prefects. Conflicts over arrest policy would be resolved jointly by the ministers of Police and Interior. But in such cases the General Inspectors could meanwhile arrest "provisionally." Special Inspectors, however, could order arrests only with permission of their superiors except for emergency reasons. Both types of inspectors might formally call out the National Guard, gendarmerie, or army in case of urgent need.

Very clearly the inspectors' comprehensive mission duplicated virtually all the customary prefectorial powers in general police. By the same token they were bound to trespass into many areas of general nonpolitical administration. To be sure, the inspectors were required to inform the prefects of all their activities that touched departmental administration. And Louis Napoleon's open letter to Maupas cautioned him to "watch everything while directly administering nothing." It also promised that the Minister of Police would "not diminish the prefect's authority because he will not share it." How to draw the line between administration and mere "surveillance," in view of the wide jurisdiction of the new ministry and the synthesis of administrative and police powers in traditional French practice, inevitably became an open, tension-laden question.

On February 11, more than two weeks before the Ministry of Police began operations, Baron Haussmann (later the rebuilder of Paris) sent a long critique to Persigny from his prefecture in the Gironde. With an acerbity unusual in official correspondence, he attacked Maupas' ministry and the import of Louis Napoleon's open letter of January 31. From his prefect's perspective Haussmann accurately isolated those sources of conflict that actually emerged in the following months. He believed that only one "political ministry" could survive. And that should of course be the Ministry of the Interior. But Louis Napoleon apparently intended that the older ministry "be stripped of what until now has been its principal importance." The police ministry's intervention in administrative routine, its surveillance over public opinion, the power to pry into everything and to recommend changes, the Minister's privilege of reporting exclusively to the chief of state —all this, Haussmann predicted, ensured that "the real leaders of the country from now on will be the Inspectors of Police." Their reports would have "the exclusive credence of the government," even though the inspectors were unburdened with the prefects' complex responsibilities. At this point, Haussmann bluntly charged that Louis Napoleon meant "implicitly to repudiate" the prefects' earlier support of his cause by a policy that showed amazing ingratitude toward men "who believed that as in the past they were invested with the government's confidence."

Indeed, the new ministry was both a spy and taskmaster unilaterally imposed upon the administration and armed with the means of undercutting even the prefects by confidential reports. In the new police inspectors' powers, Haussmann beheld "the seeds of a total political domination." In this dark prospect, he caught the glint of only one satisfying irony. No existing statute empowered the inspectors themselves legally to make arrests!

Haussmann viewed the future with both optimism and gloom. He could not believe "that the administration of General Police [would] last very long as now constituted," but meanwhile it could strike "a fatal blow" at prefectorial authority in a crucial moment of the nation's history.[11]

Maupas anticipated the prefects' fears. But in seeking to allay their distrust in advance he further stimulated it. His first policy directive to the inspectors attempted to reassure all potential critics who read it in the *Moniteur* of February 15. He admitted the existence of old animosities toward a separate police ministry. Thus the inspectors must "calm the unrest and dissipate the prejudices that will have been awakened" by revival of the institution. They must exert a "tutelary" surveillance "without in any way being involved in administration."

With rhetorical embellishments, he restated his mission in the general terms of the decree of January 30. Then, under the rubrics of "political" and "economic" action, he specified the duties he expected the inspectors to perform. Here the circular left scarcely an aspect of departmental administration untouched. Maupas again warned his agents to stay "scrupulously within those limits beyond which your authority would become oppressive or inquisitorial." In time, he predicted, "the police will be a source of dread only for the wicked," as others learned that his ministry was merely a "safeguard" for the public weal.

During March, Maupas confidentially urged his men to demonstrate by their zeal "the necessity of an institution as important as the inspectorships." On April 20, *Moniteur* readers found another circular stressing the impartial, conciliatory intent of the Ministry of Police. But again Maupas spoke of powers that must have seemed painfully universal to administrators. The inspectors were to search for "any fertile idea, any legitimate viewpoint, any significant information . . . whatever its source," and to examine "all those living forces whose development creates a powerful society."

To the prefects themselves, Maupas privately addressed words of tactful reassurance. The inspectors were depicted as "auxiliaries at your side," deferentially assisting the prefects, easing their burdens without assuming their prerogatives. The new agents would be mere "centers of surveillance" content to leave *"action* in your hands."

Persigny was advising the prefects, too. He counseled them to accept their "double duty" and to avoid clashes. But neither must they forget that their administrative powers "should be exercised freely," for they existed quite independently of the Ministry of General Police whose only legitimate task would not exceed mere surveillance and reporting. The prefects must report regularly to the Minister of Police. However, Persigny instructed that they send copies of all such reports to his own office. Special dispatches on important general police matters should come directly to himself in double envelopes marked *cabinet du ministre.*[12] The prefects willingly complied. They kept Persigny well informed on their relationships and differences with Maupas and his staff.

When the Ministry of Police began its routine activities in March, 1852, an atmosphere of administrative tension had already gathered. Conflict was built into the new institution, particularly if the prefects and other officials were to believe themselves threatened in actual practice with subordination to Maupas' agents. Such a belief promptly showed itself.

The Ministry's Activities and Conflicts

The cantonal commissaires *of police.* On March 28, 1852, Maupas sponsored a decree creating a new police jurisdiction, the "cantonal *commissariats* of police." This meant that the authority of existing *commissaires,* limited since the First Empire to their communes of residence, could now be extended over all the communes in a given canton. Or new *commissaires* with such jurisdiction could be installed in the many cantons where no commune had a *commissaire.* Budgetary problems delayed the decree's implementation until January, 1853, when a new decree established 738 new cantonal *commissariats* and extended the jurisdiction of the 630 already in existence. The cantonal *commissariat* was one of the few police innovations of the second Napoleonic era. It increased both municipal and general police coverage, especially

in rural areas. It also provided a source of bitter dissension between the Ministry of Police and other authorities.

Maupas publicly praised the innovation as a necessary support
in the pyramid of which his ministry was the "summit." The cantonal *commissaires* were "the last link of the chain that must bind
the people to the government . . . and spread security through all
levels of society" by systematic warfare against the "pernicious
doctrines" peddled by "agitators" through rural France. The
reform would provide "a new guarantee of public security." To
the prefects and the inspectors of police, Maupas further emphasized the political police mission of the *commissaires*. He
recommended that new appointments come whenever possible
from among ex-soldiers and ex-gendarmes, adding that it was
"nearly always bad" to station a *commissaire* in his home territory
lest he be tainted by local influences. Reliable political police
agents, the Minister advised, must possess not only "integrity,
morality, and energy," but an "absolute devotion to the present
government and the principles that have consecrated it." Maupas
invited colonels of gendarmerie to submit lists of candidates to
both the prefects and the Ministry of Police. In January, 1853,
the Ministry of War published a forty-one page list of eligibles,
each name annotated, for the use of the selecting authorities.[13]

The idea of cantonal *commissaires*, considered narrowly as a
local extension of administrative centralization and political police, could not fail to earn the approval of both the prefects and
the judiciary police. For example, the three *départements* under the
procureur-général at Aix-en-Provence (Bouches-du-Rhône, Basses-
Alpes, and Var) received twenty-six new *commissariats* in January, 1853. The *procureur* and his subordinates lauded "the primarily political mission" of the *commissaires*, whom they hoped
to use against political suspects and to rehabilitate pardoned
offenders through daily advice on morals and political conduct.[14]
But the question of who would control the *commissaires* was another matter.

Even before the cantonal jurisdiction was announced, the General and Special Inspectors of Police lost no time in attempting
to assume control (which their Ministry's organizational decree
of January 30 seemed to give them) over the *commissaires*. Gen-

eral Inspector Sylvain Blot, upon arriving in Marseille, sought the prefect's cooperation in his "high mission of surveillance." He assured Suleau that he wanted no "antagonism" between himself and departmental authorities. He thereupon ordered the *commissaires* to report to him on a host of matters that were ordinarily the prefect's responsibilities—ranging from secret societies to sanitary conditions and the efficiency of public functionaries. In a minute investigation of the 133 *commissaires* in his district, General Inspector Cotton at Lyon requested assistance from the gendarmerie and *procureurs*. The latter were asked to send confidential information on the officers' "morality, antecedents, aptitudes, intelligence, degree of energy, devotion, and . . . attitude since the events of December." He directed the *commissaires* themselves to make regular reports on both the obvious political police topics and purely administrative items ranging from municipal elections to fires, from stray dogs to "miscellaneous" events.[15]

The prefects, also before the advent of cantonal *commissaires,* were irritated by the inspectors' power to give orders to *commissaires* of police even on the communal level. When in January, 1853, many *commissaires'* jurisdiction was extended and the appointment of hundreds more to new *commissariats* authorized, the issue of appointment and supervision of these officers became acute. The decree of March 28, 1852, required the prefects to appoint each *commissaire* in towns of six thousand or less from lists of three names submitted by the General Inspectors. In larger cities, appointment was by Louis Napoleon on nomination by the Minister of Police. Unfortunately for administrative harmony, this measure followed by only three days a so-called decentralization decree of March 25, which greatly increased the prefects' autonomy in appointing functionaries, including *commissaires,* and in making other decisions without consulting higher authority. The "decentralization" of March 25 obliged the prefects to name *commissaires* from lists submitted by the mayors, but it was a quite different matter in prefectorial eyes to accept such lists from agents of the Ministry of Police, as provided by the decree of March 28.

So frequent were the clashes over nomination of *commissaires* that Maupas, after a conference with Persigny, yielded in August, 1852, by "reinterpreting" the rule so as to make it desirable but not obligatory for the prefects to choose *commissaires* from the police inspectors' lists. Actually, Persigny had already told the prefects to disregard the inspectors' nominees if necessary. Despite the August compromise, conflict continued. The real issue was posed by the prefect of the Cher, who asked Persigny if the prefects were or were not to lose their power.[16]

The prefects found varied reasons to reject the inspectors' nominees for the office of *commissaire*. The candidates were "unknown," they lacked competence, or were unsuited to local situations. The prefect of the Calvados, preferring to appoint men who were native to the *département,* rejected the outsiders nominated by Rancé, General Inspector at Paris, whom the prefect regarded as "an honorable man" but unreasonable on this issue. Anyway, he asked, why should not the prefect, who had to live with the results of such appointments, choose his own *commissaires*? To compound his problem, the prefect complained, the local citizenry so disliked the General Inspector's nominees that they were showing "distrust" of the new police organization altogether. However, they would gladly have accepted his own choices, to the profit of the administration. The new mode of nomination left the prefect unable to "make use of and reward the modest local devotion [to the administration] which used to be the best test for filling our little *commissariats*."[17]

At Marseille, Sylvain Blot made no headway at all with the prefect, who refused to appoint any *commissaires* whatsoever. Blot, forced into a pleading role, suffered the embarrassment of having to ask the *procureur de la république* at Brignoles to intercede with the stubborn prefect. But in the Dordogne, where the prefect fought a running battle on the same issue with Baron Frossard, General Inspector at Bordeaux, he found the Inspector unwilling to plead. Frossard blisteringly informed the prefect that he rejected his protests categorically and that he was "accountable only to the Minister" for his policy in nominating *commissaires*. Though agreeing to consider the prefect's advice "without in any way abandoning my own rights," Frossard in a final blast invited the prefect to go ahead and "denounce" him to Maupas if he wished. "But," Frossard repeated, "I cannot accept you as judge in this matter any more than I will admit your power to settle this with your own chief." Reporting a similar but less explosive dispute with Delesvaux at Bourges, the prefect of the Cher conveyed his dilemma to Persigny. To accept Delesvaux's nominee would be at the cost of his own *"real* responsibility"; to defy the Inspector would cause "regrettable conflict between two authorities who are nearly the same rank."[18]

Not only the nomination but also the discharge of *commissaires* created dissension. The decree of March 28 allowed the prefects to revoke a *commissaire* only after approval by the Minister of Police. In one instance, the prefect of the Charente discharged an officer at La Rochefaucauld neither for incompetence nor disloyalty, but because he irritated the local citizens with his "unbridled" zeal and excessive "amour propre." After suggesting that Maupas find the man some lesser employment, the prefect was "painfully surprised" when the Minister reinstated the *commissaire*. Whereupon the mayor, with all twenty municipal councilors behind him, threatened to resign unless the unpopular police officer were again removed from the community.

In a variant of the same problem, the prefect of the Bouches-du-Rhône did not protest the discharge of a certain *commissaire* in Marseille; but the mayor took up the attack against the Ministry of Police.[19]

Questions of nomination and revocation were entwined with an acrimonious conflict over the routing of the *commissaires'* police reports. Along with the prefects, many mayors became involved in this issue because of the multipartite character of the *commissaires'* administrative functions. The decree on cantonal *commissaires* deprived the mayors of any way to ensure that appointees would be amenable to local influences. In 1852, the *commissaire,* whose official life was already complex enough in his traditional tripartite role as officer of municipal, general, and judiciary police—with corresponding obligations to mayors, prefects, and *procureurs*—now had to endure a fourth claim upon his time and loyalty. To whom would he be most loyal? The prefects, with mayors often collaborating, vied with the inspectors of police for the primary loyalty of the *commissaires*. As for the latter, some avoided cooperation with the Ministry of Police while others confided principally in the police inspectors. Crucial to the outcome of this contest was the routing of information, especially in political police matters. For example, a *commissaire* at Bourg (Ain) confided to Inspector Paul Lagarde at Lyon that the mayor insisted upon full information, ignoring the rights of the Ministry of Police. Lagarde told him to continue fulfilling his administrative duties to the municipality, but to send his political police information confidentially and exclusively to Lyon.[20]

The prefects made such problems an important issue. The prefect of the Deux-Sèvres insisted that the *commissaires* report to the prefect via the subprefects and that the inspectors seek information from the prefectures. Otherwise, he maintained, to "centralize" the police action of the *commissaires* at the level of the inspectors meant domination over the prefects. In another clash between General Inspector Baylin de Montbel at Metz and the prefect of the Moselle, the former sent printed instructions to the *commissaires,* tactlessly declaring, "we form a *special administration."* A *commissaire* at Thionville thereafter refused to report to the subprefect on the grounds that he was responsible only to the Ministry of Police and no longer responsible to the prefectorial administration. Responding to the prefect's repeated complaints, Persigny advised him to discharge the *commissaire,* agreeing that "we must have this kind of thing stopped as soon as possible." Maupas stood his ground. In December, 1852, he insisted in a "very confidential" circular to his agents that *commissaires'* political police reports go exclusively to the inspectors —bypassing the mayors, judiciary police, and all other administrative authorities.

Many other issues arose. Incomplete records of the inspectors' activities and the prefects' and *procureurs'* correspondence show that Maupas and his agents were caught up in an administrative war waged on many fronts.[21] Skirmishes in the *départements* quickly reached the ministerial level.

Conflicts with other ministers. After April, 1852, the min-

istries of Justice and Police clashed over the administration of
presidential clemency measures and the police inspectors' intervention in affairs of the judiciary police. Maupas caustically
charged that Abbatucci and his hierarchy were not keeping him
informed on recommendations for pardons. He curtly demanded
cooperation, only to be rebuffed with the countercharge that his
ministry actually received all pertinent information but was too
inefficient to keep track of it. Abbatucci followed through with
criticism of the police ministry's allegedly harsh treatment of
surveillés and internees and its disregard for the niceties of
justice. Abbatucci agreed with his *procureur* at Lyon that blunder-
ing and uninformed police intervention in affairs of justice was
"deplorable." He advised the *procureur* to watch closely and
report the abuses committed by the General Inspector at Lyon.
In reply to Maupas' complaints against the "tepidity" and "indifference" of a court at Le Havre in political cases, the *procureur*
at Rouen so vehemently denied the accusation and questioned the
accuracy of police reports that Maupas, belatedly retreating,
asked to let the matter drop. Tensions multiplied between the
inspectors and *procureurs* over reporting policy, intervention in
judicial procedures, surveillance practices, and the making of arrests on scanty evidence. When the Ministry of Police was abolished, the judiciary police shed no tears. The *procureur* at Montpellier hailed its suppression as an act of "undeniable wisdom"
because of the agency's "overextensive" and undefined activities.[22]

A more serious clash arose with the nearly twenty-four thousand gendarmerie, a conflict spiced by personal animosity between Maupas and General Saint-Arnaud. Proud of their military
esprit de corps, ever sensitive to criticism or attempted control
by civilian authorities, and conscious of Louis Napoleon's favors
since 1849, the gendarmerie officers also emerged from their
December operations expectantly. Like the administration itself,
they envisioned a new era of expansion and autonomy. They, too,
were eager to bask in Louis Napoleon's "publicly expressed gratitude toward the very honorable service of the gendarmerie."[23] The
gendarmerie resented the apparent presumption of the Ministry
of Police in requesting their services and adding to their already

heavy reporting load. But the conflict was most intense over jurisdictional clashes with cantonal *commissaires* and the gendarmerie's refusal to perform secret police services.

General Saint-Arnaud branded the *commissaires'* demands upon the gendarmerie "an insult to the uniform." He deplored Maupas' "impassioned tendencies" in defending his police personnel and refusing the Minister of War's insistence upon the removal of certain *commissaires*. And he forbade gendarmerie officers to submit recommendations for cantonal *commissariats* to the Ministry of Police except through himself. The General was even more unbending on the issue of secret police activities. Such conflicts sometimes involved the police inspectors and the prefects and *procureurs*. For example, the *procureur* at Brignoles (Var) offered a sympathetic ear to General La Rüe's complaints against the *commissaires,* under the inspectors' orders, expecting gendarmes to perform secret police duties. On this issue, Saint-Arnaud played no favorites. In a stiffly formal letter, hardly concealing its icy rebuff, he informed Persigny that he had no intention of allowing the prefects, any more than the Ministry of Police, to use his gendarmes for such confidential work as compiling lists of friends and enemies of the government.[24]

In June, 1852, a sharp behind-the-scenes encounter between Saint-Arnaud and Maupas—with Louis Napoleon acting as mediator—ended in a joint circular addressed by the two ministers to both the gendarmerie and the inspectors of police. Referring to "some confusion" in the relations of the two police organizations, the circular gave Maupas a psychic victory by asserting that "the Ministry of Police is entirely substituted for the Ministry of Interior in general police." This must have been no comfort for Persigny!

Saint-Arnaud scored too, in more concrete terms. Admitting that the police inspectors had "in some cases overstepped their powers and rights," the circular precisely identified the kinds of service and reporting which the gendarmerie were obliged to render to civil authorities, emphasizing the limits thereto. "In no case," the dispatch read, "either directly or indirectly, must the gendarmerie accept secret missions of the kind to distort its true character." But the issue persisted, as Saint-Arnaud continued both publicly and confidentially to remind gendarmerie officers of their rightful position. In April, 1853, the Minister of War flatly refused Maupas' request that he order one General Carrelet on temporary duty to the Ministry of Police for "a highly confidential mission," even though the mission was at the behest of the Emperor. A military officer, Saint-Arnaud insisted, could not serve two ministers. Rebuking Maupas for even proposing such a project without prior consultation with himself, Saint-Arnaud declared, "I therefore do not have to give him orders on this matter."

In October, 1852, Saint-Arnaud assigned General La Ruë, now chairman of the Gendarmerie Committee, to make a special study of gendarmerie-administrative relationships (which were later defined in great detail in 1854). Meanwhile, the gendarmerie held its own against Maupas behind a barricade of legislation going back to 1820 and repeatedly invoked in the *Journal de la gendarmerie de France:*

The gendarmerie must take *orders* only from its officers and the Ministry of War. But it defers to *legal requisitions* issued by competent authorities responsible to the various ministries. However such authorities can in no case exercise an exclusive control over this force nor can they intervene in the internal details of its service.[25]

A few minor irritants arose between the ministries of Police and Finance, involving collaboration of police agents and the customs service in policing literary materials entering France, and police investigation of the latter ministry's functionaries. With respect to the Prefect of Police, I found only one clear instance of conflict—a sarcastic complaint by a Ministry of Police official that "this master of his own terrain has refused all cooperation" in certain matters.[26]

Maupas' ministry foundered especially on the resistance of Persigny and the prefects. The controversy stimulated much public gossip. To London, the British *chargé* in Paris reported that both Persigny and Maupas "pass for men of violent and determined character. . . ." The caustic diarist, Horace de Viel-

Castel, no friend of either man, noted that "they detest" one another to the extent that each prodded his staff into "clumsy zeal" in order to do the other harm. Maupas later accused Persigny of using all his influence to remove him and the Ministry itself and of allying for that purpose with others among Maupas' enemies, "whom my functions increased in numbers daily."[27]

The prefects' resistance. Few direct exchanges between the two ministers remain in the archives, but evidence of their rivalry abounds in prefectorial correspondence with Paris. Persigny, after ordering the prefects to keep him fully informed of their relations with the police ministry, invited suggestions for counter-measures. Resumés of the prefects' complaints were compiled. One of these included underlined "observations" which concluded that the Ministry of Police must absolutely be kept out of administration because time and precedent had made the Ministry of the Interior "the sole political ministry."[28]

The prefects responded at length to the sympathetic overtures of their chief. Generally, they portrayed the conflict as a battle for domination, right being on the side of prefectorial prerogative confronted by Maupas' empire-building. A recurrent theme held that administrative dualism violated both tradition and the canons of practicality: "a prefect administers *alone* in his *département*" as the sole voice of the executive; dual authority inevitably produced "delays, difficulties and obstacles to obstruct the normal routine" of administration. Prefect de Sainte Croix of the Deux-Sèvres (and later from his new post in the Eure) suggested a general reorganization of departmental administration, now made urgent by the "irregular" attempts of the Ministry of Police to usurp general administration. Not surprisingly, he urged that "it is only the Ministry of the Interior that must direct the police."[29]

Apart from the struggle over *commissaires* of police, the prefects' most specific grievances centered upon the handling of *surveillés,* loyalty and competence checks of functionaries, the inspectors' meddling in general administrative routine, and control of the political press.

No one was satisfied with the handling of the suddenly increased numbers of *surveillés* and internees sentenced by the Mixed Commissions. Maupas complained of lax enforcement. Prefects and *procureurs* grumbled at the magnitude of their task. Maupas warned that "the internees are trying to regroup," but his proddings elicited more irritation than compliance. The busy prefects persisted in such makeshift practices as delegating the details of surveillance to minor functionaries who often did not bother to require their charges either to report periodically or to keep their papers in order. In certain regions, the prefects and judiciary police resented the concentration in their districts of "dangerous men" in great numbers—a problem aggravated by some prefects' device of "dumping" their internees into other *départements* by enforced changes of residence. To the many protests on this score, Maupas retorted rather peevishly that one "must send them somewhere." But he forbade the further transfer of internees to other *départements,* thus mollifying certain prefects, only to earn the resentment of others who were bound to regard the regulation as a new curtailment of their own autonomy.[30]

Investigation of functionaries. Many prefects also resisted the inspectors' large-scale investigation of functionaries as a threat to their own control. Féart warned his subprefects in the Gers to forestall this bid "to deprive the departmental administration" of authority over its own personnel. Others denounced such inquiries as "intolerable" or "shocking" intrusions into their rightful terrain. The prefects knew that even they were not immune from the inquisition. On orders from General Inspector Cotton at Lyon, Special Inspector Lecourbe conducted a confidential check on the prefect of the Haute-Marne that probed into his motives in appointing certain mayors and adjoints, his degree of willingness to foster Bonapartism in municipal councils, and even the political opinions of his personal guests. Writhing a bit under the weight of this "delicate and difficult" mission, as he described it, Lecourbe carried it through.[31]

Meddling in administrative business. The prefects had no grounds for refusing the inspectors' requests for their cooperation in general police. But when Maupas' agents crossed the rigid line drawn in the prefectorial mind between mere surveillance and positive administration, the prefects complained of arbitrary and unseemly meddling. The inspectors, themselves ex-prefects, brought to their new duties a similarly unrestricted view of their proper sphere of action. Seldom did the prefects question their adversaries' sincerity; but they did charge them with incompetence. Who could preside over a *département* from afar or know its complexities as well as its own prefect? To presume otherwise was a meddling zeal that "knew no bounds," declared Haussmann in a dispute with Baron Frossard at Bordeaux.[32]

The inspectors' use of secret police agents irked the prefects, who were accustomed to controlling such agents on their own. The thought that their activities were the object of an "occult" surveillance drove many prefects to write to Persigny with an air of wounded resentment at the implication that their own means of administration were inadequate or inferior to those of their rivals. Maupas himself was drawn into a heated encounter with Prefect Suleau of the Bouches-du-Rhône during secret police investigation of the so-called *Complot de Marseille* against Louis Napoleon in the fall of 1852. Sylvain Blot, General Inspector at Marseille, imported his own secret agent whose information enabled Blot to "discover" the plot. Suleau insisted that his own undercover men had made the discovery. In the *Moniteur* on September 26, Blot and the Ministry of Police took full credit for aborting the plot, much to the wrath of the prefect. In secret police policy, Inspector Blot was in a difficult position, having been criticized severely only a month earlier by a *procureur* for not using secret agents in the Var.

The secret police issue aroused the prefects for another reason. They protested the transfer of secret funds from the Interior to the Ministry of Police because of subsequent cuts at the departmental level, ranging from 100 per cent in the Ariège, to a sum below "indispensable" need in the Var, to one-third the former amount in the Bouches-du-Rhône. From Marseille, Suleau suggested, long before the *Complot de Marseille* episode, that the police inspectors deserved no secret funds in any case because the prefects had the real police job to do.[33]

There were other issues. Persigny fully supported the prefect of the Moselle when he disobeyed orders from the General Inspector at Metz to close a drinking establishment. A similar conflict pitted Sylvain Blot against Suleau, who preferred the mayor's advice that a sudden closure of cafés and clubs in Marseille would reap only a paltry harvest of subversives while alienating many solid citizens, through resentment at the dislocation of their habitual recreation. These and other seemingly minor issues were magnified by the prefects as indications that the inspectors were assuming the prefects' role as the official spokesmen of the government in the *départements*.[34]

Meddling by the inspectors in electoral affairs was a leading prefectorial grievance. In this, their traditional domain, the prefects after December, 1851, had the all-important duty of promoting officially approved candidates. Interference in this fundamental assignment seemed intolerable. Le Provost de Launay, prefect of the Hautes-Alpes, bitterly denounced General Inspector Cotton to Persigny for daring to send him political comments on the departmental elections. He saw in this gesture "the thinly disguised intention to give my administration a directive that . . . should come only from your authority." In the Cantal, another inspector aroused a similar storm by sending electoral policy instructions to the *commissaires,* thus allegedly disrupting "a delicate and complex" local situation. When Inspector Poriquet asked a subprefect in the Sarthe for a report on electoral affairs, the prefect forbade his subordinates to correspond with the General Inspector without his own approval. From the Gard came repeated attacks against Cotton, then Special Inspector at Montpellier, and Tissot, the General Inspector, for criticizing official candidates, instructing a subprefect in electoral tactics, and questioning the political loyalty of several members of the *département's* general council. This angry prefect denied the right of an "inferior agent" to disrupt "good administration" and warned Persigny that toleration of such abuses would soon encourage the inspectors to order the prefects about. Eventually the inspectors "would replace the Ministry of Interior's action on general politics."[35]

In all such complaints, the inspectors were portrayed as clumsy outsiders ignorant of local conditions and therefore bound to upset the best-laid plans and diplomacy of the prefects. Much of the indignation of the prefect of the Gard against Tissot arose from the latter's presumption in instructing functionaries only eight days after arriving in the area. During Cotton's brief term as Special Inspector at Montpellier, the same prefect was supported by regional "notables" in attacking the appointment as "imprudent and impolitic." They charged Maupas with complete ignorance of the political situation in the Gard.

Cotton, a Protestant in a region where the non-Catholics were reputed to be "socialist, revolutionary, insurrectional, and eaten by the gangrene of secret societies," was known to favor "breaking and dissolving" the Catholic party. His appointment was interpreted as a "threat and provocation" to the Catholic-legitimist majority who otherwise, under prefectorial leadership, would support the government because of their hatred of Protestantism and Orleanism. Maupas countered by defending his inspector as "a firm man with a rare intelligence," at once a liberal and disciple of Louis Napoleon, who was specially chosen to break the legitimists' "yoke" in the Gard.

Undoubtedly the inspectors' decisions often ignored the intricacies of local situations. Even after nearly two months in office, Special Inspector Lecourbe admitted that he knew "almost nothing" of the five *départements* in his jurisdiction, partly because of his ostracism by the prefects: "I have no correspondence, I receive no reports."[36]

Control of the press. Maupas believed that his ministry's press policy provided the immediate pretext for a "veritable declaration of war" by his enemies. The issue was bound to generate conflict. Surveillance over the press had for many years been one of the Interior's crucial political police activities, particularly in electoral policy. From Marseille, Prefect Suleau voiced a very typical protest against the "personal action" of the General Inspector in trying to color the editorial outlook of the *Nouvelliste* and *Courrier,* whose editors had standing orders to take their cues from the prefect. This interference, said Suleau, was not only useless as a general police measure. Worse, it would inevitably destroy "the unity of political direction so essential to maintain" in the *départements*.[37]

Tensions multiplied when the press law of February 17, 1852, empowered the prefects and Prefect of Police to issue *avertissements*, or official warnings, three of which could result in administrative suspension of a political newspaper. Maupas' appeals for cooperation in applying this new means of "safeguarding society" did little to clarify his ministry's ambiguous position under the new law. He depended upon the prefects for necessary information on printers, editors, and publications. But despite repeated pleas, he failed to elicit satisfactory reports from either the prefects or the *procureurs*. He also differed with these officials over the use of criminal prosecutions and formal warnings against newspapers.

For punitive action against the persons of editors and journalists—as distinct from official warnings to or suppression of the paper itself—the new press law required court trials and the preparation and prosecution of cases by the judiciary police. Rather embarrassingly for Maupas, Article 10 of the Code of Criminal Procedure reserved the power officially to demand the services of the judiciary police for the prefects and the Prefect of Police. Thus the Minister of Police, as one of his officials observed, faced the dilemma of "the superior [who] cannot assign a specific mission to an officer of judiciary police . . . without the willingness of his inferior. . . ."[38] Neither the prefects nor the Prefect of Police proffered the desired cooperation.

Formal *avertissements*, Maupas insisted, were a new weapon for use only against "systematically malevolent" newspapers considered "dangerous for public order, religion, and morality." But in this case the prefects' cooperation was far too zealous for the Minister's liking, releasing a flurry of warnings to both opposition and governmental papers alike. Attempting to moderate the prefects' repressive ardor, Maupas stirred a hornet's nest with a very confidential circular of August 18, 1852. It demanded that official warnings be issued only "prudently and with reserve." Henceforth, no warnings became final without the Minister's approval. Thus Maupas advised the prefects to keep "complete silence" on their proposed warnings lest they reap the embarrassment of having their proposals rejected in Paris. Coincidentally, on the very day of Maupas' circular, even Persigny admitted the prefects' excessive rigor. He proposed that both ministries assume a joint central control over *avertissements;* with his suggestion was the reminder that the Interior was still "charged with the political direction and administration of the country." Persigny's overture collided with Maupas' unilateral action of the same day, which incensed the prefects and created resentment in the Interior's central offices. In a heavily underlined memorandum, Persigny's chief of general correspondence charged that Maupas' circular completely usurped the Interior's traditional "right of directing and regulating the action of the prefects on the periodical press" and public opinion. Because of the "absolute necessity" of reversing Maupas' decision of August 18, the memorandum urged Persigny to seek Louis Napoleon's direct intervention.[39]

Intervention came in January, 1853. Napoleon III asked Maupas to reply to a "Note" addressed to the Emperor by persons unnamed, attacking his ministry's press policy. In a long and impassioned report to the Emperor, Maupas defended his Press Director Latour-Dumoulin and denied a salvo of charges against his agency. His apologia reflected bitter internecine strife between Maupas and such intimates of Napoleon III as Saint-Arnaud, Achille Fould, and their alleged tool, Pierre Carlier, former Prefect of Police. Without naming Persigny, Maupas hinted darkly that he knew the identity of other enemies very close to the Emperor. His indignant denials ended with a historical reflection on the fates of other ministers of police: "The truth, whose organ is the Ministry of General Police, sometimes becomes too painful a mirror for some men. . . . In this above all one must seek the cause of the successive abolitions of the Ministry. . . ."[40]

After this incident, in Maupas' words, Persigny waged "all-out war" against the Ministry of Police.

Suppression of the Inspectors of Police

Maupas' inspectors were the first to fall in the war against the Ministry. Early in March, 1853, Persigny twice confidentially hinted to the prefects of a possible abolition of the inspectorships. He invited comments on the idea of replacing them by a superior *commissaire* of police in each *département* who would coordinate general police activities under the prefect's direction. On March 5, before the prefects' comments had time to arrive, a decree suppressed the police inspectorships and replaced them by new Departmental Police *Commissaires,* one in each *département,* responsible exclusively to the prefects for general police.[41] Persigny had won the field. Thereafter Maupas could only retreat.

The Inspectors of Police disappeared unmourned in administrative circles, where they had been the targets of almost universal complaint. This investigator found only three really favorable references to the luckless officials—contributed by the prefects of the Sarthe, Vosges, and Haute-Loire.

Maupas' position had been difficult from the start. In March, 1853, it became untenable. Thereafter, he was forced to work entirely through the prefects who became, technically at least, functionaries of the Ministry of Police in all general police activities. Maupas artfully pleaded for their cooperation. He admitted that the abolition of the inspectorships was intended "to fortify police action in the prefects' hands" in the name of administrative unity. "The prefects," he wrote, "are now the primary agencies of my ministry." And he had to say, "You now resume exclusive responsibility for the *sûreté générale.*"[42] Actually, the prefects continued as before to regard themselves as keystones of the Interior's hierarchy. The Ministry of Police, planned as a superstructure, now became a mere appendage of the "sole political ministry."

During his last three-months' tenure, Maupas kept his central staff in Paris. But he was reduced to only four specially appointed "high functionaries" (two councilors of state and two senators) who inspected police operations in the *départements*. Until November, 1853, months after the Ministry of Police had itself disappeared, the four new officials conducted a "grand general inspection" of the administration, reporting directly to the Emperor.[43] These "imperial *missi dominici*," as Prefect Dieu of the Haute-Saône facetiously named them, were apparently supposed to accomplish less invidiously what Maupas had failed to do—to provide the Emperor with a direct channel of surveillance over the administration. But this form of special inspection was not repeated after 1853. Meanwhile, the prefects resumed their traditional roles as decisive links between the Chief of State and the nation in all that affected the *sûreté générale*.

The Departmental Commissaires of Police

Maupas regained no more than a shadow of his provincial staff when, on April 30, fifty-five of the new departmental *commissaires,* authorized on March 5, were actually appointed from among the prefects' nominees. Directly responsible to the prefects, these new officials owed the Ministry of Police reports of their activities but little else. Maupas chose the correct pronoun when he informed the prefects that the new *commissaires* were "the chief mechanism of *your* general police operations."

Rumor had it that the Minister had tried to delay their appointment. According to *La Foi Bretonne* of May 7, he "used every effort" to stave off a reform designed "to subvert the influence" of his own agency. The departmental *commissaires* received all the usual municipal, judiciary, and general police powers (under the prefects' supervision) of the *commissariat* extended to *département*-wide jurisdiction. Specially charged with the central "direction of the various police services," they acted as coordinators at the departmental level, just as their lesser colleagues did in the cantons and communes.[44]

The prefects' view of the departmental *commissariats* was ambivalent. They combined approval of further police centralization per se with irritation at even this slight competition with their own administrative omnipotence. The new *commissaires* were, after all, still tenuously linked to the recently amputated Ministry of Police by the obligation to report to Maupas as well as to the prefects. They did so under "Ministry of General Police" letterheads until Maupas' ministry was abolished in June, 1853. Some prefects, as in the Ardennes, found them to be of "incontestable usefulness." Prefect Dieu in the Haute-Saône withheld approval unless they were attached to the *département* by even "tighter bonds . . . under the absolute authority of the prefect." He distrusted even the mere formal "separation" of police functions from the general administration because it "tended to weaken the authority" of the latter. The prefect of the Gironde feared that the new officers might attenuate the prestige of subprefects by their authority over lesser *commissaires* at local levels, thus stranding the subprefects "in a still more embarrassing position than that in which the creation of the General and Special Inspectors placed most of the prefects."

Scattered evidence suggests that the departmental *commissaires* tried to perform efficiently and avoided significant controversy. But even after the abolition of the Ministry of Police in June, 1853, removed the stigma of their earlier ambiguous link with the rival ministry, they remained unpopular. In December, 1853, the Minister of the Interior "very-confidentially" invited the prefects to criticize them and to propose ways "to give the police service more strength and unity without in any way weakening the administrative function."[45]

The departmental *commissariats* were abolished in March, 1854, ostensibly because they were "an inevitable cause of trouble, embarrassment, and regrettable slowness."[46] The prefect of the Aube believed that their demise was "generally approved" by his colleagues throughout France. Now not even the vestiges of the Ministry of Police faced the prefects. Henri Chevreau of the Loire-Inférieure, probably expressing a widespread attitude, agreed that the potential "dangers and abuses" of a special departmental police officer were too great. But he admired the *principle* of more centralized general police action provided, of course, that the prefects retained unchallenged and exclusive control.[47] The cantonal *commissaires,* survivors of the Maupas era, remained useful adjuncts to the prefects' police supremacy in the *départements.*

End of the Ministry of General Police

Left in virtual isolation after the inspectors' suppression on March 5, the Ministry of Police itself disappeared nine months before the departmental *commissaires* ended their short careers. Maupas gave in his resignation on May 6, 1853. Although he urged that the Ministry be continued under another chief, Napoleon III abolished it on June 21. All police powers returned to the Ministry of the Interior according to the status quo *ante* Maupas. Conveying his personal regrets to Maupas, Napoleon III offered the explanation: "Every day I see that the Ministry's creation has weakened instead of strengthening public authority."[48]

Thus in early summer 1853, nothing remained of the late ministry but the departmental *commissaires* (also en route to extinction) and a pile of unpaid bills, including one for the printing of two thousand copies of Maupas' budget request for 1854! The prefects celebrated their emancipation from Maupas' tutelage with congratulatory messages to Persigny, who appended them to his next weekly report to the Emperor.[49]

CONCLUSION

Launched personally by Louis Napoleon, the Ministry of Police was stultified by conflicts inherent in its very organization. From the start it was incompatible with the edifice it was supposed to crown—the prefectorial bureaucracy. Its creator erred if he expected success from an agency structured with so little foresight. Without direct evidence from the Emperor's side, we cannot know finally and exactly what he expected from the Ministry or why he gave it an organization and mission so likely to produce conflict and failure.

Two speculations seem justified. To have founded a truly monolithic, autonomous Ministry of Police probably would have also defeated Louis Napoleon's ends. Public and administrative opposition together would surely have become formidable. Perhaps also the Chief of State thought his "superstructure" ministry sufficient because he misconstrued the import of the administration's enthusiasm for his immediate objectives in the coup d'état. Administrators' vision of a "new era" in early 1852 was by no means inspired by the willingness to sacrifice their stronger position in the state for the sake of the Napoleonic tradition, of which the police ministry was a symbol.

A decisive underlying reality in 1852–53 was the particularism in thought and deed of the public administration. After fifty years of centralized existence, its contours had hardened and the attitudes of its higher officials become proprietary. Police powers were so complexly interlaced in its structure and mentality that to uproot them for the benefit of a specialized ministry seemed to spring the seams of the whole edifice. The real clash was between Louis Napoleon's plans and the functionaries' sense of their own prerogatives. Even the Emperor could not afford to ignore their corporate resistance. By defeating the Ministry of Police, the functionaries proclaimed their refusal to become partial prisoners of a situation they had done much to create. Whatever his private reaction may have been, Napoleon III yielded.

But there was no defeat for centralized police powers as such. In the prefects' hands, political police activities found a favorable environment in the revised institutional setting of the Second Empire.

Centralized General Police Operates Without the Ministry

THE PREFECTS' victory over the Ministry of Police was decisive. Outside Paris, the prefects remained the chief of state's unchallenged agents in their three most essential and inseparable political tasks: the management of elections, the supervision of political police activities, and the cultivation of a loyal, harmonious, and efficient administrative system.

New institutional arrangements fashioned by extraordinary powers and the constitution of 1852 expanded these duties. During the fifties, new legislation and administrative procedures further increased the prefects' control over the communes and enlarged the political police facilities within various branches of the public administration. Such changes concentrated formidable general police powers in the hands of the prefects and promised to assist the administration toward its twin goals—overcoming the nagging vestiges of the "red specter" and dissolving persistent "local influences" in favor of one "national" political orientation. To pursue these goals, centralized police authority need not depend upon a special ministry when the Ministry of the Interior and the Paris Prefecture of Police could serve instead.

EXTENSION OF CENTRALIZED CONTROLS

The Constitution of 1852

The new constitution focused upon executive supremacy and thereby increased the administration's relative independence. Article 58 conferred the "force of law" upon the extraordinary powers interim. Articles 3 and 6 assured the executive's initiative and independence of the legislature and in appointment of officials. These articles alone opened a wide channel of unobstructed authority leading from the Elysée through the Council of State, the ministers (the "Crown's high clerks," in Maupas' words), and into the departmental administration. All members of the public services were to swear obedience to the constitution and fidelity to the chief of state (Article 14), reviving an older practice interrupted since March, 1848.[1] Earlier laws not abrogated by the constitution (Article 56) continued to buttress administrative authority. Article 7 prolonged the traditional "separation of powers" between the administration and judiciary as a two-sided guarantee against the executive's disregard of justice in the common law sphere, and of the administrative law's immunity from judicial intervention.

Louis Napoleon thus met the promises uttered since the coup d'état and repeated in the constitution's preamble. He re-emphasized that which had never fully disappeared among the "best" institutions of the First Empire. The Prince-President stressed his commitment to administrative centralization. It was synonymous with the evolution of the French nation; but, he insisted, the new centralization was more truly national than the old. Since December, it was legitimized by plebiscitary delegation of popular sovereignty in support of the President's attempt "to assure the destiny of France by founding institutions reflecting both the nation's democratic instincts and the universally expressed desire to have a strong and respected central power." Being "responsible" to the sovereign people, the Chief of State's power "must be free and unobstructed" through the ministries, "the honored and powerful auxiliaries of his thought."[2]

A Caesarian political myth thus justified a fusion of democratic suffrage and personal rule whereby Louis Napoleon, the nation's representative, became the public powers personified. Or, to restate the myth within the context of administrative doctrine, the full exercise of general police powers in the name of the *sûreté générale* became not only the executive's prerogative but a mandate conferred by popular sovereignty as well.[3]

THE COUNCIL OF STATE REHABILITATED

To a reorganized Council of State, the traditional custodian of administrative independence, Louis Napoleon assigned an amplified role as "a veritable governmental council and basic mechanism of our new organization." The old Council, made less dependent on the executive in 1849, was dissolved the day after the coup. A decree of January 25, 1852, outlined the organization of a new Council whose position was defined in Articles 47-53 of the constitution.[4]

The core of the new Council was its authorized membership of up to fifty councilors appointed either directly or indirectly by the chief of state. In addition to a hundred and twenty other officials, the ministers received rank, seats, and a deliberative voice. At first the chief of state or his representative presided. After December 30, 1852, the Emperor named the President of the Council of State, who ranked with ministers. Jules Baroche held the office for many years. Under Article 50 of the constitution, the Council drafted projects of law, issued *règlements* of public administration, and resolved "all difficulties arising in administrative matters." The Council met behind closed doors except during hearings of administrative court cases. Publication of its deliberations was forbidden after February 1, 1852.

Thus reconstituted, the Council of State was again the executive's instrument in what critics termed a "reversion" to the First Empire. The executive controlled its composition. Absorbing the duties of the short-lived Tribunal of Conflicts of 1849, it resolved conflicts between administrative and regular court jurisdictions. It again lost the right to dispense "delegated justice," declaring in the executive's name, not its own, in administrative court decisions. The new Council of State was, in short, once again the guardian of the old administrative immunity writ larger now within the wider spaces of constitutional dictatorship. It would be more accurate, therefore, to speak of "reversion" not to Napoleon I but only to 1849. Though the Council was the executive's arm, in practice Louis Napoleon overrode none of its administrative court decisions. Under Jules

Baroche, the Council—no mere rubber stamp of imperial wishes —often resisted certain of its nominal chief's innovations, especially in economic policy.[5]

The "Decentralization" Decree of March 25, 1852

During the reaction of 1849–51, decentralization as a reform issue in the Assembly rode a momentum generated in the spring of 1848. A Committee of Thirty issued various decentralist studies and proposals. Raudot, deputy from the Yonne, drafted a plan that would have left the prefects still "agents of the government" vis-à-vis the departmental general councils; but the latter would have controlled purely departmental affairs. Raudot's proposal, still alive in November, 1851, of course passed away in December.[6]

So the prefects escaped the threat of decentralization, if indeed there ever was a serious one. But in the name of "decentralization," a decree of March 25, 1852, sharpened the actuality of *centralized* administration in the prefects' favor. Quoting an old functionaries' adage, that one could govern from afar but could administer only near at hand, the decree allowed the prefects to decide independently a host of matters formerly requiring clearance in Paris. Only a few of the prefects' new powers were concerned with police. Prefects now appointed *commissaires* of police and *gardes-champêtres* (rural policemen) in towns of six thousand and under. (Three days later, as discussed in chapter 3, the prefects briefly lost some of their new autonomy in the naming of *commissaires*.) The "decentralization" did not explicitly extend prefectorial latitude in general police, but the Minister of the Interior interpreted it in that sense. He ruled that only "important matters affecting public order, political administration, and questions of general police [involving] arrests" required preliminary ministerial approval of the prefects' actions. At first, the prefects read this more conservatively than Persigny, who had to urge them to go their own ways except in the truly "very important" questions.[7] After this, they needed no urging.

The "decentralization" of 1852 consequently benefited the prefects without essentially altering administrative doctrine or centralization itself. Eight years later, Jules Baroche could assess the prefects' status in perfectly traditional terms:

... the prefects of the Emperor are above all his representatives. He alone is judge of the degree to which it is proper to give them the right to administer in his name, with or without prior authorization on his part. As long as it is not a question of administrative measures exceeding the limits of authority and requiring a legislative act, the Emperor alone controls the extension or restriction of the delegation of his power. . . .[8]

Further Centralization over Local Authorities, 1852–1855

Any extension of the prefects' *tutelle* over municipal administration and departmental general councils automatically extended the potential for more effective political police. In theory, municipal police belonged to the commune and general police to the prefect; in practice, the two were never fully distinct. As the Prefect of Police observed in 1858, the municipal police "had never been separated from political police nor could it be now." In proportion to their control of the nomination of municipal administrators and local elective assemblies, the prefects' general police authority more deeply penetrated the country.

From the later 1790's until December, 1851, the decisive central control of the appointment and policies of mayors and the councils was modified only relatively in favor of local self-administration. In March, 1831, municipal councils became elective by a very restricted suffrage, the other councils in June, 1833. A law of July 3, 1848, lowered electoral requirements for the councils and allowed the mayors and adjoints to be selected by municipal councils in towns of six thousand and under, except in administrative capitals (*chefs-lieux*) of *départements*. The coup d'état, of course, suspended all such local autonomies.

The communes and "local influences." The whole question of local administrative autonomy was inextricable from the problem of "local influences," one of the chronic sources of prefects' and *procureurs'* complaints before and after December, 1851. "Local influences," a hackneyed term used endlessly and deploringly in administrative correspondence, referred to communal officials who were politically hostile, indifferent, corrupt, lethargic, or susceptible to the selfish or parochial biases of regional notables or oligarchies. The term embraced particularistic attitudes generally, both within and outside the administration, which no amount of centralized policing and attempted cultivation of a truly "national party" under Louis Napoleon could overcome. Mayors and municipal councils, foci of so many local administrative and police activities, were always potential cornerstones of the tenuous barrier that "local influences" could erect against the most energetic prefect.

It was, therefore, more than coincidental that during the post-December interim of extraordinary powers, the prefects conducted a great purge among municipal authorities. So many mayors were dismissed that in August, 1852, a confidential Interior circular ordered that official suspension notices cease to include explanations lest such publicity undermine "the dignity of the administration." The prefect of the Ain bemoaned the enormous task, created by his own zeal, of finding suitable replacements for 446 mayors and adjoints. His colleague in the Hérault dissolved twenty-two municipal councils and discharged forty-four mayors between December 8 and February 19 for hostility to the administration, refusal to denounce other persons, and "weakness in the face of anarchical manifestations." By the end of March he had replaced about one-fifth of all mayors in his area.[9]

Article 57 of the 1852 constitution allowed the government, through the prefects, again to appoint mayors and adjoints for their five-year terms. A mayor could be chosen from outside the municipal council and even the *département*. Prefectorial control over these officials was assured—at least in law and theory. But "local influences" intervened. Many prefects remained unhappy with even their new appointees. As late as April, in the Saône-et-Loire, municipal personnel were considered to be "deplorably" contaminated by the passions of 1848. Nearly a year after the coup, the prefect of the Dordogne planned again "to proceed . . . with a kind of purge among the mayors." The Minister of Justice relayed similar discontent to the Interior from *procureurs'* reports. From Aix-en-Provence came the plaint that many communal officials in the Var, including new mayors, had been among "the principal agents of the insurrection" in December. From Nîmes and Grenoble it was charged that many were "known enemies of the government." Agreeing, the *procureur* at Montpellier continued through 1853 to report that in rural communes the mayors were politically unreliable, incompetent, or unable to show "completely satisfactory evidence of personal morality."[10] Involvement of the mayors in "local influences" continued throughout the fifties.

The law of July 7, 1852, on elective councils. The problem of the general (departmental) and municipal councils remained. The latter especially were dissolved wholesale in the coup, but their future status had to be decided. Under the law of July, 1848, the general councils would have been renewed by one-third in July, 1851, but at that time elections were postponed pending the Assembly's decentralization studies. Again renewal was deferred in February, 1852, until the government decided what niche the councils would occupy in the new centralized polity. That decision, ratified by the new Legislative Body, appeared in a law of July 7, 1852, providing for the councils' full renewal by universal manhood suffrage but leaving them still vulnerable to central control.[11]

To prevent recurrence of the intrusion of "dangerous elements" into the councils as had occurred in 1848, the chief of state would appoint the officers of each session. If the executive used his right to dissolve a municipal or general council, its functions temporarily passed to an administrative commission appointed by the prefect. The law further decreed that if "in some localities the results [of new elections] should not satisfy the noble confidence of the Chief of State . . . the government would not hesitate to use its right of dissolution." The law made a change in the appointment procedure for mayors and adjoints. Those in administrative capitals and communes of three thousand and over were named by the chief of state, the others by the prefects. The prefects could suspend these officials; only the chief of state could dismiss them. This situation prevailed until a new municipal law brought changes in 1855.

The communes were too important in the prefects' political

mission to be allowed real autonomy. To complicate the problem, most communes were small rural entities highly susceptible to that plague of conscientious prefects—"local influences." In 1858 France contained 36,826 communes. By 1864 there were 37,510, of which 16,692 had less than 500 people and 11,630 between 500 and 100. Only 177 communes had more than 10,000 population.[12] Few of the smaller communes had a resident *commissaire* of police. The mayor, therefore, personified both local and national administrative authority. His functions thus embraced all types of police activity.

Thus the prefects envisioned control by the municipal councils as the alternative to their own control of mayors. But the councils, if no longer infiltrated by "demagogues," as so often reported before 1852, usually reflected obstructive "local influences," from the prefects' viewpoint. They were dominated by clashing factional interests, important families, the "old parties," the clergy, or simply by a static, parochial outlook. Both the prefects and *procureurs* were often led to muse pessimistically upon the contradictions between the "democratic" aspect of the imperial polity and their own authoritarian mission. Some doubted the wisdom of universal suffrage at the municipal level because it stimulated, they believed, both the radicals and more conservative but self-centered "local influences." The *procureur* at Montpellier, for example, feared that universal suffrage would "sooner or later lead to complications such as to threaten the stability of the regime, no matter how strong it may seem."[13]

Despite such worries, by July, 1852, the prefects seemed to tower over the municipalities—so much so, in fact, that the policy of the Ministry of the Interior became less rigorous than that of the prefects, whose use of their powers often seemed excessive to officials in Paris who did not daily rub elbows with "local influences."

In the Var, the prefect suspended fifteen municipal councils, newly elected in August, 1852, and replaced them with temporary administrative commissions because the elections returned men of the "democratic party." Elsewhere, a municipal council was removed because its legitimist members refused to join the public celebration of the Empire in December, 1852. In most cases, the prefects acted when the elections installed hostile majorities or councils which for any reason opposed mayors favored by the administration. In several cases, such bodies were suspended before their first meeting. Persigny cautioned the prefects against ill-considered or "premature" suspensions that would appear to be a "kind of protest against universal suffrage." Sometimes he differed with his prefects' timing, not their policy: "It is much better to await a favorable occasion. The radical passions in some of the new councils will soon provide you with one. Then you can act with more convincing authority." The prefects should patiently wait until they found "a plausible reason" for suspension on an issue so related to communal welfare that the public would applaud the disciplinary measure "as an act of good administration."[14]

Nonetheless, the prefects continued to suspend municipal councils and to ask Paris for their dissolution. Prefect Dieu defended his suspension of a council in the Haute-Saône because of its "violent and systematic opposition to the mayor" on the grounds that several months' suspension nearly always eased the return to "normal" administration. Another prefect cited the "very remarkable consequences of the suspensions" in seven communes, all of which were afterward unanimously favorable in the plebiscite of December, 1852. This confirmed Dieu's belief "that the suspension of hostile municipal councils, far from in any way impeding governmental policy, would on the contrary produce the best effect." The prefect of the Eure-et-Loir, also rejecting Persigny's suggestions, insisted that he could best serve universal suffrage by "freeing" the great majority from intimidation by municipal councils whose members included men of "the demagogic party" intent upon harassing the mayor's administration. But when this prefect wished to dissolve a council in order to thwart an uncooperative mayor, Persigny refused because "it would be impossible officially to explain your real motive in requesting it."[15]

Persigny and his successors sent repeated instructions on the issue. In 1856, Billault accused the prefects of too readily suspending councils on purely communal issues of no interest to general policy. Yet the prefects, beset by "local influences," continued the practice. As late as November, 1858, one out of every 104 of the country's 36,826 communes was without a municipal council because of suspension or dissolution.[16]

The Municipal Law of 1855

Even though they maintained formal supremacy over the municipalities and commanded the cantonal *commissaires* of police, many prefects (and *procureurs*) worried throughout the fifties over the laxity of communal police. They continually demanded still further centralized controls. The Loire-Inférieure's Henri Chevreau expressed a very typical view: "Only by surveillance of the municipal police can the most effective political police be achieved." He argued that the *commissaires* were enmeshed in too many "concurrent and sometimes contradictory" obligations. Municipal authorities, jealous of intrusions into their own local police affairs, obstructed the *commissaires'* conduct of more important police duties. At least in the larger towns, Chevreau urged, the prefects should directly control all levels of administrative police functions. Chevreau's wishes were partly realized in a definitive law of May 5, 1855, on municipal organization. In force until 1867, the new measure supplemented the controls of July, 1852, over mayors and municipal councils. It also, to the prefects' benefit, reformed and standardized the municipal police systems of larger cities.[17]

The law of 1855 retained the 1852 regulations on appointment, revocation, suspension, and election in the cases of mayors, adjoints, and municipal councilors. But it allowed the adjoints, like the mayors, to be appointed from outside the *département*. The reform in no way inhibited the tactics applied in all the municipal elections of the fifties, whereby mayors and adjoints were appointed before the voting in order to circumvent attempts of the new municipal councils to influence the choice.[18] The prefects could still suspend mayors and adjoints, but only for two months without ministerial approval. Revocations required an imperial decree. Prefects could suspend municipal councils for two months or—with ministerial approval—up to one year. Only the Emperor could dissolve them. He appointed the councils in Lyon, Paris, and other communes of the Seine. It was the prefects' new prerogative to delimit the electoral sections within the commune and to fix the number of councilors to be elected from each section provided that this be done according to the numerical distribution of registered voters.

Article 50 of the law created a new fusion of municipal and general police powers by directing that in departmental capitals of over forty thousand population "the prefect fulfills the functions of prefect of police" as in Paris or Lyon. Seventeen cities were affected. Their mayors continued as acting chiefs of municipal police "under the surveillance of the prefect." The law ordered these cities to expand their police forces and to reorganize them in a uniform way in accordance with details which had been prescribed on September 26, 1855. Financial limitations —always an obstacle to the expansion of police forces under the Second Empire—allowed complete application of the reform only in Bordeaux, Lille, Marseille, Metz, Nantes, Rouen, Strasbourg, and Toulouse.

Billault, Minister of the Interior, foresaw that the prefects' new police control in the cities affected would surely "awaken . . . the honorable susceptibilities of the municipal bodies." Consequently, he advised the prefects to deny any intention of obliterating the municipal police powers of these cities. Rather, they were to say that the municipal police now came "more particularly under the prefect's authority." The prefect would appoint and discharge municipal policemen. However, he would give them direct orders only for general police, otherwise leaving them at the mayor's disposition. Even this nominal vestige of municipal police autonomy in the seventeen cities was nullified when the Court of Cassation ruled, a little over a year later, that even in purely municipal police activities (traffic, lighting, cleaning, and so forth) a prefectorial *arrêté* superseded the municipality's authority.

The 1855 law required the specified cities to adopt a uniform organization of municipal police forces. A Central *Commissaire* of Police must be established as the "intermediary" between prefect and mayor. Communal and cantonal *commissaires* must actually be maintained in numbers (one for each ten thousand of the city's population) and conditions of service required by their founding regulations and the reform of 1854 (see chapter 6). The *commissaires* were to preside over three basic categories of subordinate police officers. The mainstays of the municipal force were uniformed *sergents de ville,* some with the rank of *brigadier,* roughly analogous to the grade of army corporal. Several *agents de police,* detectives in mufti, were allotted for criminal and political work. *Inspecteurs de police* rounded out the new forces. Under the *commissaires'* orders, they commanded the *sergents* and *agents* and administered routine and "special missions" in the city. The reform provided modest and badly needed increments in clerical help, at least on paper. In all seventeen cities, the new role of the Central *Commissaires* was actually established and the prescribed ratio of ordinary *commissaires* enforced. Otherwise, the reforms of 1855 were incompletely carried out except in the eight cities mentioned above.[19]

Political police motives did not alone dictate the reform of 1855. Since 1800, these growing cities had hardly increased their police forces. Procedures and organization—the haphazard accumulation of time—were extremely varied. The reform, even in the eight favored cities, brought no inordinate expansion of police forces, considering the routine needs of such large municipalities. In Marseille, the largest community (nearly three hundred thousand) included in the reform, the expanded police roster included one Central *Commissaire,* eighteen other *commissaires,* nineteen secretaries, five inspectors, forty-one police agents, one hundred and fifteen *sergents de ville* plus twelve *brigadiers* (and kindred ranks still designated by names peculiar to this city), one *concierge,* and one quartermaster sergeant—a total of two hundred and thirteen persons, clerks included. Lille had seven *commissaires,* two inspectors, seven agents, twenty-nine *sergents,* and one interpreter. Bordeaux's full complement was eighty-five, supplemented by a Municipal Guard of sixty-six men. Strasbourg had fifty-two, Nancy twenty-four.

The reforms of 1855 left the prefects still dissatisfied. They continued to urge an extension of the same sort of reform to smaller communities. Prefect Lorette in the Tarn-et-Garonne typically observed that "there is a nearly inevitable and permanent conflict with the municipality, which [wishes] to have its separate police." Why, he asked, was not the principle of Article 50 extended to smaller cities? In various dispatches, he pressed his point that municipal obstructionism prevented the most effective political police against "the red party. . . . A good police is the only remedy." "Good police" meant exclusive prefectorial control. But even in the cities affected by the 1855 law, no policemen's utopias emerged. Marseille remained intractable under its prefects' attempted tutelage throughout the Second Empire. Its municipal council stubbornly resisted increased police expenditures and actually cut appropriations on several occasions. Intramural conflicts, factional strife, and other symptoms of "local influences" provided rich material for complaints by various prefects and by the *procureurs* at Aix-en-Provence. Maupas himself went as prefect to the Bouches-du-Rhône in 1860 in order to achieve a more efficient police regime in Marseille.[20]

To those who complained of such problems and offered reform proposals, the Ministry of the Interior in the later fifties acknowledged receipt and promised to study all suggestions with care, meanwhile extending little aid or comfort. The government never expanded the 1855 police reform to other cities. Instead, another municipal law in 1867 returned most of the control over municipal police in the seventeen cities to their mayors.

Further Centralization of Political Police
Through Public Education

During the fifties, the prefects' political police channels cut into the Ministry of Public Instruction as well as into municipal administration. The "Falloux Law" of 1850 had increased clerical influence in the centralized hierarchy which presided over public education. Under the Ministry of Public Instruction, a Superior Council, headed by the Minister, sat at the top of educational administration. In each *département*, an Academy, under a Rector assisted by an Academic Council, determined curriculum, chose teachers, and enforced academic discipline in the secondary and primary schools. The Church had great influence at all these levels. Four bishops sat in the Superior Council, which named the Rectors. In every *département*, the Rectors' Academic Council consisted of a bishop, another cleric of the bishop's choice, a representative from each of the various religious bodies, and the prefect. The municipal councils appointed primary teachers, but only from a list drafted by the Academic Council.

Not surprisingly, the prefect often found himself a minority of one in the choice of teachers and academic policies. At such times, he confronted a special combination of "local influences"—the clergy and municipal councils—that struck to the heart of his sensibilities regarding communal affairs. The many prefects who objected to this system were moved by more than a mere compulsion toward full centralization. They regarded the schools as important political influences, either for creating sentiment for the dictatorship or for harboring and fostering resistance against it. Clerical influence or control might in a given instance serve either end; the clerics' decisions often reflected motives that were irrelevant to the prefects' immediate political objectives. They frequently protested that the political aspects of public education should be supervised by themselves as the agents of the "sole political ministry." The coup d'état and extraordinary powers permitted the prefects to purge suspected teachers along with other doubtful public servants. But they knew that after the return of "normality," the fundamental problem would remain unless the educational regime of 1850 were modified.

Administrative control of teachers. The prefects argued that Louis Napoleon's political roots were in the smaller communes, where the teachers played a role so crucial that their cooperation with the administration was indispensable. It was intolerable to allow their appointment and control to reflect the devious motives prevalent in the cleric-dominated Academic Councils. The prefects found allies in high places. Jules Baroche in the Council of State and Hippolyte Fortoul, Minister of Public Instruction, seeking a more centralized and secular control over the schools, achieved two major changes in the educational organization of 1850.[21]

A decree of March 9, 1852, reorganized the Superior Council and gave the chief of state exclusive appointive power at all levels of educational administration above secondary teaching personnel. The Ministry directly appointed secondary teachers. The Rectors named primary instructors. Fortoul made it clear to the Rectors and others that the 1852 law was intended to centralize secular control of education under the Ministry, in which clerical spirit would no longer prevail.[22] With Persigny's support, a second law of June 14, 1854, empowered the prefects to appoint primary teachers. The departmental Academies gave way to larger and fewer regional counterparts and eventually the numbers of Rectors and Academic Councils, where the administration's influence now predominated, were reduced.

The reforms of 1852 and 1854 combined to give the prefects, backed by a nonclerical, educational hierarchy, the means of decisive political influence over the teachers. Without "extraordinary" powers, they could bar or purge suspected radical republicans or other undesirables from the teaching profession. They could make varied political use of the favored teachers who were appointed. Many prefects hoped that the results would become an important force in the eventual political "re-education" of the country. To that end, for example, Prefect de Bourgoing of the Seine-et-Marne circulated detailed instructions among the primary teachers: they must emphasize religion, obedience to authority, and the truth of the Second Empire's principles and aspirations, "to which France owes its glory abroad and its prosperity at home. . . ." From the Tarn-et-Garonne, Le Vasseur reported great improvements in curriculum and teaching personnel—to which he had contributed by "replacing those teachers . . . under the influence of the deplorable doctrines of '48, whom I have eagerly discharged whenever the occasion arose." On this issue, at least, the prefects agreed with the Rectors, one of whom typically urged that the "intellectual mission" of all educators be conceived "to the profit of religion and morality" and founded upon "the duty of resolutely supporting . . . this wise and constructive government."[23]

The Rectors' political reports. The Rectors indirectly became adjuncts of the Interior's political police activities as a byproduct of the reactionary sequel in 1858 of Felice Orsini's attempt on the Emperor's life. On March 19, the Minister of Public Instruction confidentially ordered them to submit equally confidential monthly and trimestrial reports on political, religious, and moral conditions in their jurisdictions. The Rectors adapted with apparent enthusiasm to their peripheral role in the political police system, though many apologized for their amateur status and lack of intelligence facilities in comparison with the administrative and judiciary police. For at least eight years, they sent their minister periodic reports in which their own observations mingled with information supplied by school inspectors. The Minister of Public Instruction relayed at least some of the reports to his colleague of the Interior. The Rectors occasionally criticized certain of the prefects' specific actions. But on the whole, their reports revealed an authoritarian mentality strikingly like that of the *procureurs* and prefects. Stressing political themes, they dealt with public opinion, the "red specter," the activities of the clergy, legitimists, and Orleanists, and the performance of educational functionaries.

The Rectors liberally garnished their facts with personal opinions and recommendations for changes in national policies. Rector Mottet at Aix-en-Provence, for instance, found universal suffrage to be a "very dangerous" stimulant to the "lower classes [who] respect order only because they are isolated and powerless before a strong government and vigilant administration." He thought it folly to allow them any means of "conquering political power." Universal suffrage should be cast out entirely or at least be so modified that it becomes harmless.

At Grenoble, Rector Guet considered the professors "perhaps too timid," but "profoundly devoted" to the Empire. He proposed that "the great and noble political concepts" of Napoleon III be more emphasized in the curriculum. *Lycée* students, he was happy to report, were "becoming more religious," whatever their parents' opinions might be, in a hopeful trend which he equated with the students' enthusiasm for the imperial family. He attributed the new climate to the instructors' "propagation of healthy doctrines and sound values."

From Nancy, the administration, army, and clergy together

were portrayed as a "salutary dike" against social upheaval. The Rector praised the teachers' energy in spreading "healthy ideas" during elections and noted that teachers were more useful to the prefects than the mayors.[24]

The Prefects and Their Ministry: Restraints with Satisfactions

Having rejected centralization over themselves by the Ministry of Police, the prefects accepted as their due the consolidation of authority given them during the fifties. Yet many of them yearned for a more ideal autonomy and, on occasion, questioned their ministers' restrictions on their initiative. The "excessive zeal" of departmental officials was frequently criticized in the Ministry of the Interior in terms not too far removed from those used by the Empire's opponents. Persigny, a staunch advocate of prefectorial authority, was impelled to modify the laissez-faire policy he had adopted after the "decentralization" of 1852. He asked that in all but "cases of extreme urgency" the prefects obtain his approval before issuing *arrêtés* (decisions with the force of law) on "matters involving the public order, political administration, and issues of general police."[25]

On the other hand, the prefects must have gleaned satisfactions from their minister's championship of their cause against the Ministry of Police and his subsequent repeated acknowledgments of their supreme role in general police. Citing the "decisive" encounter with Maupas and the departmental *commissaires,* Persigny agreed that general police, "one of the most integral aspects of the administration," never could be separated from the prefects' control.

"It is best," he told the prefects, "to centralize everything pertaining to administrative and political surveillance . . . in the prefectures and sub-prefectures."

The prefects received certain other attentions along with reassurances from their Minister. On Persigny's proposal, the Emperor authorized them after September, 1853, to advise on all personnel changes and promotions contemplated by other ministerial bureaucracies, including recommendations to the Legion of Honor. Persigny provided the prefects with better communications and a more comprehensive view of national administration. After January, 1854, they received summaries of significant activities undertaken by their colleagues throughout the country. The Ministry also circulated copies of special directives addressed originally only to certain *départements*. In 1852, both prefects and subprefects received salary increases. Of the eighty-six prefects, in April, 1856, all but one held the rank of *chevalier* or above in the Legion of Honor, as did 108 of the 277 subprefects then in service.[26]

Despite such satisfactions and the accretion of new powers by 1855 (which, incidentally, steadily increased their work loads), many prefects still found their expanded role to be less than ideal. A prefect, wrote Mentque from the Gironde, should "dominate the municipalities, watch over all functionaries, and shepherd the people along the Napoleonic path. Such is his mission. . . ." From other *départements* came agreement that a prefect should have a police more fully integrated into the administration, exclusive power to judge the competence and political reliability of all functionaries, and still more freedom to make decisions unhampered by parliamentarians, regional influences, or the Ministry of the Interior itself.[27]

Some prefects resented the appointment of nine councilors of state to make annual inspections "in depth" of all aspects of departmental administration, "with the objective of maintaining or strengthening the unity of administrative action in every *département*." This new arrangement of 1853 no doubt was more acceptable to the prefects than surveillance by Maupas' late ministry and it was no threat to their supremacy. Moreover, Persigny emphasized that the inspectors were direct agents of Napoleon III, who expected everyone to cooperate. Still, a few prefects refused to keep silent on even this inspection by their own kind, done expressly in the Emperor's name. The prefect of the Gironde saw it undermining the prefects' "moral ascendancy" in the *départements*. No apparent results emerged from the survey when it ended in 1854.[28]

THE MINISTRY OF THE INTERIOR

Further concentration of the prefects' centralized controls and the passing of the Ministry of Police heaped new burdens upon the Ministry of the Interior—the Second Empire's closest approach to a monolithic police-state mechanism after June, 1853. The "decentralization" of 1852 cut the central paperwork in Paris. But the demands of an authoritarian regime complicated the work of an agency responsible for myriad administrative tasks other than those of general police. Because of the regime's relative parsimony in supplying and paying subordinate functionaries, the Ministry accomplished a great deal with a modestly sized central bureaucracy.

During the fifties, after Morny's brief tenure, the Ministry was dominated by Fialin de Persigny for two-and-a-half years (from the end of January, 1852, until June 23, 1854), and again in November, 1860, for another term; by Adolphe-Augustin Billault for four-and-a-half years (June 23, 1854, to February 7, 1858), and during the interim of Persigny's absence, from November 1, 1859.[29]

Persigny set the tone. Bored by his young wife's entertainments and the gaieties of life at 101 Rue de Grenelle, Persigny worked long hours to make his ministry the primary political instrument of the new order. He was an authoritarian inspired by the conviction that a new political generation must mature before France could again venture into political liberty. Always the defender of prefectorial authority, he could be both firm and flexible with the prefects. He understood the subtleties of their diverse local problems. When he left office in 1854, he seemed more satisfied than the prefects with the national effectiveness of general police. To the Emperor he reported that the wisdom of abolishing the Ministry of Police and restoring the prefects' autonomy was fully confirmed by political results:

Every day has been marked by new progress in the restoration of material and moral order. . . . At no time has the political police been exercised with more authority in the face of fewer obstacles.[30]

The Ministry's Central Organization

The fifties saw more changes in the Ministry's central offices than would be profitable to relate in detail. Frequent internal reorganizations sought retrenchment to the minimum staff and modest improvement of the employees' welfare combined with maximum effectiveness in general police operations in the *départements* without great increases in the numbers of police officers.

Morny, on Louis Napoleon's orders, began the first reorganization in mid-December, 1851. He revised personnel policies and raised some salaries among the staff of 196 people at no added cost to the state. The central offices were revamped to include a Division of *Sûreté Générale* designed as a unified national general police agency. Presented as only a first step in the Ministry's rejuvenation, Morny's reforms were interrupted by his resignation and the creation of the Ministry of General Police.[31]

With the fall of Maupas' ministry in June, 1853, agriculture and commerce returned to a separate ministry and a new Directorship of the *Sûreté Générale,* with seven divisions and thirty bureaus, arose to accommodate the general police powers now restored to their original home. Collet-Meygret, who had left the police ministry to become prefect in the Aube, headed the new Directorship. On August 21, 1854, Collet-Meygret's domain was expanded into the General Directorship of the *Sûreté Publique* plus a special commission for the censorship of the nonperiodical press. Finally, on November 30, 1859, Collet-Meygret's former directorship passed (for general police only) to the Paris Prefect of Police who, without basic changes in the Interior's central bureaucracy, now added to his own police functions the directorship of one unified service of the *Sûreté Publique* for the entire country. In effect, without the title or special bureaucracy, many of the elements of a general police ministry were thus reassembled within the Ministry of the Interior's structure.[32]

The magnitude of the Interior's national police duties was reflected in the General Directorship as it was in April, 1856, still under Collet-Meygret. The First Division consisted of four *bureaux.* The Bureau of General Correspondence and *Sûreté*

Publique presided over the following: general correspondence; archives and information; relationships with the gendarmerie; surveillance of political offenders, foreigners, and refugees; the use of the secret police funds and the granting of "indemnities" to deserving persons; and, of course, "matters relating to the *sûreté générale* of the state and to the discovery of activities dangerous thereto." The Second Bureau dealt with "special police": lotteries; meetings and associations; surveillance of cafés, cabarets, and public places; surveillance of liberated convicts; burials; and various other nonpolitical activities. The Third Bureau, for "administrative police," was the personnel office for the *commissaires* and rural policemen. It also administered passports, workers' permits, firearms, and game wardens. The Fourth Bureau regulated emigration. The Second Division in 1856 consisted of two bureaus which together regulated printing, bookselling, and the press in all its aspects including translation of foreign newspapers; publishing the official administrative paper, the *Moniteur des communes,* for the *départements*; and enforcement of copyright laws and treaties.

The Prefects' Reports

The Paris bureaucracy of the Interior would, of course, have withered on the vine without speedy and regular communication with the prefects. Technology played an important role. Morny, during the coup d'état, in constant telegraphic contact with military and administrative authorities throughout the country, might have inspired the stereotype later drawn, perhaps with a trace of begrudging admiration, by the anti-imperialist Eugène Pelletan:

> Each morning upon awakening, the Minister of the Interior rings a telegraphic doorbell from the privacy of his office and gathers all the prefects intangibly around him in order to give them the orders of the day.[33]

A decree of December 27, 1851, gave the government a monopoly over the establishment and use of the telegraph, the administration of the Postoffice and Telegraph being empowered to refuse, in the public interest, transmission of any message.

The telegraph was much used in administrative communications. But the day-to-day political policing of France rested upon routine informational and instructional correspondence up and down administrative chains of command from the ministries to the smallest communes. From the ministers of War, Justice, and the Interior, "circulars" went out to the officers of gendarmerie, *procureurs-généraux,* and the prefects—particularly to the latter. The prefects themselves, like their counterparts in the other two services, in turn issued circulars to subordinate functionaries and received regular and special reports from them. From these local and regional reports, synthesized in the prefectures, and from correspondence with the gendarmerie and the *procureurs*—and sometimes out of personal inspiration—the prefects returned periodic and special reports to Paris.

As they proved in their conflict with the Ministry of Police, the prefects were extremely sensitive to any changes in regular reporting channels that would bypass themselves as the direct agents of the executive power. After 1852, the prefects sent regular bimonthly reports (and after October, 1857, monthly plus trimestrial) on the political, administrative, economic, and moral conditions in their *départements.* More than once, ministers of the Interior tried to accelerate communications on general police by requiring direct reports from the *commissaires* to Paris. Delangle ordered such a procedure in July, 1858, but it was discontinued the following year, and the prefects were asked to relay information from the *commissaires* daily. Persigny revived Delangle's idea in September, 1862, only to modify it again a few months later. The Ministry, except for the two brief interims mentioned, thus relied almost exclusively upon the prefects for their interpretation of the facts of departmental affairs and opinion.

The periodic reports covered, or were supposed to cover, a vast range of topics basic to a comprehensive political policing of the nation. In the late 1850's, the Minister of the Interior expected to be informed by all pertinent information within the prescribed rubrics presented in abridged form below:[34]

I. Moral and Political Situation

Public opinion: its principal concerns and manifestations related to governmental policies. Attitude toward military commanders.

Political parties: their importance and activities.

Secret societies: evidence revealing or justifying suspicion of their existence.

Behavior of persons condemned for political offenses.

Political offenses: the circumstances, culprits, and prosecutions involved.

False news: information on persons circulating it.

Newspaper press: its tendencies, influence, and numbers of subscribers to political newspapers.

The book press and bookselling: activities, violations, and prosecutions.

Elections: their political characteristics; results of by-elections.

Clergy and religious organizations: their influence, activities; public complaints against them.

Civil functionaries generally: their attitudes, conflicts, and relations with the public and other authorities.

Functionaries in detail: personal conduct, performance of duties, influence, attitudes, relations with the public, complaints against them.

Teachers: appointments, dismissals, and the reasons therefor.

Gendarmerie: conduct, etc.

Public health: epidemics, mortality.

Important events: fires, crimes, noteworthy trials.

Miscellaneous: drinking establishments; direct and indirect taxes; mendacity; societies of mutual assistance; savings banks.

II. Material and Economic Situation

Agriculture, vine diseases, industry, commerce, public works, administrative affairs, thermal establishments, miscellaneous.

A summary of a better-than-average prefect's report will suggest the varied content of the periodic correspondence with the Ministry. Though some of the material obviously related to political police and some did not appear immediately relevant, almost anything in a typical report could become politically important in changing circumstances as interpreted from Paris.

Prefect Ferlay of the Drôme began a report of 1854 by reminding the Minister of the Interior of the dimensions of his *département* and its four *arrondissements*, the religious division of its 326,846 people into 289,542 Catholics, 37,079 Protestants, 63 Jews, and members of 162 other communions. He described, by *arrondissement*, the Drôme's rivers, roads, and railways. He provided general information on its 28 cantons and 364 communes (one having been recently created), commenting statistically on landholding, forests and other resources, and public revenues. He discussed the climate, public institutions, and social composition, going on to a summary of the *département*'s economy.

Against this background, Ferlay proceeded to an analytical commentary on departmental life. He remarked upon the great tact required to keep peace among Catholics and the sizable Protestant minority. Among the functionaries of other ministries, he found a satisfactory attitude despite the presence of many legitimists who, fortunately, did not let their prejudices show unduly. Ranging over his subprefects, the prefect expressed approval; one of them, he was glad to see, was "full of urbanity" as an addendum to his professional competence. His twenty-eight *commissaires* of police provided no serious complaints, nor did the gendarmerie. Like virtually all prefects, Ferlay found his 374 *gardes champêtres* (rural policemen) normally and exasperatingly inefficient, though he detected a slight improvement. The mayors, since the prefect had acquired the right to name them, were "more disciplined" and the municipal councils easier to handle, both eliciting more "deference" from the public. The councils of *arrondissement* were safely composed of successful official candidates since the last election. The general council of the *département* also consisted of devoted men, mostly "notables"; its president was a popular man who knew how to control without appearing crudely domineering. The one political newspaper, edited in "quite a governmental manner," offered no problem.

On the whole, then, public authority in the Drôme was generally respected and obeyed—"but this on the condition that it prove itself strong and just." To be sure, some political problems existed, since in human affairs there were always improvements to be made. Orleanists were relatively few, far outnumbered by legitimists. Generally the upper classes were attached to the government if only out of self-interest, "because it has given them security." In time, perhaps, more genuine, selfless attachments to the regime would evolve. The masses were widely attracted by the name Napoleon: "They have faith in him."

Still, Ferlay saw in his *département,* as elsewhere, a link between economic insecurity and demagogic radicalism or at least
serious opposition. He estimated that in December, 1851, about
twenty-five thousand secret society members were enrolled in the
Drôme. As long as dwarf landholdings prevailed in the presence
of land speculation, debt, bad harvests, and business slumps, the
danger of radicalism would remain endemic, even though the
département's well-being had improved since 1851. Patience, Ferlay counseled, and tactful listening to the public's divergent views,
were the best ways to lead back those who strayed. "But," he
said, "I do not compromise with evil passions." Four years later,
Ferlay's reports were much the same.

THE PREFECTURE OF POLICE DURING
THE FIFTIES

In Paris, Pierre-Marie Piétri, Maupas' successor as Prefect
of Police, required no further centralization to make his agency
effective, nor did he share the departmental prefects' worries over
"local influences." The Prefecture of Police itself had for a half-
century been the decisive local influence in Paris and the Seine,
where the prefect of the Seine was cast in a nonpolitical and
auxiliary role.

Piétri ruled the Prefecture for more than six years (from January 27, 1852, until March 16, 1858), the thirty-first Prefect of
Police since the office began in 1800. A Corsican lawyer and
youthful disciple of the Napoleonic cult, Piétri later became a
militant liberal under the July Monarchy, member of the Society
of the Rights of Man, and occasional associate of Ledru-Rollin.
In 1848, he served as Commissioner of the Provisional Government in Corsica and as deputy of the Left in the Constitutional
Assembly, where he abruptly reverted to earlier Bonapartist
loyalties. During the presidential campaign of late 1848, Piétri
was known as "one of the most zealous partisans" of Louis Napoleon. Among the Elysée's favorites in 1849, he was offered his
choice of prefectures, but tactfully deferred to the Minister of
the Interior's decision.

In August he was installed in the Ariège. There he assiduously promoted the Bonapartist cause, not forgetting to remind his superior that he was "attached by indissoluble bonds to Louis Napoleon Bonaparte." Requesting another prefecture, he refused that of the Doubs; but in October, 1851, he replaced Maupas in the Haute-Garonne, where he continued the latter's groundwork for the coup d'état. Still in Maupas' footsteps as the new Prefect of Police in 1852, Piétri began eight years of service which raised him through the various ranks of the Legion of Honor and earned him the title of senator in 1857.[35] In Paris, this short, thickset Corsican, with lowering brow and a vigorous moustache beneath a balding crown, presided over a police state-within-the-state whose First Empire foundations were further solidified by the Second Empire.

Organization and Personnel

Nominally under the Interior's supervision, the Paris Prefecture of Police after its origin in 1800 evolved into a virtually autonomous agency. As the state's most important political police officer, the Prefect usually enjoyed a *de facto* ministerial status, free to consult independently with the chief of state. With the Prefect of the Seine he shared—in an administrative relationship unique in France—certain nonpolitical administrative functions. Otherwise he shared very little with anyone, being supreme in municipal government and administrative police, and endowed with considerable judiciary police powers. Additionally, he also supervised the city's food supply, many other aspects of business and industry, prisons and other public institutions, public places, public health, and sanitation. He commanded all the administrative police forces directly; he could call upon special military forces when necessary. The "mayors" of the Parisian quarters were in reality hardly more than the Prefect's functionaries. His police authority penetrated the vulnerable domain of his prefectorial colleague of the Seine, who alone among French prefects had no general police powers. Actually it reached even beyond, a decision of 1801 having placed not only the Seine but three communes of the Seine-et-Oise (St.-Cloud, Meudon, and Sèvres) under the Prefect's police jurisdiction.[36]

The Prefect of Police combined the powers of a departmental prefect, a municipal administration, and a special political police officer in an urban agglomeration of more than one million people at the end of the fifties. His was the most absolute public authority in France. For a half-century before Louis Napoleon, this authority was rooted in administrative law and general police doctrine. Theorists pointed to the unique role of Paris—the "head and heart" of France—in order further to justify the unique status of its Prefect. Generations of writers have described how the capital thus lived

under the authority of a special magistrate, agent of the central power, prefect and mayor at the same time, having neither all the attributions of a prefect nor all those of a mayor, concentrating in his hands the powers of . . . general, municipal, and judiciary police.[37]

Not that the Prefect was entirely immune from a special Parisian version of "local influences"! Officially, he coexisted in a delicate web of relationship, with other municipal officials, the *parquet* of the *procureur-général,* and the prefect of the Seine—all of whom had their special enclaves in Parisian administration. The Prefecture's authority thus stood "between the judicial and the municipal functions, touching both, but retaining in their midst an independent existence . . . subordinate in law to the Ministry of the Interior but in fact accountable only to itself."[38]

Most of the Prefecture's time was devoted to nonpolitical municipal activities thoroughly interwoven with Parisian daily life. It suffered a brief eclipse during the First Restoration. The revolution of 1848 brought another abortive change. On February 24, the Provisional Government subordinated the Prefecture to a newly created mayor of Paris, then returned it to the Interior on March 20. The mayoralty of Paris survived only until July 19, whereupon the Prefecture resumed its accustomed domination. Under Pierre Carlier (November 9, 1849, to October 26, 1851) and Maupas, it played a basic role in the execution of the coup d'état.

By 1851, the Prefecture's organization and personnel, based upon Napoleonic legislation, no longer met the demands of a diversified and growing community that was increasing yearly as

more provincials arrived with their regional political tempera-
ments and grievances intact. To police over one million people,
the Prefecture had less than a thousand employees. Its moldering
quarters in the old Rue de Jérusalem along the Quai des Orfèvres
were a somber maze once occupied by the Parlement of Paris and
eventually burned in the disorders of 1870–71.[39] There, in 1852,
Piétri found a force in need of expansion and modernization. Both
were forthcoming during the next eight years. The "decentralization" decree of March, 1852, applied to the Prefect of Police as
well as to his departmental colleagues. But the Prefecture's important reforms did not begin until 1854.

The Reform of 1854

On September 17, 1854, the Paris municipal police began a
major renovation modeled on London's police system. Before the
decree, about three hundred of the city's seven hundred and fifty
sergents de ville, or ordinary policemen, were assigned to special
municipal police and administrative services, leaving only four
hundred and fifty to patrol the capital's twelve *arrondissements*
and forty-eight sections. The decree of 1854, therefore, greatly
increased the personnel and revised patrol assignments so that
Paris could be adequately covered day and night by patrolmen
on smaller beats. The total municipal police force was more
than tripled to a figure of about thirty-six hundred (compared to
London's 4,764 constables).

The twelve *arrondissements* remained as organizational units,
each under a *commissaire* of police. However, they were seg-
mented by a new "topographical division" into 850 *îlots,* or patrol
areas, each manned day and night by a *sergent de ville* resident
in the area. A central post was established in each of the forty-
eight sections of the city, with two policemen always on duty, one
standing by at the post, the other touring the section. In each
arrondissement, three *sergents* with the rank of *brigadier* were
assigned to continual inspection of the service. They, the central
posts in the sections, and the patrolmen on the streets, were commanded by an *officier de paix* on duty, under the *commissaire,* in
a central post for the entire *arrondissement.* None of these police

ranks was new. In 1854, their numbers were simply increased and
their deployment over the city reorganized and intensified. Other
men of all ranks served in the special units devoted to various administrative tasks. The *commissaires* were, as before, the mainstays of the system, the only officers with powers of both
administrative and judiciary police. The Chief of Municipal Police acted as the Prefect's executive officer, with the rank of
commissaire.

Accompanying the reform was a new regulation governing recruitment, to be supervised by a special commission which would
examine all candidates on their aptitudes and physical qualifications. Stricter personnel standards and professional discipline
rounded out the reforms of 1854.

In 1857, four new "special police inspectors" were appointed.
Each undertook the surveillance of police services in three *arrondissements*. They also were liaison officers between the Chief
of Municipal Police and the *officiers de paix;* and they performed
"extraordinary" duties, including special political police assignments direct from the Prefect, to whom they reported.[40]

Extension of Paris and the Prefect's Jurisdiction

Expansion of the Paris police personnel and the Prefect's jurisdiction kept pace with the city's growth. In June, 1853, the Prefect's powers were extended fully to all communes of the Seine.
Rapid population growth contributed to the expansion of the city
limits by a law of June 16, 1859. In 1859–60, thirteen communes
were annexed, adding eight new *arrondissements* to the earlier
twelve. The municipal police rose to 4,590 on paper, but budget
problems delayed the employment of the full complement.[41]

The General Directorship of the Sûreté Publique, *1859*

The annexations coincided with two other important jurisdictional changes in 1859. Following Orsini's attempt on the Emperor's life in early 1858 and the resultant political police reaction, rumors spread that the Prefecture of Police would be
drastically remodeled and another police ministry revived.
Neither rumor was accurate but the first came nearer the truth.

According to Baron Haussmann, Napoleon III and Delangle wished at least to create a new division of labor between the Prefects of the Seine and the Police, giving purely administrative functions to the former and leaving municipal and general police authority to the latter. The motives arose from the desire to achieve a more effective national political police and the need to resolve a long-standing conflict between the two prefects which the city's expansion now made acute. Both motives underlay the changes of 1859.

On October 10, 1859, the respective jurisdictions of the two prefects were redefined. The Prefect of the Seine gained certain administrative functions in Paris and the right to represent the city in the courts. But the Prefect of Police lost none of his essential police powers, which were reaffirmed in their original sense of 1800. Neither prefect was happy with the compromise.

A second decree, on November 30, 1859, placed the Prefect of Police at the head of the Ministry of the Interior's Directorship of Public Security. This simply meant that without organizational innovations, the Prefect of Police added to his Parisian duties the supervision of nationwide general police activities through the departmental prefects.[42] Structurally this was not a new ministry of police. As General Director of Public Security outside the Seine, the Prefect of Police operated through the Interior's office facilities in Paris. The effect, obviously, was further to centralize political police activities in France as a whole, while preserving the prefects' authority and the Ministry of the Interior's jealously guarded status as the "sole political ministry."

Billault, in a circular printed in the *Moniteur* on December 1, explained the rationale of this new concentration of general police powers. The growing importance of Paris and the dawning age of rapid communications increasingly fused the police needs of Paris and the country, Billault explained: "The same eyes must be able to follow the wrongdoer everywhere and the same hand reach him anywhere." It was only practical to combine the existing resources of the Prefecture of Police with its "skilled and devoted agents," technical facilities, and the Interior's national prefectorial organization. Billault emphasized that this was a simple administrative device to coordinate the work of two organizations without changing either, by placing "all the police of the Empire in the Prefect's hands, under the direct authority of the Minister of the Interior." The prefects accepted the new arrangement without alarm.

Boittelle, Prefect of Police, 1858–66

Except for the new link with the Directorship of Public Security, the Prefecture of Police expanded in the 1850's without essentially changing its traditional police role. Piétri, however, did not remain to enjoy the benefits of the reform period. He was succeeded by Symphor Casimir-Joseph Boittelle on March 16, 1858.

Boittelle came to Paris from the prefecture of the Yonne with a military and administrative background. A St. Cyr graduate, he left the army in 1841. Several years of gentleman farming intervened before he followed the Bonapartist bandwagon into the coup d'état, advising Morny on December 11 that he regarded Louis Napoleon as the "sole rampart against the most hideous anarchy." Having over the years come to know many men in the Prince-President's entourage—Persigny, Morny, Haussmann, Espinasse, and Castellane among others—Boittelle easily found his way into administration, beginning as the subprefect at St. Quentin early in 1852 with Persigny's support. By March, 1853, he was prefect in the Aisne, where he earned a reputation for vigor and loyalty before transferring to the Yonne in September, 1856. Though contemporary estimates varied on the personality and aptitudes of the new Prefect, they agreed on his erudition, poise, and urbanity. To Albert Vandam, a British observer, he was "essentially a man of the world in the best sense of the word," disciplined, tolerant, and fair. The Goncourt brothers graphically described a visit to Boittelle's office, where they found somewhat more than they had expected in a policeman:

This office, witness of so many redoubtable things . . . is (can one believe it?) full of blond, amorous paintings: nude hussies, coquettish young girls with pretty faces, which not only cover the walls (done in the frightful imperial paper sewn with golden bees) but which are scattered upon the chairs, desk, and other furniture, stacked everywhere! 'Yes,' Boitelle [sic] told us, 'when one sees all day, as I do, such villainous people, it is restful to have a pretty thing to look at now and then!' And then he took us into his private den, the gardener's hut in the little prefecture garden, crammed to the ceiling with paintings. Here with a sponge and basin of water, smoking cigars, he passes his freest and best hours, restoring and revivifying the soiled colors of enigmatically anonymous canvases.

The testy General de Castellane, after meeting Boittelle at a social gathering, later recorded that the new Prefect "seemed to be delighted by the way he has organized the police."[43]

The Prefecture and Political Police

From atop his administrative pyramid, the Prefect, despite the reforms of the fifties, manipulated a police force whose operations in the capital scarcely deviated from the traditional pattern. The Prefecture became more efficient; its personnel was more adequate to the demands upon it. The greatest change in the Prefect's life was his additional role as the national Director of Public Security, supervisor of general police activities throughout France. But in Paris his duties remained more those of a municipal administrator than of a political police specialist. He made daily political reports to the Emperor and regulated soft-drink hawkers in the city's streets. He kept in touch with important political police cases, of course, but meanwhile he corresponded, outside his immediate domain, with departmental prefects, mayors, judges, procureurs, justices of the peace, directors of prisons, military authorities at all levels, cemetery supervisors, public assistance officials, engineers of public works, health officers, railway officials, foreign police authorities, ministers, and many others.[44]

Political police activities, as in the départements, merged inextricably with municipal police routine. In his own office, the Prefect maintained a small section expressly for political police. Otherwise such activities might at any time involve other bureaux and personnel. The famous police de sûreté, a special service of over one hundred men, was an expert criminal detective force principally assigned to nonpolitical activities, though both its open and secret agents were always at the Prefect's disposal for political duties. In 1856, three new brigades of twenty-two men each were assembled as another special political service responsible directly to the Prefect.[45] Full-time professional and casual part-time secret agents, not listed in the public roster, also served the Prefecture but their number and conditions of service remain obscure.

Boittelle, along with his predecessors and the departmental prefects, recognized that "there could be neither judiciary nor political police without the municipal police [which] itself is in the highest degree the political police."[46] In this sense, the visible, overwhelming majority of policemen under the Chief of Municipal Police and other *commissaires* on duty throughout the city were part-time political police agents. By January, 1860, the municipal police numbered over 4,600, including 3,676 uniformed *sergents de ville* in divisions of three brigades to each of twenty *arrondissements,* patrolling, observing, and reporting during eight-hour shifts. Recruited mainly from ex-soldiers, carefully chosen and disciplined, the *sergents* were a familiar part of the Paris scene in cocked hats and bulky, silver-buttoned frock coats (or long, hooded capotes in winter) over trousers with red piping, wearing copper-hilted swords engraved with the Parisian arms, and identified by collar numbers in silver embroidery. The *sergents* obeyed an officer-hierarchy of 427 subbrigadiers and 78 brigadiers, who in turn answered to 32 *officiers de paix,* twenty of whom were posted in the *arrondissements* and others in five "central brigades" or other special services.

The aristocrats—and a prime source of political police information—of the Paris police were the 116 *commissaires* of the Seine, most of whom served in the city itself. Deployed through the *arrondissements* and special services, they performed multiple municipal, general, and judiciary police functions while serving both formally and informally as arbiters of life in the city's various quarters. The Parisian *commissaire* in tricolor sash (and on formal occasions in an ornate black uniform brightened by a stiff white shirt, white bow tie, silver buttons, silver stripes, and braid), was the mainstay of the system, as he is today. He was named by imperial decree and enjoyed direct access to the Prefect of Police and the *procureur-général* at Paris.[47]

To supplement his own forces for ceremonial guard duty or emergency service, the Prefect of Police could call upon the 2,441 officers and men (and 673 horses) of the Parisian Guard—an arm of the gendarmerie on permanent police duty in the capital. A direct successor to Napoleon's Municipal Guard of Paris organized in 1802, the force had since undergone various changes in administration, size, and name. In 1848, as the Republican Guard, its 2,600 men were for a time under the exclusive orders of the Minister of Interior and the Prefect of Police. But in 1849 the force returned to the Ministry of War and the gendarmerie, its complement cut to 2,130 men. Louis Napoleon on December 11, 1852, brought a mild renaissance to the force by increasing its complement to 2,441. The Guard remained a branch of the gendarmerie, a fact that generated friction now and then between the Prefect of Police and the Minister of War. In 1853, Piétri, for example, attacked "the pretensions of the military authorities" in questioning his right to call at will upon the Guard's services.[48] In 1859, the force was again expanded, to 2,892 men and 663 horses.

Conflict Between the Prefects of Police and the Seine

Boittelle arrived in the Prefecture just in time to defend its traditional position against the heavy attack of the irrepressible Baron Haussmann, Prefect of the Seine since June, 1853. Haussmann, the "rebuilder of Paris," brought a chronic jurisdictional dispute from a simmer to a boil in 1858–59 during preparations for extending the city limits. Deciding that the "irrational division of functions" between the two prefects had become intolerable, he demanded transfer of all nonpolice administrative powers in Paris to his own prefecture. The ensuing struggle, very acrimonious at its height, arose fundamentally from the friction often produced by the French mixture of police and other administrative functions. Friction was compounded by the unique situation of the Prefecture of Police juxtaposed with Haussmann's equally unique assignment of renovating a great capital. The decree of

October 10, 1859, which repartitioned the two prefects' jurisdictions, was a compromise in no way impairing Boittelle's police powers while giving Haussmann a relative victory short of his demands.

From the beginning of his tenure in the Seine, Haussmann fretted over "the obstacles resulting from the abnormal division of the municipal powers," as he unraveled the complexities of piercing new streets and building the Halles Centrales, the great markets of Paris, which the Prefect of Police insisted upon controlling. The "incessant conflicts," as Haussmann put it, extended to sewer, street, and lighting maintenance and related issues as Haussmann found Piétri's (and later, Boittelle's) attitude "absolutely intolerable." In 1858, the conflict assumed a triangular pattern. The Minister of the Interior supported Boittelle, as did Jules Baroche, President of the Council of State, who pursued his own feud with Haussmann on other issues. Napoleon III favored Haussmann and the formula that control over "things" should belong to the Prefect of the Seine and over "persons" to the Prefect of Police. But the Emperor let himself be swayed by partisans of both sides. In 1859, after the Italian War, he appealed to Baroche to push through the Council of State a decree redefining the prerogatives of the two contending officials. Baroche reluctantly agreed.[49]

In the ensuing crisis, political police became a fundamental issue, raised by both the Council of State and the Prefect of Police. Apparently the Emperor appointed two commissions to study the problem and prepare draft proposals before an acceptable solution was found.

One project drew criticism from the Council of State, which declared in September, 1859, that the concentrated powers of the Prefect of Police were determined by a "political and governmental interest" which it would be unwise to jeopardize. Conflicts between the two prefects, the Council advised, "appear to be the inevitable result of the necessary daily relationships" between the two and were susceptible to arbitration by the Minister of the Interior.

Boittelle summarized the Prefecture's case in a sixteen-page rejoinder to Haussmann's demands, prepared for the first study commission in April, 1858. In a long historical and legal argument, Boittelle severely questioned both the sincerity and soundness of his adversary's case. He praised the "organizing genius" of Louis XIV and Napoleon I, who, in recognition of the distilled wisdom of prolonged administrative experience, had laid the foundations from which the Prefecture of Police evolved into "the leading police institution of Europe." Boittelle loaded his biggest guns with traditional administrative and police doctrine. He argued that the police power must be intertwined with general administration if it were to exist at all, especially in Paris, where political security was synonymous with full control by the municipal police. "The most impolitic and inevitable result of the proposal," he concluded, "would be the weakening, or more exactly, the nearly complete ruin of the political police and the *Sûreté.*"[50]

With Baroche's assistance, the decree of October, 1859, achieved what would appear to have been a compromise among the views of the Emperor and the contending parties. Haussmann obtained considerable administrative powers in Paris; Boittelle retained some, and preserved his municipal police intact. But a residue of conflict remained, despite Haussmann's later comment that "after the useful reform of 1859, all conflicts ceased between the Hôtel de Ville and the Rue de Jérusalem. . . ." Haussmann interpreted the decree in his own favor with respect to the provisioning of Paris and control over the commission agents and others using the Halles. In 1860, Boittelle renewed his defense, on the grounds of political police necessity, in a thirty-four-page letter to the Minister of the Interior.

Citing his "political mission," Boittelle pointed out that the thirty-six thousand people who fed the capital through the Halles Centrales created not only a problem of public order but also a potential auxiliary for political police intelligence. If licensed by the Prefect of Police they could be persuaded to relay useful information. With proper "guidance," they could have "a very great influence upon the opinion of a great many people scattered through all France and with whom they are in constant correspondence." Particularly since he was now charged with direction of the national Public Security Directorship, the Prefect argued, it was important to exploit such a means of political influence. In this anticlimactic encounter, the Minister of the Interior mediated to render a decision giving Haussmann control of persons connected with the baking industry and leaving other users of the Halles under Boittelle's jurisdiction.[51]

At no time during the conflict had either the municipal or the general police powers of the Prefect of Police been directly at issue. Nor did the sharing of administrative functions in 1859 impair the centralization of public authority per se over the capital's life. No one has more concisely assessed the historical continuity of the Prefecture of Police than Count Kératry, who on September 4, 1870, took over the Prefecture in the mistaken belief that the Third Republic would make it essentially different from what it had previously been:

. . . the First Consul knew that the possession of Paris meant the possession of France. So he created the Prefecture of Police, concentrating in one man's hands . . . all the material and moral interests of the great capital. . . . And thus he forged the veritable key of his new political edifice. This is so true that with each change of regime the first concern of the new arrivals has been to use the means of action thus accumulated. . . .[52]

CONCLUSION

The Ministry of the Interior and the prefects, together with their close administrative relative, the Paris Prefecture of Police, were obvious beneficiaries of the constitution of 1852 and the administrative reforms of the 1850's. By the time of their semifusion for general police purposes under the Directorship of Public Security in 1859, they presented a centralized administrative ensemble of imposing proportions. As "agents of the government," the Paris Prefect and his departmental colleagues were backed by increased executive authority and the precedents of administrative law once again safely entrusted to a strong Council of State. In matters of the *sûreté générale,* they had the decisive initiative before other ministerial administrations and political command over Paris and municipal government throughout

France. The "new era" founded by the coup d'état thus increased the administrative facilities for and reduced the obstacles to a freer play of traditional political police activities.

Yet a strikingly large number of the prefects—and also the *procureurs,* who were the prefects' collaborators, observers, and occasional critics in preserving the *sûreté générale*—were unsatisfied with the relative increase of administrative centralization during the fifties. The prefects, of course, welcomed further centralization as such, even though for particularistic reasons they fought it in the form of a special police ministry. But they were not "revolutionaries of the Right." They sought no "totalitarian" rule in any ideological or nihilistic sense. Except for some professional opportunism and the decisive fact that a Bonaparte was at the time their chief of state, the prefects generally were not in this writer's opinion doctrinaire Bonapartists. But they were conservatives who, like others of the social classes from which they came, were seriously disturbed by the winds of change since 1848 and the probability of more turbulence in the future. They were also traditionalists within the special context of an administrative particularism. Their ideal society was essentially orderly and static, obedient to rational administration, receptive to immutable religious and moral principles, and respectful of property.

After the coup d'état, the prefects and other administrative chiefs expected to approach nearer their ideal once the "red specter" was contained—and to all outward appearances they did so. But after December, 1851, they found the "red specter" in part replaced by new and perhaps unexpected obstacles to the realization of the ideal administrative state. The irritation produced by the Ministry of Police soon passed with the Ministry itself. But even the other more lasting reforms of the 1850's were insufficient to eliminate the prefects' exasperated uneasiness over public lethargy, conflict among various administrative branches, the incompetence or passivity of lower functionaries, and above all, the stubborn diversity of that sobering antidote to prefectorial euphoria—"local influences" throughout the country.

After the heroic interim of extraordinary powers in December and early 1852, the poetry of administrators' great expectations was dulled by the prosaic realities of daily managing a society which, however obedient, continued to fall short of the administrative ideal.

Administrative Particularism
and Obstructive Realities

THE HIGHER functionaries who directly protected the *sûreté générale* confronted their times with a certain group consensus, informal and imperfect though it was. Talleyrand, Balzac, De Tocqueville, Deschanel, and others have perceived the self-sufficient role and spirit of the French public bureaucracy. Today, Roger Grégoire's term, *particularisme de la fonction publique,* suggests both role and spirit. The term evokes a privileged "social function" assigned by administrative law and custom, "which makes the functionary's life a separate world" and administrators "a special group."[1]

THE ELEMENTS OF ADMINISTRATIVE
PARTICULARISM

Louis Napoleon's prefects and *procureurs* displayed such a particularism. It underlay their corporate opposition to the Ministry of Police, their acceptance of additional powers as a natural right, and their expectations of assuming even more. It inspired their ideal of leading France into more willing acceptance of authority under their tutelage. From their "separate world," they interpreted their mission and measured its results. They had a tradition to continue.

The Great Revolution ripped the bureaucracy's roots from an older social structure without inhibiting the continuity of administrative particularism in the newer public bureaucracy of the nineteenth century. Louis Napoleon used that particularism to win power from 1849 to December, 1851. It was necessarily a cornerstone of his Caesarian state thereafter, whatever innovations he may have contemplated in other respects. Neither was fully satisfied with the partnership, yet Napoleon III and his administration knew that they needed one another. Midway in the Second Empire, an honored ex-prefect (on the title page of his critique of the public administration) very pointedly quoted his Emperor's echo of an old bureaucratic maxim: "You can govern from afar but you can administer only close at hand." The aphorism was incarnated in the honors given to the administrative elite whose notables ascended to the state's commanding heights —the ministries, Council of State, Legislative Body, Senate, special commissions and assignments—where they directed other administrative careerists and influenced national policies.

Of the prefects, pillars of any French government, four (Tarn-et-Garonne, Hautes-Alpes, Doubs, Finistère) defected from the coup d'état by protest resignations. Three others (Ain, Somme, Ille-et-Vilaine) shortly after resigned or were discharged for reasons that are unclear.[2] In 1852, the prefects' qualifications were reviewed in Paris. The results do not appear to confirm the assertion that the prefectorial corps was "almost entirely renewed" in the "purge of 1852." A recent study has found a striking continuity of individual careers and "administrative families" in the higher posts from 1830 to 1870.[3] Many prefects moved in early 1852, principally for political strategy. In one of the few explanations of such transfers found by this writer, the prefect of the Ain was shifted because of his easy-going collaboration with Orleanist "local influences." He and his subprefects were reassigned and new men installed to oppose the regional "coterie." Of the five among eighty-three prefects recommended for dismissal by Maupas, the "devotion" of only one was questioned. Among those transferred were some of the era's strongest: Haussmann in the Gironde, De Suleau in the Bouches-du-Rhône, De Sainte-Croix in the Eure, and Crèvecoeur in the Puy-de-Dôme. Many were criticized, mainly for blunt overzealousness in the tactless way of "the old prefectorial school."[4]

Loyal to Louis Napoleon, the higher administrative officials were neither passive civil servants nor abject subjects. The *préfet à poigne*, "heavy-handed" martinet of the authoritarian Empire, unquestioning and ruthless minion of his chosen leader, is an historical stereotype with some justification. But the reality was less simple than our inherited image.[5]

The "administrative attitude." Correspondence of the prefectorial and judiciary police hierarchies discloses a striking agreement on certain fundamental values and other preconceptions. The repetition of common opinions was so massive (though rare exceptions can be found) that it seems historically valid to speak of an "administrative attitude" in the singular, if this is limited to certain recurrent themes explicitly stated and assumed to be implicit in routine communication.[6] This attitude was compatible but not synonymous with the Bonapartism of the fifties. It co-existed with spirited intramural conflicts. But it was too patent then to be ignored now by students of the period.

The administrative attitude distrusted innovation from below or above. It mirrored the values of a conservative elite secure in its dignity and the status conferred by tradition and administrative law, convinced of its indispensability. Firm defenders of national interests and public order, the members of this elite saw themselves as natural custodians, if not the "ruling servants" of the state.[7] By their services from 1849 to December, 1851, they had won the opportunity, after the "unnatural" disorders of 1848, again to pursue their stewardship rationally and more effectively according to the "right" principles. The authoritarian fifties allowed them to postpone an enforced adaptation of their views to changing times. Intead, they grasped the chance to reclaim in French life, before it was too late, the social and political virtues that were the moral landmarks in their "separate world." Although their sense of a common mission was intensified by the "red specter" of republican socialism, they were prepared to criticize or in their devious ways even to reshape or divert the intended effects of governmental policies inconsistent with their own norms of proper administration.

It was overwhelmingly agreed that although France was momentarily under firm control, a continuing "red specter" still threatened public security. Like the procureur at Douai, even those who saw public opinion improving qualified their optimism: "the demagogic party . . . will never abdicate its implacable hatreds or its hopes of upheaval . . . ; intimidation is the only way. . . ." The secret societies seemed crushed, others agreed, but only relatively: "we must not fool ourselves" because "the calm is more apparent than real." Authorities ascribed extraordinary aptitudes to the "red" chieftains, deft technicians of invisible organization able to elicit "unquestioning obedience" from their "dupes." Skilled in deceit, indefatigable in their mania for society's overthrow, they lived in "latent but permanent conspiracy." Were the "powerful hand that now restrains them" to relax, an official told his minister, "you will soon see them throw themselves upon France all the more furiously for having had to wait a longer time."

It was axiomatic that irreligion, personal immorality, and political anarchy interacted in a reversible equation. "Political passions are geared to the moral instincts" was an iron rule: "Where you see an immoral man, a debauchee, you see also a demagogue and anarchist. Revolt against moral prescriptions and divine laws engenders revolt against society and human laws, and reciprocally."[8] Even after years of press controls, the legally circulated popular literature was among the "causes of political and moral perturbation." Novels with subtly salacious allusions and biographies with subliminal political propaganda continued to "filter the poisons of their doctrines into the people's hearts," pursuing "in a tireless and certain way their work of destruction." "Socialist" sedition, alcohol, sexual irregularity, and atheism stained the "centers of republicanism" in industrial cities. For the *procureur* at Paris in 1858, it was "easy to understand how the workers become demagogues who need but an excuse to give free reign to all their wicked passions."

Republicanism fell into the equation. A few officials distinguished between ordinary republicans and "socialists" of the secret societies, but the two were commonly fused. A *procureur* facetiously apologized for heading a subsection of his report, "The Republican Party," because: "there are no more republicans; only socialists remain." There were frequent references to "the republican party of 1848, become the army of anarchy in 1851" or to "the republican party, turned socialist while penetrating the masses." In 1857, an official at Lyon wrote: "republican ideas fan the fire of socialistic hopes [and are] the basic road . . . of all communists toward the grand destruction of the social order."

Officials confidently expected strong authority to curb revolutionary agitators. Their deeper worries concerned an obdurate susceptibility of some of the people to the wiles of even a few subversive leaders. Remembering 1848, they doubted that the masses could avoid anarchy if allowed to act spontaneously in an unpoliced, pluralistic society. Their own moral-political code, which permeated their reports, was bounded by inflexible values reminiscent of a society more static than that of the fifties. Lacking insight into the social complexities of an emergent industrial age, their impulse was to administer and police away the "red specter."

In the administrative attitude, not many men could rise above certain frailties of human nature. The common man was basically honest and appreciative of order when it was imposed. But he was the victim of a kind of Hobbesian irony. Left to himself he was inconstant, credulous, envious, and irrational. "Socialism," wrote the *procureur* at Aix-en-Provence, "survives in the minds of the unreflective. . . . It is deeply rooted in the instincts of egoism and covetousness natural to men." The French especially, "so very volatile in their impressions," accepted with "dangerous credulity" the bait of deceitful agitators able to "flatter their passions" and make them victims in quest of "vain utopias." Such human folly fed upon "the spirit of criticism so widespread in our time."

Workers were believed most liable to succumb to innate weaknesses. Despite the rural violence of December, 1851, administrators feared industrial workers more than other social groups —probably because they understood them least. A few officials sympathetically recognized that "misery is a bad counselor." But usually the workers' radical tendencies were ascribed less to real miseries than to naïve faith in fallacious promises, a predilection for debauchery, and blind envy of the rich. Perplexity often tinged the hope of re-educating workers in the social virtues through stern repression and paternalism combined. Why, the *procureur* at Douai asked in 1859, after seven years of good administration, did not workers respond to the increasingly "benevolent" attitude of employers and the "imperial solicitude in their favor"? This baffled official could only pray that time "will one day produce devotion and affection."

Urbanization was commonly deplored as a demoralizing intrusion into the good old rural ways. Life "where the houses touch each other" daily bred political and social immorality—all the more perilously because city people escaped close administrative scrutiny. Rural folk knew the lasting truths and so were "kept from socialism." Their ethics escaped the attrition of an acquisitive society whose prevalent "materialism" and "fureur du luxe" created victims among whom "the demagogy . . . daily wins recruits." The *procureur* at Nancy decried the "irresistible" fascination of cities for farm workers who were leaving the villages to "lose themselves amidst this industrial mass whose vices and detestable principles will soon infect them."

When the government's candidates suffered a few setbacks in the elections of 1857, a flurry of reports agreed with one official's conclusion that "agriculture builds morality in people . . . less exposed to the socialists and more accessible to the counsel of justices of the peace, mayors, and the large landed proprietors with whom they are in daily contact." A prefect three years earlier had warned the government in parallel terms: "The Empire has not yet entered into the thinking of either the upper classes or even into that of some of the urban bourgeoisie. . . . There would soon be new revolutions if the government were to lose the support of the rural population."

The administrative mission. The basically moral perspective from which the administrative attitude evaluated its adversaries and unwelcome social changes also affected its concept of the administration's political mission. For the ills of their time, the prefects and *procureurs* had the ideal remedy.

"With a wise and firm government whose motto is 'I proceed, follow me,' " wrote a prefect in 1852, "the public powers must resolutely assume the direction of men and affairs." To cure the contagion of 1848 would be "slow and difficult." Only "by the prolonged application of both tutelary and repressive legislation" could administrators succeed "if not in fully correcting at least in discouraging the false ideas which have troubled so many minds and perverted so many hearts." Re-education was the highest ideal goal. "A solid and profoundly religious" reorientation would "change the hearts and minds" of the gullible "perverted generation" of mid-century. All social forces devoted to "order" must be realigned as one. Officials typically assumed that, apart from industrial workers and the "demagogic" minority, most Frenchmen if not already pledged to order were re-educable to it. "France," said one, "is a democracy preferring to be organized under a leader and to feel its governing hand. The majority's instinct is for confession and an authority outside themselves."

Therefore the administration must help build "a solid front" of orderly men. "Local influences" especially must coalesce into a "national party," transcending local political divisions and the grasp of petty "oligarchies" who "share power among themselves to the Emperor's detriment and serve only their own vanity and interests."[9] Everywhere, declared a prefect in 1854, were lawful men who "cannot resign themselves to accept the government's preponderance and freedom of action." The administration should "isolate the violent partisans . . . and free itself from the compromising influence of the others." This could be done, according to the prefect of the Haute-Garonne in 1853 (who thus underlined most prefects' thorniest problem), by "imperceptibly substituting through administrative action the prefect's influence in place of all the individual and local influences which presently enervate governmental action under the pretext of aiding it."

This more independent administration could rise far above mere police repression. It would serve all groups and interests impartially. Public authorities could awaken real "feelings of gratitude" toward the regime if the government could "encourage and honor the workers in the fields," reduce their taxes, and give them that sense of security they would never find in the cities. Summarizing this administrative ideal in 1857, the *procureur* at Montpellier pictured a bureaucracy at once inspiring the religious and moral rehabilitation of the public and becoming "themselves daily more inspired by the wise energy of the central power."

How France could prosper under "justice dispensed effortlessly to a calmer public being led back into obedience by the certainty and rapidity of a repression sometimes rigorous but never excessive, sometimes indulgent but never weak, and always precisely in tune with the needs of equity!" Then surely, "all intelligent people will quit politics for their own affairs."

Despite the prevalent administrative attitude in the prefectures and *parquets,* their chiefs found ideal goals elusive in the ambient realities outside. Political police vigilance was unabated. But the "red specter," though subdued, still lived at home and abroad. Official candidates usually won elections but signs of disunity were plentiful. "Local influences" flourished. And within the administration itself, internecine dissension roughened the upward path toward an ideal administrative state.

THE CONTINUING "RED SPECTER" IN FRANCE AND ABROAD

Throughout the 1850's, officials were unable to exorcise the "red specter" from its haunts in French secret societies and refugee colonies abroad. In public or confidentially among themselves, they traced identical pictures of the threat. From their similar attitudes, they too readily deduced the existence of secret conspiracy from partial or trivial evidence. They uncritically assumed all alleged members of secret organizations to be automatically guilty of the serious legal offense of *complot,* or intent to use violence and assassination for the overthrow of government or to precipitate civil war.[10] Such extremism attested their dead seriousness in sustaining the image of secret subversion even after their repression had removed most of its tangible manifestations. The image was too universal in their private communication and it provoked too many years of intensive police activity to be plausibly dismissed as no more than a cynical propagandic exaggeration.

The Officials' Image of the "Specter"

No one more forcefully personified this aspect of the administrative attitude than Gustave Rouland, *procureur-général* at

Paris from February, 1853, until he took the Ministry of Public Instruction and Worship in 1856. Beneath the surface calm of 1853, he saw "an incessant work of revolutionary propagation emerging in the shadows" to prepare "bloody eventualities." From 1854 to 1856, as he led the hunt against some of the more notorious secret societies—the Solidarité Révolutionnaire, Commune Révolutionnaire, Marianne, Jeune Montagne, Fraternité Universelle—he continued his jeremiads to the Minister of Justice. They warned of attempted revivals of provincial secret societies centrally commanded from Paris. Their intention was violent upheaval in the apocalyptical name of the "democratic and social republic." All revolutionaries, even though at odds with one another on lesser issues, were united in their demonic vision of launching universal anarchy by assassinating Napoleon III. Rouland located the immediate center of this sinister web in Paris. But the refugees abroad, particularly in England, were the prime authors of the evil in France. Since 1848, the worst leaders of "anarchy" had retreated abroad to internationalize their subversion. The "demagogues" had learned to regroup "with a frightening simplicity" beneath what naïve observers might foolishly mistake for public tranquility.[11]

Rouland's linkage of refugees with French secret societies would have brought resounding agreement from hundreds of other political police officials had they seen his confidential reports. They too knew that the secret societies now drew their lifeblood from exiled revolutionaries who illicitly sent their literature, envoys, and subsidies into France. Officials were extremely frustrated at seeing their own careful political police surveillance regularly subverted from havens of conspiracy beyond their reach. They ascribed local signs of political ferment to the legendary "committees of London"—or Jersey, Belgium, Switzerland, and Italy. In Paris, the ministries continually received alarms like that from Aix-en-Provence that the "committee of London" was sending pardoned exiles in 1853 to organize "committees of resistance in all the large population centers." With the *procureur* at Lyon, officials bewailed the impossibility of sealing the borders against "the revolting pamphlets of Victor Hugo" and warned, as did the

procureur at Grenoble, that French secret committees were form-
ing "for correspondence with the proscribed French democrats or
foreign refugees" to prepare "a new insurrection that would bring
M. Ledru-Rollin to power." An army general was so certain that
"the socialists of London and Belgium are soliciting converts in
the regiments" that he asked help from the civilian police—for
which he drew a reprimand from his minister for inviting loss of
face.[12]

Publicly the government tried to turn tables on the refugees
by publishing some of their inflammatory manifestos and by
ridicule in the *Moniteur*. Pro-government provincial newspapers
ran Parisian "correspondence" underscoring the disunity and fail-
ures of the "socialistic refugees" whose antics made "exile itself
ridiculous" and provoked "bursts of laughter throughout Europe."[13] But little mirth showed in political police reports, which
continued to treat the refugees as a serious danger.

The greatest resentment focused against the "excessive tolerance" of dangerous men in Great Britain. There the international
revolutionary titans, Mazzini and Kossuth, collaborated with a
host of French exiles, including Ledru-Rollin, Pyat, Delescluze,
Blanc, and Leroux. Chief among the various "committees" into
which the London refugees grouped after 1851 were the Commune Révolutionnaire and the Comité Central Démocratique Européenne. These and another refugee colony around Victor Hugo
at Jersey were regarded as the worst sources of conspiracy and
dangerous writings during the early fifties.[14] Their activities were
assumed to penetrate France and to be drawing an international
revolutionary net around the country. In 1857, the *procureur* at
Lyon penned a stereotype that found widespread credence
throughout the fifties:

> One always finds the true and definitive center of this agitation in
> England. . . . Belgium, Switzerland, and Piedmont are only branches of
> this ever-active . . . center of hostility. The evil publications and projects
> are nearly always of English origin and are only seriously dangerous when
> they come from there.[15]

The Orsini Affair in 1858 confirmed French officials' fears and
renewed their frustrated Anglophobia. The venom of Charles de

Bussy's (Charles Marchal) 350-page diatribe against the European "red specter," *Les conspirateurs en Angleterre, 1848–1858,* published later in 1858, could have been distilled from administrators' reports since 1852.

Action Against Secret Societies in France

After the decree of December 8, 1851 (see chapter 2), the Second Empire enacted no new law explicitly directed against secret societies and their members. Article 13 of the law of July 28, 1848, on clubs already banned them. This stipulation remained in a new decree of March 25, 1852, which replaced the 1848 law with stricter regulation of public association and assembly.[16] Fear of secret societies was, however, a principal motive for the creation of cantonal *commissaires* (see chapter 3) and a new law on public drinking houses.

The prefects could use the decree of December 8 against anyone once convicted (by the Mixed Commissions of 1852 or in the courts) of secret society membership. But after early 1852, to obtain a first conviction they had to have the cooperation of the judiciary police, who insisted upon all legal proprieties including the rules of evidence before assenting to prosecution. Thus the number of court convictions for secret society affiliation during the fifties seems very low in proportion to the enormous attention given to the problem. The grand total of such convictions has eluded this investigator; but partial figures are suggestive. In Paris from mid-1853 until the end of 1858, 304 persons (about 80 per cent of those accused) were convicted. In the district of the *parquet* at Aix-en-Provence (Var, Basses-Alpes, Bouches-du-Rhône), supposedly an active secret society region, only about one hundred and fifty convictions were recorded through the end of 1857.[17]

The more sensational group cases were publicized in the *Gazette des tribunaux,* whose readers could ponder the prosecution's rhetorical conjurations of the "red specter" in France and beyond. But these were not merely show trials. Resisting the prefects' tendency to urge prosecutions on thin evidence, the *procureurs* avoided trial unless they were virtually sure of winning. They diligently prepared cases with great anxiety at the prospect of acquittals that could discredit the authorities. The evidence brought to court and the opinions expressed so rhetorically there were the same as those in the confidential dossiers underlying the cases. In group trials the majority were convicted, though usually there were a few acquittals. When evidence did not support a secret-society charge, the public prosecutors sought lesser offenses which might bring the suspects to trial. Otherwise they went quietly free.

The law of December 29, 1851, on public drinking houses was an indirect but highly valued administrative weapon against secret societies. Political police reports, redolent with administrative morality, consistently denounced the evils of cafés, cabarets, and kindred popular resorts "where peasants and workers go to lose their money, develop habits of sloth and debauchery, and to succumb to the most abominable demagogic principles." Officials liked to say that what the press did to corrupt the politics of the upper classes, the cabarets did for their inferiors. The new law condemned such establishments as "a cause of disorders and demoralization [and] meeting and recruitment centers for secret societies." It placed them under the prefects' full control as a measure of "public morality and sûreté générale." The prefects authorized, regulated, or closed cafés simply by general police edicts. Morny did advise them to "be very circumspect." They walked a thin line between injuring private business enterprise on one hand and risking public security on the other.[18] Police officers universally welcomed the new law, declaring it one of their best preventives against the domestic "red specter." In 1853, the government briefly applied an oblique political police technique by raising the wine tax on bottled goods so that café patrons would buy the cheaper product in casks and consume it at home. But the expedient quickly ended in a flurry of public and administrative protest especially where, as in Lyon, family custom preferred bottles over kegs.[19]

Without further special aids until the Law of Sûreté Générale in 1858 (see chapter 9), the administration pursued the real or imagined secret threat in France with their secret agents and other political police techniques throughout the 1850's. To act against the related threat of the refugees was more difficult.

Action Against the Refugees

To reduce the clandestine entry of the refugees' propaganda, messages, and secret emissaries, the French police mobilized all means of surveillance along the frontiers. Even before the Prefect of Police became chief of the national Sûreté Publique in 1859, he lent his secret agents and superior police facilities for this purpose. Special *commissaires* on the railways and at border posts collaborated with the customs service to detect seditious literature and suspicious travelers. Secret police agents plied their trade among refugees abroad. The French achieved some degree of international collaboration with foreign police, especially in Belgium and least in England. The French Foreign Ministry became handmaiden to the political police by using diplomatic facilities to pursue the refugees where the prefects could not reach. Each of these activities needs more study than can be presented here, but the extent of the anti-refugee police effort may be at least suggested.

The infiltration of "seditious literature" probably consumed more police man-hours than any aspect of the refugee problem. Regular shipments of foreign printed matter could be controlled. But the ingenious smuggling methods devised by the exiles thwarted the utmost attention given it by prefects whose police personnel were too few for the task. Maupas made the stemming of this illicit flood one of his ministry's major objectives. So did the ministers of the Interior after June, 1853. But the traffic continued. After eight years, the prefects were still receiving rehashed versions of Maupas' earlier orders to seize and immediately report any writings by persons banished, exiled, or fugitive—"of whatever nature they may be, in whatever form they may take. . . ." To increase the prefects' frustrations, the *procureurs* and the courts were allegedly too lenient toward the distributors of "incendiary" literature who were caught, creating "serious embarrassment for the administration."[20]

A particular gadfly for the Channel coast prefects was the isle of Jersey where Victor Hugo's coterie of some three hundred refugees held "fraternal banquets" and gathered to plot "and drink the great man's beer" until their expulsion in 1855. The isle was a smuggling base for their self-styled "universal press." Among other forms of printed attack against the Empire was *L'Homme*, "journal of universal democracy," which sometimes twitted the French police for the ineptitude of their secret agents on Jersey. Their smuggling was imaginative. They inscribed Hugo's broadsides in tiny letters on tissue paper of playing-card size suitable for innumerable ways of concealment. Fishermen dropped hermetically sealed boxes of their literature into coastal shallows for recovery by confederates on the French shore. Despite coordinated efforts and an occasional arrest, the prefects of the Manche and Ille-et-Vilaine had to admit defeat, which they blamed on their lack of adequate personnel and the unseemly tolerance of the British.[21]

Switzerland. Next to England, Switzerland was the most troublesome center of exiles. French officials indignantly watched from six hundred to a thousand refugees edit newspapers and conspire just across the frontier. The *procureur* at Lyon charged that Switzerland "not only tolerated but encouraged . . . a revolutionary army." Until its dispersion, Lyon and the Midi would "never know peace." The prefects of the Ain and Rhône fretted over an international "secret association" formed by a nephew of Kossuth on orders from London. The commander of the Fourth Army Corps warned of the refugees' "counter-police" against French secret agents among them.[22] All grades of police officers strove to interrupt the "correspondence of the revolutionary party" in France with the refugees. Messages entered the Isère inside statuettes; refugees and French secret society men crossed the border to confer. Seditious writings flagrantly invaded the Ain, and Lyon's special political police unit encountered Pyat's writings in double-bottomed barrels coming from Geneva.[23]

The French Foreign Ministry abetted the police effort against the refugees in Switzerland as it did elsewhere. The Legation's spies reported on the anti-French press, nocturnal infiltrations of disguised refugees into France, and the endless machinations of

Mazzini and the "committees of London." Concern over Switzerland was not confined to lower officials in the administration and the diplomatic corps. Lord Cowley, from the British Embassy in Paris, warned London that Napoleon III was personally determined to prevent the Swiss from using their neutrality "to become a focus of peril to other countries."[24]

The Refugees as an Anglo-French Diplomatic Issue

The Quai d'Orsay created a triangular diplomatic tension by demanding that London and Berne repress or expel their refugees. Attempting to mediate between France and Switzerland while politely resisting French demands, the British found their efforts further complicated by Prussian and Austrian involvement in the issue.

The British believed French fears of revolutionary "designs planned in London" were exaggerated but genuine. Cowley noted that enough similar alarm prevailed in Berlin and Vienna to inspire a "continental league" of France, Prussia, and Austria on the issue. France denied any intent of carrying the refugee question to such lengths but continued its pressure on both Britain and Switzerland. Napoleon III himself interrupted a talk on the critical Eastern Question with special envoy Stratford de Redcliffe in 1853 to declare that until the refugees were curbed it would be unsafe to relax his dictatorship.[25]

British policy was to join the French in deploring the violent aspects of refugee activity (as Palmerston had done in 1848) and to explain that without material proofs British law permitted no criminal prosecutions against the exiles. The alternative—exceptional legislation—was sure to be opposed by the British public and Parliament. However, the French were assured that the British government would "endeavour by every legal means to prevent [the refugees] from abusing the hospitality" of its laws. The Foreign Office made similar explanations to Prussia and Austria and warned the latter that it would consider an attempt to form a "continental league" on the refugee issue "unjust provocation."[26]

London seriously considered the probability of direct French intervention in Switzerland. In Paris, Cowley adopted a "helpful" policy of discussing the problem informally at the Quai d'Orsay. From London, he was instructed to explain very discreetly that although "H. M. Gvt. can only look upon Socialist Doctrines as revolting in their nature," Britain would regard any violation of Swiss neutrality to suppress such doctrines as a threat to all small states.[27] To Switzerland, London counseled restraint, prudence, and a conception of neutrality that would accept the obligation to avoid provoking either France or Austria. The Foreign Office instructed its chargé at Berne "to press upon" the Swiss their own interest in avoiding "acts which might be reasonably construed as offensive" to Louis Napoleon and to recommend concessions apt to remove "all reasonable grounds of complaint." Concurrently, Cowley was told to advise Paris that its demands for the expulsion of certain refugees from Switzerland and the removal of others from border areas were, in British opinion, unreasonable and a deviation from "the respect hitherto paid" by France to the "guaranteed independence of Switzerland."[28] The issue hung in an uneasy balance with the interruption of the Crimean War, until the Orsini plot precipitated another flareup in Anglo-French relations in 1858.

Belgium

Belgium was more cooperative with French political police objectives than either Britain or Switzerland. The Belgian police helped their French counterparts guard the frontiers against refugee envoys and propaganda. Brussels informed the prefect of the Nord of refugees' plans and activities and tolerated the circulation of French secret agents. The prefect watched a secret society form in Belgium, followed its contacts in France, and saw its refugee founder arrested and convicted in Belgium. Unlike his colleagues along the Channel or the Swiss frontier, he saw "no real danger" in Belgium except for the free press there. The prefect of the Ardennes also found the Belgian police consistently helpful. He was allowed to enter Belgium and to coordinate joint surveillance of the refugees with provincial governors and the Brussels Sûreté Publique. The Paris Prefect of Police maintained a list of refugees in Belgium, some of whom were allowed to visit France, where secret police shadowed them in hopes of discovering their contacts.[29]

With Belgian cooperation, the French Ministry of Foreign Affairs kept Paris informed on the refugee press and occasionally persuaded Belgian authorities to suppress anti-French literature. In 1855, for example, the Belgian Foreign Ministry requested the Brussels police to forbid a political refugee to found a newspaper and to order him out of the country unless he severed all connections with the venture. Brussels was equally helpful in banning a poem, "Le Deux Décembre," on request of the Paris Prefect of Police through diplomatic channels.[30] Clandestine literature (much of which originated in England) smuggled from Belgium, baffled Belgian and French police alike. French diplomatic pressure on Brussels had no apparent effect on the traffic.[31]

Italy

Few French refugees settled in Italy. The Sardinian-Isère frontier was quiet: only a handful of refugees were in Chambéry, most were in Turin and in 1853, scarcely sixty lived in Nice. But the Mediterranean littoral between Nice and Marseille presented special problems beyond the usual smuggling of seditious literature and the passage of envoys from "the committees of London." Disciples of Mazzini and other Italian revolutionaries reportedly intended to use France as a base for plots against their own homelands and to concert with French secret societies as well as the notorious schemers in London. This possibility, and the presence of a large Italian colony in Marseille, caused particular tensions in the Basses-Alpes, Var, and Bouches-du-Rhône. There the secret societies were supposed to be very tenacious. The Riviera coast was a natural transit for both French and Italian refugees and their propaganda.

The chief burden of this special problem fell upon the prefect at Marseille. His secret agents mapped the two most likely land and sea routes of illegal entry used by agents of the Comité Central Européenne, whose Italian headquarters were in Genoa and Turin, and awaited developments.[32] Other French authorities in the Southeast were also expectant. They assumed that the ineptitude of the Sardinian police would permit an "invasion" of refugees, probably from Nice. The Minister of Justice obtained diplomatic intervention in Turin for extradition of French refugees under an 1838 treaty only to discover that the agreement's terms ignored political exiles. Repeated urging by French police officials and diplomats—the consul at Nice complained that he had asked at least "twenty times"—induced the Sardinian police in mid-1852 to intern most of the refugees away from the border. The Ministry of Foreign Affairs continued to assist the French police in the political surveillance of all Italy, reporting such items as a Mazzini article on the "theory of the dagger" in a Genoa paper, or reminding Paris (where no reminder was needed) that the presence of unreconstructed rebels in nearby countries warranted "fear for the future."[33]

Italians in France

An ironic twist of the French obsession with the refugee problem arose from the presence on French soil of foreign refugees, principally Italians. Because the French government chose not to expel Italians wholesale, they were left to the administration, whose powers over foreigners stemmed mainly from a law of 1849. By a general police measure, the prefects could simply expel a foreign suspect. They could subject him to special forms of surveillance or cut off the public assistance funds provided for stranded or needy foreigners. All political refugees, without special permission, were barred from the Seine, Lyon, Marseille, and territory adjacent to their homelands. All "political" foreigners lived under the eyes of the police. During the fifties, many were expelled or refused entrance into France.[34]

Italians were a special problem. Especially in the South, many "nonpolitical" residents and even citizens of Italian origin provided camouflage for political schemers. Moreover, the flight of certain Italian refugees into France might have been merely to escape certain conditions of which French foreign policy in the Italian Question professed to disapprove. Or they might be agents of Mazzini (who throughout the fifties was frequently reported to be in France or about to enter) and other refugees in London or Geneva bent upon contacting the French secret societies. Those suspected Italians who were not expelled in 1852 were interned under surveillance outside the temptations of populous centers. Italians were subject to special scrutiny on the railways, reports by the French diplomatic service, and special police roundups during the Emperor's provincial tours.

The Marseille police considered Italians their major problem long before the coup d'état, which hardly affected their methods or intensity of surveillance. The city's daily police blotter usually included one or more Italians picked up on various charges that ranged from lack of proper papers (the most common), or wearing a red necktie (possibly a secret society symbol), to mere suspicion. Several Marseille *commissaires* specialized in policing Italians. A few secret agents operated when the prefect's budget permitted. Groups of Italians were periodically assembled for expulsion. One contingent in March, 1854, included forty Neapolitans, ten Romans, and twenty-five Piedmontese along with fourteen non-Italians. Some Italian suspects were allowed fifteen days to leave Marseille for new residences in nonprohibited areas of France. French legations in Italian states relayed information from the Italian police to the prefect of the Bouches-du-Rhône.[35]

The French government's sensitivity to the Italian refugee problem touched off several "scares" in Marseille precipitated by political police intelligence from Italy and elsewhere. Such a panic erupted in September, 1856, with all the trappings of the European "red specter." The Ministry of the Interior urgently alerted Marseille and ordered extraordinary surveillance of all Italians because of a "vast conspiracy" inspired by the London refugees. This was to be a major revolt by "all the Italian revolutionary committees" in Marseille, Lyon, Bordeaux, and Paris, who would time it with a Mazzinian rising in Italy. The leaders were said to be assembling in Marseille. Two weeks of police activity produced only the arrest of three refugees, none of whom was a ringleader of the "vast conspiracy."[36] Indeed, except for a bomb plot in 1852, Marseille political police operations had no sensational results throughout the fifties. After years of specializing in Italians, the Marseille police may (or may not) have welcomed the novelty in August, 1860, when they were warned to gird themselves for the arrival of a hundred Irishmen, "expelled from the Pontifical Army because of disorders they provoked in the towns of the Papal States. . . ."

THE PREFECTS' ELECTORAL POLICE

No routine political duty of Louis Napoleon's prefects was more important than to "make" elections at the national, departmental, and communal levels by ensuring the victory of government-sponsored "official candidates." Otherwise, the Caesarian regime's "democratic" aspects could have stultified its dictatorial features through independent or opposition control over the nation's representative bodies.

Apart from the prefect's role in selecting official candidates, his electoral function was one of political police. He had to use all legal means to help official candidates win in order to continue the executive's power. To this end he could—and indeed must, by the imperative of administrative doctrine—manipulate at his chief's behest a centralized apparatus in whose functions political police powers were integral. Between elections, he reported and analyzed everything of political import for the next balloting. With electoral strategy in mind, he deployed his considerable means of influence and control in off years. During elections he used other functionaries to elicit a favorable vote and to discourage the opposition. He aimed his general police imperium against the "demagoguery" on behalf of the *sûreté générale* and with it silenced hostile newspapers while favoring the progovernment press. As "agents of the government," he and those of his subordinates who were entitled to such privilege acted behind a shield of immunity upheld by the "separation of powers" doctrine in administrative law. His crucial political mission was to guide the decisions of nine million five hundred thousand (in 1857) voting citizens.

The System of "Official Candidature"

The Second Empire neither began nor ended the expedient of naming "official candidates" and giving them the administration's total support.[37] The system's momentary interruption in the

revolutionary springtime of 1848 coincided with other sudden
rifts in the familiar landmarks and mores of public life. Not
least of these was France's first use of direct, universal manhood
suffrage—an unfamiliar experience for voters and administrators
alike. In the ensuing reaction, official candidature revived with its
greatest *élan*. What was really novel in the official candidature
system of the fifties was the unabashed frankness of its sponsors,
the attempt for the first time to fuse the system with universal
suffrage, and the thoroughness with which administrators at all
electoral levels supported the approved candidates.

Fialin de Persigny and others candidly and loftily justified
official candidature before the public on both theoretical and
pragmatic grounds. Speaking in terms of the Bonapartist myth
of plebiscitary dictatorship, the directors of the new regime were
not ideologically compelled to mask their electoral practices. They
could say that it was the chief of state's *responsibility* as man-
datary of the popular constituent power to offer the nation's best
potential representatives for popular approval or rejection. Official sponsorship of such men was part of a recurrent plebiscite
and also a discharge of the executive's mandate. It was not only
highly proper but even obligatory that his administrative agents
assist the official nominees. Consequently, the traditional view of
the administrative mission neatly fitted into the Bonapartist concept of official candidature.

From this theoretical matrix, more pragmatic arguments were
derived. It was time, Persigny insisted, to go beyond "those futile
parliamentary agitations that have for so long paralyzed the
country's vitality" and to turn popular sovereignty into more
constructive channels for the common good. Official candidature
summoned all men of "good will" in all parties to synthesize their
aspirations and loyalties into one "great national party." "Why,"
asked Eugène Rouher, "should only the government be forbidden to speak to voters" who had full liberty of choice? In so
speaking, the executive simply "exercised its rightful influence for
the defense of [everyone's] social interests."[38]

These attitudes and the administration's interventionist duties
were highly publicized. The *Moniteur* printed most of the pre-

fects' basic instructions: the administration's assistance to preferred candidates would be proud and open; the prefects must
use all "expedient" means to advance the candidates' cause and
to warn the public against rival candidates "whose known tendencies contradict the spirit of our new institutions." The prefects
would recruit candidates likely "to receive the majority of votes."
The government would unhesitatingly "recommend [such candi-
dates] openly to the voters" regardless of their former political
identities. They need only "accept the new order frankly and
sincerely. . . ." Preferably, ideal candidates would be self-made,
practical men of "independent" views, not professional politicians. The "confidential" instructions were not essentially different from the published ones, merely more specific. The prefects
were to draw the lines of electoral districts so as best to exploit
local rivalries and other electoral peculiarities. They must keep
the opposition press "moderate" and permit no electoral meetings or committees. Official candidates should be chosen among
wealthy, influential "notables," mainly landowners and industri-
alists, known regionally for their "benevolence." The voting itself
must strictly follow prescribed procedures in order to preclude
any sort of interference. The government's decisive role preceded
the balloting, which was to remain free.[39]

Not surprisingly, the prefects and their helpmates, the *procureurs,* generally welcomed official candidature, whose underlying concepts were consistent with the administrative attitude.
These procedures also constituted a technique to domesticate and
train the potentially dangerous beast of universal suffrage loosed
in 1848 and again in December, 1851. Few officials declared flatly
against universal suffrage in principle but their views of it were
markedly ambivalent. If not in theory, in practice it clashed with
the administrators' tutelary ideal. Official candidature was a way
to make the practice safely tolerable.

There were dangers. The *procureur* at Grenoble accepted universal suffrage because Louis Napoleon's use of it was "an instrument of safety." Yet, he confessed, "I distrust its caprices . . .
and I know that if it is not well directed it will cause our ruin."
From Aix-en-Provence came the same opinion, plus the reflection
that universal suffrage had at least one advantage over partial

suffrage; the latter had magnified the influence of cities where the administration had less control. Now conservative rural opinion was a useful counterweight.[40] But even with official candidature as a safety device, the administrators typically distrusted universal suffrage as an adjunct of the "red specter."

Defeats of official candidates, most frequent in municipal elections, were typically attributed to organized secret conspiracy as if there were no alternative explanations. In an otherwise well-policed polity, universal suffrage opened a breach through which the "demagogues" might one day come marauding. This view became widespread after the voting of 1857 favored some opposition candidates. And it was not lessened by occasional write-ins of a genre illustrated by a ballot in the Isère: "I vote for the executioner who will one day pay back M. Napoleon and his administrators."[41]

No detailed description of the administration's electoral maneuvers will be attempted here. General studies have shown that the prefects used all their facilities to comply with instructions. Few legal devices were overlooked and functionaries from various ministries became involved. A sampling of archives suggests that more detailed regional studies would show that, aside from the most obvious techniques, the means of furthering official candidates varied greatly in kind and emphasis according to local circumstances. In a few *départements*, of which the Doubs was a rare instance, the prefect sometimes ran no official candidates below the national level and refrained from overt attempts to influence the voters. Such latitude was possible where the political situation already ensured the victory of progovernment candidates. One would probably find that some prefects and *procureurs* (who were right-hand men in policing elections) stretched their powers to the limit and that others held back for tactical reasons in order to impress the public with its electoral freedom.

To take only one issue—there was much dissension over the degree of tolerance that should be shown toward the opposition's circulation of electoral bulletins. Their distribution was legal if certain regulations were observed. Some officials barred them by finding technical violations of the regulations; others treated the matter more liberally. The *procureur* at Douai disapproved altogether of such bulletins, while his southern colleague at Aix-en-Provence believed they should appear freely: "Not only must the elections be free, but especially must the voters be convinced of their complete independence," or the results might undercut the official candidates.[42]

Both the prefects and the *procureurs* used even their minor functionaries in elections and retaliated against those who refused to cooperate. Very typically, the prefect of the Haute-Vienne precisely instructed every public employee to give "a public example of their devotion" lest their fitness for office be re-examined. The *procureur* at Montpellier discharged a minor employee because he "obstinately" disapproved of an official candidate. The *procureur* expressed a prevailing view of the issue: "The elections are of course free and everyone has the right to vote as he pleases—but on the condition that if he is a public functionary he begin by resigning his post."[43]

On election days, the higher officials insisted that balloting be "free." No doubt violation of this prescription—especially by lower functionaries—did occur nonetheless. If so, the administration as such had the legal advantage, but the functionary himself could risk prosecution. The Court of Cassation held consistently that electoral irregularities did not invalidate an election unless the complainant proved that the violation decisively affected the outcome. The Court also decreed that electoral services to official candidates invoked the principle of immunity for acts undertaken as "agent of the government." If an aggrieved citizen sought legal recourse against such an "agent," even for a crime or misdemeanor, his case was inadmissible in the regular courts. Recourse could be had only in the Council of State with its permission. However, if the "agent's" acts were not an essential part of his *function*, he was liable to ordinary prosecution for criminal offenses or damages—as was a mayor who called opposition candidate Anton Lefèvre-Pontalis "lazy and cowardly" during a campaign.[44]

Official candidature had its ironies. It was justified by Bonapartist theory in which the plebiscitary regime postulated a unified national will; yet it was a device to create, where none existed,

such a unified will in the sense of a Bonapartist "national party."
Theodore Zeldin has ably shown that the prefects, given their
head by Persigny, looked for and found official candidates among
regional "notables" of diverse opinions who were willing, for the
time at least, to ally with the regime though they came from its
potential opponents. Even in the authoritarian fifties, these men
were not ideological Bonapartists or uncritical puppets as members of the national Legislative Body.[45] They were less so in
the departmental and municipal councils, where regional and local
issues were involved. The official candidates were generally cooperative with the government and administration's defense of
the social order against the "red specter." But they expected in
return concessions in the localities where as "notables" they
wielded influence.

Thus it was the prefects' tactical dilemma that by discovering,
grooming, and supporting official candidates they contributed to
their ubiquitous problem of "local influences," the chief obstacle
to building that one-minded "national party" for which official
candidature was the intended means.

THE PREFECTS' WORLD OF LOCAL INFLUENCES

Between themselves and their haven of an ideal administrative
state lay the prefects' immediate environment through which they
had to "navigate as best they might among the notables, the
clergy, and the electoral mass."[46] Their course led mainly through
the towns, villages, and countryside. Cultivating official candidates and otherwise striving to create a "Bonapartism of the
notables" that would articulate the more diffused popular Bonapartism of the fifties, they were surrounded by the shifting reefs
charted in their dry official idiom as "local influences."

The semimythical *préfet à poigne,* had he literally matched his
despotic image, would have been constantly in straits in his *département* and a liability to his ministry for tactical sins which
official jargon labeled "excessive zeal." The methods of December, 1851, served in their brief time. But after March, 1852, the
time was over. With the "red specter" thrust below the surface
and driven beyond the frontiers, other divergent elements in

French society confronted the prefects with a stubborn continuity often impervious to administrative authority and rationality. The problem no doubt stimulated the prefects' wish to increase still farther their already considerable powers over the communes. But the good prefect knew that with all his formal powers he must learn to live somehow with "local influences," rational or not. Patience, tactical dexterity, and indirect methods were as vital in his success as draconian legislation and centralized police facilities. Along with shrewd insight into the subtleties of his complex situation, the prefect needed, as a *commissaire* of police once phrased it, "a velvet glove around his mailed fist."

The prefects' role was ironical. At the national level, their power sabotaged the Ministry of General Police. On occasion, they discouraged or modified other governmental inclinations toward innovation, obliging even the Emperor usually to refrain from more than an "oblique" interference in administration.[47] But unmalleable local diversities could resist the most artful prefect. The clergy, religious divisions, economic interests, organized Orleanists or legitimists, and still other sources of factionalism and special-interest pressures—often purely local and even trivial —combined with the prestige of strong-minded "notables" to complicate the prefects' world. These influences, in turn, affected the appointment, outlook, and behavior of lesser functionaries in all the ministerial hierarchies. Especially in certain problem areas, the prefects were buffeted by local balance-of-power situations that often intruded into the public administration itself. Such problems simply did not dissolve at the touch of a unilateral prefectorial edict.

Especially when Persigny, their champion, left the Interior in 1854, the prefects complained that the government itself connived in bypassing them, whether in the arranging of a pardon or by tolerating "the old local habit of obtaining everything by the intermediary influences of the parliamentary deputies." The latter, one indignant prefect believed, "should [rather] be treated as the debtors of the government which chose them." The prefect of the Aube regretfully noted that "since M. le Comte de Persigny's retirement, the government has singularly tolerated the action of local and extra-administrative influences" in an attrition of the administration's prestige. He charged further that the ministries showed "a dangerous tendency readily to grant, at the personal requests of deputies and politicians, the same favors they refuse to the prefects' written requests." No wonder then that mayors and other local functionaries preferred to deal with influential men other than the prefects, whose status dissolved as a result.[48]

Local Influences over Functionaries

If Paris catered to "local influences," how could the prefects fulfill the mission which Persigny articulated so emphatically in February, 1852? The Minister had called for the creation of a Bonapartist administration united in "perfect harmony of ideas, sentiments, and interests, for it is unity of views in the public powers that alone constitutes the strength and grandeur of nations."

A new prefect in the Vienne, quite in the spirit of his minister's words, promised to align the lower functionaries into "a veritable army corps with its hierarchy, ranks, and special unity." Two months later, he admitted his distress in trying to make the functionaries into "political men" when the bishop, the army district commander, a government engineer, and two officials of the Ministry of Finances were lackeys of the Poitiers legitimists.

Of 985 functionaries in the Haute-Garonne in 1853, the prefect could rely upon only 53 Bonapartists among 629 legitimists, 241 Orleanists, 53 republicans, and nine "unknowns." Another prefect distrusted the Rector of the Academy (who "rallied" after a warning), the chief engineer of Bridges and Roads (who was transferred), the mayor of Troyes (whose dismissal he requested), and various others.[49] The prefects detected such common political shortcomings principally in local administration and among personnel of ministries other than the Interior.

These problem-functionaries were not militantly disloyal or politically "red." The prefect of the Calvados saw "a deep-rooted vice . . . in their very makeup" which impelled lower functionaries to accept changing regimes cynically, without genuine enthusiasm, and meanwhile to keep their local connections in repair. Wearing the outward signs of "devotion," they catered as always to "local interests" who sought "clients" to favor their selfish aims whatever the current form of government. For this prefect, the solution was not a mass purge but to place all functionaries under the prefects' absolute control, where in time they would learn that only political loyalty earned "the confidence and favors of the state."[50]

Some prefects, who juxtaposed their complaints with evidence of their own tirelessness in whipping the functionaries into line, were perhaps opportunists bent upon embellishing their own service records. But generally they showed deep concern for a baffling problem candidly stated. Many prefects composed reflective and perceptive essays on the limits, as well as opportunities, facing centralized administration amid the contrary and varied forces in provincial life.

"Local influences" enmeshed the functionaries in devious ways. Their grip could be nonpolitical, involving family prestige or petty rivalry among factions. They might center on economic issues, as in a northern commune where the mayor aligned the community against the prefect by "skilfully exploiting . . . the instinctive revulsion inspired by the creation of any new tax." More seriously, local influences could be linked to obdurate political "coteries," to use another favorite term of the prefects. These stood for "order" but on issues other than the "red specter" they shunned a "national" orientation for nagging opposition rooted in Orleanist or legitimist particularism. Linked with the legitimists, the clergy was another special source of local opposition.

Orleanism was never feared. It was just troublesome, as in the Oise where many functionaries posed as "come-lately Bonapartists" without "inward faith in the present government" because of old Orleanist ties. Such hypocrisy was a chronic prefectorial grievance because it commonly infected the magistracy and judiciary police hierarchy. Many prefects were highly critical of judges, who could not be purged, and of the judiciary police, who could be. Professional rivalries with men whom they met regularly in political police duties may have colored the prefects' frequent accusation of disloyalty or passivity among the judiciary police. The prefect of the Ardennes found many magistrates "more or less doubtful and even hostile." From the Saône-et-Loire, the same charge was aimed against the *procureur-général* at Dijon and all his principal assistants, from whom "the administration has met more opposition than cooperation." Perhaps "opposition" was too strong a word, the prefect of the Loiret decided. More usual was the sort of "neutrality, if not hostility" which he observed in the bar, magistracy, and judiciary police in electoral policy. In the Meurth, functionaries of the Nancy *parquet* showed an "absence of good will regarding the Emperor," as did those in the Haute-Saône, where Napoleon III was received "merely as the present representative of order." The prefect of the Ille-et-Vilaine admitted that two justices of the peace "do not exactly deserve dismissal [but] they are not the best men in a region of opposition where . . . they are useless to us." One was an Orleanist appointee of ten years' tenure. The other was a status-seeker subservient to "all the local interest groups, and a man of the *pays* rather than a man of the government."[51]

The prefects' demands for transfer or dismissal of undesirables often caused exchanges between the ministers of Interior and Justice. These protests occasionally bore fruit, as in the Nord where the assistant *procureur* at Cambrai was dismissed for trying to sabotage the prefect's action against a local newspaper. But Persigny advised against expecting too much from the magistracy: "the members of the judiciary order cannot be completely assimilated [politically] with the administrative functionaries."[52]

Clerical-legitimist obstructionism, especially in the West, was by common agreement a far more serious form of "local influences" than Orleanism. In the Haute-Garonne, the prefect faced legitimist influence so strong that many public servants were openly hostile. From the Hérault, the unusually self-reliant Costa de Bastelica lamented his helplessness before legitimist domination of public affairs and functionaries: "Anarchy has been conquered in the streets and secret societies but it persists in official salons." Here the legitimists' influence was subtly expressed not in open defiance but as a "diversity of tendencies" reflecting "hidden hostility toward the government." Functionaries dissembled on the job; elsewhere they showed "systematic doubt" of the regime. They took governmental setbacks complacently or with "simulated regrets." As cronies of local notables and ex-functionaries "who refused to take the oath," they too listened while the army district commander extolled "the glories of monarchical France."[53]

The Clergy as a Local Problem of Political Police

Legitimist obstructionism was reinforced by the clergy, an ally with formidable influence in smaller towns and rural areas. Universal suffrage not only countered the cities with rural votes; it gave the clergy a powerful electoral role and greater ability to guide other "local influences." To forestall a clerical-legitimist alliance against the Empire and its official candidates, the administration had to woo the clerics. The resulting problems were of a very "delicate" nature, complicated by the prefects' typically ambivalent attitude toward the Church.

On some issues the administration and the Church were natural allies. They stood together against the "red specter." As a bulwark of social order, the Church was an ideal instrument of the administrative mission, wherein religious indoctrination was indispensable in the political "re-education" of the people. Moreover, the clergy and Catholic laymen almost unanimously welcomed the coup d'état and supported the new regime even before discovering its religious policy.

Conversely, cross-purposes were unavoidable. The prefects' collaboration with the clergy strengthened "local influences," challenged the prefects' ideal of administrative independence, and subverted the creation of a "national party." The prefects saw the Church as a potential state-within-the-administrative-state. Locally, the clergy tenaciously intruded into education, communal government, the lower administrative hierarchy, the press, legitimists, and other groups. Nationally, its growing opposition to the government's ecclesiastical and Italian policies in the later fifties sent repercussions directly into the prefects' local worlds. The administration's and the clergy's dilemmas were interlocked.

Each group found the other useful; but neither could realize its ideal goals if it were dependent on the other. The administration's attempted solution was an uneasy alliance coupled with close political police surveillance and indirect pressures on the ally. As a *procureur* in 1859 observed in retrospect, all relations with the clergy were "serious and ticklish" in the 1850's.

Jean Maurain has thoroughly traced the vicissitudes of Church-Government relations in the 1850's.[54] From an apparent mutuality of aims in 1851–52, the government derived valuable support in two plebiscites and its first elections. In its turn, the Church expected rewards, which to some degree it received under a relatively benevolent Ministry of Public Instruction and Worship headed by Fortoul until 1856. But the alliance wore thin on both sides after 1852. The clergy, dissatisfied with its role in such cherished areas as education and public assistance, was piqued by an unanticipated turn of the regime's authoritarianism against themselves. The government's policy fell into the hands of men who regarded the Church primarily as a political instrument. They were receptive to the specific complaints of like-minded administrators for whom clerical influence and ambitions were increasingly worrisome. In 1854–56, a perceptible "anti-clerical reaction" emerged, marked by the appointment of the more inflexible Gustave Rouland to the Ministry. In 1859, France's Italian policy provoked other differences to bring the Church-State rift into the open. Minister of the Interior Delangle candidly advised the prefects to avoid undue conflict with the clergy but to resist their meddling in local administration. It was time for clerics to understand that their mission was solely spiritual!

Long before 1859 the clergy lived under an unobtrusive but extraordinary political police surveillance. Surveillance per se was not new. Traditionally, it was an activity of the so-called *police des cultes* function in the Ministry of Public Instruction and Worship. This was essentially a routine political police activity on behalf of the state's interests in the Church's temporal affairs. Although members of the clergy enjoyed an immunity like that of administrative "agents of the government" unless waived by the Council of State, the Penal Code (Articles 201–205) had special penalties against clerics who politically opposed the government. In the 1850's these were hardly used. But as tensions increased between administrators and clerics, the normal inspection operations of the *police des cultes* were unusually supplemented and intensified by the Ministry's greater collaboration with administrative and judiciary police authorities.

In 1853 even Fortoul, whose ministerial policy was "softer" than his successor Rouland's after mid-1856, "very confidentially" asked the prefects to send secret information on the personal lives, public activities, and political opinions of the secular and regular clergy. The prefects, responding, kept their own surveillance files and fully informed their own minister as well as Fortoul and Rouland. The Ministry of the Interior compiled summaries of prefectorial complaints against the clergy's writings, sermons, and other activities. It collaborated with the Ministry of Public Instruction to discipline the offenders indirectly; the initiative in a given case might come from either ministry. For example, in the case of an abbé who said publicly that the Empire rested on weak foundations, the Minister of the Interior had the prefect tell the Bishop to warn the cleric that such behavior would not again be tolerated. In another instance, the Minister of Public Instruction directly instructed the prefect of the Bouches-du-Rhône to tell the head of a Catholic school that unless he took administrative suggestions on educational policy he would answer to the Bishop.

Napoleon III kept in active touch with this surveillance through summaries supplied by the ministries. He often made (through his secretary, Mocquard) specific queries on the basis of these reports to the Minister of Public Instruction, who in turn used information supplied by the Interior's hierarchy and the gendarmerie to reply. The Prefect of Police also shared in this collaboration. As early as 1852, Piétri, irritated by the clergy's "hostile tendencies," took it upon himself to warn the Emperor that the clergy would attempt to dominate the state. Clerics were "profoundly legitimist because government by Divine Right best satisfies their instincts toward domination and encroachment." To give them favors, he believed, would only increase their "hope of being called upon to play the first role in the state." The *pro-cureurs* contributed complaints and suspicions like those of the other police services. The *procureur* at Lyon in 1853 protested in familiar terms against clerical encroachment: "the government must keep all authority for itself; otherwise it will have conceded everything to the clergy. . . . ." However, the Minister of Justice almost always forbade legal action even when statutory violations occurred, out of fear that prosecution would chain-react into other issues at both the local and national levels.[55]

The most frequent complaint against clerics was for disparagement of the regime or the administration in print or from the pulpit. The three other leading charges also reflected the prefects' problem of "local influences": involvement in municipal affairs, noncooperation in elections, and intrigues with the legitimists. Still, the government preferred to use indirect and informal disciplinary pressures instead of direct administrative or legal action against the clergy. Thus in regions of strong clerical and legitimist leanings the clergy was relatively free to make life difficult even for seasoned prefects. Certain western *départements* offered the worst trials.

The Tarn-et-Garonne received and tested nine prefects from 1849 to 1852 and four more from 1852 through 1857. Prefect Chambaron (1852–54) found the magistracy divided and their decisions biased by their old political loyalties, both legitimist and Orleanist. Similar divisive influences ruled local functionaries, who had "escaped from all control" by the upper administrators. Effective Bonapartism was nonexistent. The narrowly personal and parochial interests of local elites penetrated even the prefecture, where office heads dared to usurp the prefect's prerogatives. During his two years' tenure, Chambaron strove by degrees to rebuild his authority by removing dubious functionaries "at every opportunity." His successor Le Vasseur carried on, recommending in vain that all public servants native to the *département* be replaced by men "absolutely foreign to the region." His increasingly optimistic progress reports were belied by his replacement, Le Provost de Launay, who in October, 1855, described the "complete moral disorganization" of the Tarn-et-Garonne as a challenge to the most ingenious administrator. When Lorette, the next prefect, submitted a more optimistic initial report in January, 1857, it was annotated in Paris with cynical marginal comments questioning the new arrival's perception.[56]

Another illustrative case-history of the fifties accumulated in the Ille-et-Vilaine. In June, 1858, Prefect Féart, who during six years in the Gers had measured up as nearly as any of his colleagues to our stereotype of the *préfet à poigne,* arrived in Rennes determined to "fortify governmental influence" by breaking "the endless abuse of local influences." As an experienced prefect he did not underestimate the hazards of his mission in an area riddled by "rival and contrary influences," where the people and most of the functionaries "had come to consider the government as its guest not its leader."

As he had anticipated, the legitimist newspapers, "the coteries of the diocesan authority," and local officials joined in "a veritable crusade" against his announced intention to forge "a great national party" in the Ille-et-Vilaine. Among three political newspapers, he found the legitimist *Journal de Rennes* "completely hostile" but skillfully evasive in avoiding or even making opposition capital out of official retaliation. "It is difficult even to give it a formal warning which it does not somehow exploit against the administration or the government," Féart conceded with some wry admiration. Thus he advised that it was "inopportune" to suspend it or to seek its suppression.

He described the few loyal functionaries as timid, hesitant, and embarrassed by his attempt to challenge the sway of "local influences," not "daring to believe" that the latter could be countered. Really zealous functionaries had long since been driven from the *département* on various pretexts. Communal authorities were completely subservient to the legitimists and the clergy. Yet Féart expediently refrained from attempting a purge. He avoided "any rigorous measures" likely to precipitate a head-on clash, preferring gradual, indirect methods. "I shall never forget what happened," he confided to the Minister, "when I insisted that the new hospital at Rennes be named the 'Napoleon III Hospital.' "

The mayor of Rennes stood aloof during the prefect's ensuing conflict with the clergy and he rebuffed Féart's advice to choose liberal bourgeois candidates for the municipal council. Indeed, the mayor, a self-confident "notable" of the region, pointedly delayed his first formal call on the prefect, scorning protocol. When the two men did meet, the mayor told Féart he was a legitimist but not of the "rallied" variety. Féart reported that he spent thirty minutes in persuading the mayor merely to say that he would live up to his loyalty oath. When the mayor finally assented, Féart doubted his sincerity. For months Féart summoned enough self-restraint to ignore the young legistimist hotheads who ostentatiously visited the prefecture wearing the fleur-de-lys in their lapels; and he overlooked the legitimist mayors' refusals to attend his social functions. He called bimonthly conferences with his sub-prefects, meeting them singly and in a group, trying to overcome their "lack of administrative initiative and political energy, even of faith in the government." He inspected the communes and found government mayors "very rare," the *commissaires* of police indifferent to political police duties, the rural police utterly useless.

Only the gendarmerie served effectively. But, Féart admitted, "with the gendarmerie I cannot discuss all the problems of special influences which must be resolved in this region." In the end he saw no hope of governmental supremacy in the Ille-et-Vilaine except through prolonged, opportunistic, tactful, and constructive administration of a kind that would eventually seem more profitable for the region's self-interests than the prevalent "local influences."[57]

Féart's case was not isolated. In the West, such problems worsened after 1859 as clerical and legitimist opposition mobilized against the Emperor's Italian policy. Official anxiety over the situation was amply attested in a series of confidential Interior circulars. In 1861 a certain Gallix, inspector of *colportage* (book peddling) who used his regular duties as a screen for confidential political reports to Persigny, toured the western *départements*. He reported that Mgr. Pie, Bishop of Poitiers, had for years dominated the Vendée, Deux-Sèvres, and Vienne through his private intelligence organization and connections with legitimist leaders and many high functionaries. In nine years, only one prefect had been able to resist the pressure; and even he had finally requested a transfer. Throughout the West, Gallix believed reliable functionaries to be in the minority.[58]

CONCLUSION

As a younger functionary, Prefect Féart of the Ille-et-Vilaine had already gained some insight into the prefects' world before he took his first prefecture in the Gers soon after the coup d'état. Vowing then to replace the "military occupation" of the Gers (which had been under siege) with an administrative *"governmental occupation"* [underlined in text], the novice prefect had the foresight to warn his minister that "we must cherish no illusions" of easy success in the presence of that corrosive parochial opposition which had undermined earlier regimes and which everywhere in France remained to eat away at the ideals of public administration from the surrounding localities.[59]

The many advantages and satisfactions of increased powers in the 1850's were not equivalent to the prefects' ideal bureaucratic state. Having "saved" France from dangers of epic proportions in December, 1851, the prefects' energies turned into less heroic grappling with very tangible and deeper-rooted realities. Specific successes had a way of intensifying related problems. With the "red specter" at bay, other indigenous wellsprings of dissension flowed once again. The triumphs of official candidature, an intended means of achieving a more obedient "national" orientation, were paid for by concessions to notables in the localities over which the prefects had formal dominance. The clergy, so useful in founding the dictatorship and "re-educating" the people to social order, turned into obstructive allies. For the prefects, all activities seemed to lead back into the dreary labyrinth of "local influences." One might even speculate that in their exasperation the officials took a certain perverse comfort from their belief that the refugees' European "red specter" still threatened France. Here, at least, the prefects knew they were the indispensable paladins of the nation on guard against a more distant adversary whose threat was all the better understood because it did not fill their daily lives.

6

Manipulation of the Provincial Press

THE PRESS was at once a weapon and a problem in the prefects' confrontation of local influences. Most provincial newspapers were voices of local attitudes and interests after the "demagogic" press expired in December, 1851. Nearly all were older than Louis Napoleon's rise to power. Their biases were mainly Orleanist, legitimist, clerical, or anti-Bonapartist republican. Despite their low circulation, by twentieth-century standards, they offered the prefects a challenge parallel to that of creating a "national party." The coup d'état left a press desirous of "order" but not reliably Bonapartist. It was the prefects' task to make it so, or at least to control the journalistic balance of power.

In that objective, the prefects were relatively successful because their superiors, up to the Elysée itself, shared provincial administrators' views on the dangers of newspapers. A new press law that ensured a commanding position over journalists was therefore enacted in early 1852.

Apart from its obvious propagandic value, the newspaper press constituted a special concern in the administrative attitude. The turbulence of unaccustomed press liberty in 1848, when new papers mushroomed by the hundreds, along with universal suffrage and other "unnatural" innovations, was etched upon officials' memories. An uncontrolled press was inseparable from the "red specter" and a tool of secret societies. After August, 1848, a series of new laws revived earlier restrictions until, not quite a year later, press controls resembled those of 1835.[1]

But these and even more sweeping regulations in the fifties failed to blur the authorities' threatening image of an unregulated press. Gustave Rouland, *procureur* at Paris until 1856, never tired of recalling that a deadly interaction of nihilistic slogans, secret organizations, and political newspapers had thrust France "to the brink of the democratic and social republic of 1848." An irresponsible press was sure to "politically debauch" the public, Rouland believed; thus "any government which allows its existence to be challenged publicly commits suicide !"[2]

Another official typically saw in the press "a machine of modern invention . . . which harbors enormous reserves of power." As uncontrolled power, it malevolently organized, said the *procureur* at Lyon, "a communist force destructive of all authority." The prefects still heard from their minister in 1859 that "newspapers are power structures organized within the state. . . ." This attitude prevailed at the very pinnacle of the state. Lord Cowley's first reports from the British Embassy in 1852 stressed Louis Napoleon's "extreme sensitiveness about the Press, which is carried to an excessive pitch." Cowley noted the same anxiety in Foreign Minister Turgot, who "used strong language when speaking of the Press, which, he said, had brought France to the verge of socialism."[3] In such a like-minded milieu, the government developed in early 1852 a press policy which armed the prefects with their best weapon against "local influences."

POLICY OF THE "BALANCED PRESS"

Like other regimes since the early 1790's, the Second Empire bowed to the principle of a free press and regulated newspapers at the same time. The controls of the fifties found their rationale in familiar administrative law and the practical argument that France's revolutionary history made an unfettered press uniquely destructive. Persigny insisted on the priority of society's right of self-defense over that of a free press. Maupas pointed to the bitterness of French partisan conflict which threatened national existence and turned the press into "an instrument of demolition . . . , the torch which lights the fire in perilous times."

Such attitudes underlay what might be called the "balanced press" of the fifties. Its formula was partial control, not full censorship, over political newspapers in a blend of "authority and liberty" protected by the Emperor's executive independence and

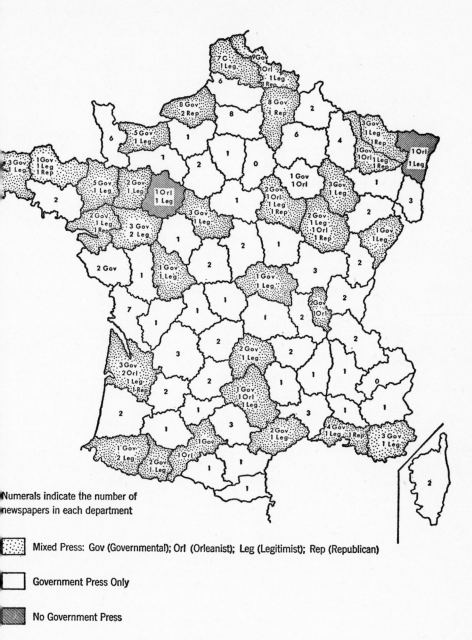

Numerals indicate the number of
newspapers in each department

Mixed Press: Gov (Governmental); Orl (Orleanist); Leg (Legitimist); Rep (Republican)

Government Press Only

No Government Press

MAP 2

Distribution of provincial political newspapers, about 1860

sanctioned by popular approval. Controls, said Persigny, were temporary but necessary until "a new political generation—young, vigorous, and independent—arises to replace minds distorted and enervated by our revolutions." For Maupas, the balanced press was the competition of various-minded newspapers within a context of "proportionate" and "variable" liberty. Except for the advocates of violence, Billault agreed, a controlled "balance of forces" permitted the free expression of legitimate differences: "not a single major political opinion is unrepresented in this continual conflict [wherein] the contenders' strengths are perfectly balanced." The directors of press police insisted that most Frenchmen in their disgust with past excesses preferred the "balanced" press to that of 1848. If asked to restore that interval of license, an official predicted, "with almost one voice the country would answer no."[4]

Provincial authorities agreed, though a *procureur* noted in 1857 that some of the urban upper classes "were forgetting past dangers . . . , lamenting the passing of that very press liberty which earlier they cursed amidst the storms." Such paltry opposition, another advised, should not deter the administration from its duty: "If we owe the people nourishment of their bodies we must also guard their minds and hearts."[5] The "balanced" press thus served the administrative mission. Newspapers, declared the governmental *La Patrie,* must address the public mind, instruct, and correct, and forge bonds "of confidence and devotion, without which government is always feeble and liberty ever dangerous." Presumably, then, the "balanced" press functioned best when unbalanced in the government's favor.

THE PRESS LAW OF FEBRUARY, 1852

Louis Napoleon, assisted by Baroche, Rouher, and Persigny, drafted the law of February 17, 1852, as the charter of the "balanced" press. It completed the post-1848 reaction in press legislation just short of preliminary censorship. Otherwise, Baroche noted, it combined elements from "all the old laws."[6] The law applied to periodical publications "dealing with political matters of social economy." Others, thereafter by definition "nonpolitical," escaped its strictures but trespassed into forbidden territory at their own peril. The crucial terms "political matters" and "social economy" went undefined; but the prefects were told to apply the law "in a rigorously uniform manner." Presumably they would act as their sense of the *sûreté générale* advised. The interpretive latitude was scarcely narrowed by the decision of the Court of Cassation that "political matters" included "all discussions whose objective is the criticism or censure of either general or local administrative activities."[7]

In essence, the law of February, 1852, multiplied the administration's means of disciplining the press without judicial process. The law neither dispensed with judicial procedures altogether nor significantly added to the existing repertory of legal offenses which could bring journalists to court.

New Means of Administrative Control

Preliminary authorization to publish political newspapers, not mere declaration of intent, became the prefects' most fundamental control after February, 1852. What the administration exclusively gave, it could refuse or withdraw. Maupas enjoined the prefects to allow the "high function" of publication only to men whose "antecedents and morality" met administrative standards.

Qualified applicants encountered heavy financial requirements. As had been the law since 1849, they must deposit "caution money" as a pledge of financial responsibility for fines that might be levied in future. In 1852, the amount of such deposits was fixed much higher than before, ranging between fifty thousand and twelve thousand five hundred francs according to frequency of publication and the size and importance of the publisher's city. Thus only men of means, presumably conservative, could finance a newspaper. Authorized journals paid large stamp taxes. A ten-page brochure in two thousand copies cost five hundred francs in stamps; a large Parisian daily's press run of forty thousand enriched the government by 876,000 francs yearly.

Newspapers made a *dépôt légal*, submitting copies of every issue to certain officials for the convenience of press surveillance. The administration authorized or forbade changes in newspapers' title, ownership, and management or editorial personnel. All articles had to carry their author's name. Many papers ran afoul of these regulations. Unless they were in the administration's favor, violations could lead to severe penalties.

Authorization did not ensure a newspaper's security even if its editors stayed out of the courts. In theory, at least, the administration need only invoke general police doctrine to withdraw authorization for sake of the *sûreté générale*. Maupas, in a circular never superseded by his successors, informed the prefects on March 30, 1852:

> Repressive measures by pure administrative decision derive from the . . . right of authorization. As soon as a newspaper ceases to observe the conditions of authorization . . . or persists in polemics that make it an instrument of disorder to the point of endangering public security, the government . . . has the right to withdraw its authorization.
>
> You will use this right with impartial severity against those journals whose editorial policies, without specifically becoming liable to judicial action, are nonetheless dangerous for public order, morality, and religion.[8]

Such doctrine governed decisions on the authorization of new journals and approval of changes in the ownership of established ones. To this writer's knowledge, it was never literally invoked outside the specific terms of the law of 1852 to suppress a newspaper. It did justify the arbitrary administrative powers in the new law, some of which could lead to suppression without any sort of due process.

The prefects received three formal means of directly penalizing newspapers. They could insert *communiqués,* official rebuttals of editorial opinion, or corrections of "false news" on the front page of an offender. The most original feature of the law of 1852 was the *avertissement,* or official warning, understated as "an invitation given a newspaper to take a more moderate course," constituting a heavier pressure and inducement for self-censorship on the part of editors. After two official warnings, whose explicatory texts must appear on the recipient's front page, a paper became liable to suspension or outright suppression by administrative decision within two months after the second warning. This third power had great deterrent potential although it was not widely used.

Novel as it was in French press legislation, the official warning (with its possible consequences) was legitimized by administrative law as a "political act" by qualified "agents of the government." The Council of State rejected appeals against it because:

the exercise of this right is neither confined to any legal form nor subjected to any of the rules of adjudication by ordinary or administrative courts. . . . The law's intent is to arm the government with a discretionary power which by its very nature excludes most absolutely the possibility of recourse. . . .[9]

Communiqués, warnings, and administrative suspension or suppression were employed as actions against a paper as distinct from the liability of its responsible personnel, who were subject to prosecution for the many press offenses under the 1852 law that were continued from the past. For conviction of a major crime, the courts of assizes, as before, could suspend or suppress the paper as well as imprison and fine its writers and managers. One other innovation in the 1852 law authorized judicial suspension or suppression after two convictions for less than felonious offenses.

Unofficial Censorship

Officials were technically correct in denying that the press law of 1852 imposed censorship. But under its sway, only a rash editor would not blue-pencil his material to some degree with an eye upon powers so formidable that the administration could usually afford to hold them in abeyance.

Informal censorship was also wielded by the ministers of the Interior and the prefects who simply informed editors that certain topics were taboo. Comprehensive ministerial instruction told the prefects in 1854 to warn publishers to avoid casting "any sort of public disfavor on the measures adopted by the Emperor's government."

Otherwise, informal censorship dealt with specifics. Notices of certain arrests, crimes, and political offenses were sometimes forbidden, as was reference to specified trials such as that of eighty-five secret society suspects at Reims in 1854. Financial and industrial news or comment, along with many other diverse items, intermittently appeared on the unofficial Index.[10]

DISCIPLINING THE "BALANCED" PRESS

Even in the authoritarian fifties, press police powers were never used to their full potential. In addition to editors' self-censorship when overawed by the administration's power-in-being, in their turn the prefects found it expedient not to use the law to the hilt. Still, a journalist's life could be rigorous if not always so agonized as that portrayed by Hector Pessard:

> Censored by himself, his copy pored over and corrected meticulously by his editor-in-chief, given a last check by the printer (who was responsible to the courts for every line that came off his press), deprived of scope and movement, drawing the thunderbolts while chained to the lightning-rod, compelled by his job to strike sparks while seated on a powder keg, the journalist of 1860 was indeed the tortured victim of the imperial regime.[11]

From the perspective of the administrative attitude, the situation appeared differently to the *procureur* at Limoges in May, 1852. He happily saw "the state of the nation completely changed . . . the journals being without influence and nearly without interest." Actually, the press lived somewhere between these two suggested extremes.

During the first six months of the new law, the prefects and *procureurs* used their powers the most severely. Thereafter, the ministries restrained their more zealous agents, who themselves learned to adapt the use of formal powers to their problems of "local influences." Paul Juillerat, an official in the press sections of the police and interior ministries, probably realistically appraised ministerial (and incidentally, prefectorial) policy in a confidential report to Napoleon III:

> The director . . . had to achieve a very difficult golden mean. He had to anticipate and forestall press excesses to avoid having to repress them, to make the law's rigors tolerable by observance of informal amenities, to direct constantly in one way or another both the governmental and the opposition press. He had to induce voluntary moderation in the latter through a liberal use of unofficial warnings before using the weapons . . . of official warnings or prosecutions, whose reverberations are always regrettable.[12]

It is not intended here to analyze the policing of the Paris press, a subject suitable for a specialized study. In the provinces, the legitimist newspapers offered the most serious opposition, which, with the encouragement of clerical protest against the French policy of assisting Italian political unification, reached a climax in 1859–60. Even earlier the prefects acted most often against legitimists.

Official Warnings

Relatively few newspapers in the fifties suffered administrative suspension or suppression. Many formal warnings were issued, however. To Maupas' alarm, during the first four months of the press law, the prefects seemed overzealous in their issuance of warnings on their own determination. Provincial newspapers, half of them legitimist, were under the most intensive attack, fifty-four of them receiving seventy warnings. Next hardest hit were progovernment journals, with eighteen warnings.

This brief period accounted for nearly 32 per cent of all warnings issued during the eight-year span from 1852 to 1860. The entire period 1852–60 produced 219 warnings; 65 in Paris, 154 in the provinces. Over half of the 219 warnings clustered in 1852–53 and 1859–60.

Official warnings sharply declined after June, 1852, and during the remaining eleven months of Maupas' ministry, only twenty-one warnings were issued. Maupas sharply rebuked the prefects for lack of "propriety and reserve," and ruled that warnings thereafter required ministerial approval. Although this action became involved in Maupas' feud with the prefects, Persigny continued the policy when his ministry recovered its police powers a year later. Of the ninety-one warnings issued under Maupas, only seven were in Paris.[13]

A press amnesty of December 2, 1852, wiped the slate clean. Between the amnesty and August, 1854, forty-nine warnings were issued to eight Parisian papers and nineteen departmental papers. The quieter intervening years averaged just under nineteen warnings annually.[14]

Provincial authorities proposed more warnings than the ministry allowed. Many drafts were filed away unsigned, as they were in Paris where *Le Siècle* accumulated more unused warnings and abandoned prosecutions in its dossier than its editors may have known.[15] The same was true in the provinces.

Most of the warnings were not charges of revolutionary tendencies. Rather, "local influences" in the form of alleged press "attacks" against the administration or its actions underlay more *avertissements* than any other single charge. Progovernment papers, like the *Charente Napoléonienne* in 1858, were by no means immune. Other recurrent motives for warnings were criticisms of the chief of state, the regime's legitimacy, or its alleged bases in popular sovereignty. These offenses were frequently charged against legitimist papers such as the *Ami de l'Ordre* at Amiens which in April, 1852, attacked popular sovereignty as the "doctrine of despotism," a mere pretext to seize power. Church-State affairs and Italian policy also earned many warnings for the legitimist press. But the *Indépendant de l'Ouest* at Laval varied the pattern; the fourth of five warnings was sent to it in the fifties for accusing the government of tolerating "revolutionary newspapers."

The administration was especially sensitive to "polemics" involving the Emperor even indirectly. The editor of another staunchly Bonapartist *Ami de l'Ordre* in the Oise too closely identified his own local views with those of the chief of state, and received a warning declaring that "it is not permitted to invoke [Louis Napoleon's] true or supposed opinions as elements of discussion." The Orleanist *Aube* at Troyes assaulted the dignity of the Legislative Body with "perfidious allusions and insinuations too obvious for authority to tolerate."

"False news" was a covering indictment in most warnings, even when departmental papers merely copied from the Paris press. In 1852, the editor of *Le Guetteur* at St. Quentin violently protested to the prefect and dared to print another broadside beneath the text of the warning he received for reproducing an article from the *Charivari* in Paris, which also had a warning. The prefect classified the *Guetteur* as "systematic opposition"; its editor's public defiance could have earned another warning. But it continued for six more years without official incident.

Some warnings concerned foreign affairs, especially during the Crimean War in 1854–56 and the Italian crisis in 1859 and 1860. Many warnings struck at financial or economic articles when the government considered them harmful to private business or public economic policies. The nonpolitical *Journal de Loudéac* in the Côtes-du-Nord was perhaps surprised in 1854 to be warned for a "polemic" on industrial oils.

It is difficult to reach general conclusions on the rationale or relative justice of the formal warnings issued during the fifties. They reflected the variant interpretations of officials who, amid differing "local influences" and the procession of larger issues, made judgments from the citadel of the 1852 press law on what was good or bad for public security.[16]

Suspensions and Suppressions

Although few newspapers were suspended or suppressed during the fifties, had Paris approved all the prefects' requests, more newspapers receiving two or more warnings would have been affected. For example, although the prefect of the Nord proposed a suspension of the legitimist *Emancipateur de Cambrai* after two warnings (one for an article ending in "Vive le roi!"), the paper survived even another because Paris decided that its criticism was compatible with a basic acceptance of the regime. At Nantes, the ultralegitimist *Espérance du Peuple,* a plague upon all prefects within its radius, survived two warnings, a proposal of suppression, and another warning in 1855 before it was finally suspended for two months in June, 1859. Within six months after its chastening, it absorbed a fourth warning.

Before 1860, the administration imposed eleven suspensions of from eight days to two months upon ten papers (the Paris Assemblée Nationale received two). Two were in the colony of Réunion. Of eight suspended papers in France, five were provincial: the governmental *Echo de l'Aude* whose editor broke with the prefect in 1855; the *Espérance du Peuple* in Nantes; the legitimist *Foi Bretonne* at Saint-Brieuc after four warnings; the clerical-legitimist *Gazette du Languedoc* of Toulouse (later suppressed in 1857); and the parliamentary-liberal *Journal de la Meuse* for unknown reasons. This eight-year record may be compared with the suspension of sixteen or more papers by the courts in 1848–49.[17]

Newspapers were not suppressed lightly. As his press office reminded the Minister of the Interior in 1854, suppression was a violation of private property and politically inexpedient if overused.[18] Nine papers disappeared by administrative decision, five of them between 1858 and 1860, including two earlier suspended. Two were in Algeria and Martinique. Of the other seven, only four were provincial: the clerical and once-Bonapartist *Bretagne* in the Côtes-du-Nord for "complete misrepresentation" of the Roman Question; the ultraclerical and legitimist *Gazette du Languedoc* after six warnings, a suspension, and convictions; and the "rallied" *Tribune de Beaune* for reasons unknown.

Amnesties periodically forgave press penalties beginning with cancellation of all warnings and remission of prison sentences on December 2, 1852. In 1854, the Interior's press director, pleased with the amnesty's ostensible results, noted a marked decline of disciplinary measures and a more moderate spirit in the press. In August, 1859, and December, 1860, the government again erased all warnings. On the latter occasion, Persigny invited the press to enjoy a "wide liberty of discussion" short of deliberate abuses and urged journalists to seize this "opportunity to show their patriotism." Nine days later, still another amnesty canceled judicial convictions for press offenses and ordered dismissal of cases then in process.[19] Other amnesties followed in the sixties.

Press Prosecutions

The personnel of newspapers untouched by administrative measures were still vulnerable to prosecution for legal violations. One or more convictions could seriously injure all but the largest and most affluent papers.

It seems doubtful that judges or the judiciary police, despite their affinity for the administrative attitude, significantly abdicated professional ethics and their sense of legality for political expediency. The authorities preferred prosecution to formal administrative action when circumstances warranted it. In flagrant cases the two could be combined. But, since prosecutions without ironclad cases could backfire through acquittals, journalists were taken to court only after cautious reflection, particularly in the Ministry of Justice, which often denied the *procureurs'* requests to prosecute. Prosecutions were sometimes undertaken only after the original charge was reduced to make the case stronger.[20] The statutory press offenses inherited from earlier regimes were sufficient for this purpose.

Incomplete evidence indicates that the press suffered less from political charges in the courts during the fifties than under earlier governments. From 1852 to 1867, about a hundred newspapers were prosecuted one or more times, including those of Paris. The correctional court at Paris heard fifty-one political cases of which one was acquitted. Many of the more numerous nonpolitical cases probably arose from political motives. Press fines (without any breakdown into political and other offenses) for two years from early 1848 alone amounted to 113,416 francs; whereas for fourteen years—February, 1852, until April, 1868—they yielded only 114,920 francs. Responding to a request for comparative statistics in 1861, all prefects outside the Seine reported a total of 383 press prosecutions under the July Monarchy, 168 during the Second Republic (with the figures from fifteen *départements* missing), and 211 for the Second Empire until May, 1861. Twenty-nine *départements* reported no cases at all from 1852 to 1861. Only the Hérault, Nord, and Somme reported more than ten.[21]

In place of harsher measures, the prefects were free to use the *communiqué* or, still better, informal persuasion. The *communiqué,* like the official warning which must also be printed on the front page, admitted government propaganda into hostile papers, which were forbidden to comment upon the contents. It was a *de facto* warning without specified consequences. The technique flourished most after 1860 during the relaxation of press controls but it was also used in the fifties. In his conflict with Maupas, Persigny won the exclusive right for the prefects to issue *communiqués.* The tactic was a "first" weapon but, like other powers, not for frivolous use.[22]

Unofficial Warnings and Advice

By far the prefects' most frequent tactic was informal conferences with editors and the occasional issuance of "unofficial warnings"—termed *officieux,* not *officiels.* On their own or by ministerial order, the prefects "invited" editors to comply with friendly advice or informal admonition. When, for example, the *Indépendant* in the Charente-Inférieure reprinted another paper's critique of press laws, the prefect conveyed his "serious observations" on the "harm of such publication."[23]

Perhaps for greater effect, unofficial warnings were sometimes delivered in a full-page format identical with that of an official warning except for its ending. One of these in 1859 concluded: "What action should be taken because of the *Gazette de France*'s article? A WARNING, or at least a notice that the administration will not let such articles pass without reflecting upon their possible consequences."[24]

MANAGING THE "BALANCED" PRESS

Management of the "balanced" press was not always the prefects' simplest chore in multinewspaper *départements.* They sought a malleable press weighted in the government's favor though not monolithic, engaged in a guidable interplay of differing opinions. Criticism must, of course, stop short of frontal attacks upon the regime or undue carping at public policies and functionaries. Outside Paris, the showcase of the "balanced" press, the problem often was ensnarled in "local influences." Coercion wore a more liberal look if partly masked by the prefects' manipulation of competition among several newspapers through informal and indirect means.

In the *départements,* as in Paris, the 1850's ended with about the same number of political newspapers as in 1852. However, the opposition's proportional strength had declined. The new era began with approximately 258 papers; by 1862 only four more were publishing (with 207,071 subscribers). About two hundred of these were listed as either dependably or expediently progovernment. In the outright opposition class were 13

Orleanist, 34 legitimist, and 13 republican papers with 75,184 subscribers. Only two *départements* (the Seine-et-Marne and the Hautes-Alpes) lacked a political newspaper compared with five in 1851. Twenty-three *départements* supported only one political journal each. Few papers boasted more than fifteen hundred subscribers. The sole political paper in the Lozère had only 40, that of the Basses-Alpes 112, and the Creuse 222.[25]

To their ministers' oft-recorded irritation and the frustration of later researchers, the busy prefects were dilatory in reporting details on the newspaper press. However, enough unsystematic evidence survives to permit the tracing of press policy beyond the technical enforcement of the law of 1852.

Subsidies

Direct subsidies from the administration's secret funds went to collaborating newspapers, but detailed evidence of this practice for the 1850's is very fragmentary. The ministry periodically asked the prefects to report their papers' financial condition as a guide to "appropriate measures of assuring the organs of governmental policy a situation befitting their lofty cause." Annual subsidies went to help found a progovernment newspaper, to assist those in financial straits, sometimes to widen favored papers' circulation by lowered subscription rates, or quietly to "buy" editors of the opposition.

In the absence of better evidence, by turning to documentation of the 1860's, three inferences can be drawn for the fifties. Departmental papers probably received less subsidy than under the July Monarchy. They received less than they did in the 1860's. During both periods, their direct subsidy was far less than that of Parisian papers. The Interior's funds for the entire French press in 1869 was two hundred thousand francs, noted as an increase over former years. Subsidies to provincial papers were obviously not lavish in the fifties. In 1852, the *Napoléonien* in the Aube received a grant of six hundred francs but budget shortages forced deferment of payment for a year.[26] Paul Juillerat, in addition to his subsidy for Parisian journalists, developed similar links with the more important provincial papers, advising their editors in personal letters and receiving "useful information" in return.[27] Further research in departmental archives might yield more detailed insight into subsidy practices than can be offered here.

The Annonces Judiciaires

The prefects had an extremely effective alternative to direct subsidy in their power to assign publication rights for the *annonces judiciaires* (legal advertisements) to preferred newspapers. No device more effectively unbalanced the "balanced" press toward the government's side. The revenue, plus the prefecture's other printing business, could seduce many provincial editors into accepting the prefects' editorial guidance. The courts assigned the *annonces* until the press law of 1852 gave the prefects the "absolute right" to allot them at will under whatever conditions they wished to impose.[28]

The prefect of the Isère, who had seen its success in Sardinia, had proposed this change before the new press law was passed. He correctly foresaw that "without any subsidy you could have a paper in every *département* devoted to the Napoleonic cause." His superiors agreed by defining the *annonces* as "an indirect means of coming to the aid of papers whose collaboration is assured."[29] The grant or refusal of this indirect subsidy could make or break many small papers whose meager advertising revenue made them depend upon printing business to augment the income from a few hundred subscribers. Disgruntled publishers who lost the *annonces* repeatedly challenged the prefects' new power. They were as many times rebuffed by the Council of State. Every year the prefects proposed a distribution of the *annonces* according to their sense of political strategy. But Paris, far away from local influences, often disagreed. This issue ignited one of the conflicts with Maupas and outlived the police ministry. In 1858, the Ministry of the Interior dulled another of the prefects' lances by directing that the *annonces* normally go to political newspapers with the largest circulations.[30]

Before this limitation, the prefects freely used the *annonces* in varied local tactical situations. In the Gard, the prefect was able to "convert" a legitimist paper and to reward a loyal Protestant competitor, both at Nîmes, bypassing another legitimist paper at Alais. He immediately clashed with Maupas' insistence that the *annonces* be more widely shared in fairness to printers and nonpolitical newspapers. Angrily protesting to Maupas that political expediency superseded all else, the prefect also complained to Persigny that Maupas' policy would only strengthen "local coteries."

In the Gers, Prefect Féart's political sense also deviated from the ministry's. He helped to ruin the Orleanist *Opinion* when it balked at supporting official candidates by withdrawing its *annonces* in favor of the *Courrier de Gers,* which had just been founded under his own sponsorship. Féart also endowed three weak, nonpolitical papers with the *annonces* until after the elections of 1852. One, the *Echo de la Baïse,* sinned by frequently criticizing the administration. The prefect withdrew the *annonces* from all three papers and gave them entirely to the *Courrier.* "It was . . . opportune," Féart explained, "to show . . . that the privilege of the *annonces* implied the obligation to serve the government in all its interests. . . ." In a sequel to this incident, publishers learned of their lack of recourse when deprived of the legal advertisements. For himself and printers of the Gers, the *Echo*'s editor hotly protested to the Emperor and Council of State. His petition failed. When he then offered to run a progovernment paper, Féart refused lest such a turnabout react undesirably on public opinion.[31]

In the Puy-de-Dôme, the Orleanist *Ami de la Patrie* resisted an invitation to collaborate, and lost its former monopoly of the *annonces.* The latter, with the prefecture's printing orders, went to the new *Journal du Puy-de-Dôme* which the prefect "not without difficulty" persuaded a printer to launch under the prefect's nominee as editor. The annual ten to twelve thousand francs involved promised to buy double value. The *Journal* would thrive, the prefect predicted, and the *Ami* would "disappear before the end of the year."

The Vosges offered no problem. There the prefect "saw no hesitation at all" when the *Courrier des Vosges* accepted the *annonces* on condition that the newspaper cut its price to gain wider circulation and "support and propagate the government's views and principles in all circumstances, through good times and bad."

Not all prefects settled the *annonces* upon one paper. The Finistère's six nonpolitical and three authorized journals shared the bounty. One of the latter three was legitimist, another neutral, and the third "reformed" by stages from "advanced" republicanism before December, 1851, to moderate opposition, then to compliance. The prefect of the Haute-Saône divided his largesse among the *département's* three papers, all tainted with a "penchant for Orleanism." Lured by the *annonces,* all cooperated though "a bit tepidly."[32]

The Propagation and Care of "Administrative Journals"

Subsidies—direct, indirect, or by the *annonces*—were intended to nurture what every prefect hoped to have: a loyal, pliant, "administrative" or "governmental" newspaper. Many editors volunteered; others could be recruited among papers of various political hues. Or, through some form of subsidy or privilege, the administration could preside at the birth of new ones.

Some prefects lived easily with only one administrative paper as their *département's* entire political press. The *Courrier des Ardennes,* which the prefect habitually called "my political journal," provided that ideal situation. Monopolizing the *annonces,* it gradually eliminated its only political competitor and outsold the Parisian papers in its domain. With a trace of pride, the prefect revealed his "system" of giving the *annonces* to one favored paper, "killing the small local sheets, and ending with only one political organ, influential and easy to manage." Prefect Dieu of the Haute-Saône was equally gratified by several newspapers "all under the administration's patronage." A few luckless prefects never acquired an administrative paper. In the Sarthe, two thousand subscribers read nothing but Orleanist and legitimist publications, which the prefect managed to stand off in a "disguised hostility" throughout the 1850's.[33]

The typical situation in a multinewspaper *département* was a "balanced" press of one or more administrative journals cultivated or founded to compete with rivals held to mild criticism or neutrality by the administrative presence. If editors did not volunteer to serve, the prefects took the initiative. Either way, official control over authorization and sundry favors was decisive. Relations with protegés were not always harmonious; administrative papers also were disciplined. If vexed enough, a prefect could abandon his favorite and woo another.

The prefects' initiative varied according to their local situations. In 1853, a prefect sponsored *Le Var* against the mildly legitimist *Union du Var*. The new paper would "receive the prefecture's communications and be known as the unofficial but regular administrative organ." It would inoculate "this somewhat refractory and long-neglected region with healthy ideas and saner attitudes toward its political and administrative interests." Lacking a political newspaper, the prefect of the Ardèche assigned a similar educative mission to a new journal which he promoted as "a powerful means of enlightening the laboring population" against the "demagogy." By 1862, the paper was enlightening 657 subscribers. Some prefects welcomed the clergy's attempts to found congenial newspapers. In the Vienne, Abbé Bessonnet easily changed his nonpolitical *Châtelleraudais* into authorized status. The *Messager de l'Ouest,* begun by the Bishop of Rennes, was patronized in the face of four other legitimist or conservative newspapers.[34]

Even nonpolitical papers could serve political ends. In the Mayenne, the prefect winked at the press law by using two unauthorized journals against the *département*'s sole political paper, the *Indépendant de l'Ouest* at Laval, which displayed five warnings by January, 1860.

A classic example of prefectorial initiative in quest of a "balanced" press was the *Moniteur de la Moselle,* founded in March, 1853, to print official news and opinion. It received the *annonces* and other printing business. But the ministry refused the prefect's project for further subsidy by requiring the Moselle's 627 communes to subscribe. It confronted the legitimist *Voeu National,* citadel of "local influences," the Orleanist *Indépendant,* and the

Cavaignac-republican *Courrier,* "a sleeping serpent" after the coup d'état. These stayed within the law. But the prefect doubted if they would ever sincerely back the new regime; meanwhile, they prolonged the "coldness" of Metz and other cities.[35]

Tolerance of opposition papers varied with the prefects' divers problems and tactical imagination. The prefect of the Vosges doggedly chipped away at the granite views of certain editors in hope of eventual conversions, accepting moderate opposition meanwhile. Indeed, he reported, "I preferred an open hostility to a crafty demeanor displaying neither the desire to combat the authorities openly nor the intention of frankly supporting them."

As a matter of fact, hostile papers in the journalistically sophisticated areas offered useful targets for the polemics of governmental papers. "In a large city," the *procureur* at Lyon reported, "amidst active parties with such diverse tendencies I accept and submit to the necessity of an opposition newspaper." In the Aisne, whose ten papers in 1852 were reduced to eight in 1860, the prefect with six governmental or "rallied" allies could tolerate four opposition papers—up to a point. The *Observateur* at Laon mirrored the *Siècle* and *Presse* at Paris. The *Courrier* at St. Quentin retained the stigmata of its former "socialism" and the *Journal de Soissons* a "prudent" liberal opposition. The prefect's heaviest cross was the republican *Guetteur* at St. Quentin, noted for its "systematic opposition against all the government's acts." However, it was tolerated (with two warnings and two prosecutions) until the court at Amiens suppressed it for promoting "the worst doctrines and inciting the working class against the established order."[36]

Toleration of opposition papers was sometimes enforced by the weakness of the prefectures' protegés. The Loire-Inférieure's prefects were caught in a delicate balance-of-power problem. Of six papers at Nantes in 1852, the government had only the dependable but uninfluential *Breton*. Two others—the fusionist *Union Bretonne* and the Orleanist *Courrier de Nantes*—tentatively "rallied." Three problem papers remained. Two of these were legitimist with different emphases: the *Alliance,* until it ceased in 1853, followed the clerical *Univers* of Paris; the ultralegitimist *Espérance du Peuple* waged a vendetta with the *Union Bretonne,* which earned both identical warnings.

To exploit this enmity between two royalist journals, the administration tolerated the third problem paper—the republican *Phare de la Loire.* This tactic and seduction of the *Union Bretonne* into governmental status in 1853 (with all the *annonces*) allowed the prefects to contain the incorrigible *Espérance.* The latter, whose suppression the prefect vainly requested of his minister, received five warnings and a suspension in eight years. The combined circulation of the *Phare* and *Espérance* outdid the pro-government papers by nearly a thousand (in 1862), but the administration accepted this as a tolerably "balanced" press. The *Phare* enjoyed considerable freedom and published such writers as Edgar Quinet and Jules Michelet.

Some administrative papers vied equally with one rival as in the Aube, where the new *Napolénien* at Troyes faced the hostile Orleanist *Aube,* whose "cautious reserve" saved it from a fate harsher than one prosecution and a five-hundred-franc fine during the fifties. In 1859, the *Napolénien* had 730 subscribers; the *Aube,* 542.[37]

The prefects and their kept press did not always harmonize. A prefect tried to mold the *Journal des Vosges* into reliability. But his "lively discussions" with the editor failed to uproot its attachment to "local influences" and an obdurate tendency to criticize and "advise" the prefect by "the most singular analyses and tangled, impracticable, and incomprehensible proposals." Despite the *Journal*'s praise of the coup d'état, its support of unofficial candidates in 1852 led the prefect to abandon it and create the *Courrier des Vosges* in his own image. The *Courrier*'s prospectus promised to eliminate political discussion and asked: "Why tire the readers with it? What does it usually lead to?"

The *Echo de l'Aude* offered a similar problem at Carcassonne. By 1855, it had two warnings and a conviction. The prefect removed its editor from the *département*'s general council as "a necessity of public morality" and helped to found the *Courrier de l'Aude* with full patronage. The *Echo* soon disappeared to leave the *Courrier* alone in the Aude with a modest circulation of about eight hundred. The prefect of the Dordogne constantly inveighed against his "loyal" *Echo de Vésone*. His colleague in the Eure was no happier with the *Courrier de l'Eure,* whose "secret, malevolent resistance to all the [administration's] political acts" cost it all favors.

Administrative papers sometimes performed well enough for many years before dissension set in. The *Journal de l'Aveyron* at Rodez fought the legitimist *Echo de l'Aveyron* for more than three years before the prefect cast it off to promote the *Aigle,* which in 1860 became the *Napoléonien.* For an even longer period, the prefect of the Côtes-du-Nord maneuvered the *Bretagne* against the legitimist *Foi Bretonne* only to assent to the former's suppression in 1860. He substituted the newly founded *Armorique.*[38]

The governmental press failed to hold its own in a few *départements,* even after nearly a decade of press controls. In the Gironde, the Napoleonic *Mémorial Bordelais,* so badly run that the prefect contemptuously dismissed it as "more compromising than useful," was not improved upon by the Orleanist *Courrier de la Gironde* whose owners did no more than "feign" a correct attitude. Other competitors were the negligible *Indicateur,* "reformed" republican, and the legitimist *Guienne,* the strongest paper. Despite its prefect's efforts, the Gironde entered the sixties with only 1,985 subscribers to governmental papers compared with the legitimist, Orleanist, and republican opposition's 8,289. In a more evenly balanced situation, the *Côte d'Or,* in spite of the administration's creation of the *Elu du Peuple* at Dijon, counted a circulation of 3,200 for two governmental papers and 3,950 for the royalist and republican opposition.

In *départements* near Paris, the local press balance was overwhelmed by the metropolitan papers, though in an erratic political pattern. In the Seine-et-Oise, the one local paper printed little but *annonces judiciaires.* In 1859, subscribers to Parisian newspapers numbered 7,865; the governmental *Constitutionnel* led with 2,293; the oppositionist *Siècle* was next with 1,325. But in the Maine-et-Loire, one legitimist paper was a "bad influence," the administrative paper was sometimes intractable, and the Parisian opposition prevailed.[39]

The "Balanced" Press in the Nord

Outside Paris, the Nord offered the greatest challenge to the art of "balancing" the press. In the eighteen months before the press law of 1852, the Nord lost at least nine "socialist" or "ultra-democratic" newspapers in one way or another. But (see chapter 2) it emerged from the coup d'état with a large press that ran through the allowable political spectrum. Four papers succumbed soon after the new law for lack of caution money. Twenty-two survived.

Prefect Besson's task was only relatively simplified. He still had to ensure the predominance of reliable papers in the principal cities. In a few smaller one-newspaper towns, Besson doled out shares of the *annonces* to such "devoted" recipients as the *Observateur d'Avesnes* and the semiclerical *Indicateur d'Haze-brouck*. The *Indicateur de Tourcoing* and, at Cassel, the *Observateur du Nord*, were uninfluential weeklies already favorable to the regime without further inducement. At Valenciennes, the *Courrier du Nord*, republican in the Cavaignac tradition, "rallied" to the extent of remaining "inoffensive" until it ceased publication in 1857. The *Impartial du Nord*, of the moderate parliamentary opposition, "rallied" in 1852 and gained influence. The legitimist *Echo de la Frontière* was "very devoted" until it strayed in the later fifties.

Dunkerque was more complex. The legitimist *Commerce* came around within a few months; in January, 1853, it became the *Vingt Novembre* under the slogan, "L'Empire c'est la Paix." *Le Dunkerquoise*, an old Orleanist paper, seemed to be "approaching us," Besson noted in 1853; but it remained unreliable and gradually declined without administrative patronage. It sold out in 1854 and its facilities passed to the new governmental *Autorité*. There remained the radical republican *Journal de Dunkerque*, which yielded to various pressures and quit in 1854. By the mid-fifties, the administration prevailed.

Cambrai posed one problem. The *Emancipateur*, clerical and legitimist, followed Louis Napoleon "quite frankly" at first, then settled into opposition. Countering it with every administrative favor was the *Gazette de Cambrai*, "devoted" since 1848. In

Douai were three opposition papers in 1852. The very weak republican *Indicateur du Nord* collapsed after two warnings in September, 1854. An unrepentant legitimist *Réformiste*, chastened by a warning in April, 1852, remained impotently hostile and hence tolerable with a negligible circulation of 150. Besson wooed and won the third and largest paper, the Orleanist *Indépendant*. It was owned by a company into which enough Bonapartists had infiltrated by 1853 to make it governmental with a satisfying share of the *annonces judiciaires*. Besson refused to recommend the requests of three successive owners of the non-political *Industriel de Cambrai* for authorization as a political newspaper. He rejected two supplicants because of their past "demagogic" associations, and the third because of a "doubtful" political background. Besson's real reason was probably the one he repeatedly gave to the ministry. Not only would another newspaper be "useless" in Cambrai—press surveillance was more effective when it could be "concentrated" on fewer targets.

Besson's real problems arose in Lille. One small, friendly weekly in December, 1852, snapped under the strain of posting twenty-five thousand francs in caution money, reducing the prefect to only one governmental paper—the daily *Journal de Lille*, well edited and at first "devoted." But during 1852 its growing penchant for criticism cost the newspaper its prefectorial support, and its presses stopped in January, 1853. Besson now needed a reliable counterweight to three opposition journals which, if not incorrigible, did withhold positive support. The republican *Echo du Nord* carried its hostility to the nether brink of the press laws, and Besson saw no point in wooing it. The ultralegitimist *Gazette de Flandre et d'Artois* was a "bad influence." More conciliatory and highly opportunistic was the widely read *Liberté*, which dexterously catered to both legitimists and Orleanists. By January, 1853, after a few overtures, Besson decided that at best the *Liberté* would give only "timid support" and would revert to opposition at the first profitable temptation.

With aid from Paris, which proved to be a mixed blessing, Besson maneuvered for control in Lille. In December, 1852, he had encouraged a Parisian business man to finance 90 per cent of *Le Nord,* a new political daily, to replace the defunct *Journal de Lille* whose subscribers it inherited. Besson groomed the *Nord* "to support the great principles of the imperial government" and to re-educate the people of Lille—"cold, apathetic, inclined to criticism and opposition, and until now lacking political direction." Meanwhile, one Edouard Reboux sought authorization for a new paper "entirely devoted to the government," provided he were assured of the *annonces* and other administrative favors. His application dragged on until 1854, when Collet-Meygret, then head of the Sûreté Générale in the Ministry of the Interior, acquired a personal interest in the proposed venture. Besson saw in this another fortuitous moment to reinforce the *Nord.* At that moment, the *Liberté* and *Gazette de Flandre et d'Artois* were being suppressed by judicial condemnations. Besson now strongly endorsed Reboux's request to found *La Vérité,* which would give the prefecture "an excellent journal in place of two hostile organs."

Actually, Besson gained two supposedly docile papers under the same management: the morning *Courrier de Lille,* which did not prosper, and the evening *Vérité,* which did. Beginning in April, 1854, under Reboux and partner Jacques Louis Lardin, *Vérité* reached a circulation of 2,500 in 1855, whereupon Besson's troubles multiplied. Lardin clashed with both Reboux and an editor specially attached to the paper by Collet-Meygret. Besson turned on Lardin because he "had only been an embarrassment and adversary for the prefecture instead of keeping his promise to be a docile and useful instrument." The prefect thereafter sniped at Lardin's papers, warning both and suspending the *Vérité* on a technicality in February, 1856. Besson meanwhile sought a new administrative paper to replace Lardin. But Collet-Meygret favored Lardin. Persisting, Besson demanded the ministry's support for a new paper and continued to pick away at Lardin's papers. He demanded warnings for both the *Courrier* and *Vérité* but the ministry refused, though Besson's warnings were actually drafted. In February, 1857, Besson had both papers prosecuted and condemned for unsigned articles; whereupon Lardin appealed directly to Napoleon III against the verdicts.

At this point, Lardin's fortunes waned. His appeal failed. He lost a lawsuit for eight thousand francs to his partner Reboux; and Collet-Meygret left the ministry. Besson at last won an official warning against *Vérité* and authorization for a new administrative journal. But when the latter had organizational problems, Besson abandoned it, had its approval canceled, and instead launched the *Mémorial de Lille* in February, 1857, as a model administrative paper under Lardin's ex-partner Edouard Reboux. Now thoroughly bypassed, Lardin lost the *Courrier* in May, 1857. The *Vérité* was suppressed in October after two judicial condemnations and the *procureur* at Douai refused to endorse Lardin's request for reinstatement through imperial clemency. As an administrative paper, the *Mémorial* had better luck. When it faced possible judicial suppression in 1858 after losing two civil suits, the *procureur* at Douai and the Minister of Justice interceded to obtain pardon. The paper remained ardently Bonapartist throughout the rest of the Second Empire and during the early years of the Third Republic. Meanwhile, by 1858 the prefect of the Nord could look upon the departmental press with some satisfaction.[40]

CONCLUSION

Until the later fifties, officialdom was a bit complacent when viewing the controlled press. In 1854 the prefects heard from their minister: "Today, happy results are evident in the press except for rare exceptions. It displays an attitude for which the government can only congratulate itself." Outwardly such confidence seemed justified, though some uneasiness was revived when the Paris opposition in 1858 printed about 8 per cent more copies than the governmental papers.

Despite its short-run success, the "balanced" press policy failed in certain essentials. Paralleling the inability to fuse "local influences" into a truly "national" or Bonapartist body politic, the controlled press never became a basically loyal or homogeneous one. A common observation on the part of the prefects concerning "rallied" and "governmental" newspapers was the prediction that in a less controlled situation they would desert their benefactor. Questioning of the Empire's doctrines, institutions, and legitimacy continued, however obliquely. It has been a justified commonplace to point out that journalists developed a flair for satirical and other critical subtleties that pricked and probed up to the limit of administrative tolerance and legality. As the *procureur* at Douai noted, certain of the opposition papers even preserved the essence of their republican aspirations. Obliged to be prudent on large issues, they gave local events "a slant designed to nourish their followers' passions." The opposition press as a whole was showing a stronger critical bent as the fifties ended.[41]

The control techniques of the fifties had some perhaps unforeseen long-range results. As a prominent journalist began to note later on, the earlier system of preliminary authorization, subsidies, and the wooing and toleration of opposition newspapers actually strengthened them financially and morally. Safe from new competition, prosperous, and acquiring public prestige by contrast with the obviously kept press, the larger opposition journals gathered confidence and momentum for a more outspoken role in the sixties.[42] This held most true in Paris, where by 1859 officials were showing their alarm at the increasing circulation of metropolitan papers in the provinces. Though enemies of the press law usually loosed their spleen on official warnings and other forms of official fiat, even these administrative powers had an ironic advantage for opposition editors. When the law of 1852 shifted most press offenses to the jurisdiction of the correctional courts whose judges were more rigidly bound to inflict prescribed penalties than were the juries of the assize courts, sentences were harsher. But the administration placed more emphasis upon its own control methods than it did on prosecutions. As a result, the surviving newspapers probably fared better financially than would have been their lot in the courts, where heavy fines and prison sentences could have driven many into bankruptcy and disrupted their organization.

A more liberal policy might have allowed the governmental press to follow a divide-and-rule tactic; a stricter one might have driven the opposition from the field. The "balanced" press policy of the fifties, unbalanced as it was in the government's favor, accomplished neither.

The *Commissaires,* Gendarmerie, and Rural Police

THE DEGREE to which the prefects could achieve a political police of high quality, capable of realizing either the repressive or tutelary ideals of the administrative mission, depended upon the lower police functionaries who were their agents in the care of the *sûreté générale.* During the Second Empire, these men, to use the administrator's cliché, "left much to be desired." They were too often wanting in the high aptitudes and zealous singleness of purpose demanded by the ideal administrative state. And, despite some modest police reforms in the fifties, "local influences" arose to thwart the prefects' hopes of building an expanded, more cooperative and efficient team of disparate police forces. The *commissaires* of police, gendarmerie, and rural policemen lived in their particular functionary's worlds which touched but did not coincide within the prefects' wider domains.

THE *COMMISSAIRES* OF POLICE

The *commissaire* rather than the more remote prefect, was, in most provincials' daily lives, the familiar symbol of the state. Town and country dwellers who could not have recited the *commissaire*'s legal status as "permanent delegate of the executive power" knew that his blue, black, and silver uniform—or more usual, simply his tricolor sash—personified the central authority. Most would probably have agreed that the *commissaires*

... are busy day and night, going everywhere in unforeseen circumstances, giving ceaseless attention to the vital interests of society. . . . Thus their function is complex . . . and their official sphere includes everything pertaining to justice and society.[1]

206

The Second Empire changed neither the *commissaire*'s traditional status nor his long working day. It broadened his territorial jurisdiction, notably in the cantonal *commissariats* of 1852, moderately increased (then decreased) his numbers, raised his pay, and tried with only partial success to adapt his services to an era of growth and change.

Appointment and Status

The *commissaire* owed his formal appointment and his obedience to the prefect, before whom he swore his oath of office. After the "decentralization" decree of 1852 and the conflict with the Ministry of Police over appointments of cantonal officers, the prefects in towns of six thousand or under named the *commissaires* on recommendation by the mayors. Elsewhere, the chief of state appointed them on the prefects' recommendation. Beginning in 1854, the Minister of the Interior kept a central list of candidates recommended by the prefects and other persons as a "pool" from which vacant positions could be readily filled.[2]

Despite low salaries, applications were numerous. No systematic mode of recruitment or professional training—beyond publication of the unpretentious but concisely informative *Journal des Commissaires de Police* after 1854—were developed during the Second Empire. Applicants wrote directly to the prefects or the ministry, preferably armed with recommendations from influential patrons, or exploited "local influences." In appointing *commissaires,* as in so much else, the prefects often tacitly yielded to the very local influences they so chronically deplored. If not, the prefect's appointees themselves soon adapted to local realities. Most prefects would have agreed with a colleague who warned Persigny that the greatest threat to good police administration arose from these underpaid officers' acceptance of the patronage and advice of influential local men. From *commissaires* "devoted to their protectors" and using police powers for their benefit, this critic believed, the administration "will know only what they deign to let it know."[3] Although new *commissaires* were not supposed to be appointed in their native regions or where they had close acquaintances, the rule was often ignored.

Preferably the *commissaires* were recruited from ex-noncommissioned army officers or the gendarmerie, ex-mayors, and minor functionaries. In 1852, Maupas defined the qualification most desired: "an unequivocal, absolute devotion to the present government and the principles that have legitimized it."[4]

For a low-salaried official recruited so casually, the *commissaire* of police had a very crucial part in the integrated mechanisms of general administration, police operations, and judiciary procedures. His office was an administrative junction for the work of prefects and subprefects, municipal officials and policemen, the gendarmerie, rural policemen, the judiciary police, and the judicial system itself. In his official relations with four kinds of authority—prefectorial, municipal, judicial, and military—the *commissaire* found conflicts built into his situation, which reflected the "interpenetration" of police functions in administrative theory. He needed tact and flexibility to keep abreast of his complex responsibilities amidst chronic tensions and clashes among various chains of command.

Service manuals and writers on police doctrine consistently stressed that *commissaires,* as "agents of the government" and general police officers, must maintain their "administrative independence." They must never forget their pre-eminent status as "political functionaries under the direct and immediate authority of the prefect." Commissaire Emile Thomas's service handbook reminded his readers that "independence is the great principle of our authority. . . . We are the *commissaires* of police of no person. We are the law. . . . The state has placed an unbounded confidence in us by declaring us absolute masters in our own office."[5]

Beyond the *commissaire's* various administrative relationships extended the further problem of public relations. Frequently sought out as arbiter, conciliator, and counselor—or approached as the "discreet confidant" of the citizenry in the privacy of his office—he became "on the civil plane what the priest is in the religious sphere." He must be available to the public "at any moment of the day or night," willing always "to hear complaints . . . and to give prompt and equitable satisfaction."[6] Obviously, a good *commissaire* must be a man of many parts. If he were not already so, there was ample literature to instruct him in self-improvement and to indoctrinate him in the highest ideals of the administrative attitude.

The Ideal Commissaire

Manuals, booklets, and articles in the *Journal des Commissaires de Police* portrayed the ideal *commissaire*. Whatever the size of his district, the busy officer ran his office usually without secretarial aid, lived harmoniously with his several official and unofficial lives, and stood ready to act against the government's political foes or to cope with fire, flood, riot, or "any other danger of the day and night."[7] He must aspire also to the higher standards the Second Empire set for its servants.

His day was long. "A good *commissaire* arises early," he was told, and should be the last to bed. The day began and ended by hearing the reports of his agents and giving them new orders for the day or night. He must see that his *sergent de ville* kept busy and "always [had] something to think about." After consulting his memoranda on current business and running through his correspondence in the early morning, the *commissaire* made an inspection, "opening his eyes and ears, seeing everything and taking notes." Along the way he should talk to anyone who wished a word and invite such persons into his office "if the matter is worth the trouble." He answered mail, received complaints, and called on the mayor, carefully making notes on the interview as soon as he returned to his own office. He called frequently upon the *curé*. He chatted at every opportunity with "experienced men" on various topics, hoping to enrich his own knowledge and perception. By bedtime, he could reflect upon a "well-filled day," with no duty neglected, all records and correspondence up to date, and no loopholes left open.

If he were a cantonal officer, the *commissaire* regularly toured all the communes of his district, "not leaving any town or village until he knows it by heart." He visited the merchants, verified weights and measures and the quality of merchandise and produce, not forgetting to peer into the cabarets in order "to warn or threaten" the more dubious establishments pointed out by the mayor or the local police. He took notes on the harvest and the political situation. After a final stroll around the town, the touring *commissaire* departed, leaving an impression of himself as the "first, faithful, and punctual representative of the constant solicitude of the Sovereign."

The editor of the *Journal des Commissaires de Police* devoted its pages to encouraging the growth of an upright, efficient, and informed police service. He predicted in one of his first issues that the *commissariat* "will increasingly merge into our customs and soon be counted among our most popular institutions." Had the *commissaires* been transfigured into the paragons of virtue and virtuosity pictured by their tutors, the prediction might indeed have come true.

Above all, the *commissaire* was enjoined to be tactful with everyone. Never forgetting his "administrative independence," he must not display it too brusquely. To mayors, the judiciary police, and gendarmerie officers he owed dignified cooperation and a pleasant mien, but no subservience. Yet he must scrupulously avoid jurisdictional disputes—"that plague of administrations!" A manual advised that "the mayors, though not our superiors, deserve our marked deference. . . . We must deal with them within the bounds of a respectful propriety," keeping strictly within the *commissaires'* assigned legal sphere. Relationships with the gendarmerie, always zealous in the assertion of their own "independence," received great attention. The respective legal functions and powers of *commissaires* and gendarmes were repeatedly defined for the former's benefit. Perhaps nodding in agreement, the *commissaire* could read in one manual:

> Without exaggerating the difficulty of maintaining good relations with the gendarmerie, it is no less true that a certain usually-involuntary suspicion . . . makes the gendarme the sworn antagonist of the *commissaire* of police.

Still, the *commissaire* must avoid conflicts and try to become "comrades without familiarity" of gendarmerie officers, never seeking close private association.

A good *commissaire* respectfully cultivated the clergy because he knew their value in propagating religion as the "safeguard" of society, thus involuntarily assisting preventive police. Whatever his inward convictions, he must always be publicly deferential to religion, never speaking lightly of God or the saints, "leaving that vile amusement to young libertines." The ideal *commissaire* was morally impeccable. He lived "a modest and dignified private life, open for all to see, transparent as the proverbial glass house." His ethics were undiluted. His integrity met "every test." He was moderate and impartially just. Communicating perceptively and sympathetically with persons of all social classes at their respective intellectual levels, he must be firm, yet absolutely impartial, and respectful of confidences, dispensing justice equally among the rich or poor, the educated or unenlightened. Toward the public generally the good *commissaire* was considerate, never domineering. This advice hummed in his ears: "The public is not our subordinate. Thus we must forego all offensive expressions, especially that air of the absolute master assumed by so many petty men."

An ideal *commissaire* was erudite and cultivated. He studied administrative, civil, criminal, and commercial law; and he must "know a little of architecture and ordinary medicine." While "studying incessantly the trends of social economy," he must at any time be able to descend from such heights to the details of traffic control, public lighting, street-cleaning, and practical politics. Poised, articulate, a man of taste, he spurned the vulgarities of life and appeared "well-reared, modest, reserved with superiors and kindly toward subordinates." A *commissaire* never mixed personally in public brawls, which would lower the dignity of his station. He relied upon subordinate policemen in such affairs. This was not a question of bravery—a *commissaire* was eminently courageous—but rather because "the man of good society has nothing to gain by direct contact with the vulgarity of drunkards and blusterers." Police business was discussed with dignity and discretion, never on the street but always in the "sanctuary" of the *commissaire*'s office.

To become an ideal *commissaire* was to embrace loneliness. Administrative independence meant the sacrifice of personal commitments or close friendship with members of the community.

Standing above all parties, factions, and local interests, the *commissaire* acted only as "the devoted, impartial, and incorruptible
agent of the government." The point was often made more forcefully:

> "Never, absolutely never, have a confidant in the locality. . . . Because of
> what he is, the *commissaire* of police has no real friends. For honorable
> though we may be, the very nature of our public office engenders distrust."
> Friends must be found only among other *commissaires*. Indeed, this would
> encourage a strong *esprit de corps* that in time would make the service "a
> veritable moral force that will be called—order!"

The *commissaire*'s prime duty was to unmask "enemies of the
government." To this end, he must regard nothing as beyond
his rightful surveillance. He must know and demonstrate that
"the state is a family, whose leader and father is the Emperor."
He must show that his police mission was "to prevent the mis-
fortunes that could fall upon a good, but credulous and impres-
sionable, people." Crude or brutal methods were disdained; the
rights of good citizens must be respected. "The political police
requires a rare tact, delicacy, and exactness of judgment. . . .
Avoid making your political police vexatious, and never earn the
name of lowly police spy!"

Numbers and Distribution

Before the introduction of cantonal *commissariats* in March,
1852, *commissaires* of police were obligatory only in towns of
five thousand or more population, and in a legal ratio of one
officer to every ten thousand people. For various reasons, principally financial, this provision was not strictly enforced before
1855. Before 1852, these cities (excluding the Seine) maintained
513 *commissaires*. On the other hand, many smaller towns in the
early nineteenth century recognized a need and voluntarily established their own *commissaires,* adding another 487. The reform
of 1852 led to the appointment of 745 more by 1855, or a total
of 1,745—of which 1,232 served towns of under five thousand
people.

Until 1855, all the increase went to the smaller towns and,
through the cantonal jurisdiction and state financial aid, indirectly

to small communes which otherwise could not have afforded their own officers. In the larger cities, the legal ratio of *commissaires* to population was more accurately maintained after 1855. In March, 1860, the number of *commissaires* of all types in France (including under a hundred "special *commissaires*" on specific missions for the Interior) reached its peak of 2,150. Only 1,886 were cantonal officers, though France had 2,850 cantons before the territorial annexations of 1860. The ultimate goal of extending the cantonal jurisdiction to the entire country was never achieved. Rather, the cantonal *commissariats* were reduced to 1,475 by 1868.[8]

Regionally, the distribution of *commissaires* was extended in the fifties but it remained uneven in many places, adding to the already formidable burden upon the capacities and time of the hard-worked *commissaires*. Of forty officers in the Bouches-du-Rhône, half were concentrated in Marseille's six cantons. In the Rhône, whose *commissaires* increased from thirty-two to thirty-four between 1854 and 1860, nineteen were in Lyon. Excepting the Seine, the Nord had the greatest number (from sixty-two to seventy, during 1854–60); the Hautes-Alpes (seven throughout the fifties) and Lozère (seven during the same period) had the fewest. Thirteen *départements* had thirty or more *commissaires*. Only four had ten or less.

Despite official hopes of eventual uniformity, the regional jurisdictions of the various *commissaires* varied greatly. At the end of 1854, some operated within only one commune or a portion thereof. Others had an entire canton, either as a portion of a large city or a cluster of rural communes. A few had two or three cantons. Many had a canton plus some communes of an adjacent canton. Occasionally two *commissaires* divided one canton, as in the Calvados, where two officers policed twenty communes. Outside large urban centers, cantonal *commissaires* might have more than five communes to administer, though the average ran somewhat less. In Nîmes, to cite one instance of regional variation, five *commissaires* resided. One had jurisdiction over an entire *arrondissement* including several cantons; another had one canton plus one commune; and a third had a canton plus two communes.

The other two *commissaires* policed two and three cantons, re-spectively. Between 1854 and 1860, forty-four *départements* in-creased their number of *commissaires;* twenty-three did not; and eighteen lost *commissariats.* After 1860, further reductions were the rule.[9]

The Reform of February, 1855

A decree of February 27, 1855, established a uniform service classification and pay scale for the *commissaires* of police. Long overdue, this had been promised in the decree of March, 1852. Until 1855, the *commissaires* of towns over five thousand were still paid the salaries fixed in 1813.

In a report to the Emperor, Minister of the Interior Billault summarized the "deplorable deficiencies" resulting from forty-two years without increases. Many officers' salaries were "well below even the most ordinary requirements of life." In smaller towns which had created their own *commissariats,* incomes were even lower. Eighty of the 1,232 *commissaires* in towns under five thousand received annually less than eight hundred francs (about $160) and only 327 received as much as fifteen hundred francs or more. The ninety-seven highest-paid *commissaires* in France received an average of three thousand francs in salary and office expenses combined. Some communes had taken the initiative to increase their *commissaires'* incomes through such devices as bonuses, extra funds for office expense, and the like. Many others had not. The results, Billault declared, were neither equitable nor conducive to an honest, efficient police force, and he proposed reform.

The *commissaires* were classified in five pay categories, accord-ing to the size and importance of their towns of residence. Their new annual salaries and office expenses combined, as compared with the old system, were 4,800 francs, or twice as much as be-fore; 3,600 francs compared with 1,950; 2,400 francs over 1,550; 1,800:1,250; and 1,440:1,000.[10] Still, for most of the *commissaires,* the full millennium had not arrived. Only 55 quali-fied for the highest pay grade. The majority—143, 168, 123, and 1,256, respectively—fell within the four lower grades. The *com-*

missaires, though better off than before, were still left short of affluence.

As the prefect of the Côtes-du-Nord pointed out early in 1855, the fifties were inflationary years, and the pay of most functionaries, meager enough in ordinary times, had become quite insufficient in a time of rising prices. Lacking a national pension plan, although a few cities voluntarily pensioned their retired officers, and without any professional organization, the *commissaires* along with other lower functionaries continued to endure economic hardship, as the prefects frequently reported.

In the Hérault, a *commissaire,* driven by acute financial need, stole watches and money from prisoners. Another, promoted to a better post in the Jura, lacked the money to move his household until the prefect arranged a small subsidy. The prefect of the Nord protested to the Minister of the Interior about the "truly insufficient" income of his *commissaires* at Roubaix, where high rents and other expenses kept those with families constantly "at grips with misery" and undermined "the dignity of the administration" itself. *Commissaires* often found it difficult or impossible to buy their besilvered uniforms; fortunately, the indispensable tricolor sash alone endowed its wearer with ample police authority. Funds permitting, the prefects and the Minister of the Interior sometimes managed small "merit" awards.[11] Although the spokesmen of police doctrine often told him that he was "the principal link between government and people," the *commissaire* of the Second Empire was coddled by neither.

Public and Administrative Criticism

Twice the salary probably would not have drawn men with the personality and virtuosity demanded of the ideal *commissaire.* Mere mortals after all, the real *commissaires* were targets of spirited public and administrative criticism. Public attitudes varied. Political enemies of the dictatorship regarded all police officers as symbols of tyranny and the *commissaires* as especially invidious because of their crucial functions. All critics found certain *commissaires* wanting in aptitude and professional skills. Some were charged with "excessive zeal," though they were chosen for political loyalty. Others were condemned for lethargy. Imperialists approved the *commissaires* as an institution while often balking at paying the costs of extending the system. Irate taxpayers abounded during the Second Empire.

Often enough it was not the officer himself but his traditional multipartite administrative role, with mayors, *procureurs,* and prefects pulling him in three directions at once, that drew officials' criticisms. That source of "embarrassments and wrangling which always hinder spontaneity and liberty of action . . . causing loss of precious time," drew the attention of many prefects who would have preferred absolute control over the *commissaires* themselves. It was usually charged that involvements with mayors and municipal police, wherein myopic local factionalism obstructed the *commissaires'* "prime duty of political police," constituted the worst abuse.[12]

Reform-minded *commissaires* could occasionally castigate their less zealous colleagues as severely as anyone. One of these, though writing just before the coup d'état, painted a broad canvas of faults that could just as well have been copied from some of the recurrent complaints of the fifties. He denounced the "intemperate and brutal" *commissaire* along with his opposite, "indolent and almost ridiculous, betrayed by his weakness and inactivity." Too many, he said, lacked proper training and were indifferent to self-improvement, merely following the uninspiring example of their equally detached predecessors. The result was a "thick-headed police, unintelligent, often culpable," that brought discredit upon the government represented by such officers. "People will not draw the fine distinction," he believed, "between law and morality as such, and the behavior of administrators themselves." What would people think of their government, he asked rhetorically, when it was too often personified by *commissaires* who tried to hide their incompetence behind arrogance and pride, or who behaved frivolously, like "superannuated charlatans," or "gadabout dandies trying to draw the besotted attention of provincial boobs"? The same writer found equally deplorable those *commissaires* "whose sole distinctions are fashionable dress, affected manners and speech, and spending most of their time in cafés, thereby neglecting their work." This disgruntled reformer-*commissaire* blamed the deficiencies of many colleagues upon inadequate pay, "which makes their positions precarious and their dispositions vicious," forcing the administration to take its *commissaires* wherever they could be found regardless of minimum qualifications.[13]

The Cantonal Commissaires *and "Local Influences"*

Until the end of the Second Empire, the cantonal *commissaires* were most criticized of all. It was not that their human frailties in an exacting, overworked, and ill-paid job were more striking than those of other *commissaires*. The cantonal jurisdiction awakened the stubborn financial resistance of the communes, heretofore not forced to tax themselves for the luxury of such police protection. This form of "local influences" prevented the establishment of cantonal *commissaires* in about a third of the nation's communes even at the peak of the institution's existence.

In 1852, one of the more sanguine functionaries had predicted that the new cantonal jurisdiction would fulfill one of "the most pressing needs of the upward progress of our times." The government expected the cantonal officers to coordinate all branches of police activity, build a better rural police, assist the gendarmerie, improve judiciary police procedures in smaller communes, and link them more closely to the prefect, especially in political police.[14] This was only partly achieved.

The prefects, and occasionally the *procureurs,* at first resented the cantonal *commissaires* as an arm of the Ministry of Police. Later they approved the concept because it strengthened the prefects' central control. Their criticism then centered less on the institution than on the human failings of certain overzealous, incompetent, or indifferent officers.

The *procureurs* criticized individual *commissaires* mainly for ignorance of judiciary police technicalities. The *procureur* at Lyon found nearly all *commissaires* in the Saône-et-Loire crudely severe, untrained, poorly distributed geographically, and generally useless to the justices of the peace. But in the Haute-Marne he approved their work in most cases, though not all of his justices of the peace would say as much. In the Côte-d'Or, his third *département*, he endorsed about half of the cantonal *commissaires*. His colleague at Montpellier questioned the competence of many; and the *procureur* at Nîmes thought some very good and others very bad. His prodding of the prefects of the Gard and Vaucluse to remove the bad officers caused the two prefects facetiously to agree to appoint anyone the *procureur* named if he could find qualified men in France. In the Var, the judiciary police accused the *commissaires* of neglect of duty and personal inability to "measure up to the demands of their mission." Such criticisms continued steadily through the 1860's. The *procureur* at Dijon rather typically concluded that "the institution of cantonal *commissaire* sins less in itself than by the men who bring it to life."[15]

The prefects made similar criticisms with less emphasis on failings in judiciary police procedure and more tolerance once the *commissaires* were dissociated from the Ministry of Police. In the Tarn-et-Garonne, Prefect Chambaron in 1853 saw little to praise: "They fail to see that the police must protect the citizens without irritating them. Either by negligence or excessive zeal, they provoked well-deserved complaints." Chambaron's successor added that far too many showed "a profound ignorance of the basic elements of their duties. Some lack the dignity demanded by their magistracy. Several leave much to be desired in temperance and morality. This corps needs to be purged." The standard locution, "leave much to be desired," was often applied to the *commissaires*.

Yet many prefects complained that more cantonal appointments were not made. This was true in the Ardennes, where the prefect liked the *commissaires'* rural police work; and in the Hérault, where the mayors of small communes improved under the scrutiny of cantonal officers. Similar reports came from the Aube, where twenty-three of twenty-six cantons had *commissaires;* and from the Haute-Saône, where Prefect Dieu wished only that he had more time for their closer supervision and coordination. In the Seine-et-Oise, the *commissaires* rendered "incontestable services" in tactfully preventing offenses as well as repressing them.[16]

The Ministry of the Interior apparently feared that too many *commissaires* displayed "inordinate zeal" unbefitting a "paternal and tutelary regime." In 1853 the Minister warned the prefects that the *commissaires* must not irritate the public needlessly. "Unfortunately," Persigny said, "all do not seem to have formed a proper concept of their mission."[17]

The Minister's sensitivity to the *commissaires'* public relations related to "local influences." Much of the prefects' grumbling on the personal shortcomings of *commissaires* and the failure to establish them in cantons where the need was clear, was related to the communes' influence in choosing the officers and in blocking appointments altogether in certain cantons. Municipal resistance was reported from all parts of France. "Everywhere . . . I have met a tendency to resist this measure," wrote the prefect of the Ain shortly after the decree of 1852, adding that he expected all the newly elected municipal councils to object.

Seven years later the same complaint was still reaching Paris. In the Vienne, for example, one of the few cantonal *commissaires,* with only two subordinate policemen, had charge of six communes and twenty thousand people. Another prefect in the Pyrenées-Orientales had two cantons and forty-two communes, while other *commissariats* were being abolished in the *département*. In the country at large, reductions began after 1860. In 1860, 1,886 cantonal *commissaires* were in service. In January, 1868, there were 1,475. Just after the fall of the Empire in 1870 they were suppressed altogether (to be quietly revived after May, 1875, under another name), on the grounds that they violated communal rights.

The rights in question were financial. Municipal councils did not necessarily oppose the idea of the cantonal *commissaires* per se. But they did oppose increasing their local taxes to pay the officers. As the ministers of Justice and Interior admitted to one another in 1854, there simply was not enough money forthcoming to extend the system of *commissariats* and attract men with the ideal qualities desired.[18]

Legally, the government could have forced the communes to support *commissaires* in all cantons. Like earlier regimes, it hesitated to use its full powers. The law of 1800, which created the communal *commissaires* in larger towns, allowed the administration arbitrarily to levy the cost on the commune in order to maintain the ratio of *commissaires* to population. As already indicated, until the Second Empire that legal ratio was not well enforced, though some communes had supported *commissaires* on their own initiative.

The reforms of the fifties suddenly threw an unaccustomed burden on smaller communes. The decree of March 25, 1852, on cantonal *commissaires* made a part of their cost obligatory on every commune in the canton—the amount to be decided by the prefect. For the first 738 cantonal officers under the 1852 law, the state paid one-quarter of the expense, slowly reducing this until by 1865 it paid only one-twelfth. Furthermore, the 1855 pay increases again weighted the burden, together with more literal enforcement of the *commissaire*-population ratio. The law of 1855 further provided that if the communes refused to pay their share the administration would invoke its full coercive powers. Nonetheless, after three years of aroused "local influences," two concessions were also made in 1855. The commune's contribution would be in proportion to its population; and the prefects were instructed to use coercion only very rarely. Before assessing any commune, the prefects must study its finances and then assess according to capacity to pay.[19] After 1855, the state less frequently forced cantonal *commissaires* on unwilling communes, regardless of need. But the significant reduction of *commissariats* began only in the late sixties.

The Central Commissaires *of Police*

Beginning at Marseille in 1823, a few larger cities designated "central" *commissaires* to coordinate urban police work and supervise the other *commissaires*. Extending the practice, a decree of March 22, 1854, authorized one central *commissaire* in each of twenty-three large *chefs-lieux* of *départements*. These officials received general police authority over the entire *arrondissement*. The Minister of the Interior carefully reassured the prefects that this relative centralization in no way violated tradition. It bore, he said, no relationship to the defunct and unlamented departmental *commissaires*, being merely an application of the doctrine that police "is one of the most intimate branches of administration" never to be isolated from prefectorial functions. In other large cities with central *commissaires*, the prefects could specially delegate their own police authority to central *commissaires* for an entire *arrondissement*. The twenty-three central *commissaires* affected by the 1854 measure and those with delegated prefectorial authority were the direct superiors of other *commissaires* only in their own city. Elsewhere in the *arrondissement* the other *commissaires*, though obligated to cooperate with the central officer in general police, remained the direct chiefs of their own men. In purely municipal police, the central *commissaire* answered to the mayor until Article 50 of the municipal law of 1855 placed those in seventeen large cities directly under the prefects in both municipal and general police.

In the mid-fifties, thirty-seven central *commissaires* were in office. Although on paper they—especially those with authority over an *arrondissement*—extended the centralization of general police, the effects were probably most felt in the municipal police of the city of residence. One wonders, for example, how much wider political police improvement was achieved by the central *commissaire* in the city and *arrondissement* of Valence, with 102 communes, 155,017 people, and only three other *commissaires* to sustain the general police function in addition to their other duties. Henri Chevreau of the Loire-Inféreieure predicted, with some accuracy, that though the central *commissaires* had their virtues, they would be too busy for effective liaison with all their subordinates. Moreover, they would complicate the administrative confusion and tensions already inherent in the *commissaires'* functions.[20]

THE SPECIAL *COMMISSAIRES* OF POLICE

The Second Empire continued to use several categories of "special *commissaires*" inaugurated by earlier regimes since 1811. These officers differed from other *commissaires* in two decisive respects. The Ministry of the Interior paid their full salary for specifically circumscribed duties that left them free of the multiple administrative involvements of other *commissaires*. But like the others, they had both judiciary and general police authority and served a variety of political police objectives arising from their special tasks. They were not included in the reform of February, 1855, for communal and cantonal officers. But in October, 1859, they were assimilated with other *commissaires* with respect to uniform, pay, and official status.[21]

Special Commissaires *for the Domestic Book Trade*

After 1810, France employed a small number of *commissaires-inspecteurs de la librairie* in Paris and the *départements* for the surveillance of printing and the book trade. These officers' duties, but not their numbers, steadily increased during the fifties.

In Paris, two officers enforced laws dealing with copyrights; the licensing, inspection, and sale of printing shops, press and type manufacturers, and bookstores; and the makers and sellers of medals, stamps, and the like. They watched for political and moral violations and submitted bimonthly statistical reports on the circulation of Paris newspapers. Victor Gaillard, the senior of the two, also reported confidentially "on everything pertaining to the press," having two secret agents to assist him.

Ten other special *commissaires* shared the surveillance of 5,278 provincial printers and bookstores. They resided in Rouen, Tours, Lille, Strasbourg, Lyon, Marseille, Toulouse, Bordeaux, Nantes, and Limoges. In both Paris and the *départements,* these special *commissaires* were comparatively well paid, averaging four thousand francs annually.[22]

Frontier Inspectors of the Book Trade

The Second Empire inherited nineteen officers with the sonorous title *inspecteurs-vérificateurs de la librairie, établis à la frontière.* Originally a force of nine, installed by a royal ordinance of December, 1842, these officials examined imported printed matter at various customs posts, following an instruction manual which the Second Empire only slightly revised in 1853. In the fifties, the *commissaires-vérificateurs,* as they were then called, evaluated incoming materials from the viewpoints of literary proprietorship, public morality, and political content. Theirs was a strategic, if narrowed, political police assignment, though insignificant routine consumed much of their time. Poorly paid, increasingly overworked despite the addition of two more inspectors in 1859, this frontier police specialty was stranded in the backwaters of police reform.

Of the twenty-one agents on duty in 1859, only ten held full-salaried appointments yielding between nine hundred and two thousand francs per year. The other eleven received only variable annual "indemnities" for their services ranging, in 1853 for example, between one hundred and five hundred francs. The quantity of material to inspect increased steadily. In 1860, Inspector Lecomte at Le Havre, the highest paid of the group, received two thousand francs after eleven years of service. He handled 67,593 pounds of printed materials in 1859. The inspector at Strasbourg, a ten-year veteran rated among the best in the service, received twelve hundred francs for inspecting over 132,000 pounds in 1859. At Bordeaux, one Alexandre Dumas, with his mere 6,700 pounds of material, enjoyed no more than three hundred francs indemnity in any year of the fifties.

The service operated on a static annual budget of eighteen thousand francs; in 1859, a request for an increase to thirty-five thousand was parried by the ministerial counterproposal that the *commissaires* of police in frontier cities could assume some of the burden without extra cost to the state. Reform came belatedly in 1860–61. Five inspectors were added; and by April, 1861, a new budget of seventy-six thousand francs allowed some long-needed but modest salary adjustments. The service was again reduced in 1864 to twenty-two inspectors, fourteen of whom received a thousand francs or less. The other eight had from two thousand to three thousand francs annually.[23]

The *commissaires-vérificateurs* lived in chronic tension with the customs officers to whose stations they were attached. Victor Francis Gaillard, a conscientious and articulate officer rated "indispensable" by the Ministry in 1852, wrote of the loneliness and vexations of his frontier inspector's life in Bastia. One of his reports, though dated in 1846, typified the complaints more fragmentarily expressed in the fifties. Gaillard believed the men of his service should at least have financial equality with the more affluent customs men. An effective inspector, he submitted, needed greater aptitude than customs agents. The work called for a high order of perception and a "highly varied and profound knowledge" of literature, lest the officer fall into "the most ridiculous and perhaps serious mistakes." Gaillard asserted that a good inspector must know foreign languages, bibliography, printing processes, kinds of type, copyright laws, and pertinent international treaties. Never should he appear boorish or ignorant in dealing with "the most educated classes of society" who usually imported books.

But, woefully paid, without hope of betterment, and consigned to the disdain of the customs service, how could the inspectors fulfill the government's expectations? The service needed men who could master their assignment without inconvenience to the public and who would command the respect of the customs agents! Of the latter, Gaillard recalled his arrival at Bastia, where he met "a cold and even discourteous welcome from most of the customs employees." Relations gradually eased thereafter, but he never really penetrated "the corporate spirit of the customs service," whose members were "so spitefully touchy in everything seeming to affect their own prerogatives." They were efficient, he admitted, in their narrowly circumscribed duties, but obtuse in the presence of literary materials: "they measure the thoughts expressed by authors as they would measure a piece of calico."[24]

Special Commissaires of the Frontier Service

For criminal and political surveillance of travelers to and from France, earlier governments had maintained around twenty special commissaires of police at the principal passenger crossings along the frontiers. The service continued during the Second Empire as the coming of the railways and the use of special railway commissaires to check international passenger traffic increasingly transformed the old frontier posts into a stagnant obsolescence.

The frontier *commissaires* took orders from and reported to the prefects and occasionally the Minister of the Interior, recording relevant incidents and miscellaneous general data. In 1860, twenty-five special *commissaires* manned posts in seventeen small frontier communes. Those at Pont du Var and at Pont-du-Rhin (Bas-Rhin) each had a "special inspector" as an assistant. The officer at Le Mont-Doré (Puy-de-Dôme) was paid by the *département,* and another at Trelazé (Maine-et-Loire) by a privately operated slate quarry.[25]

Following the excitement of the coup d'état, life subsided into pallid routine for the frontier *commissaires* in the less-frequented border points. At the two posts in the Isère—Beauvoisin and Pontcharra—the officers tasted boredom, wrote their periodic reports, did errands and investigations for the prefect, and learned to nurse chronic occupational grievances. To fill their reports, they assayed public opinion on both sides of the border, sporadically described economic and administrative conditions, and always submitted their "observations on the movements of travelers." When not alerted for the suspected passage of an occasional fugitive or shipment of subversive literature, they noted the comings and goings of clerics and Italians with particular care. In passing flashes of sympathetic perception, one of them alluded to the harsh lives of the region's migrant workers. Their complaints ranged freely, returning most often to their relationships with the customs service, the absurdity of the frontier-crossing procedures, and the perverse negligence of French visa agencies which issued incorrect passports. After mid-1852, they seldom saw need to depart except in syntax from the political conclusion: "The government's enemies, particularly the demagogues, show an exemplary reserve and discretion."[26]

Over a span of time, their reports told something of themselves as well as of these minute parts of France. Summarizing his situation and duties, Commissaire Dussert at Beauvoisin outlined a lonely career without assistants, and little but disdain for the tiny community itself. Beauvoisin, without manufacturing or anything else "important," existed mainly because of its bridge across the frontier. Dussert's workday, formally undefined, embraced all hours when travelers were crossing. Pedestrians ap-

peared at any time of the day or night. Two carriages regularly
left France at six in the morning. At noon another entered France
from Chambéry bound for Lyon. Two postal vehicles clattered
past into Sardinia in mid-afternoon. The day was punctuated at
odd hours by various commercial or private carriers, and the
night by scheduled vehicles at nine, midnight, and two in the
morning. Then there was what Dussert called his "extraordinary
service": the reception of occasional French expellees from the
custody of the gendarmerie, and reporting consummation of their
expulsion to the Prefect of Police. Sometimes the gendarmes
brought Savoyard fugitives, arrested for illegal entry, to Dussert
for the necessary judiciary police paperwork before turning over
the culprits to departmental authorities at Tour-du-Pin. The
commissaire received and filed bulletins on fugitives or on suspected smuggling of political literature.

Dussert lamented the absence of municipal police in Beauvoisin,
whose mayor seemed quite indifferent. There was not even an
adequate rural police. The one *garde-champêtre* was, of course,
"useless." Beauvoisin itself had no gendarmerie brigade, though
Dussert had requested one; the nearest brigade of a half-dozen
men patrolled fourteen other communes as well. Without assistants, Dussert could not watch the frontier every moment!
Swarms of beggars, so numerous that "one cannot take a step
without meeting some of them," swept in from Savoy. Shooed
back across the bridge, they returned an hour later when the
commissaire was occupied. One of the two civic organizations
Dussert thought worthy of mention was a politically inoffensive
mutual aid society whose honorary officers, members of the local
gentry, never attended meetings. The "high society" of Beauvoisin belonged to the Society of St. Vincent de Paul, which
offered aid to those of the area's poor who were "of good
morality—of which there are few in this place." The community
was "religious enough outwardly but really lacking in faith," the
commissaire judged, "it is a region of cold indifference, egoism,
and slanderous backbiting without end."[27]

In 1860, an inspecting officer of railway police—the era's
newest special police service—swung through the Ain and the

Isère during a survey of political police efficiency along the frontiers. Crisply efficient, he felt no nostalgia for the simpler past which he thought distressingly exemplified by the frontier *commissaires* of the region. He proposed that the government might as well turn the old frontier service over to the gendarmerie and be done with it—in an age when the railways had atrophied the older communications, leaving carriage roads desolate and the international carriages nearly empty except for the mail. At Ferney in the Ain, he saw only a few Italian working families using the old crossing, only one regular carriage in summer, none in winter. Worse, it seemed that the *commissaires* wastefully symbolized a bygone age, in contrast to the bustling new railway police officers. He could not help digressing in praise of the latter, his special charges—men of "good bearing, without peculiarities in their personal habits," part of "a great family composed of the employees and agents of the railway companies, the customs and telegraph services, and the administrators. They live together in a sort of homogeneous, self-sufficient colony. . . ." In sad contrast, he found the frontier *commissaires* "isolated among an unfriendly local population of smugglers, usually untidy in appearance, looking put-upon and tired. . . . Each is trying to compensate for his situation by certain habits. One raises silkworms, the other does flower gardening and tends his songbirds. Another plays the piano or collects insects."[28]

The Railway Commissaires *of Police*

In an evolution natural to an expanding industrial economy, the Second Empire emphasized, though not disproportionately, another of its legacies—the special *commissaires* of railway police. Originating in 1846, they and their subordinate agents, under the Public Works administration, were primarily concerned with safety and public order in trains and stations. Their duties required the rank of *commissaire* with judiciary police power to order arrests and report officially on crimes and other mishaps.[29] They were replaced in July, 1848, by so-called *commissaires et sous-commissaires spéciaux de surveillance des chemins de fer,* named by Public Works but under divided authority: the Directorship of Engineers of Bridges, Roads, and Mines for matters arising from the technicalities of railway operation, and that of the railway company inspectors with respect to passengers and stations. In this divided and more specialized status, the *commissaires* were of little use in general police and they lost their judiciary police powers. In February, 1850, the railway *commissaires* regained their judiciary police function for offenses committed within the railways' jurisdiction. They were linked administratively to the *procureurs,* again becoming useful if limited sources of political police information.

The Second Empire definitively reorganized the service. On February 22, 1855, in response to the needs of an expanding railway system and the attendant opportunities for political police operations, a new system of railway police was established. In twenty-four cities, at terminal or intermediate points on main railway lines, thirty special *commissaires* of police were appointed under the command of the Sûreté Publique section of the Interior. Paris had six, Lyon had two, and each of the other cities, one. The new *commissaires,* better paid than others, received from two thousand to eight thousand francs in salary and more liberal expense allowances. Seventy special railway "police inspectors" assisted the new *commissaires.* Because of the inspectors' initial zest for their jobs, the Ministry of the Interior had to remind them sternly of their subaltern status. By 1860, after frequent changes in their cities of residence, thirty-three railway *commissaires* were on duty: seven in Paris, two in Bordeaux, and the rest in other railway centers.

The *commissaires'* peculiar jurisdiction generated administrative clashes from the outset. After prolonged disputes, they were directed to "share" authority with the communal *commissaires,* who by a decision of 1863 were declared "auxiliaries" of the railway officers in certain situations.[30] On another plane, the railway *commissaires'* functions overlapped with the older *commissaires de surveillance administrative* of 1850, whom the reform of 1855 relegated to the status of railway company policemen under supervision of the Public Works administration.

Nor could the prefects be indifferent to a new general and

judiciary police jurisdiction steaming daily through their domains. As the complexities and importance of the *commissaires'* service grew with the railways, the question of their central control became more pressing. In March, 1855, a central *commissaire* of railway police was established in Paris, and another in July, 1862, both directly responsible to the Minister of the Interior. But less than a month after the second appointment, policy suddenly changed. Both central *commissaires* were suppressed in August. On September 1, five "divisional" *commissaires* of railway police took their places. The new divisional officers supervised the railway *commissaires* and the special inspectors explicitly under the prefects' administrative authority, presiding over districts that included all French railways. Shortly after that, the prefects learned from their Ministry that they could require the divisional *commissaires* to undertake "special missions" even outside their regular railway police duties.[31] The prefects retained the major influence over the new police service and its emergent hierarchy.

This arrangement in the sixties accorded with the Ministry of the Interior's policy since the decree of 1855. The prefects saw the tentacular growth of a new general police jurisdiction through their *départements* with the sort of concern they always felt when confronted by an innovation in centralized administration outside or above their own system. Billault launched the reform of 1855 by soothing the prefects' anxiety. The railway *commissaires* were to receive instruction from the prefects and report to them on all aspects of their duties. To the prefects, the Minister wrote that the law "places them unreservedly under your authority. These new functionaries belong to you in the same way as all the ordinary *commissaires* of police." The appointment of a supervisory central *commissaire* of railway police "for the special guidance of this personnel," Billault meticulously explained, was because of the *commissaires'* intradepartmental jurisdiction and their "delicate and extensive functions." Almost apologetically, he pointed out that ordinary reporting channels through the prefectures would be too slow and awkward in the railway age; officials in Paris would have to assemble bits of information from several prefects before seeing a problem or situation whole. Billault promised, though the *commissaires* would send copies of their reports directly to Paris, that "These various measures, Monsieur le Préfet, raise no obstacle to the exercise of the authority invested in you."[32]

One can understand why the prefects, mainstays of the "sole political ministry," were more than casually interested. Paris expected the railway *commissaires* to be important political police agents. Collet-Meygret, director of the Sûreté Publique in 1855, urged that they "should become the gendarmes of the railways." The Minister of Justice deemed them "indispensable" to the nation's political police, which he considered their prime reason for being. The government, he emphasized, must be "perfectly clear on the political opinions of the railway personnel," particularly since the Emperor was often a passenger. But the *commissaires'* political assignment was much broader, as Collet-Meygret very confidentially informed the prefects while reiterating the "multiple mission" of the new officers:

As political agents, they must investigate the personnel of the railway companies, observe the attitudes and behavior of travelers, and be sure that no seditious literature enters the country. . . . They must give attention to anything which from any point of view is politically relevant to the *sûreté générale*.[33]

Political work by no means filled all or even most of the railway *commissaires'* time. But political vigilance underlay all their routine, whether during the uneventful policing of Lyon-Grenoble excursion trains or the verbatim reporting of a casual and unsuspect remark such as that of a garrulous traveler who said that France lived "on a volcano and that without this government's strength she would suffer a political upheaval." As in other branches of police, the superiors of the railway officers found their political police work too relaxed and "incomplete." In 1860, a central *commissaire,* inspecting the system, observed that although the railways facilitated checking identities at the frontier, travelers escaped strict surveillance afterward. For one thing, the powerful railroad companies—a new sort of "local influences" on wheels—disliked harassment of their passengers. The central *commissaire* proposed the adoption of domestic passports, or "travel cards" with photographs, for all railway users, noting parenthetically the potential new business this would create for commercial photographers. Also he hoped to see railway *commissaires* linked administratively "in a more intimate and regular way" to the Sûreté Publique in Paris.[34] Neither proposal was adopted. The reaction of prefects and railway companies, for their respective reasons, would probably have been formidable.

There were tensions aplenty as it was. During incessant conflicts between the railway *commissaires* and other authorities, notably the companies' policemen (the *commissaires de surveillance administrative*), the prefects backed the *commissaires,* over whom their own influence had been ensured. Two kinds of conflict plagued the railway *commissaires*. One arose from jurisdictional clashes with communal *commissaires* of police over incidents in railway stations or along the right of way in towns. By 1863 this issue had been satisfactorily resolved by a careful redefinition of respective functions and by declaring the ordinary *commissaires* "auxiliaries" of the railway officers. The prefects would serve as effective mediators in case of need.

A second conflict, with company agents, was more difficult. The reorganization of 1855 carried over the older *commissaires de surveillance administrative* of 1850 (under the Public Works administration) as company policemen in matters arising from the technical details of railway operations. They lacked judiciary and general police powers, but in practice the line between theirs and the railway *commissaires'* functions was often blurred. The latter resisted encroachment upon their judiciary and general police powers; the *commissaires de surveillance* charged their rivals with encroachments as well. Such a conflict was foreseen in 1855 when a joint Public Works and Interior administrative directive attempted unsuccessfully to define a just division of labor. In the ensuing disputes, the ministers of Justice and Interior concurred in their resolve to prevent the company policemen from acquiring powers overlapping those of the railway *commissaires*. The Minister of Public Works explicitly agreed with their views in June, 1855. *Procureurs,* prefects, and ordinary *commissaires* of police aligned on the same side.

But the conflicts continued. Officials sometimes speculated philosophically that the trouble lay in the very nature of a situation bound to produce "mutual ill-will between the two orders of functionaries." All agreed that "the solution of all these difficulties is a delicate matter" requiring special study by all heads of services involved. The study was made, the problem continued, and during the sixties confidential circulars, conferences, and a special study commission pursued the solution of the puzzle.[35]

THE GENDARMERIE

No police organization received more unstinting praise than the gendarmerie. Administrators considered it indispensable in the villages and rural areas. This "armed magistracy" with judiciary and general police powers received such verbal tributes as: "a brigade of gendarmerie is worth more than a company of the line." Administrators also ruefully admitted the peculiar difficulties inherent in collaborating with such an elite. As members of a military corps belonging administratively to the army and Ministry of War, the gendarmerie officers were as sensitively protective of their independence as any prefect. At least in the gendarmerie's case, the prefects did not have to see efficiency impaired by "local influences." But ironically enough, the corporate particularism of the corps worked against the prefects' aspirations in the fifties.

The gendarmerie's *esprit* glowed more intensely after 1849 with the knowledge of Louis Napoleon's special interest in their branch. Gendarmes returned the favor in loyal service.They expected and received their reward in terms of accentuated autonomy and further increases of personnel.[36]

The Gendarmerie before the Coup d'Etat

No one publicly solicited and applauded interested gestures from the Elysée more fervently than Captain Cochet de Savigny, retired gendarmerie officer and very articulate editor of the corps' *Journal de la gendarmerie de France.* Through 1850 and 1851, Savigny waged a spirited editorial campaign for the gendarmerie's further regeneration. Unabashedly, he extolled the superlative qualities of gendarmes in general and Louis Napoleon's beneficence in particular, predicting an imminent and even greater rehabilitation of the force.

"It is high time," Savigny wrote, "that the gendarmerie . . . be delivered from its present inferiority . . . , especially now that it is rightly considered the army's elite."

He printed and editorially approved of "communications from readers" urging increases of personnel up to fifty thousand men. Only an expanded force, Savigny insisted, could apply the necessary "continuous vigilance and repression" against the enemies of public order. "In the labors of Louis Napoleon," gendarmes read, they would find:

a proof of a sympathy and confidence for which we should be proudly grateful, especially since his government has already improved our position.

Therefore let us take hope in him and his justice. What he has done should prove to us that he knows our needs and that they are the object of his solicitude.

By December, 1851, a kind of "tacit contract of mutual assistance" existed between the Prince-President and the gendarmerie.[37] The coup d'état consummated that understanding.

After the Coup, a Time of Rewards

The gendarmerie's energy during December earned extravagant plaudits in the press and unpublicized administrative correspondence. Accusations of political disloyalty among gendarmes were extremely rare. Captain Savigny received these encomiums with unconcealed delight. Henry Cauvain in the governmental *Le Constitutionnel* published and reprinted glowing articles on the gendarmerie during 1852, providing Savigny with rich material for quotation in his journal. In a triumphant editorial at the end of December, the Captain launched a campaign to turn praise into "a new era" of tangible rewards. The gendarmerie would now escape from the "rut" to which it had been consigned. As under the first Napoleon, it would find its deserved status under a man "who knew how to conquer and to govern." Savigny reminded Louis Napoleon that the gendarmerie had responded "as one man" on December 2. Before the month was over, he was able to

print General Saint-Arnaud's promise on behalf of the Prince-
President that rewards "proportional to their services" would be
forthcoming. In private, the Minister of War predicted a time
when an expanded gendarmerie would become "a real and very
solid army of the interior."[38]

Lists of deserving gendarmes received national recognition;
gendarmes' widows and orphans received assistance. Public sub-
scriptions showered donations upon outstanding men for their
wounds and valor. In the Loiret, for example, a group known as
the "Friends of Order" raised nearly twenty thousand francs,
most of which went to fifty-nine gendarmes for outstanding performance. For services in workers' riots at Angers in 1855, seven
gendarmes received, respectively, a cross of the Legion of Honor,
a Military Medal, and five personal citations from their Minister.[39]

The dialogue of mutual admiration between the gendarmerie
and other authorities extended through the early fifties. Savigny's
Journal, before declaration of the Empire, printed unaccustomed
poetry by gendarmes, dedicated to "His Imperial Highness,
Prince Louis-Napoleon." *Le Pays* in Paris, proclaiming that it
did so with the Emperor's approval, glorified the gendarmerie
in its issues of April 24–25, 1854. The panegyric was reprinted
as a sixteen-page pamphlet. Its author ascribed the gendarmes'
bravery to God's special favor toward a service which "even in
the midst of peace is constantly in a state of war." Such a "life of
self-sacrifice" for the nation could be sustained only by deep
"religious sentiment." Even a prefect now and then veered briefly
away from his administrative prose into a lyrical flight—as did
the prefect of the Eure-et-Loire, whose poem, "Le Gendarme,"
on the theme "without fear and above reproach" went in eight-
page reprints to all the gendarmes of his *département* in November, 1852. The prefect of the Calvados was pleased to discover
in the summer of 1852 that all the barracks walls of his *département's* forty brigades were hung with pictures of Napoleon I and
Louis Napoleon.[40]

Meanwhile, more lasting rewards developed. On December
16, 1851, the Consultative Committee of the Gendarmerie, abol-

ished in 1848, was revived as a semiautonomous governing body within the Ministry of War. Captain Savigny was elated by a measure "so keenly and impatiently desired by the entire gendarmerie," predicting that "this is the prelude to further rewards and improvements." A week later, a reorganization decree authorized substantially increased personnel in twenty-five legions and the Republican Guard of Paris. By 1853, 461 new brigades were in uniform, bringing the gendarmerie's complement to four thousand men over that of 1847.[41] About twenty-four thousand gendarmes now patrolled France.

The Reorganization Law of 1854

The "new era" of the gendarmerie received its charter in a definitive law of 645 articles on March 1, 1854.[42] Its innovations were principally in organizational details, not in concepts of police service. The reform was the work of the Consultative Committee of the Gendarmerie, headed by General of Division Count de La Ruë. It codified earlier regulations and precisely defined the relationships between the gendarmerie and civil police authorities.

Article 1 succinctly stated the gendarmerie's mission: to safeguard the "public security" by "continual and repressive surveillance" throughout the Empire, being "particularly assigned to the sûreté of the countryside and routes of communication." Twenty-six legions were provided for metropolitan France and Algeria, with five special units including a Colonial Gendarmerie, two battalions of Elite Gendarmerie (which in May, 1854, were renamed the Garde Impériale), the Garde de Paris, and a unit of "gendarme veterans."

In France, each legion patrolled several départements (except in Corsica, which had one legion) under a colonel and lieutenant-colonel. Each département had a company, under a chef d'escadron. Captains or lieutenants commanded arrondissements. Foot or horse brigades of five or six men—the basic operational units —were posted in communes or cantons under noncommissioned officers. A moderate pay increase for simple gendarmes and some noncommissioned officers appeared in 1855. Mounted noncommissioned officers kept to their earlier annual 1,136 and 1,036 francs; but their counterparts in the foot gendarmerie were raised by 150 francs to 886 and 996 francs. Unrated gendarmes of both horse and foot brigades profited by 150-franc increases to 900 and 750 francs, respectively. An 1852 estimate set 600 francs as the minimum subsistence income for a married gendarme without children.[43]

The "Mixed Regime"

Article 5 of the 1854 decree preserved the traditional *régime mixte,* or "mixed character of service" of a military unit in liaison with civilian police. Mixture was not marriage. The limits of "ordinary" and "extraordinary" service were carefully spelled out. "Ordinary" service was automatic daily routine. "Extraordinary" duties required formal written "requisition" and special orders by *procureurs,* prefects, *commissaires,* or mayors. Ordinary service included correspondence and specified reports; tours of communes and rural areas by day and night; checkups on inns, railways, fairs, markets, festivals, ceremonies; forest searches; pursuit of army deserters; and, of course, dealing with lawbreakers met during patrols. Extraordinary service meant special reports; carrying dispatches; suppressing riots; policing public occasions, the transport of prisoners, and policing elections.

The Gendarmerie and Political Police

Political police did not appear by name in the gendarmerie's service descriptions. Yet the Second Empire relied on the corps for a significant political contribution. The very nature of the "mixed regime" brought gendarmes into politically significant police work. Because of the universal inefficiency of civilian rural policemen, the administration relied heavily upon the gendarmerie in their own political police outside the larger communes. This involvement was made very explicit by General de La Ruë in a circular of 1854 to gendarmerie colonels, his directive itself being classified as "political correspondence."

Service during elections constituted a very important political contribution. Gendarmes patrolled the voting areas at election time. Often they acted as informal electoral agents for official candidates. The administration fully appreciated the psychology of country folk long habituated to regard the gendarmerie as "a sovereign power" and the *brigadiers* as courts without appeal. Fear mixed with respect; the rural populace often sought and took the gendarmes' advice.[44]

The prefect of the Ille-et-Vilaine in 1852 persuaded the Bishop of Rennes to issue a pastoral letter urging a favorable vote in the imperial plebiscite. Suspecting that some legitimist clerics would disobey and advise abstention, the prefect ordered the gendarmerie to report *curés* who disregarded the order. He planned to inform the Bishop, whom he had "obligated to prove by his severity that he is really the master in his diocese." In the same *département,* a justice of the peace was censured for complaining that "the administration always prevails because the gendarmerie takes the election by the throat." In the Sarthe, declaring the gendarmerie essential to "make" the municipal elections, the prefect requested that the Minister of War cancel a review at Le Mans so as not to divert the gendarmes from their election duties. Granting the request, the Minister telegraphed orders "not to displace the gendarmerie during these delicate operations."

In March, 1863, the gendarmerie's electoral role was suddenly canceled, at least in part, by the Minister of War. He ordered a new policy of neutrality, saying that the Emperor "does not intend that the troops of this ministry be changed into electoral agents." Even so, this was not an unequivocal departure from the past, for the Minister added that the commanders of legions could confidentially tell their higher officers to "lend their cooperation to the administration," using "such reserve as their tact and experience deem proper."[45]

The issue of secret political police brought about a major clash between the gendarmerie and other authorities. Saint-Arnaud, it will be recalled, in a victory over Maupas in 1852–53, won the gendarmerie's formal exemption from secret police work. The Minister's protests notwithstanding, Maupas and the prefects were only asking the gendarmes to do what they had done for Louis Napoleon since 1849. On November 12, 1849, Minister

of War D'Hautpoul, in a highly classified directive to his colonels
of gendarmerie, had asked them to assign undercover political
police duties (including political police reports on the civil administration) to commissioned and noncommissioned officers "fit"
for such tasks. On Louis Napoleon's behalf, Hautpoul frankly
appealed "to the gendarmerie's devotion" as "the advance guard
of the public order" against "socialism." The Minister himself
passed the gendarmerie's secret information to the Prince-President.

In 1854, Saint-Arnaud's earlier victory over Maupas was reflected in Article 119 of the reorganization decree: "In no case,
either directly or indirectly, must the gendarmerie receive secret
missions of such nature as to destroy its true character. Its action
always proceeds openly, in military uniform. . . ." Yet the prefects
kept trying to use gendarmes for secret service, probably with
some limited success or otherwise their persistence would not have
continued. In 1857, one such incident provoked a captain to protest directly to the Emperor.[46]

Actually, by deliberate policy the gendarmerie continued
throughout the Second Empire to perform secret political police
service, but not for the direct use of the prefects. The archives
of the Ministry of War show that until the late 1860's, Hautpoul's confidential instructions of 1849 were not only kept alive,
but that the practice was further justified by earlier directives
going back to 1814. In the conflict with Maupas and the subsequent withdrawal of the gendarmerie's confidential political intelligence from that of the prefects, one can trace the fine hand
of General Count Aristide de La Ruë.

Retired in 1848, La Ruë was returned to active duty as a brigadier general on the general staff. In 1851, he became one of
several inspectors-general of the gendarmerie and a general of
division. He presided over the Consultative Committee of the
Gendarmerie after its restoration in December, 1851. One of his
reports to the Minister of War in 1852 showed that during his
inspection tours he also submitted confidential reports on the
functionaries of both the ministries of Interior and Justice—an
assignment which he described as "especially necessary."[47] By

1859, General La Ruë still headed the Committee and belonged to the General Staff Committee as well. Under Napoleon III, he bypassed even the Minister of War, acting as an unofficial and confidential chief of political police by directly relaying the gendarmerie's confidential information to the Emperor. In May, 1859, Minister of War Vaillant acceded to the Emperor's request to name La Ruë "permanent inspector-general of the gendarmerie." Now a senator, La Ruë again retired to reserve status in February, 1860. But by the Emperor's wish he kept both his permanent inspectorship and the presidency of the gendarmerie Committee. At seventy years of age, he permanently retired on December 31, 1865, according to regulations. But in his own hand he informed the Minister of War shortly before his "retirement" that the Emperor "has expressed his will that the political service of the confidential correspondence of the gendarmerie continue to be carried on under my direction and that I shall retain the qualification of Senator, Permanent Inspector of the Gendarmerie," with the services of two secretaries of the gendarmerie Committee. A few days earlier, La Ruë had explained to the Minister that "Your Excellency knows that I am in no way soliciting the continuation of this mission," adding that he "must," however, do so "quietly," without attracting undesirable attention.[48]

Although the Minister of War's instructions of May, 1866, to gendarmerie officers omitted previous references to confidential political reports, a memorandum in the Ministry stated that the earlier policy "nonetheless remains quite completely valid." The last previous instruction, on June 3, 1865, had asked senior officers to carry out *"confidential"* [underlined in text] correspondence directly with the Minister of War and the Permanent General-Inspector, "conforming to the Emperor's orders."[49]

Although Napoleon III in 1853 lost the services of a police minister as a direct and confidential source of information on national political trends and his public administration, through the services of gendarmerie officers and General La Ruë he apparently salvaged some of the loss.

The "Mixed Regime" and Administrative Conflicts

Secret police was not the only issue to arouse the gendarmerie's sense of autonomy. In the "mixed regime," as in other administrative services with "interpenetration" of police functions, conflicts had been inherent since the gendarmerie's origin. Gendarmes were in the special situation of belonging to one ministry, from which they received promotions and other benefits, while taking many of their service orders from functionaries of the Interior who in no way could affect their personal welfare. Under military discipline they performed efficiently, but not in order to please the civil authorities with whom they were in daily contact. Perhaps they felt the disdain of men in uniform for civilians. Administrators made maximum demands on the gendarmerie, generally despairing of any effective services by the *gardes-champêtres* in the villages. The prefects and the departmental councils, neither being free spenders for the purpose, provided the gendarmes with living quarters whose quality provoked much barracks grousing. When the gendarme committed a crime, he was punished in a civil court. Thus the complaints imbedded in his way of life were often directed against the functionaries with whom he dealt.

Perhaps with reason, gendarmes considered themselves overworked. There were sympathetic writers who told them so: "Of all the public functions, probably the most difficult are those of the gendarmerie." They grumbled under their multiple chores— making patrols, answering calls for "extraordinary" services, assisting the administration during elections, playing nursemaids to the rural policemen. There were unending reports to write, through their own military channels as well as to the other authorities high and low. For example, a lieutenant of the twenty-first Legion in the Jura regularly reported to the prefect and the ministries of the Interior and War. Copies went to the Minister of Police, the General Inspector of Police at Lyon, the Special Inspector at Besançon, General de Castellane at Lyon, the commander of the Legion, and the commandant of the Company of the Jura. There was, of course, other incidental correspondence daily. Sympathetically, the prefect of the Aisne in 1859 reported that the gendarmerie "complain of spending more time giving account of their activities than in acting."[50]

The collapse of the Ministry of Police in 1853 in no way inhibited the gendarmerie's conflicts with other authorities. The corps stood firmly upon an official position simply stated: gendarmes took no *orders* from anyone except their own officers and the Ministry of War; they obeyed proper requisitions, within legal forms and limits, issued by competent officials; never would they tolerate outsiders' intervention in their "internal affairs."

Conflicts followed an ascending pattern of rank. The noncommissioned *brigadier* usually clashed with the *commissaire* of police, particularly after the cantonal jurisdiction of 1852 reached into the rural communes. The *procureur* at Amiens in 1853 was not alone in noticing the gendarmerie's widespread resentment against the cantonal *commissaires*. The lieutenant disputed with the subprefect, the *chef d'escadron* with the prefect. When the issue went higher, as it sometimes did, it was the Minister of the Interior's turn to have it out with the Minister of War. In one instance, the subprefect at Argentan (Orne) collided with a lieutenant who questioned the former's dismissal of a functionary in 1852. Through the prefect, the quarrel reached Paris, where Saint-Arnaud rebuffed Persigny by accusing the subprefect of reporting untruths and trying to push the gendarmerie beyond its limits of subordination to the administration.[51]

At the *brigadier-commissaire* level, the two services' respective professional journals instructed their readers on their legal status and rights. The gendarmerie's journal stressed what the gendarmes need *not* do at the *commissaires'* bidding, declaring that the gendarmerie "can be diverted from its customary service only in grave circumstances, and then only when the reasons have been formally stated in a clear and precise manner." The *commissaires'* journal concentrated on what its readers *could* require of the gendarmes through their "right of requisition" for extraordinary service, though "it should be used only with great discretion." Requisitions must be scrupulously drafted and sent through the proper officer-channels; they "must not contain any imperative term, such as *we order, we want, we enjoin, we summon.*"[52]

The burden of jurisdictional conflicts fell upon the prefects as a special adjunct to their chronic confrontation by "local influences." After the shared euphoria of the early 1850's burned itself out and the gendarmerie's eagerness to help found the new regime was satiated, the prefects looked more ambivalently upon their uniformed colleagues. Appreciative of good police work, they continued to praise the gendarmerie's effectiveness in areas otherwise poorly policed because of personnel shortages and the incompetence of available municipal and rural policemen. On the other hand, the gendarmerie's egregious spirit of independence after 1854 caused the prefects to leaven their praise with some very acid criticism.

In the prefects' context, the gendarmerie joined the other competitors with the prefects' own rightful position as departmental arbiters and agents of the "sole political ministry." The gendarmerie's cooperation in the prefects' general police system was one thing; their holding aloof on their strict legal rights was another! The prefects complained that the gendarmerie asserted its autonomy too technically and narrowly, working with but refusing to be part of the administration's police mission. Worse, they were becoming their own empire builders who did not conceal "the exaggerated importance they want[ed] to give to their own force."[53]

The result was an "isolation" of the gendarmerie's police activity from that of the administration—the principal theme of the prefects' criticism. In 1853, the prefect of the Ardennes noted the gendarmes' tendency "to isolate themselves in their own self-importance" because, he thought, of the adulation heaped upon them in 1852. At some length, he prophesied that if the trend continued, this once-admirable elite group would devour its own usefulness and decline into merely a "simple repressive force." Perhaps referring to the ambitious role of General La Ruë, the prefect accused the gendarmerie of aspiring beyond the *régime mixte*: "it wants to become a kind of independent authority . . . , the Minister of War having his secret orders and personal police." The gendarmerie knew that "the surest way to make itself important [was] to monopolize the information it gather[ed] and to send it directly to the government before informing—or even without informing—the prefects." In a sequel to this report, written less than two months after the death of the Ministry of Police, the same prefect submitted another alarmed plea for unity of police action under the prefects that could just as well have been among those earlier aimed against Maupas' ministry.

Agreeing with the prefect of the Ardennes, others reported in the same vein. The prefect of the Vienne confessed in 1858 that he had long noted the gendarmerie's tendency "to isolate [itself] from the administrative authority in everything involving . . . political surveillance and the *sûreté générale*." His colleague in the nearby Haute-Vienne also protested that the gendarmerie's action was "not intimately linked to that of the administration as it was in the old days." This critic dwelt upon the growing and "regrettable tendency" of hostility toward the *commissaires* and the waning "deference" shown to subprefects and even prefects. The junior gendarmerie officers in the Haute-Vienne openly voiced their preference for avoiding the administration. And why not? They only followed the example set by the departmental commandant and even the inspector-general of gendarmerie himself—both of whom rudely ignored protocol by omitting formal calls on the prefect during their tours. This discourtesy, the prefect declared, was unparalleled in his twenty years of experience! In the Tarn-et-Garonne, the departmental commandant withheld more than "half the facts" he collected; five years later the prefect still held to the same complaint. In the Orne, a captain was even less generous, flatly refusing to assist the prefect in political police reports. In the Dordogne, the gendarmerie's prying into the prefect's municipal policies also brought complaints, with which the Minister of the Interior agreed to the extent of declaring the gendarmes' behavior "intolerable."[54]

Even the old soldier, General Espinasse, during his brief tenure as Minister of the Interior in 1858, very confidentially asked the prefects to assess the gendarmes' loyalty, efficiency, and cooperation in general police. His request brought typically ambivalent replies, which again attested the gendarmerie's great professional potential while deploring their particularism. The prefect of the Isère sent a virtual resumé of prefectorial criticism. Between 1848 and 1852, he recalled, a "sympathetic confidence" bound the administration and gendarmerie together: "the solidarity was complete." Then the gendarmerie's glorification and the emphasis on their independence in the decree of 1854, had a "regrettable influence" on formerly ideal relationships, amounting in 1858 to a "schism." To be sure, the gendarmerie performed with technical correctness. But its spirit had degenerated into that of "isolation" from administrators and public alike. The government's elite police protegés were consequently defeating their sponsor's objectives. The Emperor's goal, the prefect concluded, "has not been attained."[55]

The Prefect of Police also entered into a sharp exchange with the Minister of War in 1853 during a dispute over control of the Garde de Paris. The scanty evidence indicates that Piétri, charging General Saint-Arnaud with trying to nullify the Prefecture's influence, took the matter to the Emperor, determined to retain "all the rights belonging to him." Apparently the Prefect succeeded. In 1859, Marshal de Castellane noted that Boittelle openly showed his resentment of the "centralized" political reports which General La Ruë was passing from the gendarmerie to Napoleon III.

The *procureurs* criticized the gendarmerie much less than the prefects, no doubt because their service contacts with the force were fewer and simpler. They continued to see the gendarme's best side—"both conciliatory and firm, active without meddling," aloof from "local passions . . . and personal pretensions." When the *procureurs* did sprinkle their praise with isolated criticisms, it was usually because of the gendarmerie officers' ignorance of proper judiciary police procedure.[56] The *procureurs* managed to detect this weakness in nearly all police officials outside their own hierarchy.

THE *GARDES-CHAMPÊTRES* AND RURAL POLICE

Clinging precariously to the lowest rung of the administrative hierarchy were the *gardes-champêtres,* village agents of the rural police. They shared the so-called *police des campagnes* with the gendarmerie, but without the training, effectiveness, and *esprit de corps* of the latter. Indeed, the *garde-champêtre* remained throughout the Second Empire what he was at its beginning—the "poor man," though not the "forgotten man," in the French police hierarchy. Never reformed, he was, paradoxically, the object of the most criticism and reform proposals.

The Gardes-Champêtres: *Status and Distribution*

Like other nineteenth-century French functionaries, the *gardes-champêtres* were the progeny of Old Regime prototypes, resurrected and retouched by Revolutionary and Napoleonic legislation.[57] Their organization remained static after 1811, except for a series of changes in their mode of appointment. After 1820, the mayors received that privilege, with the approval of the municipal councils. As part of the centralization of the "decentralization" law of March, 1852, the prefects appointed *gardes-champêtres,* but only after nomination by the municipal authorities. Because the *gardes* served under the immediate command of the mayors, the extension of prefectorial control over the communes in the fifties automatically included the rural policemen, but they counted little in general police. In 1854, they went nominally under the professional surveillance of the gendarmerie brigades, who were the only really effective rural police. Originally chosen from military veterans, the *gardes-champêtres* of the 1850's were recruited from men aged twenty-five or older, regardless of background.

Armed with a saber (at least in theory), the *garde* might carry a firearm if the prefect saw the need. He wore no uniform. He patrolled (at least in theory) his village and adjacent countryside—grossly underpaid, and subordinate to nearly everyone else in administrative life. Nonetheless, his official relationships, like those of the *commissaires,* were complex. He was supposed to inform the *commissaires* and the gendarmerie (the latter inspected and recorded his activities) on everything relating to public order. For the mayor, he undertook what in larger communes would have been municipal police duties. As his title implied, he guarded the fields against fire and vandalism. He was at the disposal of the *commissaires,* subprefects, and prefects for general police duties at any time. As a subordinate judiciary police functionary, subject in that respect to the *procureurs'* tutelage, the *garde-champêtre* had to investigate violations, make arrests, and compose *procès-verbaux* on minor offenses against rural property. Illiterate *gardes* dictated their reports before a justice of the peace or mayor. Unlike the *commissaires* and other higher "agents of the government," the *garde-champêtre* could be prosecuted in the ordinary courts without right of appeal, in cases arising from his police duties.[58]

In 1856, of 36,710 communes with rural territory, about three-fourths employed *gardes-champêtres.* In numbers, at least, this amounted to a considerable force, though one-fourth of the communes had no civilian rural policemen. In the mid-fifties they earned an average yearly salary of 211 francs, though in a dozen *départements* none exceeded 100 francs. In the Bas-Pyrenées, Haut-Pyrenées, and Vosges the *gardes'* pay averaged 38, 46, and 68 francs, respectively. Obviously, the profession of *garde-champêtre* usually had to be a part-time occupation. Compare with other wages: in a region where day-labor brought between two and three francs daily, half of the *gardes* earned less than one franc.

By the sixties, the situation had further degenerated to a national average pay of 140 francs. A *procureur* in 1864, reviewing the "derisory" situation in many communes, reported one village which rewarded its *garde* with 15 francs annually. Understandably, the turnover of rural police agents was very high, and in the consistent opinion of officials their efficiency was correspondingly low. Between March and December, 1858, in the Oise, eighty-one *gardes* were appointed, six were discharged, and forty-six resigned.[59] Against the background of such facts of life in the unenviable career of a *garde-champêtre,* the police doctrine of the Second Empire optimistically projected an ideal type:

A *garde-champêtre* must possess great exactitude, indefatigable energy, a vigilance not easily deceived, a disinterestedness raising him above all corruption. He must have besides some knowledge of the laws relating to rural police and ideas clearly enough organized to draft an official report. Finally, he must have such honesty in his functions that he will never let himself be influenced by personal likes or dislikes.[60]

Realistic portraits diverged sharply from the ideal. In 1852, a judge at Poitiers indignantly wrote directly to Louis Napoleon, depicting a pauperized, ragtail force, undisciplined, lacking effective hierarchy, not only "useless but also dangerous" for public order: "They hinder more than they assist the gendarmerie, whose auxiliaries they are supposed to be. Badly selected, poorly paid and armed, without a uniform—they cannot usually be expected to perform any useful physical or moral service."[61] The judge's description remained typical until the end of the Second Empire. For twenty years, the complaints of administrators from the ministerial level down to the commune conferred upon the *gardes-champêtres* the distinction of being the most universally criticized police officers of the day.

The Rural Police and "Local Influences"

The reason for the *gardes'* poor showing was clear and near at hand. Far more than the *commissaires* of police, they were imprisoned by "local influences." The communes held them firmly. Even though these policemen were technically appointed by the prefects, the mayor submitted nominees from whom the prefects chose. Moreover, the *gardes* depended upon the municipal councils for their pay. Here was another problem—somewhat analogous to that of the *commissaires*—which the Second Empire inherited.

Under legislation antedating the Second Republic, the administration legally could force the appointment of an adequate number of *gardes*, or increase their pay to a level considered reasonable, simply by declaring their cost an "obligatory expenditure" on the commune. From 1837 to 1852, the mayor appointed the *gardes*. But if he, with the municipal council's support, refused to appoint and pay rural policemen, the administration could do nothing but resort to "extreme methods whose application could have serious repercussions upon other aspects" of administration. The problem was one of tactical expediency, hardly solved by empowering the prefect to name the *gardes*. The more basic tactical problem of forcing the communes to increase their local taxes remained. The prefects knew that the cost of obtaining enough qualified *gardes* would impose a relatively enormous financial load upon the poorer communes, which were already resisting the cantonal *commissariats*. So they shrank from using their legal alternative. Yet nearly all administrators above the municipal level wanted reform. As the *commissaires'* professional journal observed, they were "amazed that the government has not yet provided for this need."

Administrators also knew that despite the communes' and the gendarmerie's obligations to guide the *garde-champêtre* in his duties, he was "neither directed nor supervised, but rather, as a small farmer or worker he [gave] most of his time to his land or his trade and only infrequently attend[ed] to his official obligations." He not only feared to enforce the laws against municipal officials and their friends, but he usually became "the servitor and agent of one of the coteries which divide the communes." A *commissaire* testified that he knew of many communes "where the *garde-champêtre* receive[d] as his first order the warning never to prepare an accusation against any inhabitant of the commune!" A common related complaint held that

the first-comer is accepted as a *garde-champêtre*—whomever the busy-bodies recommend the most to the ears of the municipal councillors. And the latter, mostly important landowners of the commune, choose against their own best interests that *garde-champêtre* who least enforces the law, because often enough they themselves are the first offenders.

The prefects saw no remedy until the *gardes* received adequate pay and ceased to be dependent upon the mayors and municipal councils.[62]

The *procureurs* agreed with the prefects on the ills of what one of them labeled "a vicious institution." The *gardes'* judiciary police services were "completely null," in the opinion of another, because they lived "in too absolute dependence upon the mayors and notables of each commune." According to the *procureur* at Besançon, "they scarcely prepare any *procès-verbaux* except out of personal anger or a spirit of revenge." These complaints of the early fifties echoed through the next decade, always centering on the "partiality" in rural law enforcement. For local notables, the control of the *gardes-champêtres* was said to be "the principal lever of their local influence, especially in elections; at the same time this inevitably becomes one of the most prolific sources of cleavages and enmities in the region."[63]

Abortive Reforms

A few administrators attempted sporadically to improve the rural police service within the existing system. The prefect of the Aube repeatedly but unsuccessfully tried to persuade his communes to guarantee even a minimum salary of three hundred francs. The *procureur-général* at Paris introduced training sessions in technique and morale for the *gardes,* conducted jointly by justices of the peace and *commissaires.* Despite slight improvements he considered his effort a failure.[64]

Such isolated attempts at reform were insignificant. But a flood of proposals calling for an entirely new system came from private citizens and administrators. Baron de Vincent, ex-prefect and Councilor of State, declared in 1858 that "all serious and thinking people conclude that it is indispensable to change the system." The favorite recommendation, in addition to that of higher salaries, was for some form of *embrigadement,* or reorganization into units and an officer hierarchy resembling that of the gendarmerie. But there was little agreement on the details of such a reform, as a Senate committee discovered in 1857 and again during the 1860's.

Baron de Vincent outlined a system of uniformed brigades of ten to fifteen ex-soldiers each. At the communal level, the brigades would be commanded by *brigadiers* of rural police, under the unified command of a cantonal *garde-champêtre,* who in turn would report to a *garde d'arrondissement.* His total national force would have included 36,000 local *gardes* at 400 francs yearly, 25,000 *brigadiers* at 500, 2,850 cantonal *gardes* at 700, and 363 *arrondissement* officers at 900 francs. The revised pay scale would have cost the communes 15,581,500 francs, compared with the actual current expenditure of 6,300,000 in 1858—less than half the proposed amount. Vincent rather casually backed away from the financial problem and "local influences" by predicting that his plan would require no increases in communal levies. The difference would be made up in police fines, hunting licenses, and dog taxes!

Other proposals envisaged a corps of *"gardes-*gendarmes" (entirely composed of ex-gendarmes) as a special branch attached to, but not integrated in, the gendarmerie. The *procureur* at Paris offered a variant of this plan, proposing the formation of a "rural gendarmerie" commanded directly by the regular gendarmerie, doubling the numbers of the latter for the defense of society. Prefect Ferlay of the Drôme envisaged still another sort of "rural gendarmerie" of ex-soldiers equipped with uniforms, sabers, and carbines, operating under the joint authority of the gendarmerie, mayors, and, of course, the prefects. One can imagine the administrative conflicts this plan would have generated! Ferlay's force, together with the existing gendarmerie, would form "an army of the interior" forty thousand strong, a firm dike against "evil passions." Those who wanted some degree of fusion of the *gardes-chanmpêtres* and the gendarmerie got little encouragement from the Ministry of War. The Ministry apparently did not deviate from a policy statement by General Saint-Arnaud issued in 1852, opposing such integration because of its probable dislocating effects upon military discipline and organization.[65]

CONCLUSION

The several reforms of 1852–55 affecting departmental police personnel changed these officers' lives and duties very little in substance. Materially, the *commissaires* and *gendarmes* gained modestly, the *gardes-champêtres* not at all. The chief beneficiaries were the thirty-odd railway *commissaires,* related as they were to a new dimension of police authority consonant with the Second Empire's chief lasting achievement of industrialization. From the perspective of police organization, the railway *commissaires* and inspectors, the cantonal *commissariats* and the central *commissaires,* along with the standardized municipal police reforms in the larger cities, were all assimilated without any essential change in the traditional authority and outlook of the prefects. The same could be said for the gendarmerie reform of 1854, despite the stiffened pride displayed by that organization. All of these reforms, or their equivalents, were certainly overdue by non-political criteria in a police system that had scarcely changed in fifty years. The undeniable strong motives of political police which accompanied the reforms would have been true before Louis Napoleon, since political police had long permeated the French administrative system.

The Second Empire emphasized the political police function more overtly than any regime since the First Empire. But in retrospect, the increases in personnel directly involved in political police hardly seem inordinate, in view of the existing need for the other functions which that personnel also performed, The uncompleted—and by the later 1860's, retrenching—cantonal *commissaire* system, plus the failure to improve the rural police and the self-chosen "isolation" of the gendarmerie within their own specified duties, all joined with other forms of "local influences" to thwart the prefects' ideal objectives. And they added to the load of the *commissaires'* working day at a time when the imperial prefects were making more ambitious demands upon their personnel. One wonders, therefore, how much more nearly omniscient the imperial police became than their predecessors under earlier regimes.

The directors of the Second Empire aspired to higher standards in both nonpolitical and political police. They probably achieved a relative success in both, but the reality seemed far short of the aspiration. And, for a "police state," the Second Empire was hardly a bountiful era for police agents below the prefectorial rank. In this respect, at least, the public—expressing itself through "local influences"—got just about the quantity and quality of police services that it desired.

Secret Political Police

G EORGE SAND'S oft-quoted remark that half of France denounced the other half after December, 1851, was akin to that of an American in Paris soon afterward:

The streets swarm with mouchards, or police spies, in every sort of disguise. Gentlemen noted for their Republican principles are dogged by policemen wherever they go. . . . Individuals visited by them become at once suspected, and thenceforth share the attentions of the police. . . .[1]

Even if not taken literally, the stereotype is probably misleading if it ascribes secret police methods uniquely to the Second Empire or asserts their tremendous expansion as a political instrument. The subject, with its melodrama and despotic symbolism, has intrigued many writers. Out of political bias or a taste for sensationalism, they have perpetuated an interesting mixture of fact, unverifiable (and often incredible) anecdotes, and creative imagination. Such accounts obscure the fact that most political police work continued to be done by very visible administrative functionaries.

Both the sensationalist and serious researcher must do without abundant evidence, because of the very nature of secret police and because officials often destroyed secret records. For the Second Empire, this problem was compounded by wholesale destructions of documents in 1870–71. Most of what did not expire in the curling smoke seen rising from the Prefecture of Police at the Empire's end succumbed later in the Communards' revengeful flames at both the Prefecture and the Ministry of the

Interior. Therefore the present findings, incomplete and tentative, depend upon indirect evidence and meager records in the archives or in print.

THE INCIDENCE OF SECRET POLICE

All regimes before 1852 routinely used secret police agents and informers for both political and ordinary criminal intelligence. Undoubtedly the Second Empire's relative emphasis on political police included the secret variety. Dictatorship no doubt inspired more unsolicited voluntary informers, anonymous and otherwise, to offer their services. But available evidence suggests, without accurately measuring, only very moderate increases in secret police personnel in the fifties. Secret methods did not significantly displace the established pattern of general police activity. Apparently, as Maupas later insisted, "the staff of what is conventionally called 'the secret police' [remained] more limited than generally supposed. . . ."[2]

To justify its use of secret political police, the Second Empire had no need to break with administrative tradition. Responsible nineteenth-century administrative analysts and jurists unhesitatingly invoked the "legitimate defense" doctrine to defend the practice as a political necessity. Alexandre François Vivien, eminent mid-century authority on administrative usage and outspoken opponent of abusive police power, insisted that the political police function legitimately became in part "secret by its very nature" as long as society's enemies themselves operated clandestinely.[3] He and others also recognized the abuses apt to accompany an overemphasis on secret police.

A *commissaires'* service manual typically argued that secret political police was "simply an extension of the term, surveillance" and a self-evident duty: "The nation needs this part of the police, when it is well run, as much as the vital air it breathes." The responsible secret agent stood as an "obscure sentinel against society's mortal enemy." But he was denied his soldier's right to glory. Badly run, the same manual warned, secret police techniques bred "an evil worse than the sickness" they strove against. Vivien argued that the government should frankly recruit professional agents rather than haphazardly to rely on irresponsible amateur informers. Anyway, the authorities would be damned if they did, because of the secret method, and damned if they did not, because of the disasters that would ensue if the method were not used.[4]

Secret Funds

There was nothing secret, then, in the justification of "well run" secret police. Whether Louis Napoleon's government created a greatly expanded secret police activity, as has usually been assumed, might be indicated by the amount of money given to it. Compared with earlier regimes, the Second Empire probably spent more but its expenditures were not sensationally larger. The sources, all too incomplete, that were open to the investigator, may be misleading. Those who have specified or suggested astronomical secret expenditures have offered no evidence beyond the assertions themselves.[5]

It has also been said that secret funds were not carried in the national budget, which is misleading. Every budget did show an allotment to secret funds; but no breakdown of specific disbursements was published. For the detailed use of secret funds the Minister of the Interior accounted only to the Emperor. His own detailed records, except for a few fragments, have eluded this writer in the archives. But available records do show that by no means all the secret funds went for secret police agents. They were used to subsidize newspapers and provide sundry gratuities for many kinds of services in addition to cloak-and-dagger activities. The general budget figures, together with the prefects' references to the secret funds which they could touch, may throw a little light on the question.

Documents published after 1870 showed an annual average of about 2.3 million francs in budgeted secret funds between 1852 and 1866. The highest expenditures were in 1858 and 1860—3.3 million and 3.2 million francs, respectively. That for 1852 was 1.8 million francs. Otherwise the funds ranged between two and two-and-one-half millions yearly. For 1865, the Sûreté Publique's total budget of 7,667,575 francs included 2 million francs for secret expenses. These figures suggest only a small apparent increase over the years 1828–32, 1835, and 1848, for which partial figures exist. For example, in the unusual month of February, 1848, 31,908 francs went for secret police, compared with the monthly average of 19,166 francs for the Second Empire.[6]

When the Ministry of Police was created in 1852, the Ministry of the Interior kept 832,000 francs of its secret funds and transferred 632,000 to Maupas' agency. The latter sum, unanticipated in the budget for 1852, was increased 505,333 francs in special credits assigned to sûreté générale uses generally. Thus the sums labeled "secret" in the possession of both the Interior and Police ministries, plus the extraordinary allotments, came to 1,969,333 francs, reasonably close to the 1.8 million shown in the published documents cited above.

The customary partition of secret funds may be indicated by the figures available for a year when about 2 million francs were allotted (out of the Interior's total budget of 184,257,845). The Prefect of Police received the lion's share of 600,000 francs (compared with the Prefect's 3,847,000 for the Municipal Police in the same year) ; the departmental prefects, 223,400 (an average of about 508 francs each, excluding the Seine) ; the military and judiciary police, 67,600; the press service, 297,540; a miscellaneous fund for private indemnities, awards, and the like, 334,710.

There remained 487,850 francs still at the free disposal of the Minister of the Interior to spend on his own secret agents and to disburse among the other categories according to need. Accounts were kept of the very small, as well as large, sums paid to individual agents, but the records are incomplete.[7] They do show that affluence in secret police resources was centralized, like the administration itself, in Paris.

The prefects' correspondence is clear evidence that the Ministry of the Interior held the départements to a strict and slender secret funds budget. The Minister could augment needy prefects' allowances from his central fund. But he did not do so lightly. Many prefects protested what they regarded as politically foolish parsimony in secret police compared to earlier times. Such complaints were plentiful after 1848; they multiplied after 1851. In 1850, the veteran subprefect at Aix-en-Provence bemoaned his inability to pay for even a minimum secret police and recalled the palmier days "after the revolution of 1830" when his predecessor had more adequate secret funds. Even Pierre Carlier, Prefect of Police from 1849 until the eve of the coup d'état, was said to have added from his private income to his inadequate secret police budget.[8]

As Minister of Police, Maupas further tightened the secret purse strings by diverting a large share of the budgeted total from the prefects to his own new staff. In 1853, the prefect of such an important *département* as the Haute-Garonne received 200 francs monthly for secret expenditures. From the Ariège, whose 1,800 francs per year the Minister of Police withdrew, the prefect appealed vainly to the Interior (whose own funds had been divided with Maupas) for money to pay secret agents along the Spanish frontier. In a similar complaint the following year, the prefect of the Var vented the frustration induced by his inability to support "indispensable" secret surveillance.[9]

These prefectorial grievances by no means ended with the Ministry of Police. They formed a strand of discontent that lengthened into the sixties. In the Bouches-du-Rhône, where Marseille posed a considerable political police problem, the prefect had "for years" before 1852 received 6,000 francs annually for secret expenses. That sum had never been enough, he said, because of the sizable "demagogic party" and secret societies in the region. In April, 1852, Maupas cut him to 2,400 francs. In 1853, the prefect's 6,000 francs (or $1,200) were restored, doled out by the quarter; in 1854, payment was by the month. "Despite the greatest economy," the prefect complained, he would become insolvent if he maintained an adequate secret police. On occasion, he and other officials had to pay secret agents from their own pockets. His entreaties for supplementary allowances usually failed.[10]

That the Marseille prefect's problem was general was acknowledged by three Interior circulars in 1854–55. The Minister admitted that the "fixed sum" allotted to the prefects for secret expenses, plus the rule that all stay within their budgets, did not always serve the varying needs. Beginning in July, 1854, he introduced a more flexible allocation of funds every two months on the basis of need, provided the prefects could thoroughly document their requirements. With assurance of repayment, the prefects could commit small sums on their own initiative. A *département*'s surplus at the end of a two-month period was not added to his next period's regular allowance. The Minister hoped that the new system would allow "greater latitude . . . in the justification of expenses" and avoid the fixing of "any advance limit on your means of investigation."[11]

Even the Minister lacked budgetary flexibility. In 1861, when the budget allowed 2.2 million francs in secret funds, the Minister had only 439,000 left at the end of August. His comptroller opposed his chief's desire to transfer 500,000 more from other budget categories because such a move was illegal. New secret monies required a special decree. The comptroller therefore suggested that the Minister avoid "the inevitable embarrassments that must be anticipated." The sequel appeared in a "very confidential" circular of November 26 which ordered the prefects until further notice to cease "all expense for secret police, except in cases of urgent and absolute necessity." Nor could the prefects be repaid for advances from their personal funds until a new annual budget came to the rescue.[12]

Outside Paris and Lyon, many officials reported a chronic shortage of skilled secret agents even when there was money to pay them. Considering casual informers and local *indicateurs* unreliable, they usually tried to borrow experienced agents from Paris. If the problem seemed important, they were sometimes accommodated. In 1856, Rogniat in the Vienne, alarmed because he had no undercover agents to spy on a suspected branch of the "Marianne" secret society at Poitiers, borrowed two agents from Paris. But for years Rogniat vainly relayed the pleas of his subprefects, especially the one at Châtellerault, for secret agents to cope with secret societies among local workers, some of whom volunteered to become paid informers. The officials refused such overtures lest these amateurs become "traitors on both sides." The harassed prefect supported his subprefects' complaints by polling the *département*'s gendarmerie officers, the *procureurs,* and the central *commissaire* at Poitiers—all of whom agreed that "the lack of secret police" jeopardized the *sûreté générale* in the area. Rogniat proposed a "permanent system instead of the sporadic and very rare use of secret agents . . . in cities such as Poitiers and Châtel-lerault." But as late as 1858 the latter city of fifteen thousand people had no secret agents and depended still upon one *com-missaire* and two municipal policemen for its political police.[13]

If a prefect succeeded in borrowing an agent, he was unsure how long the man would stay on the job or whether he would fully obey orders. In 1856, during a national rash of prosecutions against several secret societies, Paris generously dispatched secret agents to the Rhône, Loire, Jura, and a few other areas, in order to gather evidence by infiltrating the societies. One of the Interior's agents performed this service in the Jura. But he refused to further the postarrest investigation by posing as one of the prisoners in jail, declaring flatly that he worked for the Minister, not the prefect. The *procureur* later blamed his six acquittals out of seven cases on the lack of follow-up secret agents.[14]

SECRET POLICE ORGANIZATION

Only Paris and Lyon appear to have maintained permanent, specialized secret police establishments. At Lyon, *Commissaire* Bergeret, as Secretary-General of Political Police, headed a special office under the prefect. Not all his duties were secret or even political. Bergeret's political operations included surveillance of public opinion and the press, public establishments, secret societies, ex-political offenders, and foreigners. He directed six "open agents of the political brigade" and between six and eight full-time secret agents. In earlier years, Lyon had had from six to ten. Bergeret wanted at least ten secret agents for what he regarded as minimum needs. His maximum request was for twelve men in order to add "a secret police of clubs and salons" against legitimists and Orleanists. But this last he admitted was a "very expensive" luxury. Bergeret also had a list of 58 part-time *in-dicateurs* outside his regular staff. His men were active, according to frequent prefects' reports in the fifties. But the organization did not expand during the Empire's existence. Bergeret's successor in 1870 complained that his insufficient staff now included only six secret agents. Citing Lyon's special needs, as Bergeret had done eighteen years before, he again asked for the same minimum of ten agents. Only in July, 1870, did he realize this wish.[15]

If the Lyon establishment may be considered a limited one, the only really major secret police organizations were at Paris in the Prefecture of Police and the Ministry of the Interior. In the Prefecture, as indicated in chapter 4, control of the open and secret political police was centralized in the Prefect's office, with two specialized municipal police units available for such work when needed. Destructions of the Prefecture's archives in 1870–71 have left the details of its secret police activities obscure and conclusions based upon scraps of evidence quite tentative.

Most generalizations about the Second Empire's secret police have probably referred to the exploits of the Parisian agents. The name most mentioned—and the most elusive for researchers—is Clément Fabre de Lagrange, the so-called real chief of political police during the Second Empire. Lagrange has been made the protagonist of some rather incredible incidents and credited with a fabulous salary and hidden power. His reputation soared soon after the Empire. Count Kératry, who took over the Prefecture of Police in September, 1870, later testified during investigations by the Government of National Defense that Lagrange was "the most dangerous man for public order" in all France. Kératry accused him of faking plots, manipulating a host of *agents provocateurs,* and masterminding all the iniquities often attributed to secret police agents.

Lagrange did exist. His name appeared for years in the annual administrative directory. From 1852 to 1859, as an *officier de paix,* he was an office chief in the Prefecture's General Secretariat. In the later sixties, he emerged as *"commissaire* of police in charge of special services" attached to the Prefect's office. Today his dossier in the Prefecture's archives contains only two newspaper clippings telling of his arrest in 1871 after he returned from his haven in London. Lagrange appears in many routine dis-

patches involving the lending of Paris secret agents to departmental prefects, especially in the Rhône.[16]

In what seem to be the most reliable accounts, Lagrange's stel-
lar role in the Paris political police came only in the later sixties.
Félix Rocquain, who examined the Prefecture's surviving records
in 1870 (before later destructions), described Lagrange as a
fanatical Bonapartist patriot convinced that without urgent secret
cases "he was failing in his job." But in some 150,000 political
dossiers (dating from 1830 to 1870), Rocquain found none of
the sensational material he had apparently expected. He believed
that the Prefect had two groups of secret agents. One performed
officially; the other consisted of informers known only to himself,
who were his personal intelligence network in the upper social
strata. Some of these, including women who presided over fashionable salons, may have served without pay. Rocquain's findings
in this respect were supported by Maupas, who with fewer details
admitted the same dual system's existence in the fifties.[17]

Another secret force operated in the Ministry of the Interior's
political section. Its relationship to that of the Prefecture is unclear, but no doubt the professional secret services of the two
agencies were at least partly integrated. From 1853 through 1856
the Interior's agents answered to Pierre Marie Collet-Meygret,
an urbane administrator who in 1857 fell into disgrace and endured an official investigation of his various dubious enterprises
including alleged misuse, bordering on blackmail, of his powers
as director of political police. Collet-Meygret testified that the
Prefecture of Police directed the secret police of conspiracies and
secret societies and that the Interior's agents specialized in knowing "what goes on in the upper classes and in following the trends
in public opinion" as techniques of preventive police.[18]

A third secret service guarded the Emperor. This so-called
police du château, or Tuileries police, has inspired much sensational and scandalous anecdotal writing, probably compounded of
both truth and romance. One reads of strong-arm Corsicans,
properly swarthy, leading or following Napoleon III through
hair-raising escapades of the most diverse sort, stilettos between
their teeth or laid handily by. Griscelli de Vezzani, one of these

agents, used the pseudonym of Baron de Rimini to fill his baroque memoirs with breath-taking incidents and the boast that he personally commanded all the French police and gendarmerie when the Emperor traveled. Griscelli and another legendary Corsican, one Allesandri, protected the Emperor with "a sort of canine fidelity," according to Anna L. Bicknell, an Englishwoman in the Tuileries household. She pictured the *police du château* trying not to look like themselves during entertainments at the palace. Groups of men lounged about the entrances, "conversing together carelessly, with an assumed indifference . . . dressed to look as much like ordinary gentlemen as they could." Obviously plainclothesmen! Her woman's intuition told Miss Bicknell that "they were not men whom it would have been prudent to offend in any way by misplaced haughtiness. . . ." By other accounts, agents of the *police du château* posed as waiters and kitchen employees.[19]

The visible *police du château*, officially the *Commissariat* of the Imperial Residences, was a special thirty-man unit of the Prefecture of Police on detached duty. Through most of the Second Empire this force was headed by Louis Alphonse Hyrvoix, who survived the collapse of 1870 to die of apoplexy en route to a commemorative mass for Napoleon III in 1890. An active Bonapartist to the end, he was followed by secret police for years after 1870—ironically enough, by some of his own former agents. Like Lagrange, he has left in the archives only an insignificant trace of his professional career. In 1853 Hyrvoix was assistant chief of the Paris Municipal Police. On June 1, 1854, he became *commissaire* with the special title of Inspector General of Police of the Imperial Residences, with full police powers in any part of France where the imperial family found themselves. He, not Griscelli de Vezzani, headed the *police du château* in Paris or on the road.[20]

Writers of the cloak-and-dagger school have asserted that, in addition to the three Parisian secret police units already mentioned, various dignitaries from the Emperor on down had their personal "police" for unofficial spying on each other. Kératry and other enemies of the Second Empire made the charge in testimony before the Government of National Defense in 1871; the names most frequently mentioned were Napoleon III, Empress Eugènie, Rouher, and Prince Napoleon—in addition to officials such as M. M. Piétri and Collet-Meygret.[21] But for serious undercover work of a general nature, there were only two organizations— those of the Prefecture and the Ministry of the Interior.

SECRET POLICE PERSONNEL

A coherent view of the secret agents and their way of life cannot be recaptured in reliable detail. But enough scattered evidence exists to convey some impression of these shadowy servants of the *sûreté générale*. *Mouchard* was the popular and opprobrious general term for police spies of all types, political or nonpolitical. Many other more colorful words, coined mainly in the underworld, described the specialized techniques of various kinds of secret agents. For our purposes, agents used for political police may be reduced to three categories, none new to the Second Empire.

The professionals—full-time special police inspectors—were concentrated principally in Paris in much smaller numbers than the public imagination often supposed, according to the testimony of both friends and enemies of the regime. Unsolicited volunteer informers and anonymous denunciators contacted the police in large numbers. Regular officers generally distrusted this type but often followed the leads they suggested. A third group were the *indicateurs,* a motley lot of part-time semiprofessionals who continued their normal, unofficial lives while spying on the side for pay according to value received or, in some cases, for small retainers. These undoubtedly were the principal force of *mouchards* during the fifties, as they had been long before. Count Kératry referred to the *indicateurs* when he declared in 1870 that besides the relatively few professional secret police there existed "an absolutely undetermined number of exterior agents unknown to the agents of the bureaus and unknown to one another." They served in all ranks of society according to need, known only to a few high functionaries to whom they reported, often under assumed names.[22] In a regime chronically short of police funds the *indicateurs* were economical; and they projected secret surveillance far more widely than otherwise would have been possible.

Varied motives impelled more applicants to seek the *indicateur*'s role than the police could use. Some were in dire financial need or simply wanted extra money for luxuries. A woman might volunteer to cover her "foolish" expenses, a student to obtain tuition; or a secret society member, regretting his affiliation and yet fearing to break it, might buy immunity from the police by informing. Some were prompted by patriotism and a sense of civic duty; others informed without pay out of obscure motives.[23]

Whatever their reasons, the *indicateurs* most stimulated the widespread public antipathy evoked by the word *mouchard*. In his caustic *Lanterne*, near the end of the Empire, the journalist Henri Rochefort spiced every issue with sarcastic allusions such as that of May 31, 1868:

And you know that once called a *mouchard*, a man—though he mount the scaffold for his opinions—would never succeed in regaining public confidence. Men would be found who would declare they saw the executioner, while lifting him onto the fatal plank, slip his last quarter's pay into his hand.

There seems to be no way to unravel the pay system for secret agents. In most cases it could not have been very rewarding. A full-time professional on loan to the Bouches-du-Rhône in 1853 received 300 francs per month, plus 130 francs for expenses during the period June to September. This exceeded, to be sure, the income of many *commissaires*. Bergeret's men at Lyon received 1,200 francs per year. *Indicateurs*' pay was highly varied. The Emperor once ordered payment of 500 francs to an agent for special services over an undetermined period, during which he had reported "conspiracies" and brought "several people" to justice. A list of payments in 1867 (no similar list was found for the fifties) to sixty-six of Lagrange's *indicateurs* in France, London, Turin, New York, Belgium, and Switzerland shows one payment of a thousand francs. The others ranged between five hundred and one hundred francs, without indication of the length or nature of services rendered. Most payments were between two hundred and one hundred francs. A usually well-informed Englishman claimed to have learned from a Prefecture official that the relative shortage of secret funds forced the maximum use of criminals who could be made to serve without charge. Unpaid volunteers were plentiful according to Maxime du Camp: "At Paris there are people who would not go to bed before writing the Prefect of Police all they have heard and seen during the day." Such informers might be paid for especially useful information.[24]

THE USES OF SECRET POLICE

Indicateurs supplied useful random information from many quarters. But the police also regularly assigned secret agents to certain types of specific missions. As the prefects' reports show, they helped determine the loyalty of suspected functionaries. They supported frontier surveillance by tracing the routes of illicit literature and persons illegally crossing borders. In some cases they apparently spied on private electoral meetings.[25] They associated with Parisian students. Two secret agents regularly assisted the special *commissaires* who inspected bookselling and printing in Paris. Secret agents were, of course, in the crowds greeting visiting statesmen and sovereigns. They worked in strikes and centers of workers' unrest. For example, Prefect Henri Chevreau in 1854 borrowed two agents from Paris for undercover surveillance of agitators among the workers of Nantes. One agent posed as a factory worker; the other took a roving assignment to seek contact with "men whose antecedents and relationships suggest as being leaders of the socialist party." Secret agents circulated among political refugees, particularly in England and the Channel Isles, where *indicateurs* lived among the exiles to tempt them on occasion with subversive "proposals" or simply to report their doings. Charles Delescluze, returning secretly to Paris in 1853, remained for two months before walking into the waiting arms of the police, "sold by one of those miserable beings who eat the bread of betrayal."[26]

Secret Police Against Secret Societies

The chief use of secret agents was to penetrate secret societies. Few official files on secret society cases lacked at least one informer —an agent put there by the authorities, a venturesome *indicateur,* or a genuine member turned spy before or after arrest. *Le Figaro* in October, 1870, quoted an ex-*commissaire* of police whose obvious exaggeration had a degree of truth: "In a group of ten secret society members there are always three *mouchards,* six well-meaning imbeciles, and one dangerous man."

Volunteer *indicateurs* in the secret societies were in the long run probably as useful as professional agents. Indeed, they were the main source of recruitment for the latter. In the case files of the Ministry of Justice are many instances of secret society members who informed after arrest, were convicted, and served part of their sentences before being rewarded by early clemency. Afterward, some took *indicateur's* status and a few became regular secret police professionals. The convicted informer's reward was seldom complete forgiveness, even when he collaborated with the police after his voluntary initiation. Nor was he always offered further police employment. Sometimes he enjoyed full pardon of fine and prison sentences; sometimes these penalties were merely reduced. He almost always had to endure, at least for a time, the customary loss of civil rights that accompanied heavy prison sentences. For example, Isidore Ramade, a leader of La Marianne, volunteered information that earned a remission of his fine and two of his four years in prison. Three months later the remaining two years were canceled. But his five years' suspension of rights remained. When newly incriminated informers gave accurate information already known by the professionals, they were often pardoned after serving part of their sentences, but not necessarily sooner than noninformers who were similarly favored. Authorities were alert for false informers such as a Jean Vittet who, when arrested at Lyon, pretended unsuccessfully to have been a public-minded *indicateur* all along.[27]

Indicateurs and spontaneous informers were indispensable as cheap and often fortuitous sources of information. But officials preferred experienced professionals when possible. Gustave Rouland appreciatively followed "step by step" the adroit tactics of "devoted agents" who learned the secret plans of the Fraternité Universelle in 1855, presumably just in time to foil "a frightful *jacquerie.*" Rouland admired this expert performance, "without the least trace of provocation—such is a good and useful police!"

At Lyon, Bergeret aspired to have two agents in every secret society, unknown to one another so that their reports served as a "control" over both. If no secret agent chanced to be among an arrested group, the authorities tried to plant agents among the prisoners during the interrogation period. Sometimes professionals from Paris concealed their true identities from the prefects even while assisting them—to the point of enduring arrest and even trial before being quietly freed.

Such professional work was concentrated on what might be called the "Paris-Lyon Axis," where radical activity was greatest and police collaboration frequent. But relations were not always harmonious between the police of the two cities, as illustrated in 1856. At the Sûreté Publique's request, Lagrange sent several secret agents to Lyon and St. Etienne to collect proofs of a conspiracy involving London refugees and revolutionaries in Paris and Lyon. The agents followed orders to conceal their identities from the Lyonnaise authorities until the *dénouement*. Certain officials in Lyon resented Lagrange's deception and the tactics of his agents. The *procureur-général* refused to prosecute some of the incriminated men on the grounds that Lagrange's men had acted as *agents provocateurs*. At least one Parisian secret agent was among the thirty-eight men arrested and the twenty-eight condemned to prison. In a few days he was transferred from Lyon's jail to Paris and released without the knowledge of the Lyon *procureur,* who in the next year recommended that the man not be considered for pardon. The *procureur*'s sole consolation was that Lagrange's technique was "a good lesson" to Lyon's administrative police, who were caught napping.[28]

Secret police methods were not always successful against secret societies. Agents' information was often too imprecise to provide material evidence in court. As officials knew all too well, secret agents tended to exaggerate. Prefects, and especially *procureurs,* regarded secret evidence cautiously, though they let themselves be misled on occasion. Even the veteran Bergeret at Lyon raided a reported "new secret society" and found nothing more suspect than "legitimist portraits" on the premises. The judiciary police, sticklers for correct legal procedure, refused to prosecute cases incorrectly prepared, much to the annoyance of prefects who lost the money invested in preliminary secret surveillance. Mistakes in identity could fool even the old professional, Lagrange. His agents arrested a banker with the same surname as a secret society firebrand who was the real suspect. The victim's protests to the Emperor forced Lagrange to admit "a regrettable error."[29]

AGENTS PROVOCATEURS

Among the bitterest charges hurled at the Empire's secret police in 1870 was the accusation that virtually all the underground activity and "plots" were cynical inventions of *agents provocateurs* by policemen who wished to keep their jobs and to frighten the public into acceptance of the police state. Kératry charged that provocation was the principal activity of the imperial police and that "all the seditious affairs of the last ten years have been machinations of the secret police." Eighty years later, this accusation has been inflated into the surprising conclusion that there was "not a single anti-government action" under Louis Napoleon "which had not been inspired by the police itself."[30] That such assertions are grossly exaggerated is an understatement.

However, the imperial secret police, in the manner of their predecessors, did engage in some provocative activity. Charges of provocation usually have been confined to the Paris secret police. The scanty evidence does not indicate that the prefects deliberately followed the practice. Certainly it was never condoned in police doctrine. Certain *procureurs* vigorously condemned provocative tactics and on several occasions refused to prosecute cases resting on evidence supplied by agents who they believed were *provocateurs*. In one such instance, Rouland defended a colleague's rejection of a case: "it would be evil, immoral, and reprehensible to push these unfortunates into criminal offenses which they did not intend to commit." He added that in no political prosecution in his experience had the defense had reason to charge provocation.[31]

Three factors probably accounted for secret police provocation. The tradition was old among French secret police.[32] Actual or would-be *indicateurs* probably resorted to it in order to show

impressive results or to win employment as a secret agent. Unfortunately for the romantic image of mid-century revolutionaries, denunciations and baiting of their supposed comrades by
ex-political *condamnés* or fellow secret society members was very
common. In the Var, for example, an *indicateur* was "one of the
principal organizers of the secret societies." The administrative
police more readily than the *procureurs* took evidence where they
found it. Thirdly, if secret agents ever reflected upon the matter
at all, they must have wondered how to draw the line between
posing as an active revolutionary (always defended as legitimate
in police doctrine) and playing the *provocateur*'s role. Even the
highest officials could not always decide among themselves if their
agents had crossed the line.[33]

Some of the cruder charges of provocation under the Empire
are hard to believe. One anecdote tells of a group of *provocateurs*
in workers' dress who transparently pretended to throw up a barricade in a Paris street as they called upon bystanders for
aid. When the knowing crowd refused, jeering and shouting
"Mouchard!" the secret agents snatched clubs from their clothing
and charged the spectators. More plausibly, the Lyon police were
supposed to have "kept" a certain secret society because its police-
spy leaders were "men whom they could imprison or let go free
according to the needs of governmental policy."[34]

Except for Felice Orsini in 1858, and two or three others,
Louis Napoleon's alleged would-be assassins have been dismissed
as figments or victims of police inventions fabricated to nourish
the "red specter." No attempt is made here to explore the au-
thenticity of even the more publicized "plots."[35] But some general
observations seem justified.

If the more famous plots were hatched by the secret police, that
secret itself was amazingly well kept from the nation's ordinary
police officials. Each alarm was preceded or followed (or both)
by extensive investigations, reams of correspondence, and serious
confidential discussions of the wisdom of publicizing such affairs.
One may, of course, speculate that the prefects, *procureurs,* and
others disbelieved in all this; but that would be to assume that
those officials were playing, straight-faced, a twenty-year game

of nationwide political charades in which no one faltered in his role. It was, of course, characteristic of the administrative attitude to leap to conclusions about the "red specter." There were enough real secret agitators to encourage the tendency by extravagant propaganda and threats which the police regularly intercepted and introduced to one another in evidence.

If the imperial police had valued "plots" only for publicity, they could have had far more of it. Their files hid scores of reports of unpublicized *complots* against the Emperor or society itself. Many such reports were labeled false or dubious upon arrival, but *procureurs* and prefects routinely relayed them to Paris. Investigation sometimes uncovered suggestive evidence, sometimes not. In less than two years during 1861–62, thirteen out of twenty-eight *procureurs* reported one or more alleged plots against the Emperor's life. Some of these led to arrests and convictions without publicity; others were reported in the press. Behind scenes, officials disagreed on the political wisdom of publicizing even those *complots* they believed genuine. The "Conspiracy of the Reine Blanche" case was tried and publicized in the staid *Gazette des Tribunaux* after three months' intensive investigation in 1852. The prefect of the Haute-Garonne approved the relatively reserved mode of publicity provided the case had to be broadcast at all, but he thought the government should rarely go so far. According to the prefect of the Hérault, group conspiracies should always be kept quiet and their repression handled individually to avoid injustices and alarms. In 1854, the Minister of the Interior vetoed Gustave Rouland's wish to publicize the case of eighty-five persons arrested and tried on *complot* and secret society charges after prolonged secret police investigation, though the case had the classic features—plans for large-scale social violence and links with refugees in London, Jersey, and Belgium.[36]

THE CABINET NOIR

In January, 1852, the Duc de Morny cautioned a friend, "Be careful how you write to me; one must be very much on guard with a man like M. de Maupas heading the police." Morny referred to the "black cabinet," the legendary place and procedure of secret policy spying into private correspondence. Certainly no invention of Louis Napoleon's era, the clandestine opening, reading, and forwarding of private mail undoubtedly continued through the Second Empire. Surveillance of the mails actually was of two kinds: that done legally and openly by competent authorities following specified procedures; and that of the true *cabinet noir,* done illicitly behind closed doors by the secret police. The legal method, without doubt the more extensive, was clear enough; the *cabinet noir* remains, true to its name, obscure and thus the more dramatically sinister. The immediate successors of the Second Empire attacked the *cabinet noir* with particular spleen, vowing to destroy it with as much determination (and perhaps comparable success) as other reformers in 1830 and 1848.[37]

Accounts of the *cabinet noir* have variously located it simultaneously or at different times in the Prefecture of Police, the Ministry of the Interior, the Tuileries, the telegraph headquarters, and in Paris postal offices. There has been consensus on its existence but on little else. To hazard a guess on the basis of conflicting testimony, the *cabinet noir* existed with the postal authorities' collusion in the Ministry of the Interior until Collet-Meygret's tenure ended in 1856 and his office was fused with that of the Prefect of Police in 1859. Afterward it operated in the capital's main post office.

At the Interior during the fifties, a functionary named Saintomer copied letters obtained from *concierges,* domestics, and postmen, then returned them for regular delivery. According to a witness in the ministry, Collet-Meygret used the system with "passion" and "calculation" to spy on important people and thereby contributed to his disgrace and investigation in 1858.[38] In the sixties, the *cabinet noir* reportedly operated in a room of the main post office. There a postal employee named Simonel (one account spells it Simmonet) reigned, not in a dark closet, but in a large room equipped to open and copy letters of persons named by the Sûreté Publique, to reseal them expertly, and to send them on their way again within a few hours. Maxime du Camp described Simonel (perhaps with some poetic license) as "small, puny, sickly, consumptive, spitting—but endowed with matchless energy." From an ordinary postal employee at fifteen hundred francs he supposedly rose to an office "chief" with no one to supervise but himself. His six-thousand-franc appointment was supplemented by gratifications and "californias," the functionaries' term for overtime pay.[39]

Obviously Simonel's work, if it existed as described, was not a wholesale surveillance of the mails. It probably was confined to a few political suspects and to prying into the affairs of certain "notables." The latter were alert against the *cabinet noir*. In 1852, Eugène Rouher wrote critically of some aspects of governmental policy to a friend, who noted that the letter arrived late with signs of tampering. He sent a true copy to Morny in case Rouher's enemies chose to make an issue of the letter by distorting its contents.[40]

Secrecy was the only advantage of the *cabinet noir*. Officials in charge of political police activities could always legally seize and open printed materials or private letters in the mails by following certain prescribed formalities. Because of the rumors concerning the *cabinet noir*, the public may have confused secret surveillance with its legal counterpart. The postal service's General Instructions allowed prefects and the Prefect of Police by formal requisition to order any functionary with judiciary police authority to seize letters. Each seizure required a special report; the post office took a receipt for every item. When the pieces were returned to the mails, they were resealed by the officer ordering the seizure and stamped, "Opened by the authority of justice." This procedure was employed to detect mail frauds and to intercept illegal lottery tickets as well as for political police purposes. It drew many complaints. In 1854, the Ministry of Justice compiled a special dossier on twenty-eight cases of "illegalities attributed to the prefects" in legal seizures.[41]

The right to order legal mail seizures was unexpectedly challenged in 1853 by the Court of Cassation's technical ruling that no law specifically empowered anyone to open letters. As a brief flurry of alarm spread among the prefects, the Minister of Justice invoked administrative law to advise that the prefects had "as administrative functionaries an incontestable right of surveillance [as] agents of the government" regardless of statutes or their judicial interpretation. Before the year was up, another Cassation decision fully upheld the Minister's doctrine. Officials were thereafter assured that as long as they observed the correct procedures they might continue to seize (or to delegate the power to judiciary police officers) "all letters or correspondence presumed reprehensible . . . from the viewpoint of the *sûreté générale* and public order."[42] This instruction prevailed despite press protests and the opposition's attempted interpellations on the issue in the Legislative Body during the sixties.

CONCLUSION

In France as a whole in the fifties there appear to have been no very significant departures in secret police expenditures, organization, or techniques. Indeed, to prefects outside Paris, long accustomed by doctrine and practice to secret surveillance, governmental policy was static, even regressive. Their disapproval probably sprang from their administrators' attitude toward the refugees and secret societies after 1848. These new problems called for more intense use of all police techniques. But new or expanded secret police activities must have been limited to the Paris police organizations. There were probably more *indicateurs* on the lists; and more counterspying against refugees and the secret societies along the Paris-Lyon "axis."

Why did the prefects not receive greater secret police resources? Without knowledge of the government's inner councils, one must speculate. Paris may have hesitated to provoke "local influences" by asking for more taxes to increase the secret funds. Furthermore, the "unusual" aspects of political police in the 1850's were not secret. They were the relatively stronger executive power, heavier administrative centralization, and the new laws which directed the administration's routine, "open" security operations more freely along well-worn paths. Apart from the compulsion to watch the refugees and to bore into underground societies, secret methods offered only incidental advantages in the broader realm of political police. And mid-nineteenth-century secret agents, untrained in our contemporary sense, had their limitations.

Marseille, the nation's third largest city, provides a case in point. As a great seaport and metropolis of the Midi, where much of the coup's violence erupted, and with its large Italian colony, Marseille could hardly be ignored in political police surveillance. Yet the archives of the Bouches-du-Rhône reveal more vigor in "open" political police activities than in abnormal emphasis on secret police. Even after the police ministry, the prefect's restored annual secret funds budget was only that of the pre-December period: six thousand francs, or slightly under twelve hundred dollars at the 1855 rate of exchange. Marseille had no special bureau of political or secret police; these were left to a *commissaire* along with his other duties. Judging from a series of reports by three secret agents (one a professional on loan from Paris) in 1852–54, secret surveillance was not very productive. Even the professional from Paris found little of value and spent his time in financial worry and great anxiety lest his identity become known. Reviewing the decade 1849–59, the *commissaire* in charge of secret police concluded that the technique "has not always been skillful enough to conceal itself," and had only the merit of keeping the quarry on guard so that in public, at least, the *indicateurs* since the early fifties no longer heard "a single word with serious political significance."[43]

The French Police State of the 1850's

ON JANUARY 14, 1858, Felice Orsini and two other Italian refugees from England hurled three baseball-sized grenades at Napoleon III outside the Paris Opéra. Their target escaped. But eight dead and one hundred and fifty wounded paid for an action that later changed the history of Orsini's Italy. Orsini also triggered the greatest political police reaction since December, 1851, in France and inspired the extraordinary Law of *Sûreté Générale*. That law ironically brought general police powers to their apogee and also foreshadowed their attenuation in the sixties.

The Law of Sûreté Générale *and the Reaction of 1858*

Orsini's bombs brought the "red specter" tragically to French soil and momentarily rekindled the police *élan* of 1851–52. Officials vented their pent-up resentment against British coddling of what a *procureur* called "the abominable doctrine of political assassination." Prefect of Police Piétri depicted the exiles poised for "a triumphal return to France" through doors smashed in by regicide. The same shocked Anglophobia unsettled the general public. In Marseille, as in the far north, one heard "murmurs against the English from nearly every mouth."[1] From the Elysée down, there was also criticism aplenty for French police officials. The incident of thirty-three policemen who were hit by the explosions of January 14 did not soften charges of police negligence. The Paris police reportedly knew of Orsini's arrival; they surprised his fourth cohort with a bomb only thirty minutes before the crime. Two years earlier, a foreign official had warned French authorities that Orsini was a "dangerous emissary" of international conspiracy.[2]

Official heads had to roll. On February 7, the inflexible General Espinasse replaced Billault and took the novel and lengthier title, "Minister of the Interior and of *Sûreté Générale*." Whereupon Madame Baroche predicted, "the reign of the saber is beginning." The General's performance until his brief tenure ended on June 14 seemed designed to realize her prediction. Piétri, already suspect to extreme conservatives because of his youthful liberal taint —General Castellane thought him "half red"!—yielded to Boittelle on March 16. Piétri meanwhile acted as go-between for the Emperor and Orsini in their reconciliation on Italian policy. Against the opinion of all the ministers, he recommended pardon for the condemned assassin and leniency for his associates. While recognizing that Orsini's execution would appear just to the public, Piétri philosophically took leave of the Prefecture with the observation that it was "unhappily all too true" that great penalties for large crimes did not deter their occurrence.[3]

Before either Billault or Piétri departed their offices, a political police campaign swept France and crossed the frontiers. A flurry of "urgent" and "confidential" dispatches passed between French police and their counterparts in Prussia, Bavaria, Switzerland, Belgium, and the Italian states. But, as always, the French were obsessed with the refugee problem in England. In 1858, Britain was publicly and confidentially more helpful than at any time since the French had made the refugees a chronic diplomatic complaint. Amid polemical storms on either side of the issue, Palmerston offered Parliament a "Conspiracy to Murder Bill" which anti-French feeling helped to defeat. The government also prosecuted Simon Bernard, Orsini's alleged bomb-maker, after rejecting a French request for his extradition. His acquittal probably owed much to the jury's Francophobia. For London meanwhile "very confidentially" aided the French police in investigating his case and the Orsini Affair generally. Charles Yardley, a high English police official, personally brought to Paris the evidence seized in the conspirators' quarters. Commissaire Lagrange crossed the Channel in April with three police agents and eight civilian experts to collaborate in the Bernard case with London's Chief Commissioner of Police. Admitting that it "went beyond the prescriptions of the English law," the British government importuned Paris to keep its police collaboration secret.[4]

In France, as secret expenditures jumped to an unusual high, Orsini's attempt precipitated the closest collaboration by the police forces of three ministries since the coup d'état and the "mixed commissions" of 1852. For several months the prefects sent their minister obligatory daily political reports. From these, extracts and summaries went to the Ministry of Justice to be correlated with the *procureurs'* political reports. The nebulous evidence yielded by this spate of paperwork encouraged the Ministry of Justice briefly to conclude that the Orsini plot involved French conspirators to whom the Emperor's assassination would have been the signal to touch off risings in thirty-three *départements*.[5] Joining the Interior-Justice political surveillance, the army on January 27 superimposed five "superior commands," each under a marshal (a sixth was added in May), over the normal military districts in order to prepare for war in Italy and to join in a special political police effort with the two civilian ministries. By the Emperor's order of February 9, the marshals, already receiving political reports from the gendarmerie, were supposed also to have the full prefects' reports on anything relevant to public security. Actually the prefects kept their minister more fully informed than the marshals; and they gave him copies of their special reports to the military. Still, these arrangements more closely linked the political police facilities of the three ministries.[6]

The joint attempts to connect Orsini and French political suspects were only a prelude. At the Emperor's insistence, a more systematic instrument of political police was assembled in the Elysée, Council of State, and parliament. On February 27 it became the Law of *Sûreté Générale*.

True to its title, the new measure specified a more stringent use of the administration's discretionary general police power. Showing its authors' inability to shake off the "red specter" of 1848–51, it expanded the principle of the decree of December 8, 1851—of which the law's preamble called it the "natural consequence." The Minister of the Interior, advised jointly by the prefects, *pro-*

cureurs, and military district commanders, might now by "measure of *sûreté générale"* intern in France, expel from the country, or transport to Algeria anyone who had already endured these same penalties because of the events of May–June, 1848, June, 1849, or December, 1851. Still others, formerly judicially condemned for certain political offenses, now became liable to the same three penalties by administrative decision. These powers were valid for seven years. For suspects without records of earlier punishment, the new law was as ominously vague as the doctrine of *sûreté générale* which it embodied. Article 2 authorized judicial prosecution of anyone who "has undertaken activities or correspondence with the intention of troubling the public peace or inciting hatred or mistrust of the Emperor's government" either in France or abroad.

The one limitation on the administration's use of its new powers was itself so vaguely phrased as again to stress the Draconian spirit of the law. Past offenders whom the law placed in double jeopardy would suffer only if "serious new facts" made them appear dangerous. The Ministry of Justice at this point introduced one other qualification by interpretation: the "new facts" must occur only *after* passage of the new law. Otherwise, in response to many queries the Ministry (after consultation with Espinasse) refused to define the term "serious new facts" other than as "a general and indeterminate expression" whose practical meaning would be left to officials' "enlightened evaluation" of the "degree of gravity and peril" attending each suspect's case. The law was so reminiscent of the 1852 "mixed commissions" that in the Pyrenées-Orientales the prefect, *procureur,* and general called themselves a "Mixed Commission"; they had to be curtly reminded that theirs was merely an advisory function. Only the Minister of the Interior made final disposition of the cases submitted to him.[7]

General Espinasse began operations even before the Law of *Sûreté Générale* was completed. On February 8, he reassured the nation that the forthcoming political police actions would combine "force with right" only against those seized by "anarchist passions." Confidentially he ordered the prefects, after conference with the *procureurs* and generals, to submit two annotated lists of suspects. One list named persons affected by the new law and recommended one of the three specified punishments in each case. The second list, apparently Espinasse's own idea, named persons unaffected by the law who should be under surveillance "because of the part they might take in case of an insurrectional movement." The prefects' responses were not stern enough for Espinasse. He rebuked them severely for insufficient arrests, luke-warm cooperation with the *procureurs* and generals, negligence in updating lists of suspects, and failure to see that "new leaders of the demagogy have emerged who are even more dangerously active" than the old.[8]

This investigator has failed to find documentation for Emile Ollivier's allegation that Espinasse ordered the prefects to meet arbitrary "quotas" of arrests in each *département*. There was no apparent uniformity of arrests from one *département* to another; nor were the prefects' recommendations proportional to the number of punishments in their *départements* in 1852. Espinasse's instructions were not always fully understood or followed. Prefects and *procureurs* often clashed; the latter as usual accused the prefects (whom Espinasse considered too lax) of overseverity. Espinasse himself ultimately followed only some of the prefects' punitive recommendations. He sent 428 persons to Algeria, most of whom were earlier victims of the coup d'état. Before the general amnesty of August, 1859, 207 were already back in France, leaving 209 transportees to benefit from the amnesty. Perhaps Espinasse moderated his decisions because of pressure from above. In June he resigned with obvious dissatisfaction, accusing the Emperor of sharing the "misgivings" of his many critics. With a parting shot at the administration's leniency, he stoutly insisted that the "horror of republican anarchy" in 1858 was as deadly as in 1851.[9] His successor Delangle became simply "Minister of the Interior" without the addition "and of the *Sûreté Générale*."

The reaction of 1858 was losing momentum long before the first *proscrits* sailed for Algeria. After the initial shock of Orsini's violence, public criticism of Espinasse and his expected "reign of the saber" increased. Disapproval also spread among the Empire's notables and in the administration. General Fleury professed to be "literally sick with chagrin." Such misgivings went beyond the iron personality and immediate severity of Espinasse.

When the Law of *Sûreté Générale* was first proposed to the Council of State, Baroche had to jockey it through much opposition. Even at this stage, the government accepted more qualifications of the administration's theoretically unlimited *sûreté générale* powers than had been intended. To obtain the Legislative Body's approval, further qualifications were written into the project: the seven-year limit upon the administration's arbitrary powers; and the requirement that the prefects make their recommendations in consultation with the *procureurs* and generals. Even so, nineteen conservative deputies voted with the opposition's five against the law. The nonelective Senate was more complaisant. But the sole articulate opponent of the measure was General MacMahon, soon to become one of the commanders of the six special military divisions of 1858.[10]

The *procureurs* most strongly objected, not to severity toward real conspirators, but against this further abandonment of judicial procedures which, however justified in theory, might alienate the public and become a Pyrrhic victory. Even Chaix-d'Est-Ange, Rouland's authoritarian successor in the Paris *parquet,* bluntly protested that a law so hastily "improvised in the first moments of grief and panic" reflected "the government's fears rather than really protecting the public security." France needed "not recourse to extreme measures," he declared, "but a firmer administration felt evenly throughout the Empire." A colonel of gendarmerie feared that by appearing to "threaten everyone," the law ironically confirmed what the regime's worst enemies were saying.[11] General police theory notwithstanding, many of its practitioners in 1858 agreed that its practical limits had been exceeded.

After the spring of 1858, the Law of *Sûreté Générale* fell nearly into disuse. The administration's unique powers expired in May, 1865, leaving only those provisions involving judicial procedures until these, too, ended in October, 1870. The brief political police reaction of 1858 only mimicked the spirit of the coup d'état and its aftermath of early 1852. The "red specter" was senescent even before Orsini gave it a transitory stimulant. Reams of political police paperwork showed no vital links between the refugees and conspiracy in France by the late fifties. The events of 1859 in Italy turned the major attention of French police authorities toward the clergy and legitimists as the general political amnesty of August brought most of the aging exiles home. Thus the Law of *Sûreté Générale,* if not itself a turning point, was the prelude to one. It completed the legal arsenal of the Empire's political police. But during the sixties, the repressive weapons of Louis Napoleon's "police state" were gradually dulled in limited though significant degree by the evolution of a so-called Liberal Empire.

General Conclusion

If the relative term "police state" connotes a preponderant executive in command of a centralized bureaucracy whose edicts supersede the voice of local government and which systematically uses decisive police controls over the expression and organization of public opinion, then the Second Empire was a police state. Indeed, France, except during several revolutionary interims, was in varying degrees a police state long before Louis Napoleon made it the most noticeably so since the First Empire. The repressive legislation and political police activities of the fifties embodied historical continuity more than they anticipated twentieth-century totalitarian models. The outlook of police officials was traditional. The administrative law, doctrine, and practice upon which their power rested were preserved from the past. The coup d'état, of course, ruptured legal continuity. But its authors and executors found its rationale in the entrenched and unbounded principle of the executive's responsibility for the *sûreté générale* —which in 1851 would probably have carried much conviction even without the addition of the Bonapartist plebiscitary mystique. After extraordinary powers ended in March, 1852, traditional political police concepts and techniques operated more freely but without essential innovations within a revised constitutional and legal setting.

The police state of the fifties drew its distinctive features from the conjunction of four interacting forces. By 1849, the traditional administrative and police system was available as a potential instrument for Louis Napoleon's expedient realization of his ambitions—if he could appeal to and manipulate the particularistic attitude of higher administrative officials. The "red specter" of 1848 was the fourth and catalytic element of the combination.

Louis Napoleon's exploitation of the "red specter" and the administrative system is obvious enough. But for lack of first-hand evidence, this study has failed to discover his attitudes toward the administration, his personal reactions to such apparent setbacks as the undermining of the Ministry of General Police, and the extent to which he tried to intervene in routine administrative and political police activities.

What we have called the "administrative attitude" was a crucial contribution to the founding of the Second Empire. At mid-century, the directors of political police displayed a new dynamism of resistance against the kinds of political and social change symbolized by the international "red specter" of 1848 and by less fearful aspects of increased popular participation in public life. To a particularistic and conservative bureaucracy, these were intruding abnormalities which must be overcome on behalf of values better suited to a more static and orderly era. Fear and hope together generated a crusading spirit in the cause of destroying the sources of fear and more definitively reasserting the traditional administrative function. To these ends, the prefects and *procureurs* prepared the stage for Louis Napoleon after 1849 and helped him seize full power in December, 1851. They expected him to clear the way for a more nearly ideal realization of a "normal" administrative state. They hoped to recapture and perfect their roles as stern but benevolent guardians of a society stabilized by obedience to traditional religious and rural virtues.

Today one is tempted to dismiss the administrative attitude as a reactionary stereotype that was blind or at least irrelevant to the social problems of 1848. Twentieth-century observers bred in the liberal tradition might also too easily take the republic of 1848 as an accomplished democratic standard by which to assess

and condemn the reaction of the fifties as a retrogressive stifling
of freedom. This would be to judge one stereotype by another.
Peter Amann has recently recalled the profound complexities of
the French revolution of 1848, its social divisions, cross purposes,
and confusing welter of unrealizable hopes. The revolutionaries
also failed to relate their aspirations meaningfully to the very
problems that perplexed and repelled the officials. They too drew
on "a largely irrelevant tradition."[12] In their own way, the officials sensed this essential failure of 1848. Their image of the
"red specter" and its "vain utopias" was both an oversimplified
explanation of the problem and a specific enemy to combat in
defense of traditional norms. No revolutionaries of the Right,
they sought to bolster institutional continuity against unusual dangers.

That objective seemed ensured by the polity of the Second
Empire. Political police officials used their prerogatives sternly.
But very few of their procedures were new to French experience
since 1800. Political police action was most accentuated by the
executive's constitutional predominance, prefectorial *tutelle* over
the communes, and a repertory of laws mostly continued or revived from earlier regimes. The ability to warn, suspend, and
suppress political newspapers was a novelty. The decree of December 8, 1851, and the Law of *Sûreté Générale* in 1858 were
innovations in that they extended to specified political offenders
a kind of double punishment long applied routinely to convicted
criminals under French law. After 1852, the authorities grew
increasingly critical of the decree of December 8 and applied it
less to political offenders than to common criminals and vaga-
bonds. In 1860, a critic of the regime found that the severest
restraints upon individual liberty—such as legal surveillance, internment, and "preventive" arrest or detention after arrest—
owed less to the Second Empire's exceptional legislation than
to the Code of Criminal Procedure of 1808. Indeed, the Second
Empire began a liberalization of the Code by easing the conditions of preventive detention between 1855 and 1865.[13]

After March, 1852, political police officials implemented their
legally expanded assignments with a severity that stayed within

the limits of traditional administrative usage, by which it should be judged. Stern though it was, the administrative attitude had its ethical code and a keen sense of professional integrity. Charges of unusual brutality or illegal violence were significantly rare among the many criticisms aimed at the police. The authorities investigated such charges and punished offenders. The *procureurs* were vigilant guardians of legality conceived in an absolute, not instrumentalist, sense. Administrative police officials, whom the *procureurs* often accused of stretching their powers to the limit, acted more expediently as agents of "the sole political ministry." But, with the *procureurs,* they wished to indoctrinate subordinates in the ethics as well as the technicalities of their functions. The *Journal des Commissaires de Police* exhorted its readers to uphold objective legal standards and to temper their authority with common sense and the integrity of high-minded public servants. Writers on "doctrine" periodically reminded the *commissaires* that their power should "be present everywhere without being obtrusive." They should know "what it is better to overlook than to punish" and that individual rights "must be scrupulously respected." When the public interest was at stake, police investigations and arrests must proceed "only under legally-prescribed forms." Their journal frequently offered the *commissaires* articles on the law of arrest, the privacy of domicile, and the penalties for "denial of justice," "illegal violence," or improper violation of the secrecy of the mails.[14]

Neither increased powers nor their determination to improve the police services lured the prefects and *procureurs* into the illusion that they had achieved the ideal administrative state. The "red specter," now driven abroad, prolonged the urgent spirit of service to the *sûreté générale* which had launched the new regime. Police state techniques could control the press and reduce conspiracy in France to underground fragments. But formal powers were less triumphant over "local influences," administrative conflicts, and the widespread lethargy, opportunism, and incompetence of lesser functionaries who were seldom exemplary representatives of the administrative mission.

Their chronic and universal complaints against "local influ-

ences" cloaked police officials' begrudging recognition that a
police state had its limits. In the contexts of countless administrative reports, this hackneyed term denoted some perverse and alien
intruder with which even prefects and *procureurs* had to find a
modus vivendi. The catch-all phrase "local influences" symbolized
years of detailed prefectorial frustrations. It also implicitly admitted that everyday life was too stubbornly diversified to fit
the orderly compartments and categories of the administrative
state as conceived in the prefectures and *parquets*. Traditional
ways also persisted outside the administrators' particularism.

Administrative conflicts themselves reflected a special sort of
"local influences" problem within the public bureaucracy. At a
generalized level prefects, *procureurs,* and gendarmerie officers
shared the same hopes and fears and alike aspired to the goals of
a police state. They spontaneously acted together against the
short-lived Ministry of Police. But each group viewed the details
of administering the police state from differing perspectives. The
gendarmerie was the most removed within its own elitist outlook.
The *procureurs,* in their daily legalistic routine, were much closer
to the prefects. Yet the two most often clashed with one another
because of the prefects' primary concern with political expediency.
Commissaires, mayors, and rural policemen likewise viewed di-
versely their shares of a supposedly common task. In relations
with other ministerial bureaucracies—Public Instruction, Public
Works, Marine, and Finances—the prefects felt even more isolation. Other officials sometimes disregarded the prefects' new
decision-making powers under the "decentralization" decree of
1852. Despite an imperial order in 1853 that all ministries consult the prefects on all their personnel actions, 90 per cent of the
prefects complained that they were too often ignored.[15]

As the most powerful agents of the police state, the prefects
were in a curious position. Beset by "local influences" and often
involved in administrative conflicts, those prefects who attacked
their problems too bluntly had to face restraints from their own
minister and the *procureurs'* criticism of their "excessive zeal."
But as they looked down their own hierarchy they often had to
join the *procureurs* in the same charge—or its opposite—against

commissaires, mayors, and rural policemen. From the officials' view, police inefficiency was another element of historical continuity in France.

During the fifties, both the public and the administration composed endless variations on the theme, "the police service leaves much to be desired." The Empire's political opponents presented the police both as a terribly efficient symbol of despotism and as clownishly incompetent for purposes of satire. Ultraconservatives castigated police weakness and timidity. Central officials of the Interior and Justice ministries could agree with the opposition, the *procureurs,* and many prefects that the "excessive zeal" of certain police officers alienated the public. They agreed with fearful reactionaries when deploring the weaknesses and incompetence of others. The prefects and *procureurs* joined in denouncing the grip of "local influences" on many *commissaires,* municipal policemen, and of course the *gardes-champêtres.* The situation at Nîmes in 1854—where all municipal councilors allegedly had "some protegé" in the police, who thus were "imbued with local passions and revoltingly partial in their surveillance"—had its reported counterparts elsewhere throughout the fifties. From the heights of his *parquet* at Paris, Gustave Rouland found the administrative police nearly everywhere outside the Seine inefficient, badly organized, and obstructive to good judiciary police service. Similar criticisms inspired pamphlets and books with conclusions like that of a brochure by a veteran *commissaire* at Rodez: "In most *départements* the police has for long been badly managed, often powerless, and even derisory." An ex-prefect's published critique of police efficiency in the hopeful "new era" of 1852 was echoed in 1860 by Count Rodolphe d'Ornano, another ex-prefect and official of the Emperor's Household. D'Ornano cited "conflicts, injurious rivalries, and delays that are enormously harmful to public welfare and the expedition of business." Lack of professional training, woefully inadequate pay, and the blight of "local influences" continued to make the profession of administrator or police officer "the most precarious of all careers. . . ."[16]

Most critics agreed that inefficiency was inevitable until the number of police officers was increased and better men attracted by adequate payment. For a frankly constituted police state, the Second Empire did very little in either respect. The Paris force after 1854 underwent a major and long overdue expansion modeled in part upon London's police system. Otherwise, only the number of *commissaires* was greatly expanded from about one to two thousand between 1852 and 1860. Even so, more than a third of the nation's cantons lacked *commissaires*. The municipal reform of 1855 modestly increased the police staffs of a few large cities. The rural police remained notoriously unreformed and impoverished.

Financially, the Second Empire moderately assisted its civil servants but left most of them still in pinched circumstances compared with earlier regimes. Until mid-century, the salaries of most functionaries remained the same as in 1800 or 1806. By 1860, the franc bought only half of what it had in 1800. Contemporary estimates set the minimum needs of an unmarried functionary at 1,500 francs per year and that of a family man with three children at 2,700.

Beginning with the prefects and subprefects, in 1852 the government launched a series of salary increases. The prefects in 1822 had received from 18 to 40,000 francs. This range was cut in 1848, then raised in 1852 to 20 to 40,000. Still, only 26 prefects received salaries higher than the minimum. Before March, 1852, only 48 of the country's 278 subprefects received more than 3,000 francs per year, from which they paid the rent for their official quarters and moving costs when they were transferred. In March, 1852, they were placed in three pay grades between 4,500 and 8,000 francs; only 52 were in the two top grades. Even after similar increases in 1855, the majority of *commissaires* earned just under 1,500 francs.

From 1857 to 1860, the Emperor and Council of State sponsored the allocation of 13 million francs for pay rises for all lower functionaries of the various ministries. The Ministry of the Interior received only 350,000 francs of this supplement, leaving it on a par with the Ministry of Justice as one of the two ministries whose employees received the lowest salaries of the country's civil functionaries. In 1864, a survey by Minister of State

Rouher disclosed that nearly half of about twelve thousand Interior functionaries earned less than 2,000 francs per year. In 1859 the central ministerial administrations in Paris employed only two hundred more persons than in 1847, at an average annual salary increase of no more than 35 francs each.[17]

In administrative practices and attitudes, and in the number, quality, and welfare of the personnel who ran France's police state, it is difficult to find great differences between the Second Empire and earlier regimes. Indeed, after another interlude of reaction against "Bonapartist" centralization following the Empire's fall in 1870, the essential features of the traditional police system returned, partly to remain until the present day. The cantonal *commissariats,* suppressed in 1870, appeared under another name by 1875, as did the special frontier *commissaires,* the fusion of the Prefecture of Police and the national Sûreté Publique, and the special police regime in Lyon. Kératry's proposal in 1870 to "liquidate" the unique concentration of police powers in Paris died within the year when other leaders of the Third Republic disagreed that the Prefecture's traditional powers were "superfluous under a liberal regime." The immunity of "agents of the government," supposedly abolished by decree in September, 1870, survived when the doctrines of the *sûreté générale* and "separation of powers" plus the provisions of the civil and criminal codes proved stronger in the eyes of the courts.[18]

However, a study of the last decade of the Second Empire would discover that one of the most significant breaches in the nineteenth-century police state was opened by that citadel of the administration's predominance during the fifties, the Council of State. The softening of repressive legislation during the 1860's is well known; and Theodore Zeldin has recently shown the Legislative Body's increasingly autonomous role in achieving the Liberal Empire of 1870. At the same time, the Council of State initiated a trend which by the twentieth century would ensure citizens legal recourse against administrative actions before courts in which the executive and administration were no longer judges in their own case.

After 1862, private citizens' access to prefectorial councils was widened by the establishment of simpler and explicit rules of judicial procedure, specific guarantees to justiciables, and public sessions. Costs of actions before the Council of State were lowered. The Council and the Court of Cassation assigned more administrative cases to the regular courts. The Council became less willing—especially in the political policing of the press—to define certain types of cases as political "acts of government" and hence immune from any kind of recourse. Most of the 20,272 cases of recourse against administrative acts which the Council of State permitted during the Second Empire occurred between 1860 and 1870.[19]

Thus a regime that exploited the traditional prerogatives of the executive power in general administration and political police itself took some of the first steps toward dislodging one of the police state's cornerstones. That, however, is another story. Perhaps the Council of State in the sixties reacted to the previous decade's police state as did the *procureur* at Rouen who concluded that such discretionary powers placed upon the administration "moral obligations that it cannot fulfill in spite of all its good intentions."

Notes

ABBREVIATIONS USED IN NOTES

Archives

Archives Nationales, Paris	*AN*
Archives Départementales (city of *dépot*)	*AD* (city)
Archives de la Préfecture de Police, Paris	*APP*
Bibliothèque de la Préfecture de Police	*BPP*
Bibliothèque Nationale	*BN*
Bibliothèque Thiers (Institut de France)	*BT*
Public Record Office, London	*PRO*
Service Historique de l'Armèe, Vincennes	*SHA*

Officials

Ministers cited by name of ministry only: e.g., Interior.
Prefects cited by name of *département:* e.g., Rhône.

Procureurs-généraux	P.G. (city)
Procureurs de la République	P.R. (city)
Procureurs-impériaux	P.I. (city)
Commissaires de Police	C.P. (city)
Inspecteurs-généraux de Police	Insp. G. (city)
Inspecteurs-spéciaux de Police	Insp. S. (city)
Préfet de Police	P.Pol.

Publications

Le Moniteur Universel	*Moniteur*
Gazette des Tribunaux	*Gaz.Trib.*
Journal de la gendarmerie de France	*J.Gend.*
Journal des Commissaires de Police	*J.C.P.*

Jean Baptiste Henri Duvergier (ed.), *Collection complète des lois, décrets, ordonnances, règlements, et avis du conseil d'état* (Paris, 1790–1908), 108 vols.

Duvergier

Chapter 1. Introduction: The Administrative Legacy, Instrument of Dictatorship

1. Théophile Ducrocq, *Cours de droit administratif* (7th ed.; Paris, 1897–1905), I, ix.
2. Léon Aucoc, *Conférences sur l'administration et le droit administratif* (2d ed.; Paris, 1878–82), I, 87–90; G. M. Dufour, *Traité général de droit administratif appliqué* (3d ed.; Paris, 1868–70), I, 31.
3. Ducrocq, *op. cit.*, I, 21–30.
4. Dufour, *op. cit.*, I, 7, 31–32, 111.
5. Louis Lépine, "Police," in Léon Béquet (ed.), *Répertoire de droit administratif* (Paris, 1882–1911), XXII, 262, 268; Cotton d'Englesqueville, *La police et les commissaires de police* (Paris, 1859), p. 7; Alexandre F. A. Vivien, *Etudes administratives* (3d ed.; Paris, 1859), II, 112; quotation from Thierry by Félix Brayer, *Procédure administrative des bureaux de police* (Arras, 1866), p. i.
6. Aucoc, *op. cit.*, I, 180.
7. Aulois, avocat-impérial, before the Tribunal Correctionnelle of the Seine, Feb. 12, 1869, quoted in *Gazette des Tribunaux* (hereafter cited *Gaz.Trib.*), Feb. 20, 1869, p. 172.
8. Vivien, *op. cit.*, II, 114–39.
9. Henry Basset, *Le colportage des imprimés* (Paris, 1938), pp. 64–65; see also Lépine, *op. cit.*, p. 268, Léon Duguit, *Traité de droit constitutionnel* (3d ed.; Paris, 1930), III, 738–39, and Aucoc, *op. cit.*, I, 442.
10. Undated note on the police of the Restoration, *AN, F18 310*; see also Vivien, *op. cit.*, II, 118, 124.
11. E.g., E. Daudet, *La police politique; chronique des temps de la Restauration* (Paris, 1912), pp. i–v.
12. Interior, circular Aug. 10, 1865, *AN, F1a 2123^A*.
13. Germain Deshaires, *Traité de l'administration départementale et communale* (Paris, 1866), p. 43.
15. Paul Deschanel, *La décentralisation* (Paris and Nancy, 1895), pp. 59–60.
16. The point is emphatically made by Roger Grégoire, *La fonction publique* (Paris, 1954), p. 22.
17. Aucoc, *op. cit.*, I, 15.
18. Bernard Schwartz, *French administrative law and the common-law world* (New York, 1954), pp. 2–3.
19. Aucoc, *op. cit.*, 2 vols.; Béquet (ed.), *op. cit.*, 28 vols.; Ducroq, *op. cit.*, 7 vols.; Dufour, *op. cit.*, 8 vols., and *Droit administratif appliqué* (Paris, 1854–57), 7 vols.; E. L. J. Laferrière, *Traité de la juridiction administrative et des recours contentieux* (2d ed.; Paris, 1896), 2 vols.; and Vivien, *op. cit.*, 2 vols.
20. Aucoc, *op. cit.*, I, 389–442, 661–63; Duguit, *op. cit.*, III, 738–39;

Laferrière, *op. cit.,* I, 7–8; and Charles E. Freedeman, *The Conseil d'Etat in modern France* (New York, 1961), pp. 115–16. Article 75 was repealed by the Government of National Defense on Sept. 19, 1870.

21. Quoted by Duguit, *op. cit.,* III, 739.

22. Ducrocq, *op. cit.,* II, 20. But the Council did admit many actions for recourse against other types of administrative acts.

23. Aucoc, *op. cit.,* I, 666–70.

24. For the Paris policemen, Avocat-Impérial Aulois, Tribunal Correction-nelle of the Seine, Feb. 12, 1869, *Gaz.Trib.,* Feb. 20, 1869, pp. 171–72; on the same point see Freedeman, *op. cit.,* pp. 116–17 and Duguit, *op. cit.,* III, 739. On the *Gazette's* case, Interior to Council of State, Feb. 18, 1866, *AN,* F18 354; the Council rejected the case on Nov. 27, 1865.

25. Laferrière, *op. cit.,* I, 10–11, 188–90; Dufour, *Traité général* . . . , I, 30, 100; Ducrocq, *op. cit.,* III, 290; Duguit, *op. cit.,* III, 31–55.

26. Dufour, *Traité général* . . . , I, 30.

27. Duguit, *op. cit.,* III, 36; Schwartz, *op. cit.,* pp. 42–43; Freedeman, *op. cit.,* pp. 1–5.

28. Aucoc, *op. cit.,* I, 412–13; Duguit, *op. cit.,* III, 36–37.

29. Duguit, *op. cit.,* III, 48–49; Freedeman, *op. cit.,* p. 7; Laferrière, *op. cit.,* I, 255. Decree of Jan. 25, 1852, *Moniteur,* Jan. 26, 1852, p. 137. The meticulous care taken to return to the spirit and structure of the First Consul's Council of State is apparent in the notes made by Jules Baroche during the drafting of the decree: *BT,* Baroche papers, 1017.

30. Dufour, *Traité général* . . . , I, 183, 185; Ducrocq, *op. cit.,* I, 167; Brayer, *op. cit.,* pp. 3–4; and Emile Thomas, *Le livre des commissaires de police* (Montdidier, Somme, 1864), p. 71.

31. Ducrocq, *op. cit.,* I, 169. Arrêté by prefect of the Haute-Marne, Oct. 27, 1851, *AN,* F3 I 15. Such actions were frequent and routine.

32. Pierre-Henry, *Histoire des préfets* (Paris, 1950), pp. 143–46, 155–62; Brian Chapman, *The prefects and provincial France* (London, 1955), pp. 163–64; Emile Monnet, *Histoire de l'administration provinciale, départementale et communale en France* (Paris, 1885), p. 402; and C. H. Pouthas, "La réorganisation du ministère de l'intérieur et la reconstitution de l'administration préfectorale par Guizot en 1830," *Revue d'histoire moderne et contemporaine,* IX (Oct.–Dec., 1962), 241–63.

33. Ducrocq, *op. cit.,* I, 271–79.

34. Quotation from prefect of Loire-Inférieure to Interior, Sept. 14, 1854, *AN,* F1c III Loire-Inférieure 8. General authorities: Emile Miriel, *Des rapports des municipalités et du pouvoir central en matière de police* (Paris, 1897), pp. 1–133; E. G. Perrier, *La police municipale* (Paris, 1920), pp. 5–33, 69–100, for texts of laws from the Revolution through

the Second Empire; and Emile Arnaud, *La police municipale et rurale et les gardes champêtres* (Paris, 1928), pp. 7–13.

35. René Philippe Millet, *La France provinciale* (Paris, 1888), pp. 248–49.

36. The *commissaire*'s lineage and functions are concisely treated by P. Truy, "Commissaires de police: leur origine, leur organisation . . . ," J.C.P., 6e Année (1860), pp. 389–97.

37. M. David, "Appréciations générales de la police en France . . . ," memorandum of Feb. 15, 1850, *APP*, D B/353. Also see Ducrocq, *op. cit.*, I, 429.

38. Quotations from: Arrêt of March 2, 1838, as quoted by F. Euvrard, *Historique de l'institution des commissaires de police* (Montpellier, 1911), pp. 21–22; Interior (Billault) circular, Dec. 12, 1854, J.C.P., 1er Année (1855), p. 88; Thomas, *op. cit.*, pp. 47, 71.

39. *AN:* lists and memoranda in the ministries of Police and Interior, F18 10ᵃ, pièces 563, 578, and F1b I 267¹.

40. Béquet, *op. cit.*, XXII, 271; Perrier, *op. cit.*, pp. 167, 182–93.

41. The two founding enactments were the Law of 28 Pluviôse Year VIII and the Consular Arrêté of 12 Messidor Year VIII (July 1, 1800). The lineage could be traced even farther back to the Capetian office of Provost of the King in the tenth century: Edmond Mouneyrat, *La préfecture de police* (Paris, 1906), pp. 12–20.

42. Maurice Block and Henri de Pontich, *Administration de la ville de Paris et du département de la Seine* (Paris, 1884), p. 766.

43. Details of the Prefecture's functions in: the Arrêté of 12 Messidor Year VIII, Duvergier, XII (Ans 8–9), 250–54; and an ordinance of the Prefect of Police, 23 Thermidor Year VIII (April 16, 1800), *APP*, B/D1. Quotation from Moneyrat, *op. cit.*, p. 5. A good description of the Prefecture's operations is that of Maxime du Camp, "La Préfecture de police et la sûreté publique à Paris," *Revue des deux mondes*, 2d series, LXXXII (July 1, 1869), 152–91.

44. The legislation is summarized by Perrier, *op. cit.*, pp. 61–63. Quoted phrases from an address by the President of the Republic to the National Assembly, *Moniteur*, Nov. 5, 1851, p. 2756.

45. Baron Georges Eugène Haussman, *Mémoires* (3d ed.; Paris, 1890), I, 328–30, 413–14. For a brief treatment of the gendarmerie's history see: M. Hamelin, "La gendarmerie," in Béquet, *op. cit.*, XVII, 396–409; and H. Delattre, *Esquisse historique de la gendarmerie française* (Paris and Limoges, 1885), pp. 1–84.

46. François Cudet, *Histoire des corps de troupe qui ont été spécialement chargés du service de la ville de Paris depuis son origine jusqu'à nos jours* (Paris, 1887), pp. 63–104; and *J.Gend.*, No. 213 (July 1, 1851), p. 212.

47. The judiciary police system is concisely described by Eugène Blanchet, "De la police," J.C.P., 3d Année (1857), pp. 31–42. The system's daily

operations in the Paris *ressort* is described by Maxime Du Camp, "Le Palais de Justice à Paris," *Revue des deux mondes,* 2d series, LXXXII (Aug. 15, 1869), 841–76.

48. The *procureurs'* periodic and special reports in the BB30 series of the *AN* and the regional archives of the various *ressorts* are valuable sources for the study of political police, particularly because of the destruction of many Ministry of the Interior documents for the Second Empire period.

49. Quotations from: Mrs. Russell Barrington (ed.), *The works and life of Walter Bagehot* (London, 1915), I, 79–80; and P.G. Douai to Justice, Aug. 5 and Oct. 8, 1851, *AN,* BB30 377.

50. Robert Schnerb, *Rouher et le second empire* (Paris, 1949), pp. 30–34.

51. To Justice, May 1, 1851, *AN,* BB30 318.

52. P.G. Grenoble, June 10, 1851, *AN,* BB30 378.

53. P.G.'s to Justice, 1851: Limoges, Aug. 9, Douai, Jan. 18, Nancy, March 1, *AN,* BB30 378, 957, 318.

54. P.G. Montpellier to Justice, April 9, May 7, Aug. 12, 1851: *AN,* BB30 380.

55. Charlemagne-Emile de Maupas, *Mémoires sur le second empire* (Paris, 1885), I, 139–40; various documents in Maupas' personal dossier, *AN,* F1b I 167.

56. All material in this section, unless otherwise indicated, is based on: Adrien Dansette, *Louis-Napoléon à la conquête du pouvoir* (Paris, 1961), pp. 257–341; and Howard C. Payne, "Preparation of a *coup d'état:* administrative centralization and police powers in France, 1849–1851," in Frederick J. Cox *et al.* (eds.), *Studies in modern European history in honor of Franklin Charles Palm* (New York, 1956), pp. 179–202.

Chapter 2: The Coup D'Etat and an Interim of Extraordinary Police Powers

1. Dec. 4, 12, 14, 1851, *AD,* Bouches-du-Rhône (Marseille), M6 41; Jan. 11, 1852, *AN,* BB30 396, pièce 10; circular Dec. 7, modifying that of Dec. 2, *Moniteur,* Dec. 9, 1851, p. 3047.

2. Adrien Dansette, *Louis-Napoléon à la conquête du pouvoir* (Paris, 1961), offers a recent concise summary of the coup. Monographs on the event in the provinces are few and scattered. Two books of Eugène Ténot, though anti-Bonapartist, remain useful: *Paris en décembre 1851* (3d ed.; Paris, 1868) and *La province en décembre 1851* (3d ed.; Paris, 1868). Ténot's essential accuracy was indicated by the prefects' compliance with a ministerial instruction of Nov. 13, 1868, to compare his account with their own records: *AN,* F18 308. Dispatches of the coup concerning 63 *départements* are in *AN,* F7 12654.

3. Telegram, *AN*, BB1a 10.

4. *Moniteur*, Dec. 17, 1851, p. 3110. Philippe Vigier, in *La Seconde Ré-publique dans la région alpine* (Paris, 1963), II, 307–37, deals only with the Isère, Drôme, Vaucluse, Basses-Alpes, and Hautes-Alpes. For the dissolutions, *AN*, F1a 131¹⁰ and 132¹; and BB1a 10, Recueil . . . , No. 22.

5. Interior's policy, relayed to functionaries by the prefect of Saône-et-Loire, Oct. 10, 1851, *AN*, BB1a 10, Recueil . . . , No. 22.

6. P.G. Aix to Justice, Dec. 20, 1851, *AN*, BB30 P438; divisional order, Fifth Military Division, Besançon, Dec. 10, 1851, *AN*, BB12 10. Other illustrative directives are in the latter carton.

7. Mlle. Georges Vergez-Tricom, "Les événements de décembre 1851 à Lyon," *La Révolution de 1848*, XVII (1920–21), 229–30. War to Interior, Dec. 14, 1851, *AN*, F7 12654.

8. Report by Chef de Bataillon De France, Dec. 9, 1851, *AN*, F18 308. Correspondence on the columns is plentiful in *SHA*, Jan.–Feb. 1851–52, F1 56–57; and *AD*, Bouches-du-Rhône (Marseille), M6 100 and (Aix-en-Provence) 14.U.48.

9. Morny's instructions, *Moniteur*, Dec. 14, 1851, p. 3085. Dispatches concerning their mission are in *AN*, F1a 131¹⁰, F7 12654, and 45 AP 3.

10. Esprit-Victor de Castellane, *Journal du Maréchal de Castellane, 1804–62* (Paris, 1895–97), IV, 346–52; and *AD*, Bouches-du-Rhône (Marseille), dossiers in M6 366. Samples of such records are given by L. Remusat, "Les fiches secrètes du Coup d'Etat (documents inédits)," *La Revue* (Paris), LIII (1904), 429–40.

11. J. Tchernoff, *Associations et sociétés secrètes sous la deuxième république, 1848–1851* (Paris, 1905), pp. 1–396.

12. B. A. Granier de Cassagnac, *Souvenirs du second empire* (Paris, 1879–82), I, 258.

13. To Maupas, *Moniteur*, Dec. 17, 1851, p. 3110; e.g., circular of Jan. 2, 1852, *AN*, BB30 396 P440, pièce 9.

14. Jean Fontane, "Autour du coup d'Etat, souvenirs d'un paysan," *La Révolution de 1848*, VI (1909), 164–70.

15. Correspondence of Dec., 1851 and Jan., 1852, *AN*, BB30 403 P606 (Rouher's remark is from a ministerial "Note" of Jan. 3), and *Moniteur*, Dec. 17, 1851, p. 3110. Maupas' interpretation in Police circular, March 22, 1852, *AN*, F1a* 2120.

16. Circular, Dec. 20, 1851, printed in *Documents pour servir à l'histoire du second empire . . . 1851–1870* (Paris, 1872), pp. 28–29; *AN*, BB30 396 P440, pièce 8; and Tchernoff, *Associations et sociétés*, pp. 33–41.

17. Police circulars, March 22 and Sept. 1, 1852, *AN*, F1a* 2120 and 2121, respectively; Interior circular, Dec. 20, 1851, *AN*, BB30 396 P440, pièce 8.

18. Interior to Justice, Aug., 1854, BB30 462. This total was accepted by

Charles Seignobos, "Les opérations des commissions mixtes en 1852," *La Révolution de 1848*, VI (1909–10), 65. The other figure of 26,642 reported by Maupas, after some difficulty in obtaining data from other ministries, seems incorrect because of errors in addition. The official total itself was no doubt only approximate. Cf. V. Schoelcher, *Le gouvernement du 2 décembre* (London, 1853), p. 64; and H. Magen, *Histoire de la terreur bonapartiste* (4th ed.; Paris, 1872), p. 170.

19. E.g., for the Hérault, where arrests ran very high, Vergez-Tricom, *op. cit.* (who used the military's figures), counted 2,840; Seignobos, *op cit.* (who used the same figures plus archival data), also counted 2,840. But the *procureur* ("Etat numérique . . . , *AN*, BB30 403 P608) reported 2,513; and the prefect (April 3, 1858, F1c III Hérault 15) reported 2,565.

20. Justice, "Etat numérique, par dépts., des individus inculpés à raison des événements politiques du mois de décembre 1851," *AN*, BB30 403 P608. This summary did not include the Calvados, Manche, Orne, Corrèze, and Creuse.

21. *AN:* Moselle to Interior, Dec. 30, 1851, F1a 353–361^3; Gers to various officials, March–April 1852, F1a 333–342^2 and F1c III Gers 11.

22. E.g., Georges Eugène Haussmann, *Mémoires* (3d ed.; Paris, 1890), I, 514–15 for a typical prefectorial view; P.G. to Justice, Jan., 1852, *AN*, BB30 396 P440; and Army of Lyon, "Resumé des devoirs des membres des commissions militaires," Jan. 12, 1852, *AD*, Isère (Grenoble), 52.M.31.

23. *AD*, Isère (Grenoble), 52.M.29, Sept. 9, 1852; e.g., gendarmerie correspondence 1852–53, *SHA*, F1 56–60 and G9 1–7.

24. Alexandre Zévaès, "Les proscrits français en 1848 et 1851 à Londres," *La Révolution de 1848*, XX (1923–24), 345–75; Jean-Baptiste Boichot, *Souvenirs d'un prisonnier d'Etat sous le Second Empire, 1854–1859* (new ed.; Leipzig, 1869), pp. 3–5.

25. *AN*, BB30 957; P.G. Nancy to Justice, May 1, 1851, BB30 318.

26. For relevant documents see Georges Bourgin, "Mazzini et le Comité central démocratique en 1851," *Il Risorgimento italiano*, VI (1913), 353–71; and *Travail sur le mouvement démagogique antérieure au 1er décembre 1851*, reprinted by Tchernoff, *op. cit.*, pp. 279–387. Also *PRO*, F.O. 27/905. Draft to Normanby, Dec. 6, 1851, No. 601.

27. E.g., Chef du Service Maritime at Dunkerque to Marine, Dec. 4, 1851, and telegrams among Morny, Nord, Persigny, and the Belgian Ministry of Foreign Affairs, F1c III Nord 6.

28. E.g., telegrams Dec., 1851, *AN*, F7 12654 and F1c III Nord 6.

29. The general's remark was reported confidentially by Normanby to London, Dec. 17, 1851, No. 414, *PRO* F.O. 27/905. See also: F.O. instructions to Chargé d'affaires Paris, Jan. 13, 1852, No. 8; Walewski's statement to the Chargé, reported to F.O., June 21, 1852, No. 24; and

other documents in F.O. 27/924 series. Normanby's prediction, to F.O., Dec. 4, 1851, No. 367, 27/905.

30. Circular, Dec. 12, 1851, *AD*, Bouches-du-Rhône (Marseille), M6 41.

31. On the background, see Irene Collins, *The government and the newspaper press in France, 1814–1881* (Oxford, 1959), pp. xiii–xiv, 1–81. Both continuity and innovations in press laws after 1789 are graphically shown and annotated by Gustave Rousset, *Nouveau code annoté de la presse* (Paris, 1856), pp. 1–296. Also, P.G.'s comments to Justice in *AN:* Jan. 17 and Feb. 17, 1851, BB30 370; Lyon, June 7, 1850, BB30 379.

32. *AN,* P.G. to Justice: Aix, May 15, June 7, Aug. 6, 1851, BB30 370; and Lyon, June 7, 1850, BB30 379.

33. Circulars of Dec. 6, 1851, *AN,* F1a* 2119; and of Dec. 13, 1851, *AD,* Bouches-du-Rhône (Marseille), M6 41.

34. Duvergier, LI (1851), 533. The decree also included verbal offenses, such as "seditious cries."

35. *AN,* various dispatches, Dec. 2–17, F7 12654; Côte d'Or examples in *ibid.,* and F7 3480 and 3481.

36. Correspondence, Jan.–Feb., 1852, *AN,* F7 3480.

37. Georges Bourgin, "Historical bibliography of the press; enquiry of the subcommittee for the history of the press," in International Committee of Historical Sciences, *Bulletin V* (March, 1934), pp. 36–37.

38. This statistical summary is derived from reports by 83 prefects to the Interior in response to two ministerial circulars of Dec. 15, 1851, and June 22, 1852, *AN,* F7 3480–3481.

39. A. Brémond, *Histoire du coup d'Etat . . . dans la Haute-Garonne (1851–1852)* (Toulouse, 1870), p. 112. *AN,* prefects to Interior: Haute-Garonne, May 3, Oct. 8, 1852, F7 3481; Basses-Alpes, Dec. 19, 1851, F7 3480; Hautes-Alpes, Dec. 24, 1851, F7 3480; Ardennes, Sept. 14, Dec. 18, 1850, F18 262 and June 28, 1852, F7 3481.

40. Prefect to Interior, Sept. 17, 18, 1850, *AN,* F18 263; and March 19, June 28, 1852, *AN,* F7 3481.

41. Prefect's Dec., 1851, dispatches to Interior, *AN,* F1c III Nord 6; and his summary report of July 9, 1852, F7 3481.

42. To Interior, Dec. 24, 1851, *AN,* F7 3480.

43. *AN:* request by the editor of *Le Propagateur* to Ardennes, undated, F7 3480; and Puy-de-Dôme to Interior, March 30, 1852, F7 3481. On the Marseille press, P.R. Marseille to P.G. Aix, May 3, 1852, *AD,* Bouches-du-Rhône (Aix), 12.U.19.

44. Interior, confidential circular, Feb. 15, 1852, *AN,* F1a* 2119.

45. To Interior, Dec. 20, 22, 1851, *AN,* F7 3480.

46. Doubs to Interior, Dec. 5, 1851, *AN,* F7 12654; Interior circular, Dec. 11, 1851, BB1a 10, Recueil No. 43.

47. J. Tchernoff, *Le parti républicain au coup d'Etat et sous le second em-*

pire (Paris, 1906), pp. 82–95. Tchernoff does not present, nor could the present writer find, evidence for the statement that a "no" vote often condemned such suspects to transportation by administrative measure.

48. Justice of the Peace at Roquevain to P.G. Aix, Dec. 19, 1851, and Justice circular Dec. 6 and P.G. Aix circular Dec. 10 to P.R.'s: *AD,* Bouches-du-Rhône (Aix), 14.U.48. Various documents in *AN,* BB1a 10, Recueil No. 44 (1851), including quotation from the Sarthe.

49. Charlemagne-Emile de Maupas, *Mémoires sur le second empire* (Paris, 1885), I, 569.

50. "D'un ministère de la police," *Revue des deux mondes,* III (July 1, 1849), 179–84.

51. Quoted by Edouard-Ferdinand de Beaumont-Vassy, *Histoire intime du second empire* (Paris, 1874), p. 79.

52. Granier de Cassagnac, *Souvenirs,* II, 54–56. Decrees, *Moniteur,* Jan. 10, 1852, p. 45. P. Wauwermans, *Les proscrits du coup d'Etat en Belgique* (Brussels, 1892), pp. 21–22.

53. *AN,* BB30 396 P440: confidential Justice circular, Dec. 29, 1851 (pièces 4–5), and Interior circular, Jan. 11, 1852 (pièce 10).

54. *AN,* BB30 396 P440. E.g., P.G. Bordeaux, comments on 83 cases from the Gironde, Dordogne, and Cher.

55. "Tableau des attentats, crimes et délits à rechercher à l'occasion des derniers événemens," undated (early 1852), *AN,* BB18 1504.

56. *SHA,* F1 57. Eight military commissions had also operated in July, 1848, freeing 6,000 of the 15,000 persons included in the Assembly's June 27 decree of transportation en masse. Castellane's instructions in "Resumé des devoirs des membres des commissions militaires," *AD,* Isère (Grenoble), 52.M.31.

57. *AD,* Isère (Grenoble), 52.M.31. *AN:* prefect to Interior, March 25, 1852, F1c III Eure-et-Loire 9; P.G. Montpellier to Justice and P.R.'s, Jan. 17, 1852, BB30 396 P440, pièce 194; P.G. Nîmes to Justice, Jan. 4, 1852, *ibid.,* pièce 123. *SHA,* War to generals commanding divisions and subdivisions, F1 57.

58. *AN:* BB30 396 P440, pièce 11; prefect to Interior, Sept. 7, 1853, F1c III Hérault 9. Also Granier de Cassagnac, *op. cit.,* II, 73; and Vergez-Tricom, *op. cit.,* XIX, 351.

59. Circular, March 2, 1852, *AN,* F1a* 2119.

60. *Moniteur,* Feb. 4, 1852, p. 189.

61. Granier de Cassagnac, *op. cit.,* II, 74; and A. Quentin-Bauchart, *Etudes et souvenirs sur la deuxième république et le second empire* (1848–1870), (Paris, 1901–02), I, 454.

62. Interior to Justice, Aug., 1854, *AN,* BB30 462. The notes used by Baroche in 1858 in preparation of the Law of General Security set the total at 19,461: *BT,* 1112. These figures may be compared with 11,003 transported to Algeria by the Assembly's decree of June 27, 1848.

63. P.G. Aix to Justice, Feb. 29, 1852, *AN,* BB30 370. Generalizations are mainly from Seignobos, *op. cit.,* pp. 59–67. Typical complexities of these proceedings are suggested by the "Rapport adressé par la Commission Mixte des Bouches-du-Rhône . . . ," March 5, 1852, *AD,* Bouches-du-Rhône (Marseille), M6 100.

64. *AN:* Police circulars, March 12, 18, 21, 1851, F1a* 2120. *AD:* Bouches-du-Rhône (Marseille), Maupas' telegram to prefects of the Midi, April 14, 1852, and dispatch to Bouches-du-Rhône, June 19, 1852, M6 100. Decree of March 28 in Duvergier, LII (1852), 379.

65. To the Isère, Feb., 1852, *AD,* Isère (Grenoble), 52.M.29; to Bouches-du-Rhône, *AD* (Marseille), M6 100. During December and January some 7,000 refugees entered Belgium alone, then moved on to England and Switzerland. About 800 remained in Belgium: Wauwermans, *op. cit.,* p. 7. On the plight of *proscrits* and exiles, see the bibliography in Tchernoff, *Parti républicain,* pp. 96–148; and Paul Merruau, "Les déportés politiques en Afrique et à la Nouvelle-Calédonie," *Revue des deux mondes,* 2d series, CIV (April 1, 1873), 689–710.

66. Police circulars: April 14, Sept. 1, 1852, in *Moniteur,* April 16, Sept. 5, 1852, pp. 590, 1359; and March 8, 1852, *AN,* F1a* 2120. Maupas to prefects, *AD:* Dec. 30, 1852, Isère (Grenoble), 52.M.47 and Sept. 2, 1852, Bouches-du-Rhône (Marseille), M6 100.

67. P.G. Rouen to Justice, Sept. 14, 1852, and Justice to P.G., Oct. 12, 1852, *AN,* BB30 405 P790.

68. The Committee's documents are in *AN,* BB30 462. Decree of March 26, 1852, on the *commissaires,* Duvergier, LII (1852), 263–64.

69. Camille Odilon Barrot, *Mémoires posthumes de Odilon Barrot* (Paris, 1875–76), III, 216; Emile Félix Fleury, *Souvenirs du général comte Fleury* (Paris, 1897–98), I, 139; Quentin-Bauchart, *op. cit.,* 454–64; Granier de Cassagnac, *op. cit.,* II, 77.

70. Report undated, *Papiers et correspondance de la famille impériale* (Paris, 1871), I, 160–64.

71. Sénéca, Director of Criminal Affairs and Pardons, to Justice, no date, and other documents, *AN,* BB30 462.

72. A vast amount of dossiers, through 1856, are in the *AN* series BB22 129–89; a day-by-day list (year 1853 missing) of individual pardons recommended and granted is in BB30 481, dossiers 1–3.

73. Decree in Duvergier, LII (1852), 268–69. Maupas circular, *AN,* F1a* 2120.

74. Comte de Hübner, *Neuf ans de souvenirs d'un ambassadeur* (Paris, 1904), I, 53, dated Jan. 12. *AN:* Piétri report, July 30, 1852, ABXIX 174, dossier 142; Ille-et-Vilaine to Interior, Dec. 14, 1851, F7 12654.

75. P.R. Marseille to P.G. Aix, May 3, 1852, *AD,* Bouches-du-Rhône (Aix), 12.U.19.

Chapter 3: Administrative Conflict and the Demise of the Ministry of General Police

1. V. des Aubiers, *De l'administration et de ses réformes* (Paris, 1852), pp. 11–12.
2. Nos. 4 and 6, Jan. 23, Feb. 29, 1852.
3. To Interior, *AN,* Fic III series: July 4 (Rhône 5) and Nov. 7 (Dordogne 11), 1852. Eugène Anglade, *Etude sur la police* (2d ed.; Paris, 1852), pp. ii–iii. P.G. Douai to Justice, Feb. 9, April 13, 1852, *AN,* BB30 377.
4. Approximated from accounting records, *AN,* F7 12246; and *arrêtés* involving personnel, F1a* 782, pp. 323 ff.
5. Decree of Dec. 15, 1851, *Moniteur,* Dec. 18, 1851, p. 3114.
6. Maupas, circular, Jan. 31, 1851, *AN,* F1a* 2120. Suleau to Interior, Jan. 30, 1852, *AD,* Bouches-du-Rhône (Marseille), M6 276.
7. Organization decree, Jan. 30, 1852, *Moniteur,* Jan. 31, 1852, p. 161. In order of their cities of residence, the inspectors were: De Rancé, Cazelles, Baylin de Montbel, Bérard (at Lyon, with the title General Director; replaced May, 1852, by Cotton, Special Inspector at Montpellier), Blot, Chopin d'Arnouville, Frossard, Poriquet, Delesvaux (till May, 1852, when he became Director-General; replaced by Lagarde, Special Inspector at Tournai).
8. Appointed by decree, March 1, 1852, *AN,* F1a 132³; changes were made on March 22 and May 22. In order of cities, the Special Inspectors were: Petit, De Croze, Dubois, Lecourbe, Cotton (until May 22, when he became General Inspector at Lyon; replaced by Tissot), De Peybère, Vialon, Lalone (until March 22, when he transferred to the Prefecture of Police; replaced by Gallix), L. Arnaud (replaced March 22 by Guilhem), P. Lagarde (until May 22, when he became General Inspector at Bourges; replacement unknown), Amyot, and Le Breton (May 22, replaced by Gadrat).
9. Budget figures in *AN,* F1a 132²; expenses regulated by decree, Jan. 30, 1852, and Police circular, Feb. 15, 1852, F1a* 2120. Rank defined in regulation of Feb. 13, 1852, Duvergier, LII (1852), 387.
10. Pierre-Henry, *Histoire des préfets* (Paris, 1950), p. 177; Edouard-Ferdinand de Beaumont-Vassy, *Histoire intime du second empire* (Paris, 1874), p. 79.
11. Feb. 11, 1852, *AN,* Fic III Gironde 9.
12. Maupas to prefects, Feb. 23 and Persigny to prefects, Feb., 1852, *AN,* F1a* 2120 and 2119, respectively.
13. The two decrees, *Moniteur,* March 29, 1852, p. 511 and Jan. 19, 1853, p. 73; Maupas to colonels of gendarmerie, *ibid.,* Nov. 30, 1852, p. 1991. Maupas to inspectors and prefects, May 31, 1852, and Feb. 5, 1853,

respectively, *AN,* F1a* 2121. Copy of Ministry of War's list, *AD,* Bouches-du-Rhône (Marseille), M6 276.

14. P.I. Draguignan to P.G. Aix, March 30, 1853, *AD,* Bouches-du-Rhône (Aix), 12.U.21 and documents in 35.U.3.

15. Blot to prefect, March 1, 1852, and circulars of March 3, 29, 1852, *ibid.* (Marseille), M6 276. Cotton to P.G.'s, confidential, July 19, 1852, *AN,* F7 12164; a mass of their reports on *commissaires* is in this carton.

16. Police circular, Aug. 7, 1852, *AD,* Bouches-du-Rhône (Marseille), M6 276. I did not find Persigny's authorization of July 9 in the archives, but several prefects mention it: e.g., Calvados to Interior, July 10, 1852, *AN,* F1c III Calvados 9; and Cher to Interior, April 9, 1852, F1a 353–361[3].

17. To Interior, June 27 and July 10, 1852, *AN,* F1c III Calvados 9.

18. P.I. Brignoles to P.G. Aix, Oct. 7, 1852, *AD,* Bouches-du-Rhône (Aix), 12.U.20. *AN:* Frossard to Dordogne, July 8, 1852; prefect to General Inspector, July 2, 1852, and to Interior, Aug. 20, 1852, F7 3008[1]; Cher to Interior, April 9, 1852, F1a 353–361[3].

19. Charente to Police, Oct. 22, 1852, *AN,* F1a 353–361[3]. The ex-*commissaire* to P.G. Aix, May 25, 1852, *AD,* Bouches-du-Rhône (Aix), 12.U.19.

20. *AN,* F7 12166: e.g., *commissaire-central* at Besançon to General Inspector at Lyon, Nov. 25, 1852 (other correspondence shows this was a widespread problem); correspondence of Aug. 18–21, 1852, dossier "Ain."

21. *AN:* Deux-Sèvres to Interior, April 2, 1852, F1a 353–361[3]; Interior to Moselle, Aug. 4, 1852, and reply, with documentation, July 28, 1852, F7 3008[1]; Police circular, F1a* 2121. Substantial records of only the Inspector at Lyon, for 13 *départements,* have been preserved, in F7 12164 through 12169.

22. *AN:* correspondence of March, 1852, to July, 1853, in BB30 380 and 462, BB18 1515 dossier A2 2746 and 1517 dossier A2 2982, F7 12164 dossier "Correspondance avec les *procureurs-impériaux."*

23. Editorial, *J.Gend.,* No. 231 (Jan. 1, 1852), pp. 421–27.

24. Correspondence, Feb.–March, 1853, *SHA,* G9 1, 2. War circular to legion commanders, Dec. 4, 1852, in *J.Gend.,* No. 265 (Dec. 11, 1852), p. 416. *AN:* correspondence Dec., 1852, F7 12166, and April, 1852, F1a 333–342[2]. P.R. Brignoles to P.G. Aix, Aug. 18, 1852, *AD,* Bouches-du-Rhône (Aix), 12.U.20.

25. War and Police, joint circular, June 12, 1852, *AN,* F1a* 2121. *SHA:* General Fourth Military Division to War, Oct. 7, 1852, and La Rüe's study, F1 66 dossiers 7, 26; Saint-Arnaud's letter on Carrelet, G9 2 (actually Carrelet undertook the mission but on Maupas' request

alone). *J.Gend.:* War to generals of military divisions, No. 250 (July 15, 1852), pp. 233–37; editorial, No. 281 (May 21, 1853), p. 160.

26. *AN:* Police and Finances exchange, Dec. 18, 1852, and Jan. 29, 1853, F18 2349; correspondence of General Inspector at Lyon, Special Inspector at Besançon, and *commissaire* at Bourg (Ain), Oct.–Nov., 1852, F7 12164; on the Prefect of Police, undated "note," F18 570. Since the destruction of archives, almost nothing exists in relations with the Prefecture of Police.

27. *PRO:* Chargé (Jerningham) to F.O., No. 87, F.O. 27/929. Viel-Castel, *Memoirs,* tr. Charles Bonsfield (Covent Garden, 1888), I, 145; Maupas, *Mémoires sur le second empire* (Paris, 1885), I, 605–06. See also Honoré Farat, *Persigny, un ministre de Napoléon III* (Paris, 1957), p. 144.

28. Among the few exchanges in *AN:* Aug. 13, Sept. 2, 1852, dispute over control of theaters; Interior to Police, Aug. 31, 1852, dispute over "the direction of public opinion," F21 1046 and F7 3008^1. Persigny's countermeasure circular, June 23, 1852, some replies to which are in F1a 353–361^3 and F7 3008^1; in the latter carton also "Note relative aux difficultés survenues entre les préfets et les agents du Ministère de la Police Générale," Oct. 22, 1852.

29. Examples in *AN,* F1a 353–361^3 and F7 3008^1; Sainte Croix quotations, March 5 and June 27, 1852, F1c III Eure 13.

30. Police circulars to prefects: *AN,* March 24–25 (F1a* 2120) and Sept. 1, 1852 (F1a* 2121); *AD,* Bouches-du-Rhône (Marseille), M6 100. A typical *procureur's* complaint was by the P.G. Paris to Justice, May 13, 1852, *AN,* BB30 383.

31. *AN:* Féart to subprefects, very-confidential, March 26, 1852, copy to Interior, F1c III Gers 11; prefects to Interior, F1c 353–361^3 and F7 3008^1; Cotton and Lecourbe, correspondence Nov., 1852, F7 12166.

32. Haussmann, *op. cit.,* I, 513–14. This was a very common complaint against the inspectors.

33. *AN:* examples in F7 3008^1, F1c III Haute-Garonne 14, Indre 8, Ariège 6, Var 10, Bouches-du-Rhône 12. *AD:* correspondence of Aug.–Oct., 1852, Bouches-du-Rhône (Marseille), M6 50, and (Aix), 12.U.20 and 14.U.65.

34. Correspondence Sept., 1852, *AN,* F7 3008^1; various examples, F1a 353–361^3. Correspondence, March, 1852, *AD,* Bouches-du-Rhône (Marseille), M6 344.

35. *AN:* De Launay, July 19, 1852, and Gard, March 29, July 15, 1852, F1a 353–361^3; Cantal, July 25, 1852, and other complaints against Tissot, F7 3008^1; Sarthe, Sept. 12, 1852, F1c III Sarthe 10.

36. On Cotton's appointment, two police ministry "notes," *AN,* F1c III Gard 13; Lecourbe to Inspector at Lyon, June 29, 1852, and other

correspondence in the dossier, "Lettres de l'Inspecteur-Général à l'Inspecteur-spécial de Besançon," F7 12166.

37. To Interior, July 28, 1852, *AN,* F1c III Bouches-du-Rhône 12.

38. Police to prefects, March 30, 1852, *Moniteur,* April 3, pp. 533–34. *AN:* Maupas' requests for information, F18 300, and circulars to prefects, April, June, July, Aug., 1852, F18 3; quotation from undated Ministry of Police memorandum, "Modifications utiles à introduire dans les lois et règlements de l'imprimerie et de la presse," F18 570.

39. Maupas to prefects: March 30, 1852, *Moniteur,* April 3, pp. 533–34; and Aug. 18, 1852, *APP,* D B/206. Persigny to Maupas, Aug. 18, 1852, and memo of De Col to Interior, dated Sept., 1852, *AN,* F7 3008[1].

40. "Rapport à Sa Majesté l'Empereur," (copy), Feb. 4, 1853, *AN,* AB XIX 175–76, dossier 21.

41. Maupas to prefects: Feb. 26, March 1, 1853, *AD,* Isère (Grenoble), 56.M.7; March 6, 1853, *Moniteur,* March 6, 1853, p. 261.

42. Maupas to prefects, *AN:* March 6 and 15, 1853, F1a* 2121; April 30, 1853, F7 12246.

43. Decrees of March 5, 1853, Duvergier, LIII (1853), 76 and of April 8, 1853, *Gaz.Trib.,* April 10, 1853, named Villemain, Dubessey, Marchand, and Gen. Carrelet. On their appointment see Edouard-Ferdinand de Baumont-Vassy, *Histoire de mon temps. Deuxième série* (Paris, 1864), I, 272–73. I found archival material only for the work of Carrelet, 23 of whose reports are in *SHA,* G9 3, 4; two prefects' accounts of his visits are in *AN,* July 10, 1853, F1c III Hérault 9 and Nov. 4, 1853, F1c III Haute-Saône 9.

44. Appointment decree in *Moniteur,* May 4, 1853, p. 497; Maupas' circular, March 15, 1853, F1a* 2121. Their functions were defined in detail by a Police circular, April 30, 1853, *APP,* D B/353, pièces 78–85.

45. *AN:* prefects to Interior, F1c III series, Aug. 5, 1853, Ardennes 6, March 22, 1853, Haute-Saône 9, May 18, 1853 (to Police, copy to Interior), Gironde 9. Interior circular, Dec. 30, 1853, *AD,* Isère (Grenoble), 56.M.7.

46. Decree March 22, 1854, and comment in Interior circular, April 3, 1854, *AD,* Bouches-du-Rhône (Marseille), M6 276. They remained in the Bouches-du-Rhône, Haute-Garonne, and Gironde because of impending reorganization of municipal police in Marseille, Toulouse, and Bordeaux. But their police powers were confined to these cities. The titles were abolished on June 2, 1855.

47. Prefects to Interior, *AN,* F1c III series: Jan. 11, 1855, Aube 4; Sept. 14, 1854, Loire-Inférieure 8.

48. Maupas, *Mémoires,* II, 56–57; abolition decree, *Moniteur,* June 22, 1853, p. 686.

49. Marginal note on dispatch of prefect of Tarn-et-Garonne, June 24, 1853, *AN,* FIc III Tarn-et-Garonne 7.

Chapter 4: Centralized General Police Operates Without the Ministry

1. Robert Catherine, *Le fonctionnaire français* (Paris, 1961), pp. 110–11.
2. Preamble to the nation, Jan. 14, 1852, *Œuvres de Napoléon III* (Paris, 1869), III, 287–89.
3. Henry Berton, *L'evolution constitutionnelle du second empire* (Paris, 1900), pp. 28–35; Gabriel Dufour, *Traité général de droit administratif appliqué* (3d ed.; Paris, 1868–70), I, 3–7.
4. Quotation in *Œuvres,* III, 292: decree in *Moniteur,* Jan. 26, 1852, p. 137.
5. Léon Duguit, *Traité de droit constitutionnel* (3d ed.; Paris, 1930), III, 36–37; Jean Maurain, *Un bourgeois français au XIXe siècle: Baroche, ministre de Napoléon III* (Paris, 1936), pp. 133–213; Edouard Laferrière, *Traité de la juridiction administrative et des recours contentieux* (2d ed.; Paris, 1896), I, 257–59.
6. Odilon Barrot, *De la centralisation et de ses effets* (Paris, 1861), pp. 15–17; *Moniteur,* July 13, Aug. 3, Nov. 6, 1851; Emile Monnet, *Histoire de l'administration provinciale, départementale et communale en France* (Paris, 1885), pp. 399–402.
7. Decree in Duvergier, LII (1852), 253–56; circulars March 7, May 6, 1854, *AD,* Isère (Grenoble), 53.M.3.
8. Baroche papers, *BT,* 1103.
9. *AN:* circular Aug. 7, 1852, FIa* 2119; Ain to Inspector-General at Lyon, July 19, 1852, F7 12166 dossier "Ain." Louis Peuch, *Essai sur la candidature officielle en France depuis 1851* (Paris, 1922), p. 55.
10. Prefects to Interior, *AN,* FIc III series: April 3, 1852 (Saône-et-Loire 13), Nov. 7, 1852 (Dordogne 11). P.G.'s to Justice, in order mentioned, *AN,* Jan. 10, 1852 (BB30 542), June 8, 1852 (BB30 382), Sept. 10, 1852 (BB30 378), July 8, 1853 (BB30 380).
11. Duvergier, LII (1852), 461–65.
12. Ministry of the Interior, tableau, 1865, *AN,* 45 P 5.
13. To Justice, Oct. 12, 1852, *AN,* BB30 380.
14. *AN:* P.G. Aix to Justice, Sept. 12, 22, 1852, BB30 370; P.G. Montpellier to Justice, Jan. 13, 1853, BB30 380; Interior confidential circular, Sept. 18, 1852, FIa* 2119.
15. To Interior, *AN,* FIc III series: Jan. 14, 1857 (Haute-Saône 9), Jan. 1, 1853 (Doubs 12), Sept. 29, Oct. 4, 1852 (Eure-et-Loir 9). Interior to prefect, Oct. 13, 1852, *ibid.*
16. *AN:* e.g., circulars July 31, 1854, Nov. 20, 1856, FIa* 2119; note of Nov. 7, 1858, written in the Interior's Division of General and Departmental Administration, F18 546².

17. Chevreau to Interior, Sept. 14, 1854, *AN,* Fɪc III Loire-Inférieure 8. Law of 1855, Duvergier, LV (1855), 136–45.
18. Persigny to Emperor, Aug., 1865, *AN,* AB XIX 175 dossier 30.
19. Duvergier, LV (1855), 334–35 and tables annexed; *J.C.P.,* II, année 3 (1857), 229–31. Examples of the incompleteness of the reform in nine cities: the *commissaires* got no secretaries in Amiens, Besançon, Limoges, Nancy, Nîmes, and Orléans; no police inspectors were placed in Caen or Orléans; no agents of police in Angers, Besançon, Caen, Limoges, Montpellier, Nancy, Nîmes, and Orléans.
20. Oct. 4, 1856, July 3, 1857, report dated Jan., 1858, *AN,* Fɪc III Tarn-et-Garonne 5. Much documentation on the Marseille situation is in *AD,* Bouches-du-Rhône (Marseille), M6 247, 276, 1884 and (Aix), 12.U.48 and 35.M.3.
21. For the background and general effects of the measures of 1852 and 1854, see J. Maurain, *La politique ecclésiastique du second empire de 1852 à 1869* (Paris, 1930), *passim,* and *Baroche,* pp. 147–50. Typical prefects' arguments, *AN,* Fɪc III series: Oct. 8, 1852 (Moselle 15) and April 16, 1853 (Gers 11).
22. Berton, *op. cit.,* p. 142. Fortoul circular, March 12, 1852, *Moniteur Administratif,* No. 7, March 15, 1852.
23. *AN:* to Interior, Jan. 11, 1855, Fɪc III Tarn-et-Garonne 5; Seine-et-Marne, circular May 1, 1858, to primary teachers, and Rector at Clermont, April 3, 1858, to Public Instruction—both in F17 2649.
24. Public Instruction circular, and incomplete collection of Rectors' reports from 1858 to 1866 in *AN,* F17 2649–2650. Reports from Aix, Grenoble, and Nancy dated, respectively, Aug., May 20, and April 6, 1858. I found no reports later than 1866; neither did I find evidence of their official discontinuation.
25. E.g., of one opponent, Sébastien Commissaire, *Mémoires et souvenirs de Sébastien Commissaire, ancien réprésentant du peuple* (Lyon, 1888), II, 173. Persigny circular, March 7, 1854, via Collet-Meygret, *AD,* Bouches-du-Rhône (Marseille), M6 296.
26. Interior circulars: March 7 and April 3, 1854, *AD,* Bouches-du-Rhône (Marseille), M6 296 and 276, respectively; Jan. 26, 1854, *Moniteur,* Jan. 26, 1854. The prefects' advice on personnel policies was ordered on Persigny's proposal to Napoleon III, who let his will be known through a Sept., 1853, circular of the Minister of State. I found no copy of the circular, but correspondence in both *AN,* Fɪa 11 and 12 amply verifies its content.
27. *AN:* Gironde to Interior, Sept. 15, 1853, Fɪa 11; and in the Fɪc III series, July 22, 1852, July 3 and Sept. 15, 1853 (Haute-Saône 9 and 12), "Mémoire for Louis Napoleon," July 1, 1852 (Calvados 9).
28. Decree Feb. 2 and Persigny's circular, *Moniteur Administratif,* No. 24

(July 31, 1853); Persigny's report to the Emperor, *ibid.,* No. 206 (June 30, 1854). Also Berton, *op. cit.,* p. 133.

29. Other appointments were: Espinasse, Feb. 7 to June 14, 1858; Delangle, June 14, 1858, to May 5, 1859; and the Duc de Padoue, May 5 to Nov. 1, 1859. During Billault's first term, Abbatucci, Minister of Justice, served an interim term between Aug. 25 and Sept. 10, 1854.

30. Honoré Farat, *Persigny, un ministre de Napoléon III, 1808–1872* (Paris, 1957), 127–28, 142–46, 156–57. Fialin de Persigny, *Le Duc de Persigny et les doctrines de l'empire* (Paris, 1865), pp. 51–52.

31. Decree Dec. 15, 1851, *Moniteur,* Dec. 18, 1851, p. 3114; and related documents in *AN,* Fıa 634, Fıa* 2119. E.g., opinion on intent of the reorganization, Amédée de Cesena, "Réorganisation du Ministère de l'Intérieur," *Moniteur Administratif,* No. 2 (Dec. 22, 1851), p. 1.

32. Decrees Feb. 21, June 21 and 23, *Moniteur,* Feb. 25, June 21 and 24, 1853. "Décret d'organisation du 21 juillet 1853," and other documents in *AN,* Fıa 634.

33. *Droits de l'homme* (2d ed.; Paris, 1867), pp. 291–92.

34. *AD,* Isère (Grenoble): circulars July 16, 1858, May 5, 1859, and Interior summary of policy, Feb. 10, 1859, 56.M.7 and 52.M.38. Circulars Sept. 24, Oct. 20, 1862, *AN,* Fıa 2122ᴮ.

35. Piétri was the 31st Prefect including Sylvain Blot, who was acting Prefect from Jan. 23 to 27, 1852. Data on Piétri from his personnel dossier, *AN,* Fıb I 170¹⁵. See also Alphonse Brémond, *Histoire du coup d'état dans . . . la Haute-Garonne* (Toulouse, 1870), pp. 23–29.

36. *Arrêté* of 3 brumaire Year IX (Oct. 25, 1801). The extension was upheld in 1839 by the Council of State after a challenge following administrative reforms in July, 1837: Interior to Prefect of Police, July 22, 1839, *APP,* D B/1.

37. Edmond Mouneyrat, *La préfecture de police* (Paris, 1906), pp. 5–10. For a concise analysis, see E. Laurent, "La préfecture de police," in Léon Bequet and others (eds.), *Répertoire du droit administratif* (Paris, 1882–1911), XXII, 306–54.

38. Achille Rabasse, "Police Municipale" (bound MS dated 1872), pp. 8, 17, in *APP.*

39. On its history: Mouneyrat, *op. cit.,* pp. 33–39; Maurice Block and Henri de Pontich, *Administration de la ville de Paris et du département de la Seine* (Paris, 1884), pp. 25–26. A consular *arrêté* of 12 messidor Year VIII created the Prefecture and defined its powers; it was implemented by the Prefect's ordinance of April 16, 1800 (23 thermidor Year VIII), *APP,* D B/1. Louis Chevalier, *La formation de la population parisienne au XIXe siècle* (Paris, 1950), traces the demographic-political aspects of the population movement into Paris. On the Prefecture after Sept., 1870, see E. Cresson, *Cent jours du siège à la Préfecture de police* (Paris, 1901).

40. Decree, *Moniteur,* Sept. 26, 1854, p. 1061, supplemented in detail by the Prefect's *arrêtés* of April 14, 1856, and Dec. 17, 1857, in *Police. Documents divers,* II, 2117–2196 and 2295–2297 Registres 20/29 and 20/30 respectively, *APP.*
41. Decrees of Nov. 1, Dec. 8 and 17, 1859, and Jan. 7, 1860: Duvergier, LIX (1859), 371, and LX (1860), 33–37. By 1870 the municipal force numbered about 6,000. For statistics of 1854 to 1892 see G. Graux, "La police à Paris et la réorganisation de la police parisienne," *Revue politique et parlementiare,* VII (Jan.–March, 1896), 242.
42. Haussmann, *op. cit.,* II, 157. Decrees in Duvergier, LIX (1859), 343–45 and LX (1860), 34.
43. Boittelle's personnel dossier, *AN,* F1b I 156³⁰. Albert Vandam, *An Englishman in Paris* (3d ed.; London, 1892), II, 127–28. Edmond Louis de Goncourt, *Journal des Goncourt* (Paris, 1887–96), II, entry for June 25, 1863, 127–28. *Journal du Maréchal de Castellane, 1804–1862* (Paris, 1895–97), V, entry of Dec. 23, 1859, 274.
44. An incomplete collection of political reports from 1852 to 1867 is in *AN,* AB XIX, 174, dossiers 32, 142, 175.
45. "Règlement général du service ordinaire de la police dans la ville de Paris," April 14, 1856, *Police. Documents divers,* Registre 20/29, 211–2196, Art. 91, *APP.*
46. Prefect of Police, "Note en réponse au mémoire de M. le Préfet de la Seine . . . ," (Paris, April, 1858, 16-page brochure), p. 6.
47. For details of the Prefecture's operations see: Alexandre François Vivien, *Etudes administratives* (3d ed.; Paris, 1859), II, 167–228 for the pre-1854 period; and Maxime Du Camp, "La préfecture de police et la sûreté publique à Paris," *Revue des deux mondes,* 2d series, LXXXII (July 1, 1869), 152–91 for the postreform period.
48. Decree of Dec. 11, 1852, Duvergier, LII (1852), 763–64; note of April 18, 1853, by the *chef du cabinet* of the Minister of War, for the Bureau of the Gendarmerie, *SHA,* G9 3.
49. Haussmann, *op. cit.,* II, 215–38; Maurain, *Baroche,* pp. 201–11.
50. Baroche notes, *BT,* 1168, including an "Extrait du registre des délibera-tions" of the Council, sessions of Sept. 22–23, 1859. Prefect of Police, "Note en réponse au mémoire de M. le Préfet de la Seine . . . ," *APP,* D B/1.
51. Haussmann, *op. cit.,* II, 236. Piétri, March 26, 1859; also another letter of Dec. 20, 1859; and Interior to Prefect of Police, Dec. 27, 1859, *APP,* D B/1.
52. *Journal officiel de la république française,* Oct. 6, 1870, p. 1621.

Chapter 5: Administrative Particularism and Obstructive Realities

1. *La fonction publique* (Paris, 1954), pp. 26–28.
2. Pierre-Henry, *Histoire des préfets* (Paris, 1950), p. 162, mentions the four defectors. On the others, various dispatches, *AN, F7 12654* and notes on copies of decrees naming new prefects in the Ain and Somme, F1a 131[10].
3. Quotation from J.-J. Chevallier, *Histoire des institutions politiques de la France de 1789 à nos jours* (Paris, 1952), p. 274. Cf. Pierre-Henry, *op. cit.*, pp. 147–94.
4. Interior, "Note administrative et politique sur le département de l'Ain," July 18, 1852, *AN, F1c III Ain 8*. Commission chargée de réunier, classer et publier les papiers saisis aux Tuileries, *Papiers et correspondance de la famille impériale* (Paris, 1871), II, 4–21. Transfers through Feb., 1852, are in *AN, F1a 131[10], 132[1], 132[2]*.
5. Marcel Blanchard, *Le second empire* (Paris, 1950), pp. 32–33, raises the possibility that the type was a republican myth.
6. Unless otherwise noted, the quoted phrases used to illustrate generalizations on the "administrative attitude" and mission are drawn from reports between 1852 and 1859 by the *procureurs-généraux* to Justice, *AN*, series BB30 370 (Aix), 377 (Douai), 378 (Grenoble), 379 (Lyon), 380 (Montpellier), 381 (Nancy), 382 (Nîmes), 383 (Paris); and from prefects' reports in series F1a 12 and F1c III for the same period.
7. Quoting the suggestive title of Eric Strauss, *The ruling servants; bureaucracy in Russia, France—and Britain?* (New York, 1961).
8. P.R. Toulon, circular Dec. 12, 1851, to justices of the peace, *AD, Bouches-du-Rhône* (Aix), 14.U.48.
9. P.I. Tarascon to P.G. Aix, Jan. 22, 1858, *AD, Bouches-du-Rhône* (Aix), 12.U.20.
10. E.g., a typical example of this assumption by Avocat-général Croissant, Feb. 26, 1852, before the Cour d'Assises de la Seine, case of the "Complot Allemand," *Gaz.Trib.*, Feb. 27, 1852, p. 203.
11. Nov. 26, 1853, and April 6, 1855, *AN*, BB30 383 and 409 P112-bis.
12. *AN*: Aix, April 17, 1853, BB30 370; Lyon, Nov. 14, 1852, BB30 379; Grenoble, May 10, 1852, BB30 378, Commander Third Military Division to War, July 15, 1853, *SHA*, G9 4.
13. E.g., *Moniteur*, Nov. 15 and 17, 1852, pp. 1871–72, 1887; *L'Ami de l'ordre* (Digne), June 24, 1852, p. 105; Prefect of Police, to Emperor, Oct. 19, 1856, *AN*, BB30 366, dossier 2, pièce 182.
14. E.g., P.G. Paris to Justice, April 16, 1853, *AN*, BB30 409 P1143. Also Marcel Dessal, *Un révolutionnaire jacobin: Charles Delescluze, 1809–1871* (Paris, 1952), pp. 190–91.
15. *AN*, P.G. Lyon to Justice, Jan. 3, 1857, BB30 379; see also earlier

reports of his predecessor. Other typical examples of the stereotype: Interior memorandum based on prefects' reports, July 5, 1852, and dossier on the "Association alliance des communistes," 1852, both in F7 3008[1]; report of July 3, 1852, on the "Vengeurs," F1c III Seine-et-Oise 9; and on the "Jeune Montagne," in 1854, BB24 548–561 S.58–4771.

16. *Moniteur,* March 26, 1852, p. 482. For an analysis see Théophile Ducrocq, *Cours de droit administratif* (7th ed.; Paris, 1897–1905), III, 216–20.

17. Lists submitted by P.G. Paris, *AN,* BB30 383; and by P.I.'s to P.G. Aix, *AD,* Bouches-du-Rhône (Aix), 14.U.89.

18. Decree in Duvergier, LI (1851), 542–43. Other quotations: P.G. Aix to Justice, March 11, 1852, *AN,* BB30 370; and Interior circular Jan. 2, 1852, *Moniteur,* Jan. 3, 1852, p. 11.

19. On the response to the new law, e.g., extracts from subprefects' reports in various *départements* compiled in the Ministry, *AN,* Fla 9; and *commissaires'* reports to General Inspector at Lyon, 1852–53, dossier "Cafés et cabarets," F7 12165. On the wine tax, P.G. Lyon to Justice, Feb. 7, April 9, 1853, BB30 379.

20. Cf. Maupas' circular to 25 border prefects, March 4, 1852, *AN,* F18 3; and that of Interior, May 13, 1861, F18 2342. Typical smuggler's tricks are described by Léon Deries, "Policiers et douaniers contre Victor Hugo," *Grande revue,* LXXXV (June 25, 1914), 635–44. On judicial leniency, Collet-Meygret to Justice, April 3, 1854, *AN,* BB30 405 P802.

21. H. Dechère, "Les proscrits du Deux-Décembre à Jersey, 1852–1855," *Etudes religieuses,* CLI and CLII (1917), 601–25, 730–64, 44–65, 192–211; and Deries, *op. cit.* Correspondence of 1852–53 in *AN,* F1c III, Manche 13 and Ille-et-Vilaine 12.

22. *AN:* P.G. Lyon to Justice, March 4, April 9, 1853, BB30 379; correspondence 1852, F1c III Rhône 5 and Ain 6. *AD,* Isère (Grenoble): Fourth Army bulletin to Isère, Dec. 30, 1858, 52.M.39; this and carton 52.M.40 have many bulletins on the refugees through 1862.

23. Correspondence 1854, *ibid.,* 52.M.35; 1852–56, *AN,* F7 12164 and F1c III Ain 6. Trib. Corr. Lyon, audience of Jan. 23, *Gaz.Trib.,* March 12, 1856, p. 246.

24. E.g., Minister at Berne, report Sept. 29, 1855, passed by Foreign Affairs to Interior, *AN,* F18 549, dossier "Messager de Genève." *PRO:* Cowley to F.O., confidential No. 124, March 7, 1853, F.O. 27/964.

25. *PRO:* correspondence Jan., 1852, F.O. 27/924, and March, 1853, F.O. 27/964; Viscount Stratford de Redcliffe, "Mem. Paris March 14th 1853," sent by F.O. to Cowley, March 18, 1853, No. 39, F.O. 146/465.

26. *PRO:* F.O. draft to Chargé d'Affaires Paris, Jan. 13, 1852, No. 8 and

draft of Clarendon's private letter to Cowley, Feb. 24, 1852, F.O. 27/924; Nos. 11, 18, 22, 30 (copies of correspondence with Vienna and Berlin, for information to Cowley), March, 1853, F.O. 146/464.

27. *PRO:* Cowley to F.O., Feb. 25, 1852, No. 20, F.O. 27/929; and F.O. draft to Cowley (confidential), March 5, 1852, No. 9, F.O. 27/924.

28. *PRO:* Granville to Cowley, Feb. 20, 1852, No. 12 (confidential), F.O. 27/924; F.O., copy No. 2, instructions to Chargé at Berne, March 15, 1853, sent to Cowley for information, March 15, 1853, No. 36, F.O. 146/465.

29. *AN:* correspondence 1852–55, F1c III Nord 14, F1a 11, BB24 500–506 S. 56–6434, BB30 366 dossier 2, BB30 410 P1161. For the refugees' side, Martin Nadaud, *Mémoires de Léonard* (Bourganeuf, 1895), p. 363 and *passim*.

30. *AN,* F18 300: Foreign Affairs to Interior, April 3, 1855, relaying a report from the French legation at Brussels; Interior to Foreign Affairs, Sept. 29, 1853.

31. P. Wauwermans, *Les proscrits du coup d'état en Belgique* (Brussels, 1892), pp. 52–53, 97–98. Amédée Saint-Ferréol, *Les proscrits français en Belgique* (Brussels, 1870), I, 231.

32. P.G. Aix to Justice, Aug. 12, 1853, *AN,* BB30 370. Bouches-du-Rhône confidential to Var, Sept. 7, 1855, with reports of secret agent, *AD,* Bouches-du-Rhône (Marseille), M6 366.

33. *AD,* Bouches-du-Rhône (Aix): correspondence Jan.–April, 1852, 14.U.55 and June–August, 1852, 14.U.64. *AN:* July 9, 1852, to Interior, F1c III Var 12; P.G. Grenoble to Justice, Nov. 18, 1852, BB30 378; Foreign Affairs to Justice, Sept. 7, 1853, BB30 405 P802, and to Interior, June 30, 1853, and Aug. 8, 1857, F18 300.

34. Basic policy in Police circular, Feb. 25, 1852, F1a* 2120. Illustrative cases in *AD,* Bouches-du-Rhône (Marseille), M6 123, and Isère (Grenoble), 52.M.35. Interior circular on enforcement to frontier prefects, June 1, 1858, in *ibid.,* 52.M.36.

35. *AD,* Bouches-du-Rhône (Marseille): prefect's *arrêté* of Sept. 15, 1851, M6 3449; lists of expellees, secret police reports for 1853–54 and other documents, M6 39. Daily arrest records in Archives Communales (Marseille), I^1 513.

36. Pertinent documents Sept.–Dec., 1856, *AD,* Bouches-du-Rhône (Marseille), M6 67 and M6 948.

37. Alexandre Pilenco, *Les mœurs du suffrage universel en France (1848–1928)* (Paris, 1930), pp. 1–312.

38. The theoretical context is analyzed by Louis Puech, *Essai sur la candidature officielle en France depuis 1851* (Paris, 1922), pp. 26–33. For Persigny's role and concepts: Paul Chrétien, *Le Duc de Persigny, 1808–1872* (Toulouse, 1943), pp. 99–110; Fialin de Persigny, *Le Duc de Persigny et les doctrines de l'Empire* (Paris, 1865), p. 159.

Rouher's "Note pour l'Empereur," 1863, in Çerçay papers, *AN,* 45 AP 1.

39. E.g., circulars in *Moniteur:* Jan. 20, 1852, p. 103; Feb. 12, 1852, p. 230; May 31, 1857, p. 593; June 20, 1857, p. 669; Aug. 10, 1860, p. 965. Confidential circulars in *AN,* F1a* 2119: Jan. 8, 16, and 18, 1852; Feb. 15, 1852; June 1, 1857. On voting procedures, e.g., May 30, 1857, with detailed enclosure, F1a 48.

40. P.G.'s to Justice, *AN:* Grenoble, Dec. 3, 1856, BB30 378; Aix, June 28, 1857, BB30 370.

41. For samples of the nearly unanimous response in 1857 see the *procureurs'* reports from Douai and Paris, *AN,* BB30 377 and 383, and the special collection of comments on the elections in BB18 1567 I–II.

42. Puech, *op. cit.* On the policy in the Doubs: P.R. Besançon to General Inspector at Lyon, Aug. 18, 1852, *AN,* F7 12166 dossier "Doubs." Quotation from P.G. Aix to Justice, Jan. 26, 1857, BB30 370.

43. Haute-Vienne to Interior, Nov. 13, 1852, misfiled in *AN,* F1c III Vienne 8; P.G. Montpellier to Justice, June 30, 1857, BB30 380.

44. Decisions of Council of State and Court of Cassation in various cases, *AN,* F18 302, dossier 24.

45. Theodore Zeldin, *The political system of Napoleon III* (New York, 1958), pp. 5–45.

46. Blanchard, *op. cit.,* p. 34.

47. *Ibid.,* p. 24.

48. Prefects to Interior, *AN,* F1c III series: July 8, 1852, Ariège 6; March 6, 1852, Haute-Saône 12; April 10, 1858, Aube 4.

49. Interior circular, Feb. 11, 1852, *Moniteur,* Feb. 12, 1852, p. 230. *AN,* to Interior: Vienne, May 23, 1854, F1a 12; and F1c III series—March 7, 1854, Vienne 8; June 27, 1853, Ariège 6; April 26, 1853 (to Police), Haute-Garonne 9.

50. To Interior, July 1, 1852, *AN,* F1c III Calvados 9.

51. To Interior, *AN,* F1c III series: July 19, 1852, Oise 7; July 22, 1852, Ardennes 6; Aug. 18, 1852, Saône-et-Loire 13; July 23, Aug. 17, 1852, Ille-et-Vilaine 12. To Interior: Loiret, Meurth, and Haute-Saône (analyses), Sept. 7, 8 and Oct. 4, 1853, F1a 11.

52. *AN,* F1c III series: Nord, Interior, and Justice, Dec., 1851, Nord 6; Interior to prefect, Aug. 24, 1852, Ille-et-Vilaine 12.

53. *AN,* F1c III series: Sept. 4, 1852, Haute-Garonne 14; March 29, Nov. 8, Dec. 5, 1854, Hérault 15.

54. *La politique ecclésiastique du second empire de 1852 à 1869* (Paris, 1930), especially pp. 3–82, 156–79, 220–45, 320–24, on which the generalizations in this paragraph mainly rest.

55. Such collaboration is documented in *AN,* F19 series, including cartons 2649, 2650, 5589, 5605, 5606 (Prefect of Police); throughout the BB18 series for the period; and in *AD,* Bouches-du-Rhône (Marseille),

M6 55 and 33.V.1. Quotation of P.G. Lyon, April 9, 1853, *AN*, BB30 379.

56. Correspondence, 1852–57, *AN*, F1c III Tarn-et-Garonne 5.
57. Confidential reports, Jan. 11, April 10, 1859, *AN*, F1c III Ille-et-Vilaine 8.
58. E.g., Interior circulars, Aug. 3, 1861, March 21, 1862, April 12, 1866, *AN*, F1a 2122ᴬ and 2123ᴬ; Gallix, "personal" to Persigny, Niort, Oct. 20, 1861 (copy), *AN*, F18 297.
59. To Interior, April 4, 1852, *AN*, F1c III Gers 11.

Chapter 6: Manipulation of the Provincial Press

1. For a chronological treatment of law and practice, see Irene Collins, *The government and the newspaper press in France, 1814–1881* (London, 1959), pp. ix–xiv, 1–117; continuity and change in press laws are analyzed by Gustave Rousset, *Nouveau code annoté de la presse* (Paris, 1856), pp. 1–296. Henri Avenel, *Histoire de la presse française depuis 1789 jusau'à nos jours* (Paris, 1900), pp. 388–436 traces the setting without research of details.
2. Confidential to Justice, Jan. 10, 1856, *AN*, BB18 1552 A2 6777; cf. another of his typical warnings, confidential to Interior, Aug. 11, 1853, F18 417, dossier "Siècle."
3. Quotations in order from: undated Interior press division memorandum, c. 1853, *AN*, F18 570; P.G. Lyon to Justice, July, 1857, BB30 379; Interior circular Sept. 18, 1859, *Gaz.Trib.*, Sept. 19–20, 1859, p. 909; Cowley to F.O., Feb. 19 (No. 1) and March 1 (No. 6), 1852, *PRO*, F.O., 27/929.
4. Persigny, various speeches and circulars, reprinted in Fialin de Persigny, *Le Duc de Persigny et les doctrines de l'Empire* (Paris, 1865), pp. 118–26, 179–95, 200–01; Charlemagne-Emile de Maupas, *Mémoires sur le second empire* (Paris, 1885), I, 580–87. These were also Louis Napoleon's views according to Bernard Adolphe Granier de Cassagnac, *Souvenirs du second empire* (Paris, 1879–82), II, 84–85. Billault to Corps Legislatif, June 18, 1861, *Discussion de la loi sur la presse....* (Paris, 1861), pp. 7–8, in *B.Nat.*, Le⁸³.143.
5. *AN*: P.G. Grenoble to Justice, Dec. 10, 1857, BB30 378; P.G. Nancy to Justice, Feb., 1853, BB30 381.
6. Decree in Duvergier, LII (1852), 104–07. A more severe law for the colonies appeared on Feb. 20, *ibid.*, 156–57. Algeria came under the Feb. 17 law on March 14, 1855: see A. Behaghel, *La liberté de la presse. Ce qu'elle est en Algérie* (Paris, 1863), pp. 1–16. For background, Granier de Cassagnac, *op. cit.*, II, 87–93; Baroche papers, *BT*, 1135, pièce 4 and others.
7. Quotations from Cassation decisions of 1852, 1865, *Gaz.Trib.*, July

12–13, 1852, p. 670 and March 10, 1865, p. 235. In *AN,* statement of
official doctrine with notes on several cases, F18 302; interpretation of
"social economy," Interior circular Oct. 9, 1854, F18 4.

8. *Moniteur,* April 3, 1852, pp. 533–34.

9. Quotation from: Interior to Président of the Section du Contentieux,
Council of State, Feb. 18, 1866, *AN,* F18 354, dossier "Gazette de
France"; also "Note relative à la prescription des avertissemens," Feb.
14, 1857, F18 302, dossier 26.

10. *AN,* circulars of the 1850's in F18 4; correspondence in F7 3480, F18
300 and 301. *AD,* Bouches-du-Rhône (Marseille), 33.V.1, Interior
circular, April 4, 1853.

11. Hector Pessard, *Mes petits papiers, 1860–1870* (Paris, 1887), pp. 8–9.

12. Director of Printing and the Book Trade [at this time, Juillerat], unsigned, 1856: *Documents pour servir à l'histoire du second empire*
(Paris, 1872), pp. 187–93.

13. Statistics from Maupas to Emperor, Feb. 4, 1853, *AN,* AB XIX 175–
76 dossier 21. Also Léon Vingtain, *De la liberté de la presse* (Paris,
1860), pp. 153–427. The political bias of papers affected I compiled
from prefects' reports in various archival series. Maupas' and Persigny's
policies in Police circular Aug. 18, 1852, *APP,* D B/206, and in *AN:*
Police and Interior correspondence Aug., 1852, F7 3008[1] and F18 300;
Interior circular July 28, 1853, F18 3; Maupas to Emperor, Feb. 4,
1853, *loc. cit.*

14. Three writers deal extensively with the warnings but they differ on
details: A. Germain, *Martyrologe de la presse, 1789–1861* (Paris,
1861); Edouard Laferrière, *La censure et le régime correctionnel* (2d
ed.; Paris, 1868); and Vingtain, *op. cit.* I have tried to correct differences by comparison with each other and with documents in the *AN:*
Interior, Bureau of Press and Colportage, notes for an amnesty, Aug.,
1854, F18 570; Director of the Press, notes for "Compte-rendu de la
situation de l'Empire," Jan. 21, 1864, F18 294. Cf. also Persigny's
report, June 20, 1854, *Moniteur,* June 21, 1854, p. 673.

15. *AN,* F18 417, dossier "Siècle."

16. Texts of most of the warnings of the period are reprinted by Laferrière
and Vingtain, cited above.

17. General data on suspensions, Germain, *op. cit.,* p. 273.

18. Interior, "Note" on Article 32 of the 1852 law, May 15, 1854, *AN,*
F18 310.

19. Press director's project of amnesty, Aug., 1854, *AN,* F18 570. Persigny's remarks and later amnesty, *Gaz.Trib.,* Dec. 20, 21, 1860, pp.
1218–19, 1221.

20. E.g., correspondence through the Second Empire, *AD,* Bouches-du-
Rhône (Aix), 16.U.4 through 9.

21. Finances to Justice, May 13, 1850, and April 29, 1868, *AN,* BB18

1770, A4 8661; responses to Interior circular May 22, 1861, are in
F18 264. See also Laferrière, *op. cit.*, pp. 9, 241–49.

22. Interior circulars: July 12, 1852, *AN*, F18 3; Aug. 21, 1861, and
June 4, 1862, F18 6. Prefect to Interior, July 28, 1852, FiC III
Bouches-du-Rhône 12.

23. For the Charente-Inférieure and similar incidents, *AN*, Interior register, entry Jan. 4, 1858, F 5770, p. 300 and *passim* in this and other
registers.

24. *AN*, F18 354, dossier "Gazette de France."

25. Summary data in Interior, "Etat statistique . . . ," Sept., 1862, *AN*,
F18 294.

26. Inferences for the fifties based on internal evidence in memorandum of
Sept. 15, 1867, *Documents pour servir . . . ,* pp. 197–221, and *AN:*
"Note à l'appui des propositions de subventions," 1869, F18 307; De
La Guéronnière, press director, very confidential, May 31, 1861, F18
16.

27. Report to Emperor, *Documents pour servir . . . ,* pp. 187–93; also
Maupas, report to Emperor, Feb. 4, 1853, *AN*, AB XIX 175–76,
dossier 21.

28. *AN*, F18 302 dossier 19. The right was twice reconfirmed by the Council of State in 1854 and 1860. A Justice note, undated, to Baroche said
that the judges raised no objections to the transfer because they were
ill-informed on the press: Baroche papers, *BT*, 1142.

29. Isére to Interior, Jan. 10, 1852, *AN*, F7 3480; Police circular Dec. 27,
1852, F18 3, and very-confidential to General Inspectors, Dec. 18,
1852, F7 12165.

30. E.g., Vingtain, *op. cit.*, pp. 205–06, 283–84. Circular Sept. 15, 1858,
AN, F18 571.

31. *AN*, FiC III series: to Police and to Interior, May 4, 1853, Gard 13;
and in Gers 11—to Police, Jan. 6, April 29, 1853; M. Dupony to
Napoleon III, Condom, March 8, 1853; commission of petitions of
Council of State to Interior, March 22, 1853.

32. To Interior: Puy-de-Dôme, March 30, 1852; Finistère, June 28, 1852,
Haute-Saône, June 26, 1852—all in *AN*, F7 3481. Vosges to Police,
March 10, 1853, FiC III Vosges 10.

33. *AN:* FiC III series, to Interior, April 16, 1859, Ardennes 6 and July
5, 1858, Haute-Saône 9; Sarthe to Interior, June 28, 1852, F7 3481.

34. *AN:* FiC III series, to Police, April 16, 1853, Var 12 and to Interior,
July 8, 1854, Vienne 6; Ardèche to Interior, June 22, 1852, F7 3481.
Also, Germain, *op. cit.*, p. 205.

35. *AN:* Mayenne to Interior, Oct. 7, 1852, F7 3481; exchange, Moselle
and Interior, March–Oct. 1852, F7 3480 and 3481 and FiC III
Moselle 15; Moselle to Police, June 24, 1852, FiC I* 3^{12}.

36. *AN:* Vosges to Interior, July 7, 1852, F7 3481; P.G. Lyon to Justice,

Dec. 28, 1864, BB30 379; Aisne to Interior, June 29, 1852, F7 3481 and July 10, 1858, Jan. 29, 1859, F1c III Aisne 11.

37. *AN:* Loire-Inférieure to Interior, June 27, 1852, F7 3481, and various reports 1853–1859, F1c III Loire-Inférieure 8; Aube to Interior, June 30, 1852, F7 3481, and Aug. 13, 1853, F1c III Aube 4; P.G. Paris to Justice, Aug. 20, 1858, BB30 383. Vingtain, *op. cit.,* pp. 331–32.

38. *AN,* F7 3481: Vosges to Interior, July 7, 1852, and the *Courrier's* prospectus, July 6, 1852; Aude (June 28, 1852), Aveyron (July 1, 1852), Côtes-du-Nord (June 30, 1852) to Interior. Other *AN* series: P.G. Montpellier to Justice, Jan. 29, July 20, 1855, BB30 380; De la Tour, owner of *Bretagne,* to Interior, May 10, 1854, F1a 12; to Interior and Police, various reports 1852–1853, F1c III Dordogne 11; to Interior, Aug. 26, 1852, F1c III Eure 13.

39. Prefects to Interior: Gironde, June 28, 1852, *AN,* F7 3481; Jan. 15, 1859, F1c III Seine-et-Oise 9; Loire, Jan. 12, 1859, printed under title, "Le département de Maine-et-Loire en 1859," *Anjou Historique,* XXXIX (April, 1939), 120–24. Circulation figures here and subsequently are from "Etat statistique . . . ," *AN,* F18 294.

40. Material on the Nord in *AN:* prefect to Interior, July 9, 1852, F7 3481 and Sept. 15, 1850, F18 263; to Interior and Police, Jan. 8, 1853, F1c III Nord 14; P.G. Douai to Justice, July 29, 1856, July 22, 1857, Feb. 2, 1858, BB30 377; dossiers of the département's newspapers, F18 485^A-H series.

41. P.G. Douai to Justice, July 29, 1856, *AN,* BB30 377. Philip Spencer, "Censorship by imprisonment in France, 1830–1870," *The Romanic Review* (New York), XLVII (Feb., 1956), 30–38; J. Tchernoff, *Le parti républicain au coup d'état et sous le second empire* (Paris, 1906), pp. 265–68; Eugène Hatin, *Histoire politique et littéraire de la presse en France* (Paris, 1859–61), I, 294–98.

42. E. Hervé, "La presse et la législation de 1852," *Revue Contemporaine,* Feb. 28, 1866.

Chapter 7: The Commissaires, *Gendarmerie, and Rural Police*

1. P. Truy, "Commissaires de police," *J.C.P.,* III, 6e année (1860), 389–97, is a concise analysis of their history and duties.

2. Interior circular Aug. 30, 1854, *AD,* Bouches-du-Rhône (Marseille), M6 276.

3. Letter of Delmarre, ex-prefect of the Creuse, April 18, 1853, *AN,* F1a 12.

4. Circular to prefects, May 31, 1852, *AN,* F1a* 2121.

5. Interior circular, Dec. 12, 1854, *J.C.P.,* I, 1er année (1855), 87–88; Emile Thomas, *Le livre des commissaires de police* (Montdidier, Somme; 1864), pp. 81–82, 85, 136.

6. Quotations from a Parisian and a cantonal *commissaire:* Achille Ra-basse, *Police municipale* (bound MS, 1872), *APP,* 398/3, p. 22; Thomas, *op. cit.,* p. 109.

7. Sûreté Publique instruction of 1858, *J.C.P.,* II, 4e année (1858), 210–22. Other material on the ideal officer is drawn from Thomas, *op. cit.,* Rabasse, *op. cit.,* and various official instructions and articles of doctrine in *J.C.P.* during the 1850's.

8. Interior, report to Emperor with decree of Feb. 27, 1855, and circular March 10, 1855: *J.C.P.,* I, 1er année (1855), 97–102, 105–08.

9. *J.C.P.:* "Tableau indiquant l'organisation au 31 décembre 1854," I, 1er année (1855), 5–71; statistical data, III, année 6 (1860), 61–63, 167–73.

10. *Ibid.,* I, 1er année (1855), 97–102.

11. Decree, Feb. 27, 1855, Duvergier, LV (1855), 107–08. *AN:* to In-terior, Jan. 5, 1855, Fɪc III Côtes-du-Nord 11; examples of *commis-saires'* problems in correspondence of 1850's and 1860's, F7 12166, 12243, and 12709. Other such information in Germain Deshaire 43-page brochure, *Considérations sur l'administration départementale* (Paris, 1858), copy in *AN,* Fɪc III Tarn-et-Garonne 7. Cf. the *Com-missaires'* income with that of the prefects after March, 1852: 40,000, 30,000 and 20,000 francs. The Prefect of Police received 50,000.

12. E.g., to Interior, Sept. 14, 1854, *AN,* Fɪc III Loire-Inférieure 8.

13. M. David, unpublished MS dated Feb. 15, 1850, "Appréciations générales de la police en France," *APP,* D B/353.

14. Thomas, *op. cit.,* pp. 109–10; and outline of their duties in *J.C.P.,* II, 4e année (1858), 212–13.

15. *AN,* BB30 series, P.G.'s to Justice: Dijon, Aug. 19, 1853 (550); Montpellier, July 8, 1853 (380); Nîmes, Aug. 19, 1857 (382). Also, P.I. Brignoles to P.G. Aix, Oct. 29, 1854, *AD,* Bouches-du-Rhône (Aix), 12.U.22.

16. *AN,* Fɪc III series, to Interior: Chambaron, Sept. 30, 1853, and Le Vasseur, 1854 (noted received Paris, Nov. 22), Tarn-et-Garonne 7; Aug. 5, 1853, Ardennes 6; April 8, 1857, Hérault 9; Aug. 13, 1853, Aube 4; Sept. 15, Nov. 4, 1853, Haute-Saône 9; July 11, 1854, Seine-et-Oise 9.

17. Pierre Carlier, inspector of prefectures, referring to the Ain, to Interior, Oct. 4, 1853, *AN,* Fɪa 11; circular Dec. 6, 1853, *AD,* Bouches-du-Rhône (Marseille), M6 276.

18. *AN:* Ain to General Inspector, Lyon, July 13, 1852, F7 12166; sub-prefect of Châtellerault to Interior, Jan. 1, 1859, Fɪc III Vienne 6; Justice–Interior exchange, July 28 and Aug. 7, 1854, BB30 378.

19. Policy outlined by Police circular, Feb., 1853; and by Interior circulars, March 19, 1853, and March 10, 1855: respectively, in *AN,* Fɪa* 2120, Fɪa 47, and *J.C.P.,* I, année 1 (1855), 105–08.

20. Interior circular, April 3, 1854, *AD*, Bouches-du-Rhône (Marseille), M6 276. *J.C.P.: commissaires'* organization chart, I, 1er année (1855), 5–71; and "Instruction" of the General Director of the Sûreté Publique to *commissaires*, II, 4e année (1858), 211–14. *AN:* central *commissaire* of Valence to General Inspector at Lyon, July 2, 1852, F7 12166; to Interior, Sept. 14, 1854, F1c III Loire-Inférieure 8.

21. Police circular, April 30, 1853, *APP*, D B/353 pièce 83; decree Oct. 26, 1859, *J.C.P.*, III, 5e année (1859), 313; E. G. Perrier, *La police municipale* (Paris, 1920), pp. 167–68.

22. Memorandum and "note" prepared in Interior, both undated (1852), *AN*, F18 10^a pièces 563 and 574; undated (1853) memorandum, F1b 267^1.

23. *AN:* data and instruction manuals, F7 12246, F18 252-bis; undated memorandum (c. 1854) in Interior, F18 10^a pièce 578; various documents in F18 2349; report of Interior, Aug. 1, 1864, 45 AP 11.

24. Gaillard's personnel dossier, *AN*, F1b I 267^1; and Gaillard to Interior, undated (1846), F18 10^a pièces 583–85.

25. List of frontier *commissaires*, *J.C.P.*, III, 6e année (1860), 168.

26. Various dossiers, *AD*, Isère (Grenoble), 52.M.15 and 35; *commissaire* at Beauvoisin to General Inspector at Lyon, Sept. 29, 1852, *AN*, F7 12168.

27. Report, July 3, 1852, *AN*, F7 12166.

28. Central Commissaire of Railway Police Pauphille, "Notes à la suite de tournée d'inspection," May 4, 1860, *AN*, F7 12243.

29. Pertinent legislation from 1846 through the Second Empire is reproduced by Perrier, *op. cit.*, annexes, pp. 182–93.

30. Various documents, *AN*, F7 12243; list of *commissaires* in *J.C.P.*, III, 6e année (1860), 167. Sûreté Publique circulars June 4, 1856, and April 17, May 31, 1863, to railway *commissaires*, *AN*, F7 12243.

31. The names and jurisdictions of the central railway *commissaires* are listed in *J.C.P.*, IV, 83 année (1862), 262–64. Their number was reduced to three in July, 1864. Interior circular on "special missions," Oct. 1, 1862, *AN*, F1a 2122^B.

32. "Instructions relatives au service . . . ," Jan. 27, 1856, *J.C.P.*, I, année 2 (1856), 12.

33. *AN:* circular May 31, 1863, and Pauphille quoting Collet-Meygret, to General Director of the Sûreté Publique, Paris, Dec. 20, 1860, both in F7 12243; two "notes" in Justice: one on the decree of Feb. 22, 1855, the other dated Dec. 27, 1857, both in BB30 953.

34. Railway *commissaire* at Grenoble to Isère, March 28, 1864, *AD*, Isère (Grenoble), 53.M.15; e.g., a dossier of reports to the Sûreté Publique for 1858, *AN*, F7 12709 and Pauphille to Sûreté Publique, Paris, Dec. 20, 1860, F7 12243.

35. *J.C.P.*, I, 1er année (1855), 175–77. *AN:* joint Public Works-Interior

circular, June 1, 1855, BB30 953; Justice, "Note sur les commissaires spéciaux . . . ," Dec. 27, 1857, and P.G. Paris to Justice, July 15, 1856, both in BB30 953 in which (together with F7 12243) see this and other aspects of the conflict in dossiers of correspondence from 1853 through 1865.

36. Howard C. Payne, "Preparation of a coup d'état: administrative centralization and police powers in France, 1849–1851," in Frederick J. Cox (ed.), *Studies in modern European history in honor of Franklin Charles Palm* (New York, 1956), pp. 180–81.

37. *J.Gend.*, Nos. 198, 209, 217 (1851–52), pp. 32, 159–62, 256–58, respectively. Ernest Leblanc, *La gendarmerie, son histoire et son rôle,* reprint from *Nouvelle Revue* (Paris, June 1, 1880), p. 18.

38. War, circular to legion commanders, *J.Gend.*, No. 230 (Dec. 21, 1851), pp. 418–19 and subsequent issues; Saint-Arnaud to State, Sept. 25, 1852, *SHA,* F1 65.

39. Loiret to Interior, June 7, 1852, *AN,* F1a 333–342²; War (Bureau of the Gendarmerie) to Justice, Dec. 8, 1855, BB30 413 P1247 pièce 97. Many other areas reported similar activities.

40. To the Prince-President, July 1, 1852, *AN,* F1c III Calvados 9.

41. Decree and editorial comment, *J.Gend.*, No. 230 (Dec. 21, 1851) and No. 231 (Jan. 1, 1852), 421–27; Leblanc, *op. cit.*, p. 18; Duvergier, LI (1851), 534–35.

42. Duvergier, LIV (1854), 111–73; *J.Gend.*, No. 313 (April 11, 1854), pp. 109–10.

43. Organizational information in *J.Gend.*, Nos. 249 (July 1, 1852) and 953 (April 12, 1872), pp. 222 and 149–51, respectively.

44. La Ruë's circular, Jan. 6, 1854, *SHA,* 2003. Leblanc, *op. cit.*, pp. 24–36 for details. Also, *Papiers et correspondance de la famille impériale* (Paris, 1871), II, 22–27.

45. *AN,* F1c III series to Interior: Nov. 12, 1852, Aug. 1, 1853, Ille-et-Vilaine 12; Sept. 7, 1852, Sarthe 10. *SHA:* War to Inspector-General Gauthier de Laverderie, Sept. 10, 1852, F1 65; War, confidential circular to colonels of legions, March 30, 1863, G9 152, dossier dated May 10, 1869.

46. *SHA,* 2003, "Correspondence directe." E.g., Vienne to Interior, July 5, 1856, complaining that he can no longer get the secret police cooperation he had in the past: *AN,* F1c III Vienne 6. The captain's protest, Jan. 8, 1857, *Papiers et correspondance . . . ,* II, 22–27.

47. *SHA:* "Note pour le ministre: des rapports politiques fournis par la gendarmerie," undated (1866 or afterward), 2003; La Ruë's personnel dossier, GD 1245; report to War, Aug. 1, 1852, F1 64.

48. The General's personnel dossier, *loc. cit.* I gratefully acknowledge the aid of Gendarmerie Captain Saurel, stationed at Savigny-sur-Marne in

1954, who was most helpful in obtaining this information in the archives at Vincennes.

49. "Note pour le ministre . . . ," *SHA*, 2003. Argument over whether the gendarmerie did secret work was still alive in the 1880's. E.g., a comment in *Moniteur de la Gendarmerie*, 2d année, No. 59 (Oct. 16, 1881), p. 23, which implied that the prefects of the Empire erred in their allegations and were merely trying "to domineer" over the gendarmerie.

50. Leblanc, *op. cit.*, pp. 5–7. A. Germond de Lavigne, *La gendarmerie, ses relations, ses devoirs, son avenir* (Paris, 1857), p. 5. *SHA*, F1 64, reports for Aug., 1852. To Interior, April 15, 1859, *AN*, F1c III Aisne 11.

51. Statement of the gendarmerie's position, *J.Gend.*, No. 281 (May 21, 1853), p. 160. General account of conflicts in Lavigne, *op. cit.*, pp. 1–47. In *AN:* P.G. Amiens to Justice, Aug. 16, 1853, BB30 550; for the dispute in the Orne, correspondence June, 1852, F1a 333–342².

52. *J.Gend.*, No. 281 (May 21, 1853), p. 161. *J.C.P.*, I, 2d année (1856), 349–59 and II, 4e année (1858), 210–22. Quoted statement italicized in the original.

53. To Interior, April 1, 1859, *AN*, F1c III Aube 4.

54. *AN*, F1c III series, to Interior: Aug. 5, 1853, Ardennes 6; April 8, 1858, Vienne 6; Jan. 1 and April 6, 1859, Haute-Vienne 8; Jan. 1, 1854, and Jan. 5, 1859, Tarn-et-Garonne 5; correspondence of mayors, prefect, and Interior, July, 1859, Dordogne 11. Also Orne to Interior, April 28, 1852, F1a 333–342².

55. Interior, very-confidential circular, April 10, 1858; Isère's reply, April 23, 1858: *AD*, Isère (Grenoble), 52.M.36.

56. On relations with the Prefect: "Note pour la direction du personnel, bureau de la gendarmerie," April 18, 1853, *SHA*, G9 3; and Maréchal de Castellane, *Journal du Maréchal de Castellane* (Paris, 1895–97), V, entry for Jan. 23, 1859, 274. *Procureurs'* quotations from *AN*, P.G. Douai to Justice, July 29, 1856, BB30 377; typical criticisms in the *procureurs'* inspection reports for 1853, BB30 550.

57. Similar agents before 1789 were known as *gardes messiers* or *bangards*. A decree of Sept. 28, 1791, created the *gardes-champêtres;* legislation from 1795 through 1811 fitted them into the Napoleonic system. See Emile Arnaud, *La police municipale et rurale et les gardes champêtres* (Paris, 1928), pp. 467–73.

58. See a concise statement of their status and duties in P. Subercaze, "Les gardes. Historique et législation," part 3, *Moniteur des gardes champêtres*, No. 3 (March 15, 1868).

59. *J.C.P.:* "De la réorganisation . . . des gardes champêtres," II, 3e année (1857), 260–66; P.I. Orange, *mémoire* on the Senate's studies of the problem, 10e année (1864), 15. *AN*, F1c III series: to Interior,

April 15, 1859, Aisne 11; reports, March through December, 1858, Oise 7.

60. Eugène Blanchet, "Des gardes-champêtres," *J.C.P.*, III, 6e année (1860), 180–84.

61. *Mémoire* by Lavaur, Président of the Court of Appeal, July 8, 1852, summarized by State, Sept. 20, 1852, to War: *SHA*, F1 65, dossier Sept. 20, 1852.

62. *J.C.P.*: II, 3d année (1857), 260–66; 10e année (1864), 7–21. Baron de Vincent, *De l'organisation des gardes-champêtres* (Paris, 1858), p. 7. Also, e.g., *AN*, F1c III series: July 11, 1854, Seine-et-Oise 9; July 10, 1859, Loiret 12.

63. *AN*, BB30 series, P.G.'s to Justice: Montpellier, July 8, 1853 (380); Aix, June 19, 28 and July 1, 1853 (550); Besançon, July 31, 1853 (550); Paris, Feb. 18 and report for 4th trimestre, 1858 (383); Bastia, Dec. 20, 1864 (366, dossier 3, pièces 296–97).

64. *AN*: to Interior, Oct. 11, 1857, and April 1, 1859, F1c III Aube 4; P.G. Paris, 1st trimestre report, 1859, BB30 383.

65. De Vincent, *op. cit.*, pp. 1–30. Other proposals in sequence from: Ferdinand Jacques, *De l'embrigadement des gardes champêtres,* reprint from *Revue pratique de droit français* (Paris, Sept. 15, 1859), pp. 1–27; P.G. Paris, report 1st trimestre, 1857, *AN*, BB30 383; to Interior, Feb. 10, 1858, F1c III Drôme 8. War to State, minute, Sept. 25, 1852, *SHA*, F1 65.

Chapter 8: Secret Political Police

1. *Tricolored sketches in Paris* (New York, 1855), p. 105.
2. Charlemagne-Emile de Maupas, *Mémoires dur le second empire* (Paris, 1885), I, 249.
3. *Etudes administratives* (2d ed.; Paris, 1859), II, 192.
4. Emile Thomas, *Le livre des commissaires de police* (Montdidier, Somme; 1864), pp. 117, 127–28. Vivien, *op. cit.*, II, 193, 198–99. Identical arguments were advanced by prefects, *procureurs,* and the Prefect of Police: e.g., P.G. Paris to Justice, June 30, 1856, *AN*, BB30 417; and the deposition of P.-M. Piétri, in *Actes du gouvernement de la défense nationale* (Paris, 1876), V, 115—hereafter cited as *Actes*.
5. The dubious, ten-volume *Mémoires de Monsieur Claude* (Paris, 1881) of uncertain authorship, have perpetuated many unsubstantiated, sensationalist stories of the secret police. Apparently this work supplied some material for Jean Galtier-Boissière, *Mysteries of the French secret police,* tr. Ronald Leslie-Melville (London, 1938) [hereafter cited as *Mysteries*], with respect to secret funds and other data. Galtier-Bois-

sière's original work was a special number of *Crapouillot* (Paris) for July, 1936; the period 1848–70 is on pp. 113–35.

6. *Documents pour servir à l'histoire du second empire* (Paris, 1872), p. 298 [hereafter cited as *Documents pour servir*]. *AN:* tables of the Division de la Comptabilité, Interior, 1865, F18 2367; états of secret expenses, Interior, F4 2697.

7. Decrees of Feb. 1 and March 21, 1852, Duvergier, LII (1852), 64–65, 305. Three books of such records from 1855 to 1864 labeled "Lettres d'avis d'ordonnances de paiement réunies en borderaux et déposer au trésor," are in *AN*, F4 2697.

8. Loire to Interior, Nov. 20, 1849, *AN*, F1a 333–342[2]. Subprefect, Aix-en-Provence to Bouches-du-Rhône, July 6, 1850, *AD*, Bouches-du-Rhône (Marseille), M6 344. Reference to Carlier in Louis Canler, *Mémoires de Canler, ancien chef du service de sûreté* (Brussels & Leipzig, 1862), p. 346.

9. *AN*, F1c III series: to Police, April 26, 1853, Haute-Garonne 9; to Interior and reply, Sept. 6, Oct. 13, 1852, Ariège 6; to Interior, April 25, 1853, Var 10.

10. Correspondence 1852–55: *AN*, F1c III Bouches-du-Rhône 12; and *AD*, Bouches-du-Rhône (Marseille), M6 40 and 55.

11. Circulars, July 4, Aug. 26, 1854, and Feb. 14, 1855: *AD*, Isère (Grenoble), 52.M.35.

12. *AN:* Marie, Cassier Central at the Interior, reports of May, Aug., Sept., 1861, to General Director of Personnel, F1a 12; the Nov. circular, F1a 2122[A].

13. To Interior, July 5, 1856; subprefect at Châtellerault to prefect, July 1, 1856, March 31, 1857, and March 31, 1858: *AN*, F1c III Vienne 6. E.g., similar problems: very-confidential to Police, April 26, 1853, *AN*, F1c III Haute-Garonne 9; P.R. Brignoles, dispatches to P.G. Aix, Aug.–Sept., 1852, *AD*, Bouches-du-Rhône (Aix), 12.U.20.

14. *AN:* P.G. Besançon to Justice, Feb. 16, 17, 29, 1856, and correspondence with Jura, BB30 416 P1329; P.G. Lyon to Justice, May 6, 1856, and "loans" of agents to Lyon in 1856 in copy of Prefect of Police secret report to Interior, June 27, 1856, sent by P.G. Paris to Justice, June 30, 1856, all in BB30 417 P1371.

15. Documents Nos. 3 and 9, 1852 and 1870, in Ville de Lyon, Conseil Municipal, *Pièces saisies aux archives de la police politique de Lyon* (Lyon, 1870), pp. 8–11, 23–25: B.Nat., Lb56.471. Various reports to Interior in 1850's, *AN*, F1c III Rhône 5.

16. Depositions of Kératry and Didier, *Actes*, V, 300–01, 448. *Gaz.Trib.,* June 18, 1871, p. 241. Galtier-Boissière, *Mysteries,* p. 228. Martin Nadaud, *Mémoires de Léonard, ancien garçon maçon* (Bourganeuf, 1895), pp. 355–56. *AN*, F1a* 782, register, p. 330.

17. Félix Rocquain, archivist and historian, was after Sept. 4, 1870, ordered

by Jules Simon, Minister of Public Instruction, to investigate the Prefecture's records. His *Notes et fragments d'histoire* (Paris, 1906) has a chapter on the Second Empire's political police; its content and structure indicate that Rocquain also wrote an anonymous earlier article, "Les agents secrets sous le second empire," *La revue politique et littéraire,* 2d series, V (Aug. 16, 1873), 158–63, which has some details not in the later work. Hereafter, Rocquain's contribution is cited "Les agents." His facts check with Kératry's more generalized account in *Actes,* V, 295–315. See also Maupas, *op. cit.,* I, 320.

18. Robert Schnerb, *Rouher et le second empire* (Paris, 1949), p. 236. The extent of his involvements came out in interrogation between Sept. 4 to Oct. 8, 1857; the results are in *AN, AB XIX* 273, dossier 42.

19. J. Griscelli de Vezzani, *Mémoires de Griscelli de Vezzani dit le Baron de Rimini* (Brussels, 1867), 360 pp.; Anna L. Bicknell, *Life in the Tuileries under the second empire* (New York, 1895), pp. 30–31, 53–54, 88, *et passim;* E. A. Vizetelly, *The court of the Tuileries, 1852–1870* (London, 1907), pp. 120–21.

20. Hyrvoix dossier, *APP,* B A/1122 and E A89–8. He left only a few routine nonpolitical reports in *AN:* e.g., F7 3008[1] dossier 12 and F1a 9; his functions are shown in BB18 1533 A2 4706.

21. *Actes,* V, 200–05, 301, and other depositions.

22. *Journal officiel de la République française,* Oct. 6, 1870, p. 1621: Kératry report on Prefecture of Police. Also Rocquain, "Les agents."

23. Vivien, *op. cit.,* II, 194–95 for a brief analysis based on experience since 1830. For an indication of the social backgrounds of *indicateurs* and some reprinted letters of application for secret police employment (some from the 1850's but most from the next decade), see *Le pilori des mouchards. Liste nominative . . . des individus qui ont demandé des emplois de mouchards sous l'Empire . . . , APP,* 278–41.

24. To Interior, Sept. 8, 1853, *AD,* Bouches-du-Rhône (Marseille), M6 40; payment list, *AN, AB XIX* 273 dossier 72. Count Kératry, *Le 4 septembre et le gouvernement de la défense nationale* (Paris, 1872), p. 164. Albert Dresden Vandam, *An Englishman in Paris* (London, 1892), II, 148–50.

25. *AN,* BB18 cartons 1786 through 1793; and 1795[1-2].

26. *AN:* F18 10ᵃ pièce 574; to Interior, Sept. 14, 1854, F1c III Loire-Inférieure 8. Charles Delescluze, *De Paris à Cayenne* (Paris, 1869), p. 22; Marcel Dessal, *Un révolutionnaire jacobin: Charles Delescluze, 1809–1871* (Paris, 1952), pp. 174–75. A similar betrayal trapped Jean-Baptiste Boichot, as related in his *Souvenirs d'un prisonnier d'état sous le second empire, 1854–1859* (new ed.; Leipzig, 1869), pp. 5–9.

27. E.g., in *AN,* F1c III series: to Police and Interior, June 27, 1852, Rhône 10; Oct. 12, 1855, Loire-Inférieure 8. Also documents in BB24 478–483, S.55–4003; 489–493, S.56–1389; 548–561 dossier 8037;

these and other cartons in the BB24 series contain dossiers of applicants for imperial clemency, with much evidence on informers in secret societies scattered through.

28. *AN:* Rouland to Justice, confidential, April 6, 1855, BB30 309 P1112-bis; Fıc III series, to Interior: June 1, 1853, Loire-Inférieure 11 and Sept. 14, 1852, Rhône 5. Lyon, *Pièces saisies . . . ,* No. 3, pp. 8–11. E.g., correspondence of Isère, the *commissaire* at Grenoble, Gen. de Castellane, and Interior: Dec., 1851, and Jan., 1852, *AD,* Isère (Grenoble), 52.M.32. On the Paris-Lyon operations in 1856: in *AN*—Prefect of Police, secret to Interior, June 27, 1856 (copy sent confidentially by P.G. Paris to Justice, June 30, 1856), and other documents, BB30 417 P1371, BB24 507–15, S.56–7058; and in *AD,* Bouches-du-Rhône (Aix), 14.U.77. The pattern of operations at Lyon is suggested by F. Dutacq, "La police politique et les partis d'opposition à Lyon et dans le Midi en 1852," *La Révolution de 1848,* XX (July–Aug., Nov.–Dec., 1923), 234–51, 325–31.

29. E.g., *AN,* BB30 series: correspondence June, 1854 (409, dossiers P1113, P1121; P.G.'s Limoges, Dijon, and Lyon to Justice, July 18, Aug. 10, Oct. 13, 1857 (418, dossiers P1510 and P1511). Also various documents, Aug.–Sept., 1857, BB18 1570 A2 8787.

30. Hannah Arendt, *The origins of totalitarianism* (New York, 1951), footnote, p. 401, which refers to Gallier [sic]–Boissière [i.e., Galtier-Boissière], *Mysteries,* p. 234. Such charges were originally made almost exclusively against Lagrange's men in Paris.

31. Piétri's deposition, *Actes,* V, 115. P.G. Paris to Justice, June 30, 1856, *AN,* BB30 417; cf. a similar case in 1855 also involving the P.G. at Lyon, BB30 410 P1194.

32. E.g., Auguste Jean Marie Vermorel, *Les mystères de la police* (new ed.; Paris, 1867), III, 1–315.

33. P.I. Brignoles to P.G. Aix, Aug. 27, 1852, *AD,* Bouches-du-Rhône (Aix), 12.U.20. E.g., correspondence among Prefect of Police, Justice, Interior, and P.G. Lyon on the question of provocation, Dec., 1856, to Feb., 1857, *AN,* BB24 507–15, S.56–7085.

34. Galtier-Boissière, *Mysteries,* pp. 212–13; Sebastien Commissaire, *Mémoires et souvenirs de Sébastien Commissaire, ancien réprésentant du peuple* (Lyon, 1888), II, 173.

35. Eleven such attempts are described in the anonymous *Attentats et complots contre Napoléon III* (Paris, 1870), 176 pp.

36. E.g., *AN* BB18 series includes many of these cases, specifically those mentioned for 1861–1862, in items 1661, 1756, and 1638 A3 5527. Other data: P.G. Paris to Justice, July 9, 1852, BB30 404 P719; Fıc III series to Interior—July 7, 1852, Haute-Garonne 14; July 9 and 11, 1856, Hérault 9; correspondence on the Reims case, F18 300. In *APP,* D B/513 are many references to investigations of plots against

the Emperor based on Parisian *commissaires'* records later destroyed.

37. Morny's remark quoted by Henry William Lansdowne, *The secret of the coup d'état of Napoleon III* (London, 1924), p. 200. On the problem in 1830 and 1848, see Eugène Vaille, "Etienne Arago, la direction de l'administration générale des postes et le cabinet noir en 1848," Pierre Renouvain *et al.* (eds.), *Actes du congrès historique du centenaire de la révolution de 1848* (Paris, 1948), pp. 303–14.

38. *AN,* AB XIX 273, dossier 42, interrogation of Collet-Meygret. Edouard-Ferdinand de Beaumont-Vassy, *Histoire intime du second empire* (Paris, 1874), pp. 76–77, 327–31.

39. Emile Lambry, *Les mystères du cabinet noir sous l'empire et la poste sous la Commune* (Paris, 1871), pp. 1–70. Maxime du Camp, *Souvenirs d'un demi-siècle* (Paris, 1949), I, 168–69, claimed to have his information directly from J.-M. Piétri, the last imperial Prefect of Police. Varying in many details, these two accounts agree on the substance of Simonel's service, which was corroborated by Rampont, the new Director of the Postal Service in September, 1870, whose testimony before an investigating commission is in *Actes,* V, 348.

40. Letter of Mouillard to Rouher, Aug. 14, 1852, in Cercay papers, *AN,* 45 AP 3.

41. E.g., Police to Justice, April 4, 1853, on general policy, *AN,* BB30 405 P802; dossier on illegalities, BB18 1529 A2 5315.

42. *AN:* BB30 406, P881, pièces 1–19. *Gaz.Trib.,* May 29, 1853, p. 514 and July 30, p. 726. Circulars, Interior Feb. 21 and Justice March 26, 1854, in Lucien Munsch (ed.), *Répertoire général des circulaires et instructions du ministère de la justice* (Paris, 1900), p. 678.

43. *AD,* Bouches-du-Rhône (Marseille): reports by agent Davalon, April–May, 1852, M6 344; of another agent, June–Aug., 1853, M6 356; and of agent Ballerini, 1853–54, M6 39; (Aix), special *commissaire* of the prefecture to P.G. Aix, May 12, 1859, 12.U.34.

Chapter 9: The French Police State of the 1850's

1. *AN,* BB30 series, P.G.'s to Justice, 1858: Paris, Aug. 20 (383), Douai, Feb. 2 (377), Aix, Jan. 17 (419, P1540). Prefect of Police, Feb. 6, 1858, AB XIX 174 dossier 142.

2. Consul-General of Austria at Marseille to prefect, May 14, 1856, *AD,* Bouches-du-Rhône (Marseille), M6 67.

3. Celeste Baroche, *Second Empire, notes et souvenirs de seize années, 1885 à 1871* (Paris, 1921), p. 90. Georges Eugène Haussmann, *Mémoires* (Paris, 1890), II, 157. Esprit-Victor de Castellane, *Journal du Maréchal de Castellane, 1804–1862* (Paris, 1895–97), V, 239–40. Jean Maurain, *Un bourgeois français au XIXe siècle: Baroche, ministre de Napoléon III* (Paris, 1936), pp. 173–74. Piétri, very-confi-

dential to Justice, March 11, 1858, *AN,* BB30 440 S58–1086, pièce 11.

4. Transactions with foreign police, *AN,* BB30 419 P1540 dossier 3.

5. Unless otherwise indicated, conclusions on the reaction are based on documents in *AN,* BB30 419, and 440 through 446; see also Justice circulars Jan. 19 and Feb. 18, 1858, BB30 455 dossier 2.

6. Jacques Louis Randon, *Mémoires du maréchal Randon* (Paris, 1875–77), II, 46–49. The gendarmerie's role is shown in *SHA, G9* 47. Emperor's order of Feb. 9 relayed to the prefects by Interior, March 23, 1858: *AD,* Isère (Grenoble), 52.M.41.

7. The law in *Moniteur,* March 2, 1858, p. 273. Interpretation: *AN,* BB30 477 A2 9481, Interior to Justice, March 25, 1858 (pièce 22), and Justice circular April 15, 1858; for the Pyrenées-Orientales situation, pièces 214–216.

8. Interior circular, Feb. 8, *Moniteur,* Feb. 9, 1858, p. 169. *AN,* BB30 477 A2 9481: Interior to Justice, Feb. 20, 1858, pièce 10; Interior to prefects, Feb. 7 and March 23, 1858; Justice circular, April 15, 1858.

9. Official total of transportees in *J.C.P.,* II, 5e année (1859), 239. A general though incomplete coverage of the law's application is in Eugène Ténot and Antonin Dubost, *Les suspects en 1858* (Paris, 1869), pp. 1–327. Espinasse's resignation letter is in *Papiers secrets brûlés dans l'incendie des Tuileries* (Brussels, 1871), Part 2, pp. 53–58.

10. Emile Félix Fleury, *Souvenirs du général Cte. Fleury* (Paris, 1897–98), I, 404–05; A. Quentin-Bauchart, *Etudes et souvenirs sur la deuxième république et le second empire* (Paris, 1901–02), II, 205; Maurain, *op. cit.,* pp. 157–58; Pierre de La Gorce, *Histoire du second empire* (Paris, 1904–06), II, 232–38.

11. *AN:* P.G. Paris to Justice, Aug. 20, 1858, BB30 383; P.G. Douai, April 6, 1858, BB30 377; other *procureurs'* reactions in BB30 477 A2 9481. *SHA:* Colonel 12th Legion (Lot) to General of 12th Military Division at Toulouse, March 3, 1858, G9 47.

12. Peter Amann, "The changing outlines of 1848," *The American Historical Review,* LXVIII (July, 1963), 938–53.

13. The continuity of such powers is shown by: Célestin Auzies, *De la surveillance de la haute police* (Paris, 1869), pp. 9–50; Auguste Frémont, "La surveillance de la haute police de l'état," *Revue critique de législation et de jurisprudence,* XXXIII (No., 1868); Félix Brayer, *Procédure administrative des bureaux de police* (Arras, 1866), pp. 301–20; Gustave Dutruc, *Le code de la détention préventive* (Paris, 1866), pp. 29–166. The *procureurs'* retrospective critique of *haute police* methods and the decree of Dec. 8 is in *AN,* BB18 1633–1637 A3 5048.

14. Quotations from typical articles by Eugène Blanchet in *J.C.P.:* "De la police," 3e année (1857), 31–42 and "Des abus d'autorité," 8e année (1862), 117–29.

15. A collection of such complaints in 1853–54 is in *AN*, F1a 11 and 12 in response to Interior circular, Sept. 10, 1853.

16. *AN:* P.G. Nîmes to Justice, Aug. 5, 1854, BB30 382; P.G. Paris to Justice, Feb. 18, 1854; to Interior, Sept. 14, 1854, F1c III Loire-Inférieure 8. S.-A. Tarrade, *Coup d'oeil rapide sur l'organisation de la police en France* (Rodez, 1853), pp. 1–8. Critiques by the two ex-prefects: V. des Aubiers, *De l'administration et de ses réformes* (Paris, 1852), pp. 1–151; Rodolphe d'Ornano, 31-page pamphlet, *De l'administration de l'Empire* (Paris, 1860), in *BN*, 8°Lf96.52.

17. The functionaries' income is analyzed in great detail in two works by Paul Dupont: *Insuffisance des traitements en général et de la nécessité d'une prompte augmentation* (Paris, 1859), and *Etudes administratives. Un dernier mot sur les traitements . . . pour toutes les administrations centrales* (Paris, 1860). Also, figures compiled by Interior in *AN*, F1a 634; and Rouher's 1864 survey in 45 AP 11.

18. Léon Aucoc, *Conférences sur l'administration et le droit administratif* (2d rev. ed.; Paris, 1878–82), I, 181, 298, 673–78. Georges Graux, "La police à Paris et la réorganisation de la police parisienne," *Revue politique et parlementaire*, VIII (April–June 1896), 70 ff. On the frontier police, *AN*, F18 2349.

19. Theodore Zeldin, *The political system of Napoleon III* (New York, 1958), pp. 98–142. On the reforms sponsored by the Council and their later evolution, see: Edouard Laferière, *Traité de la juridiction administrative et des recours contentieux* (2d ed.; Paris, 1896), I, 247–59; Léon Duguit, *Traité de droit constitutionnel* (3d ed.; Paris, 1930), III, 36, 48–49; and Bernard Schwartz, *French administrative law and the common-law world* (New York, 1954), pp. 42–43 and elsewhere.

Selected Bibliography

This is not a general bibliography on Louis Napoleon or the Second Empire. Most published studies of the period deal only casually, if at all, with the political police. Only those books and other published materials which have been most useful for providing background material or information on specific aspects of the subject are listed. Many other titles, cited only once or very occasionally, are here omitted, together with numerous periodical articles and brochures which appear in the footnotes. Except for Chapter One, the present study is based primarily upon French archival sources.

Archives

Archives Nationales, Paris. Seres: 45 AP (Çerçay Papers of Eugène Rouher), AB XIX (Tuileries Papers), F1a (general administration), F1b I (personnel dossiers), F1c III (prefects' reports and correspondence with the Minister of the Interior), F3 I (municipal and rural police), F7 (general police), F17 (Ministry of Public Instruction), F18 (press), F19 (*police des cultes*), BB18 (Ministry of Justice, general correspondence of the Criminal Division), BB22 (amnesties and requests for pardons), and BB30 (political affairs, correspondence, and periodical reports of the *procureurs-généraux*).

Archives de la Préfecture de Police, Paris. Nothing significant remains of a confidential or political nature. Useful for its collection of circulars, instructions, and ordinances of the Prefect of Police, and for materials on the Boittelle-Haussmann conflict.

Service Historique de l'Armée, Vincennes. Gendarmerie, Series F1 (personnel dossiers, G9 (political correspondence), and 2003 (political reports).

Bibliothèque Thiers, Paris. Baroche Papers, in Series 1100.

Archives Départementales, Bouches-du-Rhône (Marseille, prefectorial archives, Series M6; Aix-en-Provence, archives of the Parquet, Series U); Isère (Grenoble, prefectorial archives, Series M).

Public Record Office, London. Used only for correspondence on the question of political refugees, Series F.O. 27/900 and 146/400.

Published Documents

Bourgin, Georges. "Mazzini et le Comité central démocratique en 1851," *Il Risorgimento Italiano,* VI (1913), 353–71.

Documents pour servir à l'histoire du Second Empire. Circulaires, rapports, notes et instructions confidentielles. 1851–1870. Paris, Lachaud, 1872.

Duvergier, Jean Baptiste Henri (ed.). *Collection complète des lois, décrets, ordonnances, règlements et avis du conseil d'état.* 108 vols. Paris: Société du Recueil Sirey, 1790–1908.

France. Commission chargée de réunir, classer et publier les papiers saisis aux Tuileries. *Papiers et correspondence de la Famille Impériale.* 2 vols. Paris, Garnier Frères, 1871.

France. Gouvernement de la défense nationale. *Actes du Gouvernement de la défense nationale (du 4 septembre 1870 au 8 février 1871).* 7 vols. Paris, Cerf et fils, 1876.

Lyon, Ville de. Conseil Municipal. *Pièces saisies aux archives de la police politique de Lyon.* Chez tous les libraires. Lyon, 1870.

Munsch, Lucien (ed.). *Répertoire général des circulaires et instructions du ministère de la justice (1er octobre 1790—1er septembre 1899.* Paris, Librairie de la Societe du recueil general des lois et des arrêts, 1900.

Paris. Préfecture de Police. *Recueil officiel des circulaires émanées de la Préfecture de Police.* Vol. II (1849–80). Paris, Imprimerie Chaix, n.d.
———. *Ordonnances et arrêtés émanés du Préfet de Police.* Paris, Bocquin, n.d.

Periodicals

La Gazette des Tribunaux. Paris, 1851–60.
Journal de la Gendarmerie de France. Paris, 1850–60.
Journal des Commissaires de Police. Paris, 1855–60.
Le Moniteur Administratif [new title *La Réforme Administrative,* Aug. 31, 1853, through May, 1855]. Paris, 1851–55.
Le Moniteur Universel. Paris, 1851–60.

Administrative and Constitutional Law and Organization

Aucoc, Léon. *Conférences sur l'administration et le droit faites à l'École des ponts et chaussées.* 2d ed. revised. 3 vols. Paris, Dunod, 1878–82.

Béquet, Léon and others (eds.). *Répertoire du droit administratif.* 28 vols. Paris, P. Dupont, 1882–1911.

Berton, Henry. *L'Evolution constitutionnelle du Second Empire.* Paris, Félix Alcan, 1900.

Block, Maurice and Pontich, Henri de. *Administration de la ville de Paris et du département de la Seine.* Paris, Guillaumin, 1884.

Des Aubiers, V. *De l'administration et de ses réformes.* Paris, P. Dupont, 1852.

Deshaires, Germain. *Traité de l'administration départementale et communale.* Paris, P. Dupont, 1866.

DuCamp, Maxime. *Paris: ses organes, ses fonctions et sa vie dans la seconde moitié du XIXᵉ siècle.* 7th ed. 6 vols. Paris, Hachette, 1883.

Ducrocq, Théophile. *Cours de droit administratif et de législation française des finances, avec introduction de droit constitutionnel et les principes du droit public.* 7th ed. 7 vols. Paris, A. Fontemoing, 1897–1905.

Dufour, Gabriel Michel. *Traité général de droit administratif appliqué.* 3d ed. 8 vols. Paris, Delamotte, 1868–70.

Duguit, Léon. *Traité de droit constitutionnel.* 3d ed. 5 vols. Paris, E. de Boccard, 1930.

Freedeman, Charles E. *The Conseil d'État in modern France.* ("Columbia Studies in the Social Sciences," No. 603.) New York, Columbia University Press, 1961.

Grégoire, Roger. *La fonction publique.* Paris, Armand Colin, 1954.

Laferrière, Edouard L. J. *Traité de la juridiction administrative et des recours contentieux.* 2d ed. 2 vols. Paris, Berger Levrault, 1896.

Monnet, Émile. *Histoire de l'administration provinciale, départementale et communale en France.* Paris, A. Rousseau, 1885.

Schwartz, Bernard. *French administrative law and the common-law world.* New York, New York University Press, 1954.

Vivien, Alexandre François Auguste. *Études administratives.* 2 vols. Paris, Guillaumin, 1859.

Police Organization, Practice, and Doctrine

Anglade, Eugène. *Étude sur la police.* 2d ed. Paris, Claude-Gérard, 1852.

Arnaud, Émile. *La police municipale et rurale et les gardes champêtres.* Paris, Jouve, 1928.

Auzies, Célestin. *De la surveillance de la haute police.* Paris, E. Thorin, 1869.

Bertrand, Ernest. *De la détention préventive et de la célérité dans les procédures criminelles en France et en Angleterre.* Paris, Cosse et Marchal, 1862.

Brayer, Félix. *Procédure administrative des bureaux de police à l'usage des préfectures, sous-préfectures, mairies et commissariats de police.* Arras, Rousseau-Leroy, 1866.

Cudet, François. *Histoire des corps de troupe qui ont été spécialement chargés du service de la ville de Paris depuis son origine jusqu'à nos jours.* Paris, Léon Pillet, 1887.

Dutruc, Gustave. *Le code de la détention préventive.* Paris, Cosse et Marchal, 1866.

Euvrard, F. *Historique de l'institution des commissaires de police, son origine, leurs prérogatives.* Montpellier, Firmin, Montane et Sicardi, 1911.

Galtier-Boissière, Jean. *Mysteries of the French secret police.* Trans. by Ronald Leslie-Melville. London, Stanley Paul, 1938.

Lambry, Émile. *Les mystères du cabinet noir sous l'empire et la poste sous la Commune.* Paris, Dentu, 1871.

Larrieu, Général. *Histoire de la Gendarmerie, depuis les origines de la Maréchaussée jusqu'à nos jours.* 2d ed. revised. Paris, Charles-Lavauzelle, 1933.

Le Clère, Marcel. *Histoire de la police.* Paris, Presses Universitaires de France, 1947.

Miriel, Émile. *Des rapports des municipalités et du pouvoir central en matière de police.* Paris, Librairie de la Société du recueil général des lois et des arrêts, 1897.

Mouneyrat, Edmond. *La Préfecture de Police.* Paris, Bonvalot-Jouve, 1906.

Pelatant, Léopold. *De l'organisation de la police.* Dijon, J. Berthoud, 1899.

Perrier, E. G. *La police municipale.* Paris, M. Giard et E. Brière, 1920.

Rocquain, Félix. *Notes et fragments d'histoire.* Paris, Plon, 1906.

Stead, Phillip John. *The police of Paris.* London, Staples Press, 1957.

Thomas, Émile. *Le livre des commissaires de police.* Montdidier, Imprimerie administrative de Radenez, 1864.

Memoirs

Baroche, Celeste. *Second Empire, notes et souvenirs de seize années, 1855 à 1871.* Paris, Les Editions G. Gres, 1921.

Beaumont-Vassy, Edouard Ferdinand de la Bonninière, Vicomte de. *Histoire de mon temps. Deuxième série: Présidence décennale. Second Empire.* 2 vols. Paris, Amijot, 1864–65.

———. *Histoire intime du Second Empire.* Paris, Sartorius, 1874.

Bicknell, Anna L. *Life in the Tuileries under the Second Empire.* New York, The Century Co., 1895.

Canler, Louis. *Mémoirs de Canler, ancien chef du service du sûreté.* Paris, J. Hetzel, 1862.

Castellane, Esprit-Victor, Maréchal Comte de. *Journal du Maréchal de Castellane, 1804–1862.* 5 vols. Paris, Plon, Nourrit, 1895–97.

DuCamp, Maxime. *Souvenirs d'un demi-siècle.* 2 vols. Paris, Hachette, 1949.

Fleury, Émile Félix, Comte. *Souvenirs du général Cte. Fleury (1837–1867).* 2 vols. Paris, Plon, 1897–98.

Granier de Cassagnac, Bernard Adolphe. *Souvenirs du Second Empire.* 3 vols. Paris, E. Dentu, 1879–82.

Haussmann, Georges Eugène, Baron. *Mémoires.* 3 vols. Paris, Victor-Havard, 1890.

Hübner, Comte de. *Neuf ans de souvenirs d'un ambassadeur.* 2 vols. Paris, Plon, Nourrit, 1904.

Maupas, Charlemagne-Émile de. *Mémoires sur le Second Empire.* 2 vols. Paris, E. Dentu, 1885.

Persigny, Jean Gilbert Victor Fialin de. *Mémoirs.* Paris, Plon, Nourrit, 1896.

Quentin-Bauchart, A. *Études et souvenirs sur la Deuxième république et le Second Empire (1848–70). Mémoires posthumes publiés par son fils.* 2 vols. Paris, Plon, Nourrit, 1901–02.

Vandam, Albert Dresden. *An Englishman in Paris.* 3d ed. 2 vols. London, Chapman and Hall, 1892.

Véron, Louis D. *Mémoires d'un bourgeois de Paris.* 6 vols. Paris, G. de Gonet, 1855.

Other Books

Arnaud, René. *Le coup d'état du deux décembre.* Paris, Hachette, 1926.

Beaumont-Vassy, Edouard Ferdinand de la Bonninière, Vicomte de. *La préface du deux-décembre.* Paris, Amyst, 1853.

Blanchard, Marcel. *Le Second Empire.* Paris, Armand Colin, 1950.

Boichot, Jean-Baptiste. *Souvenirs d'un prisonnier d'état sous le Second Empire, 1854–1859.* 2d ed. revised. Leipzig, C. Muquardt, 1869.

Calman, Alvin R. *Ledru-Rollin après 1848 et les proscrits en Angleterre.* Paris, Presses universitaires de France, 1958.

Chrétien, Paul. *Le Duc de Persigny, 1808–1872.* Toulouse, F. Boisseau, 1943.

Christophe, Robert. *Le Duc de Morny, "empereur" des Français sous Napoléon III.* Paris, Hachette, 1951.

Collins, Irene. *Government and the newspaper press in France, 1814–1881.* Oxford, Oxford University Press, 1959.

Commissaire, Sébastien. *Mémoires et souvenirs de Sébastien Commissaire, ancien réprésentant du peuple.* 2 vols. Lyon, Meton, 1888.

Dansette, Adrien. *Louis-Napoléon à la conquête du pouvoir.* Paris, Hachette, 1961.

Delescluze, Charles. *De Paris à Cayenne, journal d'un transporté.* Paris, A. le Chevalier, 1869.

Dessal, Marcel. *Un révolutionnaire jacobin: Charles Delescluze, 1809–1871.* Paris, Riviere, 1952.

Duprat, Pascal. *Les tables de proscription de Louis Bonaparte et de ses complices.* 2 vols. Liége, Redoute, 1852.

Farat, Honoré. *Persigny, un ministre de Napoléon III, 1808–1872.* Paris, Hachette, 1957.

Germain, A. *Martyrologe de la presse, 1789–1861.* Paris, H. Dumineray, 1861.

Guillemin, Henri. *Le coup du 2 décembre.* 2d ed. Paris, Gallimard, 1951.

Hatin, Eugène. *Histoire politique et littéraire de la presse en France.* 8 vols. Paris, Poulet-Malassis et de Broise, 1859–61.

Laferrière, Edouard Louis Julien. *La censure et le régime correctionnel.* 2d ed. Paris, Armand le Chevalier, 1867.

Maurain, Jean. *La politique ecclésiastique du Second Empire de 1852 à 1869.* Paris, Félix Alcan, 1930.

———. *Un bourgeois français au XIXe siècle: Baroche, ministre de Napoléon III, d'après des papiers inédits.* Paris, Félix Alcan, 1936.

Mermet, Émile. *La presse, l'affichage et le colportage. Histoire et jurisprudence.* Paris, Marpon et Flammarion, 1882.

Nadaud, Martin. *Mémoires de Léonard, ancien garçon maçon.* Bourganeuf, A. Doubouéix, 1895.

Persigny, Jean G. V. Fialin, Duc de. *Le Duc de Persigny et les doctrines de l'Empire.* Paris, Plon, 1865.

Pilenco, Alexandre. *Les moeurs du suffrage universel en France (1848–1928).* Paris, 1930.

Puech, Louis. *Essai sur la candidature officielle en France depuis 1851.* Mende, Henri Chaptal, 1922.

Rousset, Gustave. *Nouveau code annoté de la presse.* Paris, Imprimerie et librairie générale de jurisprudence Cosse, 1856.

Saint-Ferréol, Amédée. *Les proscrits français en Belgique, ou la Belgique contemporaine vue à travers l'exil.* 2 vols. Brussels, C. Muquardt, 1870.

Schnerb, Robert. *Rouher et le Second Empire.* Paris, Armand Colin, 1949.

Simpson, F. A. *Louis Napoleon and the recovery of France, 1848–1856.* London, J. Murray, 1923.

Tchernoff, J. *Associations et sociétés secrètes sous la Deuxième République, 1848–1851.* Paris, Félix Alcan, 1905.

———. *Le parti républicain au coup d'état et sous le Second Empire, d'après des documents et des souvenirs inédits.* Paris, A. Pedone, 1906.

Ténot, Eugène. *Paris en décembre 1851.* 4th ed. Paris, Armand le Chevalier, 1868.

———. *La province en décembre 1851.* 3d ed. Paris, Armand le Chevalier, 1868.

———, and Dubost, Antonin. *Les suspects en 1858.* Paris, Armand le Chevalier, 1869.

Vingtain, Léon. *De la liberté de la presse.* Paris, Michel Lévy Frères, 1860.

Vizetelly, Earnest A. *The court of the Tuileries (1852–1870).* London, Chatto and Windus, 1907.

Wauwermans, P. *Les proscrits du coup d'état en Belgique.* Brussels, Société Belge de Librairie, 1892.

Weill, Georges Jacques. *Histoire du parti républicain en France de 1814 à 1870.* Paris, Félix Alcan, 1900.

Zeldin, Theodore. *The political system of Napoleon III.* New York, St. Martin's Press, 1958.

Index

333